D0229021

FLORENCE AND TUSCANY

Sheila Hale

Third
edition
of the
American
Express
Pocket
Guide

Mitchell Beazley

The Author and Contributor
Sheila Hale is also the author of *The American Express Pocket Guide to Venice*. She was born in New York, but has lived in Italy and England since 1962. A writer and journalist, she contributes to a number of newspapers and magazines, including *Connoisseur*, the *New York Times* and the London *Observer*. Burton Anderson contributed the section on Tuscan wines.

Acknowledgments
The author and publishers thank the following for their invaluable help and advice: Burton Anderson, Professor Andreis of the Italian Institute of Culture, Lisa Beveridge, Julia Crosse, David Ekserdjian, Caroline Elam, Rosaria Falivene, Pamela Fiori, J.R. Hale, Italian State Tourist Department, Countess Aloisia Rucellai, Stella Rudolph, Ila Stanger; for the second edition, Sally Hood, Charles Hope, Monica Loni, Nicolai Rubinstein; for this revised edition, Nicos Pervanidis, Philip Uzielli; and David Arnold, editor of the original edition.

Quotations
The author and publishers are grateful to those listed below for their kind permission to reprint the following extracts: Phaidon Press Ltd (UK and US) for the quotations from *Piero della Francesca* by Sir Kenneth Clark (p130 and pp182-3); Laurence Pollinger Ltd and the Estate of the late Mrs Frieda Lawrence Ravagli (UK) and Viking Penguin Inc. (US) for the quotation from *Aaron's Rod* by D.H. Lawrence (p47).

General Editor   David Townsend Jones
Art Editor   Nigel O'Gorman
Designer   Christopher Howson
Illustrators   Jeremy Ford (David Lewis Artists), Illustra Design Ltd, Illustrated Arts
Map Editor   David Haslam
Jacket illustration   Henri Galleron
Indexer   Hilary Bird
Proof-reader   Sue McKinstry

Edited and designed by Mitchell Beazley International Limited, Artists House, 14-15 Manette Street, London W1V 5LB

© American Express Publishing Corporation Inc. 1983, 1987 (reprinted 1987)
New edition © American Express Publishing Corporation Inc. 1990
All rights reserved including the right of reproduction in whole or in part in any form
Published by Prentice Hall Trade Division
A Division of Simon & Schuster, Inc.
Gulf & Western Building
One Gulf & Western Plaza
New York, New York 10023
PRENTICE HALL is a trademark of Simon & Schuster, Inc.

Library of Congress Cataloging-in-Publication Data
Hale, Sheila
    The American Express pocket guide to Florence and Tuscany / Sheila Hale
        p.   cm.
    ISBN 0-13-027012-1 : $10.95
    1. Florence (Italy)—Description—1981- —Guide-books.
    2. Tuscany (Italy)—Description and travel—1981- —Guide-books.
    I. American Express Company.
    II. Title.   III. Title: Pocket guide to Florence and Tuscany.
DG732.H24 1990
914.5'504928—dc20   89-36974
                                CIP

Maps in 2-color and 4-color by Clyde Surveys, Maidenhead, England.
Typeset by Castle House Press, Llantrisant, Wales.
Typeset in Garamond and Univers.
Linotronic output through Microstar DTP Studio, Cardiff, Wales.
Produced by Mandarin Offset. Printed and bound in Malaysia.

Contents

How to use this book

The American Express Pocket Guide to Florence and Tuscany is an encyclopedia of travel information, organized in the sections listed on the previous page. There is also a comprehensive *Index* (pages 216-223) and a useful *Index of restaurants in Tuscany* (pages 223-4), and there are full-color *Maps* at the end of the book.

For easy reference, all major sections (*Sights and places of interest*, *Hotels*, *Restaurants*), and other sections where possible, are arranged alphabetically. For the organization of the book as a whole, see *Contents*. For individual places that do not have separate entries in *Sights and places of interest* or the *Tuscany A to Z*, see the *Index*.

Abbreviations and floors

Standard abbreviations used include days of the week and months, points of the compass (N, S, E and W), San, Santa or Santo (S.), Santi or Santissima (SS.), Saint (St), rms (rooms), C for century, and measurements. Throughout, "first floor" refers European-style to the floor above ground level, "second floor" to the floor above that, and so on upward.

Bold type

Bold type is used mainly for emphasis, to highlight items of special interest or importance. It also picks out places — shops or minor museums, for example — that do not have full entries of their own. In such cases it is usually followed in brackets by the address, telephone number, and details of opening times, printed in *italics*.

Cross-references

A special type has been used for cross-references. Whenever a place or section title is printed in *sans serif italics* (for example *Bargello* or *Basic information*) in the text, this indicates that you can turn to the appropriate heading in the book for further information.

How entries are organized

Hood House

1411 Lincoln Ave., Lincoln Green, Sherwood Forest
☎ *426-5960 (house), 426-5961 (group tour reservations).*
Map *8J11* 🔳 ✕ *Open Apr-Sept 9am-5pm, rest of year 9am-4pm. Closed Christmas, New Year's Day. Metro: Bow & Arrow.*

Robin Hood (?1149-1205) was the leading spokesman for the poor and downtrodden in their struggle for freedom and justice under the Plantagenets. He lectured and wrote books about his own early life as a serf, campaigned endlessly for human rights, helped recruit peasants to the Civil Service, and finally settled down to a distinguished old age in Sherwood Forest. He lived first in A St. (see *National Museum of Outlawed Art*), then bought Sheriff Villa, which he renamed Hood House, a handsome white dwelling on a height overlooking the Trent Valley. All the furnishings, except for curtains and wallpaper, are original. Hood's library and other belongings are still *in situ*, and the whole house is redolent of the spirit of a very remarkable man. In the **Visitors' Centre** at the foot of the hill you can see a film about Hood's life.

Cross-references in this typeface always refer either to sections of the book — *Basic information*, *Planning*, *Hotels* — or to individual entries in *Sights and places of interest*, such as *Accademia* or *Uffizi*.

For easy reference, use the running heads printed at the top corner of the page (see, for example, **Carmine** on page 53 or **Florence hotels** on page 106).

Map references

Each of the full-color maps at the end of the book is divided into a grid of squares, identified vertically by letters (A, B, C, D, etc.) and horizontally by numbers (1, 2, 3, 4, etc.). A map reference identifies the page and square in which the street or place can be found — thus *Siena* is located in Map **11**G6.

Price categories

Price categories are denoted by the symbols ▭ ◫ ◫ ▥ and ▥, which signify cheap, inexpensive, moderately priced, expensive and very expensive, respectively. In the cases of hotels and restaurants these correspond approximately with the following actual prices, which give a guideline at the time of printing. Although actual prices will inevitably increase, in most cases the relative price category — for example expensive or cheap — is likely to remain more or less the same. Prices are usually lower outside Florence.

Price categories	Corresponding to approximate prices	
	for **hotels** *double room with bath and breakfast; singles are usually one-third less*	for **restaurants** *meal for one with service, tax and house wine*
▭ cheap	under $45	under $15
◫ inexpensive	$45-65	$15-20
◫ moderate	$65-85	$20-35
▥ expensive	$85-250	$35-60
▥ very expensive	over $250	over $60

Bold blue type for entry headings.

Blue italics for address, practical information and symbols. For list of symbols see page 6 or back flap of jacket.

Black text for description.

Sans serif italics used for cross-references to other entries or sections.

Bold type used for emphasis.

Entries for hotels, restaurants, shops, etc. follow the same organization, and are usually printed across a half column.

In hotels, symbols indicating special facilities appear at the end of the entry, in black.

Pullman
2600 Express Ave., Orient City 20037 ☎ *299-4450* ⑰ *299-4460. Map 2F4* ▥ *238 rms* ⬛ ⬛ ⬛ *Metro: High Standard.*
Location: On a height overlooking the Universal Trade Center. Part of a large conglomeration overlooking the seafront, this luxurious hotel is set in attractively landscaped grounds and is run with clockwork precision. Its restaurant, the **Simplon**, is highly regarded.
⬛ ⬛ ⬛ ⬛ ⬛

Key to symbols

☎ Telephone	💳 MasterCard/Eurocard
⊕ Telex	*VISA* Visa
⊛ Facsimile (fax)	🚗 Secure garage
★ Recommended sight	🍴 Meal obligatory
☆ Worth a visit	🏠 Quiet hotel
❀ Good value (in its class)	⬍ Elevator
i Tourist information	⓹ Facilities for disabled people
🚗 Parking	📺 TV in each room
🏛 Building of architectural interest	📞 Telephone in each room
† Church or cathedral	🐕 Dogs not allowed
⊡ Free entrance	⚘ Garden
🔳 Entrance fee payable	⋐ Outstanding views
■ Entrance expensive	≋ Swimming pool
📷 Photography forbidden	🏖 Good beach nearby
✗ Guided tour	⚲ Tennis court(s)
🍽 Cafeteria	✤ Golf course
✤ Special interest for children	🏇 Riding
☞ Hotel	🎣 Fishing
🏠 Simple (hotel)	🏛 Conference facilities
🏨 Luxury (hotel)	🍸 Bar
▭ Cheap	🍴 Restaurant
▨ Inexpensive	🍴 Simple (restaurant)
▨ Moderately priced	🍴 Luxury (restaurant)
▨ Expensive	🍴 A la carte available
▨ Very expensive	🍱 Set (fixed-price) menu available
🛁 Rooms with private bathroom	🍷 Good for wines
❄ Air conditioning	🍽 Open-air dining
🏠 Residential terms available	⊙ Disco dancing
AE American Express	🎵 Nightclub
CB Carte Blanche	⊛ Casino/gambling
⊙ Diners Club	♫ Live music
	♪ Dancing
	💃 Revue

A note from the General Editor

No travel book can be completely free of errors and totally up to date. Telephone numbers and opening hours change without warning, and hotels and restaurants come under new management, which can affect standards. We make every effort to ensure that all information is accurate at the time we go to press, but are always delighted to receive corrections or suggestions for improvements from our readers, which if warranted will be incorporated in a future edition. We are indebted to readers who wrote to us during the preparation of this edition.

The publishers regret they cannot accept any consequences arising from the use of the book or from the information it contains.

Tuscans in Tuscany

Tuscans quite properly regard themselves as the most civilized of Italians. They speak the purest Italian, their culture is the oldest in Italy, and they were responsible for creating the first Renaissance. They will also admit to being the least cosmopolitan of Italians and the most afflicted with *campanilismo*, the Italian word for provincialism, which means, in the literal sense, excessive attachment to everything within sight of one's native bell tower.

Florence, the little city which helped to transform Western European civilization and which still possesses many of its supreme artistic achievements, is capital of a region that is predominantly rural. That harmonious trio, the vine, the olive and the cypress, climbs up to the walls of many Tuscan towns and villages and slips into the conversation of the most sophisticated city dwellers. "They argue endlessly about *language*," observed the French writer Stendhal, who understood the Tuscan character better than most foreigners; "they argue no less about the price of various oils."

They are in fact an argumentative and factious people; lack of consensus has been their undoing in the past and causes trouble even today. Nowadays, they argue also about the tourists, who are drawn to Florence in ever-increasing numbers. Some see mass tourism as a gold mine, others as an affliction: organizations exist both to promote and to discourage it. They argue about the traffic: some would ban all motor traffic permanently from central Florence; others, the shopkeepers in particular, would prefer a motorized free-for-all.

But the most serious and difficult argument is about the conflict between a long and weighty past that must be honored, whose monuments, most would agree, must be preserved, and the requirements of a modern-minded people who enjoy change and need new buildings, new roads. And so in the late 1980s the Roman foundations dug up beneath the Piazza della Signoria remain exposed while the government argues about what to do with them; and the skyscrapers of *Firenze nuova* rise above arguments about their cost to the environment.

Tuscans neither romanticize their countryside nor do they create artificial barriers between city and country. There is no Tuscan tradition of landscape painting or landscape gardening. If you come across an ornamental tree or herbaceous border in a suburban garden, the chances are that it was planted not by a native but by a homesick foreigner, probably English-born.

Two-thirds of mainland Tuscany is hilly, one-fifth mountainous, one-tenth plain. The cultivated land is extraordinarily productive thanks to naturally fertile soil and an abundance of both sunshine and rain. Farming in modern Tuscany is nevertheless not without its problems. Methods have changed drastically in the last 30 years: the white oxen that pulled the plows until 20 years ago have been replaced by machines in all but the most remote areas; the feudal *mezzadria* system by which the landowner gave a tenant farmer tools, seed and half the profit in exchange for labor died out in the 1960s and has not yet been satisfactorily replaced. The cost of agricultural labor today makes the wonderful Tuscan olive oil nearly as expensive as the liquid green-gold it resembles. In the industrialized vineyards beyond Pontassieve and above Siena disease-proof concrete vine supports have proliferated like tombstones. Elsewhere, wine growers, suffering the consequences of over-production, have turned their fields over to easy crops, such as tobacco and sunflowers.

Such changes are esthetically regrettable, but they have not

7

fundamentally altered the appearance of a landscape which has been ordered over centuries by collaboration between man and nature. Tuscans have imposed their own character on their countryside: their methods are conservative, enlightened and motivated by a not unnatural desire to make a profit. The result is that the ecological balance remains relatively undisturbed and that Tuscany still looks, as Goethe noticed almost 200 years ago, the way Italy ought to look, and promotes a sense of well-being in most foreigners.

The countryside still shelters a profusion of rare wild flowers, butterflies, birds and indigenous animals. The *macchia*, the dense Mediterranean scrub characteristic of the Tuscan coast, is now officially protected in designated areas, where it acts as a sanctuary for migrating birds, roebuck, deer, partridge and wild boar. In the wild mountains on the Umbrian border you may still sometimes hear the lethal moan of a wolf or the cough of the hoopoe. Some of the noble mountain forests of fir and beech have been maintained by monastic foundations for centuries. Elsewhere the woods are protected by their very utility. The chestnut trees, which attain magnificent proportions on the lower mountain slopes, produce chestnuts for flour; the beech trees which grow at high altitudes shed mast on which pigs are grazed; pine trees produce pine nuts; and the scented yellow *ginestra* is used to make brooms. In late summer and fall the forest floor is a treasure trove of luscious mushrooms and white truffles.

Below the surface of this productive landscape is a wealth of minerals, mineral springs and building materials. The soil of Elba contains 150 different minerals, and its iron mines produce much of Italy's total requirement. The hills which form a ridge running toward the coast from just below Siena are called the Colline Metallifere after the copper, zinc and lead they contain. Monte Amiata is one of the major sources of mercury in the world, and half a million tons of Carrara marble are quarried each year from the Apuan Alps. Then there are the colored marbles — red from the Maremma, dark green from Prato, yellow from the Montagnola hills west of Siena, which have supplied the festive dressing for many great Tuscan churches.

Tuscan towns are made out of the Tuscan countryside. No one town or village or city is like another because the shape, color and texture of each is determined by the contours and building materials of its particular site. Siena is built of burned-Siena bricks from the clay hummocks found to its southeast, Cortona is a brown sandstone city, Volterra is honeyed limestone, and Florence is gray-brown *pietra forte*.

Tuscans themselves are, as they were in the Renaissance, hardworking, inventive and commercially tough-minded. If you visit a busy, well-kept town such as Prato or Arezzo, you will see the consequences of modern prosperity, negative as well as positive. The center may be clogged with tourist buses, the old walls may have been torn down to make way for beltways with factories and industrial suburbs beyond. And the days when you could live in Tuscany for next to nothing or buy an abandoned farmhouse for a song are over.

But before complaining about Tuscan commercialism, do remember that it was the unprecedented success of Tuscan commercialism that fueled and paid for the Renaissance art and architecture that you may have come to admire. Remember too that despite their native commercialism — and their factiousness — Tuscans have preserved their beautiful landscape and historic centers far more conscientiously than have most countries.

Before you go

Documents required

For citizens of the USA, EEC and British Commonwealth, a passport is the only document required for visits not exceeding three months. For longer visits, and for most other nationals, a visa must be obtained in advance in the country of departure. Vaccination certificates are not normally required, but if you are traveling from the Middle East, Far East, South America or Africa, you should check when buying your ticket.

To drive a car in Italy, you ideally need an International Driving Permit, obtainable from the AAA. But a translation obtainable from an Italian Government Travel Office (there are offices in New York, Chicago and San Francisco) will suffice. If you are bringing your car into the country, you must carry the vehicle registration document (logbook) and an insurance certificate or international green card.

Travel and medical insurance

It is advisable to travel with an insurance policy that covers loss of deposits paid to airlines, hotels and tour operators, and the cost of dealing with emergency requirements, such as special tickets home and extra nights in a hotel, as well as a medical insurance policy.

The nearest American hospital that accepts certain US medical insurance is in Rome. Always consult your own insurance company for advice when going abroad.

Money

The monetary unit is the lira (plural lire). There are coins for 50, 100, 200 and 500 lire, and notes for 1,000, 2,000, 5,000, 10,000, 20,000, 50,000 and 100,000 lire. There are no restrictions on other currencies or travelers cheques taken into the country, but if you intend exporting more than 1 million lire-worth of any currency you should complete form V2 at customs on entry.

Carry cash in small amounts only. Travelers cheques issued by all major companies are widely recognized. Make sure you read the instructions included with your travelers cheques. It is important to note separately the serial numbers of your cheques and the telephone number to call in case of loss. Specialist travelers cheque companies such as American Express provide extensive local refund facilities through their own offices or agents.

Eurocheque Encashment Card holders can cash personal checks in most banks, and there are machines that exchange foreign bills for lire. The principal cards accepted in Florence and increasingly in provincial Tuscany are American Express, Diners Club, Eurocard and Visa.

Customs

Any items clearly intended for personal or professional use may be brought into the country free of charge.

In the following list, the figures in brackets are the increased allowances for goods obtained duty- and tax-paid in the EEC. In all cases the allowances apply only to travelers over 17yrs old.

Tobacco   If you live in an EEC country, you are allowed 300 cigarettes *or* 150 cigarillos *or* 75 cigars *or* 400g tobacco. If you live outside Europe, you are allowed 400 cigarettes *or* 200 cigarillos *or* 100 cigars *or* 500g tobacco; however, if you live in a non-EEC European country you are allowed half this amount.

Basic information

Alcoholic drinks   1 (1.5) liters spirits (over 22% alcohol by volume) *or* 2 (3) liters of alcoholic drinks of 22% alcohol or less; *plus* 2 (4) liters of still wines.

Perfume   50g/60cc/2 fl oz (75g/90cc/3 fl oz).

Other goods   Goods to the value of 500,000 lire.

When returning, you can export up to 1,000,000 lire's worth of goods. To export works of art, apply to the Export Department of the Italian Ministry of Education.

Getting there

By air: The main Tuscan airport is Pisa, which receives European and domestic flights. More convenient for Florence is La Perètola, which is only about 10mins from the city center, but takes only domestic and European short-haul flights. (The restaurant at La Perètola is excellent and inexpensive.) Some European flights arrive at Bologna.

Passengers returning to Pisa can now check in at the British Airways and Alitalia air terminal at Florence station, track 5. Passengers from outside Europe will have to make a transfer stop or fly direct to Milan or Rome. A new hourly train, using the *linea direttissima*, takes 2hrs from Rome.

By train: The two main trans-European trains to Florence are the *Palatino* from Paris (couchettes and sleeping cars only) and the *Italia Express* from London stopping at Lille, Strasbourg, Basel, Milan and Bologna. Both carry first- and second-class passengers and reservation is obligatory.

By bus: International Express (☎ *(01) 439-9368*) run a frequent comfortable bus service to Florence from London traveling via Turin, Genoa, Venice and Bologna.

By car: Two highways (autostrade) enter Tuscany from the N: the A12 along the coast from France via Genoa, and the A1 over the Apennines from Bologna, now being doubled in width, which continues s to Rome.

Climate

The weather in Florence is more variable than in most Italian cities. The temperature ranges from a brisk average of 5.8°C (42°F) in Dec, Jan and Feb to a sticky 25°C (77°F) in late July and Aug. It can rain at any time of the year but rarely for prolonged periods in summer. The wettest months are Jan, late Nov, Oct and Apr, in descending order. On the Versilia winters are much milder.

Clothes

Be sure to pack one comfortable pair of shoes for sightseeing. In summertime light, loose clothing is essential for comfort. In spring and fall bring a sweater or light coat and umbrella. In winter you will need full protection as it can become cold, particularly at night. Florentines are justly famous for their sense of fashion, but their style is extremely understated. Informal day clothes will take you virtually anywhere. Italian men do tend to wear ties on most occasions, but there is no rule about wearing ties in restaurants. Evening dress is rarely seen these days except in private houses.

General delivery

Correspondence marked *Fermo Posta* plus the name of the town and province will be held at the central post office. A small fee is payable on collection, and you will be asked to show your passport.

Getting around

From the airport to Florence
At Pisa incoming and departing flights are served by direct trains to and from Florence station at S. Maria Novella; the journey takes about 1hr. Taxis are available but are expensive.

Public transportation
Buses
City and inter-city buses are cheap and efficient. In Florence the city lines, run by the ATAF bus company, are explained in the Yellow Pages telephone directory. One ticket is good for up to 70mins of travel. For most buses, tickets much be purchased in advance from bars or tobacconists, in the form of a *biglietto semplice*(one-way ticket) or a *biglietto multiplo* (book of eleven tickets). There are also new buses which accept exact change only; these are marked by a hand holding a coin. There are two main bus companies operating outside Florence.

LAZZI   Piazza Stazione 4-6 ☎(055) 294178 (serves Tuscany and Liguria)

SITA   Via Sta Caterina da Siena 15 ☎(055) 211487/214721 (serves most parts of Italy)

The possibility of bringing subway trains into central Florence is under investigation.

Railroad services
The Florence station at Santa Maria Novella is one of the busiest and best connected in central Italy. The information office is open from 7am-10pm (☎ *(055) 278785)*. There are usually long lines at ticket counters, but American Express Card holders can buy their tickets from automatic machines. There are stations at or near all the provincial capitals. Fares are quite reasonable by European standards, but they do vary according to the speed and type of train. Trains are often very crowded, so reserve in advance to be sure of a seat. Trains are classified as follows:

Super-Rapido: Luxury first-class-only trains running between the main Italian cities; a special supplement is charged and seat reservations are obligatory.

Rapido: Fast inter-city trains. Some carry only first-class coaches; a supplementary charge is made. Seat reservations are sometimes obligatory and for this too there is an extra charge.

Espresso: Long-distance express trains stopping only at main stations and carrying both first- and second-class passengers.

Diretto: Trains stopping at most stations; both classes.

Lócale: Trains stopping at all stations; both classes.

Taxis
Taxis do not usually respond to being hailed but it is worth trying. There are stands in many of the main squares of Florence, but you will be lucky to find a taxi waiting anywhere. For radio taxis in Florence ☎4390 or 4798. Extra charges are made for this service, also for each piece of luggage, for journeys made between 10pm and 7am, and on Sun and public holidays. The driver is not required to take you outside the city limits; if he does, the fare increases. Taxis are now so expensive that Florentines no longer tip unless the driver is particularly helpful, in which case give 10 percent.

Getting around by car
Having a car in Tuscany is obviously a great advantage but be prepared to cope with Italian driving, which is skillfully aggressive. International road signs are in use and vehicles drive

11

on the right; unless signposts indicate otherwise, cars must yield to traffic coming from the right. Carry a warning triangle.

The standard of the roads is variable and roadwork on autostrade (highways), many of which are being widened or extended, can cause delays. Tolls payable on the autostrade can be a considerable expense, but this is partly compensated for by the high standard of such roads. Gas stations often close between noon and 3pm and after 7pm. Maximum speed limits are 50kph (32mph) in built-up areas, 110kph (70mph) on country roads and 140kph (85mph) on highways. Heavy, on-the-spot fines are strictly enforced for breaking these limits.

Tourists who have rented cars elsewhere in Europe are entitled to gas coupons and highway vouchers. These can be bought in the country in which the car is rented and at Italian frontier points from the Italian Automobile Club (ACI) — but not within Italy. They can be refunded only by the issuing office.

Florence is served by highways in four directions. They are: the A1 running N to Bologna and SE to Rome via Arezzo and Chiusi; the Florence-Siena link; and the A11 for Pistoia, Lucca, Pisa and the sea. The stretch of highway, A12, along the coast from Marina di Carrara to Livorno, will eventually be extended to Florence and Rome. For traffic information ☎ (055) 577777.

It is wise to leave your car outside the historic center of the city you are visiting. Most cities are provided with attended parking lots for this purpose. Many centers are now zoned against traffic; where traffic is allowed it is directed through one-way systems that baffle even the natives.

The ACI will give free assistance to members of affiliated touring clubs such as the AAA, AA or RAC. Obtain the pamphlet *Offices to Serve you Abroad* from the AAA, listing all cities where members can be serviced.

Renting a car

The major international companies have branches in most cities and airports, and offer various reduced-rate schemes for cars reserved in advance and paid for outside Italy. Companies can arrange to have a car waiting for you at your point of arrival. Cars rented from local agencies are often still somewhat cheaper, but try to arrange for unlimited mileage: the charge per kilometer can be exorbitant.

Basic insurance is normally included in the rental charge with extra cover optional at fixed charges, and some companies require drivers to be aged over 21. Most firms require a deposit equivalent to the estimated total cost of rental. Value Added Tax (IVA) at 18 percent will be added to the final bill.

Mopeds

Mopeds can be rented in many towns if you have a driver's license. The Azienda Autonoma has lists of local companies.

Getting around on foot

All Tuscan towns and cities, including Florence, are small enough to be seen on foot, and many have now created traffic-free zones (*zone pedonale*) in parts of their centers. In Florence inessential traffic is now theoretically banned from the center for most of the day. Nevertheless, the motorcycles, taxis and private cars that defy the law are still a nuisance for pedestrians, especially along the *lungarni*. In Italy, as elsewhere in Europe, pedestrians have precedence over vehicles at uncontrolled zebra crossings.

Walking in rural Tuscany, where some of the prettiest landscape and monuments have been bypassed by the modern road network, is still a delight. See *Sports, leisure, ideas for children* for information.

On-the-spot information

Public holidays

Jan 1; Easter Monday; Liberation Day, Apr 25; Labor Day (*Festa del Lavoro*), May 1; Assumption of the Virgin (*Ferragosto*), Aug 15; All Saints Day (*Ognissanti*), Nov 1; Conception of the Virgin Mary (*Immacolata*), Dec 8; Dec 25 and 26. Shops, banks and offices close on these days. Feast days in honor of local patron saints are not official bank holidays, but many shops close in Florence on the Feast of St John the Baptist, June 24.

Time zones

Italy is 6hrs behind Eastern Standard Time and from 7-9hrs behind the other time zones in the US.

Banks and currency exchange

Banks are open Mon-Fri 8.30am-1.20pm, and closed on Sat, Sun and national holidays. You will need your passport when cashing travelers cheques. Personal checks may be cashed by Eurocheque Encashment Card holders, and foreign bills can be exchanged for lire in cash machines. Most hotels cash travelers cheques, but the rate is less favorable than at a bank. Foreign exchanges (*cambio*) are open during office hours.

Shopping and business hours

Shops are normally open 9am-1pm and 3.30 or 4 to 7 or 7.30pm, although some in central Florence now stay open all day. Not all shops close Sun. In winter most shops in Florence close on Mon morning, except for food stores, which close on Wed afternoon. In summer some bigger stores close all day Sat, but remain open on Mon morning.

Post and telephone services

Stamps may be bought from tobacconists (indicated by a **T** sign) and hotels as well as at the post office. The central post office in Florence can be found at Via Pietrapiana 53-55.

Mailboxes are colored red and are marked *Poste* or *Lettere*; collections may be erratic outside towns.

Public telephones, to be found in post offices, tobacconists, bars and at some newsstands, are still sometimes operated by *gettone* (tokens obtained from tobacconists and bars but often used as currency), which must be inserted when the caller answers. Each province has its own code, which must be used if ringing from outside that province (see *A-Z* entries for codes); the Florence code is **055**. Trunk calls can be dialed direct from boxes marked *Interurbano*.

Most hotels now have fax and/or telex.

Public rest rooms

In Florence there are public rest rooms in the basement of the Palazzo della Signoria, off the courtyard of the Pitti and in the station. Otherwise, they hardly exist. Most of the larger bars have rest rooms, which may be used in exchange for the price of a coffee. *Signori* means "men" and *Signore* "women." Leave a tip.

Basic information

Electric current

Electricity in most places is 220V AC. The standard two-pronged plugs or adapters can be purchased in most countries. Tecnica Radio (*Porta Rossa 39* ☎ *(055) 283184*) is a fully stocked electrical store in central Florence.

Laws and regulations

Italy possesses one or two unusual bureaucratic laws. One is the rarely observed requirement to register with the police within three days of entering Italy, which then entitles you to stay in Italy for three months; if you are staying at a hotel this will be done for you. There is a strictly enforced requirement that passports should be produced when registering at hotels. But these laws may be abolished in 1992.

If you are driving do not leave the vehicle registration book or rental agreement in the car; if the car is stolen or towed away the police will not co-operate unless you can produce proof of your right to drive the car.

If you leave your bill behind in a restaurant the waiter may run after you into the street and press it into your hand. This is because a new law requires that each customer leaves the premises with evidence that a taxable sum has been paid.

Topless sunbathing, though illegal, is common in many resorts; if you see topless Italian girls you can assume it is acceptable.

Customs and etiquette

When visiting churches, it is important to remember that they are not museums and it is offensive to interrupt services even in the cause of seeing a major masterpiece. Women may wear pants but are expected to cover their shoulders.

Tuscans pride themselves on their egalitarian manners. In restaurants and hotels, a friendly handshake and even the clumsiest effort to speak Italian will often work wonders. Children are welcome even in the smartest restaurants; indeed they often get better service than adults.

At times, Italian friendliness can be rather a nuisance, particularly when directed toward women traveling on their own. A firm but courteous rebuff (*Va via, per favore*) is the most effective way of dealing with such attentions, which are generally just playful and rarely sinister.

Tipping

In a restaurant, if service is not included on the bill, leave 15 percent; if service is included, a small note per person is an adequate supplement. The usher who takes you to your seat in the theater, movie theater or opera will expect a tip. If a sacristan or custodian does you any special favors, such as opening parts of a church or museum that are normally closed, you should be more generous. Tip porters, hairdressers and taxi drivers also.

Disabled travelers

Italian legislation regarding premises for the disabled is not enlightened. Many hotels are located in old buildings not equipped with elevators, but the Italian State Tourist Office (ISTO) publishes an *Annuario Alberghi D'Italia*, which marks suitable hotels for disabled visitors with the wheelchair symbol.

Some major galleries, such as the *Uffizi*, are accessible to wheelchairs, but many are not. Remember that marble floors can be hazardous for crutches or calipers and cobbled streets are not ideal for wheelchairs. Most restaurants are happy to accommodate wheelchairs with advance notice.

For further information and details of tour operators specializing in tours for handicapped people, write to the Travel Information Service, Moss Rehabilitation Hospital (*12th St. and Tabor Rd., Philadelphia, Pa. 19141*), or to Mobility International USA (*P.O. Box 3551, Eugene, Or. 97403*).

Local publications
The daily newspaper of Florence is *La Nazione*, but the new "Cronaca Firenze" section of *La Repubblica* is more interesting. The bi-monthly magazine *Firenze Oggi/Florence Today*, available free from the Azienda Autonoma and many hotels, is written in both Italian and English and contains useful local information.

Useful addresses

Tourist information
American Express Travel Service (*Via Guicciardini 49 ☎ (055) 278751/218032/218179*) is a valuable source of information for any traveler in need of help, advice or emergency services.

The Azienda Autonoma di Turismo (*Via Tornabuoni 15, 50123 Firenze ☎ (055) 216544/5*) provides city maps and information about special events and opening times in the city. The Ente Provinciale Turismo (*Via Manzoni 16, 50121 Firenze ☎ (055) 2478141*) provides information about the province of Florence. The other eight provincial capitals, Arezzo, Grosseto, Livorno, Lucca, Massa Carrara, Pisa, Pistoia and Siena, have their own tourist information boards.

Arezzo Piazza Risorgimento 116 ☎(0575) 20839
Grosseto Viale Monterosa 206 ☎(0564) 22534
Livorno Piazza Cavour 6 ☎(0586) 33111
Lucca Via Vittorio Veneto 40 ☎(0583) 43639
Massa Carrara Via Garibaldi, Carrara ☎(0585) 70894
Pisa Piazza Arcivescovado ☎(050) 560464 and Piazza Stazione ☎(050) 42291
Pistoia Piazza Duomo ☎(0573) 21622
Siena Via Fiorentina 89 ☎(0577) 50044

Renting a cottage or villa
Agriturist (*Piazza S. Firenze 3, 50122 Firenze ☎ (055) 287838*) provides information about all aspects of rural Tuscany, from walking to renting farmhouses.

Airline companies
Alitalia Lungarno Acciaioli 10-12, 50123 Firenze ☎(055) 263051/2/3. Reservations ☎(055) 2788. Via Veneto 9/10, 50047 Prato ☎(0574) 29220/33220
British Airways Via della Vigna Nuova 36-38, 50123 Firenze ☎(055) 218655
Pan Am Lungarno Acciaioli 10, 50123 Firenze ☎(055) 282716
TWA Piazza S. Trìnita 1, 50123 Firenze ☎(055) 284691

Airports
Pisa Airport ☎(050) 28088
La Perètola Airport ☎(055) 3498

Automobile club
Automobile Club d'Italia (ACI) ☎(055) 24861

15

Basic information

Post offices
Central Post Office (Posta Centrale)   Via Pietrapiana 53-55, 50121 Firenze ☎(055) 212305, and at Via Pellicceria, 50123 Firenze ☎(055) 216122

Tour operators in Florence
American Express   Via Guicciardini 49, 50125 Firenze ☎(055) 278751/218032/218179
CIT   Via Cavour 56-59, 50123 Firenze ☎(055) 294306

Major libraries in Florence
Biblioteca Comunale Centrale   Via S. Egidio 21 ☎(055) 282863
Biblioteca Nazionale Centrale   Piazza Cavalleggeri 1 ☎(055) 244441
British Institute Library   Lungarno Guicciardini 9 ☎(055) 284031
French Institute Library   Piazza Ognissanti 2 ☎(055) 298902
German Institute Library   Via Giusti 44 ☎(055) 2479161
Vieusseux Library   Palazzo Strozzi, ☎(055) 215990

Major places of worship in Florence
St James's (American Episcopal Church)   Via Rucellai 9 ☎(055) 294417
St Mark's (Church of England)   Via Maggio 16 ☎(055) 294764
Synagogue   Via L.C. Farini 4☎ (055) 245252

Consulates
Austria   Via dei Servi 9 ☎(055) 215352
Belgium   Via dei Servi 28 ☎(055) 282094
Denmark   Via dei Servi 13 ☎(055) 211007
France   Piazza Borgognissanti 2 ☎(055) 213509
Netherlands   Via Cavour 81 ☎(055) 475249
Norway   Via Piana 8 ☎(055) 2280316
Spain   Via G. La Pira 21 ☎(055) 217110
Sweden   Via della Scala 4 ☎(055) 296865
Switzerland   Piazzale Galileo 5 ☎(055) 222434
UK   Lungarno Corsini 2 ☎(055) 212594
USA   Lungarno Amerigo Vespucci 38 ☎(055) 298276

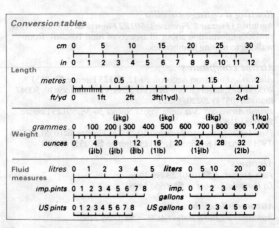

Emergency information

Emergency services
Police   ☎ 113.
Ambulance } You will be asked which service
Fire   you require.

Hospital emergency departments in Florence
Camerata   Via Piazzola 68 ☎ (055) 575807
San Giovanni di Dio   Borgognissanti 20 ☎ (055) 278751
Santa Maria Nuova-Careggi   Ponte Nuovo ☎ (055) 27741

Other medical emergencies
If your complaint does not warrant an ambulance, telephone
the *guardia medica* (doctor on call) (*☎ (055) 477891*). A list
of English-speaking doctors and dentists is published in
Firenze Oggi. The police can also be telephoned on 4977.

Late-night pharmacies
Every *farmacia* (pharmacy) has the late-night roster
displayed in its window. This information is also published in
La Nazione and can be obtained by telephone (*☎ 110*).

Automobile accidents
—Do not admit liability or incriminate yourself.
—Ask any witness(es) to stay and give a statement.
—Remember to use your warning triangle.
—Exchange names, addresses, car details and insurance
   companies' names and addresses with the other driver(s).
—Report the accident to your insurance company.

Car breakdowns
—Put on flashing hazard warning lights and place warning
   triangle 50m (55yds) behind the car.
—☎ 116 and tell the operator where you are, with plate
   number and type of car. The ACI will bring assistance.

Lost passport
If you lose your passport you should immediately report the
loss to the police and contact your consulate (see *Consulates*
p14) for emergency travel documents.

Lost travelers cheques
Notify the local police immediately, then follow the
instructions provided with your travelers cheques, or contact
the issuing company's nearest office. Contact your consulate
or American Express if you are stranded with no money.

Lost property
If you lose anything it may be handed in at the lost property
office (*☎ (055) 216341*). If you do not find it, report the loss
to the local police, as many insurance companies will not
recognize claims without a police report.

Emergency phrases
Help!   *Aiuto!*
There has been an accident.   *C'è stato un incidente.*
Where is the nearest telephone/hospital?   *Dov'è il*
   telefono/l'ospedale più vicino?
Call a doctor/ambulance.   *Chiamate un*
   dottore/un'ambulanza.
Call the police.   *Chiamate la polizia.*

Time chart of Tuscan history

8th–4thC BC	Area called Etruria after the Etruscans, the most ancient of the indigenous Italian tribes, skillful artisans and seafaring tradesmen.
6thC BC	Etruscan civilization reached from Po valley to Bay of Naples; federation of autonomous kingdoms or "lucomonies" included Arezzo, Cortona, Chiusi, Fiesole, Populonia, Roselle, Vetulonia, Volterra.
351BC	Etruria annexed by Rome.
3rd–2ndC BC	Roman roads (the Aurelia, Clodia, Cassia and Flaminia) built across Etruria; Roman colonies included Ansedonia, Fiesole, Roselle and Volterra.
91BC	Roman citizenship extended to Etruscans, whose cultural identity was gradually absorbed.
570AD	Tuscany occupied by the Lombards, a Germanic people, whose dukes ruled from Lucca.
774AD	Tuscany annexed to Charlemagne's empire and administered, still from Lucca, by a succession of imperial margraves. The countryside was held by feudal landlords, lay and ecclesiastic; the Benedictine Abbadia S. Salvatore was the most powerful of the religious foundations.
11thC	First crusade opened trade with eastern markets and stimulated religious feeling; city life revived with formation of new class of merchants and artisans. Reforming religious orders founded at Vallombrosa and Camaldoli. Powerful warlords, such as the Guidi, Aldobrandeschi and Malaspina, still held large tracts of country in fee.
1115	Countess Matilda, the last of the Germanic margraves, died, leaving her lands to the Pope. With Papacy and Holy Roman Empire locked in conflict, the nascent Tuscan cities asserted their independence; experimental republican governments were administered from public buildings fortified against the unrepresented majority and jealous feudal landowners. From the end of the 12thC, a magistrate or *podestà*, usually a foreigner, was responsible for law and order. The most prosperous early communes were Arezzo, Florence, Pisa, Pistoia and Siena; a strong economy developed based on commerce, especially the cloth trade, and banking.
1125	Florence took Fiesole, the first, most violent conquest in the gradual takeover of Tuscany.
1215	Tuscan participation in long-standing conflict between Pope and Emperor was sparked off by a feud between the Buondelmonti and Amadei clans, according to legend. The words "Guelf" and "Ghibelline," for supporters of the Pope and Emperor respectively, were not used for several decades. By 1266 the Guelfs prevailed in Florence, with the two main factions after 1300 named the "Blacks" and the "Whites."
1293	The Ordinances of Justice consolidated the political power of the major guilds, excluding the nobility from government .
1338	The chronicler Villani recorded Florence's population as 90,000. It was Europe's richest city. The Palazzo Vecchio, the churches of S. Maria Novella and S. Croce had been built, and the Duomo begun. Internal politics in the merchant oligarchy were chronically unstable.

Dante's comparison of his native city to a sick woman tossing and turning in her bed, searching in any direction for rest and relief, still held.

1342	First of the Florentine bankruptcies after King Edward III of England defaulted on large debts. To reconcile civil factions, a foreigner, Walter of Brienne, Duke of Athens, was granted executive authority, but was expelled within the year.
1348	The Black Death killed off more than one-third of the population of Tuscany.
1378	Armed uprising in Florence of the *ciompi*, the lowest-paid employees in the wool industry, seeking guild representation. After initial concessions, the result was a tightening of the merchant oligarchy.
1384	Arezzo fell to Florence, which, always at war with Milan and Naples, continued its imperial expansion, gaining Montepulciano (1390), Pisa, the great prize (1406), Cortona (1411) and Livorno (1421). Chroniclers increasingly referred not to Tuscany but to the "Florentine Empire."
1434	After a brief exile, Cosimo de' Medici, from a rich business family, became unofficial leader of Florence, initiating a period of unprecedented stability, prosperity and achievement.
1469	Lorenzo the Magnificent, although only 20, was called upon to take charge of the city after the brief reign of Piero, Cosimo's son.
1478	Francesco and Jacopo Pazzi, encouraged by Pope Sixtus IV, made an ill-judged bid for power by plotting the assassination of Lorenzo and his brother Giuliano at High Mass in the Duomo. Giuliano was stabbed to death; Lorenzo escaped. The Pazzi family and its supporters were exiled or executed with the enthusiastic backing of the Florentine public. Sixtus served an interdict on Florence and excommunicated Lorenzo.
1492	Death of Lorenzo.
1494	Charles VIII of France invaded Italy, took rebellious Pisa under his protection and entered Florence. The Medici were expelled and Florence governed according to a new, broader-based republican constitution supported by Savonarola, Dominican prior of S. Marco and a puritanical preacher. Some 3,000 citizens were enfranchised.
1498	Savonarola burned at the stake in the Piazza Signoria as a heretic, with the connivance of the Borgia Pope, Alexander VI.
1502	The democratic constitution proved an inefficient instrument at a time of unremitting war. Piero Soderini was elected head of government for life.
1503-4	Leonardo and Michelangelo commissioned to fresco the walls of the council chamber of the republic with representation of past Florentine victories; but neither work has survived.
1509	Reconquest of Pisa.
1512	The Medici were reinstated as leaders of Florence, and their control subsequently fortified by two Medici Popes, Giovanni as Pope Leo X, and Giulio as Pope Clement VII.
1525	Accademia degli Intronati, the first of the modern

	literary academies, founded in Siena.
1527	As imperial mercenaries sacked Rome, Florence again expelled the Medici and reinvoked the Savonarolan republican constitution.
1530	Florence besieged by imperial forces. Alessandro de' Medici installed as head of the defeated republic.
1531	Alessandro created first Duke of Florence.
1532	First (posthumous) publication of Machiavelli's *The Prince*.
1537	Cosimo I, from a lateral branch of the Medici family, created Duke of Florence, after assassination of Alessandro. He ruled until 1574.
1555-9	Florentine conquest of Siena and its territories. The concept of Etruria was revived to emphasize the cultural and political unity of Cosimo's enlarged empire.
1563	The Accademia del Disegno, the first fine arts academy in Europe, founded with Cosimo I as its patron.
1569	Cosimo I created Grand Duke of Tuscany by Pope Pius V. Of the six grand dukes who succeeded Cosimo, only his grandson Ferdinand I (reigned 1587-1609) inherited his gift for leadership.
1582	The Accademia della Crusca, a scholarly body responsible for the purity of the Tuscan language, began work on a definitive Italian dictionary.
1589	Galileo demonstrated the first principles of dynamics at Pisa.
1593	The free port of Livorno, established by Cosimo I, was opened to all immigrants.
1610	Galileo discovered the satellites of Jupiter, the "Medicean Planets," and was made court mathematician to Cosimo II.
1737	Gian Gastone, the last of the Medici, died without an heir; the Tuscan grand duchy passed to the house of Lorraine, under whose enlightened rule Tuscany became known as a liberal oasis in a Europe otherwise suffering from despotic and inefficient governments. Administrative procedures and religious foundations were reformed and rationalized; agricultural improvements included draining swampy coastal plains and the Valdichiana.
1753	The Accademia dei Georgofili was founded and supported an agricultural economy.
1799-	French occupation interrupted rule of House of
1814	Lorraine, now head of Austrian Empire.
1815	Restoration of Ferdinand III of Lorraine, who continued to implement progressive policies. The Congress of Vienna ceded Monte Argentario, Piombino and Elba to Tuscany. Lucca and Massa Carrara were still separate duchies.
1847	Lucca ceded to Tuscany.
1848	Uprisings spearheaded by middle-class radicals. Leopold II retired to Gaeta but was recalled in a year.
1860	Tuscany voted to be annexed to the united Italy emerging from the wars. The following year, a United Kingdom of Italy was officially proclaimed.
1865-71	Florence capital of Italy. Part of the old city rebuilt as Piazza della Repubblica.
1944	German bombs destroyed Por S. Maria, Ponte Santa Trìnita and Borgo San Jacopo. Outside Florence the most severe war damage was inflicted on Grosseto,

	Livorno, Pisa and along the "Gothic Line" from the Versilia through the Mugello into Romagna.
1966	Florence suffered its most severe flood in recorded history. The low-lying Santa Croce area was the worst affected. Some 1,000 paintings and 500 sculptures were damaged or destroyed.

The Renaissance

The first writer to popularize the idea that art was reborn in central Italy shortly after 1300 was Giorgio Vasari in his Lives, first published in 1550 at the end of the period he was describing. According to Vasari's anthropomorphic chronology, each art had its own life cycle: in painting Giotto was the representative genius of vigorous youth, Masaccio of early maturity, Michelangelo and Leonardo of perfected prime. Vasari contended that with these late Renaissance masters, art, hitherto devoted to reproducing the appearance of the real world, had finally triumphed over nature and become its own master.

It was not, however, until the publication of the French historian Jules Michelet's La Renaissance in 1855 that the word "renaissance" was applied not only to art but to an entire historic period. Michelet was, in fact, describing 16thC France; but five years later Jacob Burckhardt picked up the term and attached it to the spirit of Italian history from 1300-1550. And there, dazzlingly and maddeningly, it has stuck ever since.

The word is out of favor with modern historians. They argue that all period labels are misleading because history is a continuum, not a series of neatly packed "ages," and that this particular label is worse than most because it refers to the activities of an unrepresentative elite minority.

A common reaction to all clinical historiography of the Renaissance is rather like that experienced by the character in E.M. Forster's novel Where Angels Fear to Tread. He was forced to think of a dentist operating among the medieval towers of a Tuscan hill town, and found it painful and disgusting to accept "False teeth and laughing gas and the tilting chair at a place which knew . . . the Renaissance, all fighting and beauty!" The Renaissance is a sensitive subject because it contains the roots of our own civilization; yet we do need the dentist-historians because it is also one of the most complex of historic periods.

Fighting and beauty, yes, but also crises within municipalities, wars between city states, invasion from without. Deference to the ideas and achievements of ancient Rome and Greece set standards that stimulated every form of thought and practical endeavor. Through the weight of investment, the technique of business practice and the geographical reach of commerce, capitalism emerged in something very like its modern form.

If to these developments we add transformation in the arts — music and literature as well as painting, sculpture and architecture — then we have a revolution. But a revolution cannot last for 250 years. So we use a label: the Renaissance. Modified, the label came to describe the outward flow from Italy: the English Renaissance, the French Renaissance, and so forth. Inwardly, however, the pulse rate had certainly been set by Tuscany.

Tuscan architecture

Etruscan

Few non-mortuary buildings survive, but evidence suggests Etruscan origins for the atrium, the central courtyard of the Roman house, and a remarkable similarity between the Etruscan villa type and that of 15thC Florentine palaces. The Tuscan order was characterized by plain rounded columns and capitals. Sections of city walls built with huge irregular blocks remain at Volterra, Cortona and other Tuscan towns. Outside the walls, rock-cut underground tombs were constructed.

See *Route 4* in **Planning**.

Roman

The Romans, superb engineers, developed the Tuscan arch as a central structural element, the Classical Orders being used mainly for decoration. They were master town-planners, and the most complete city remains are at Fiesole, Roselle and Cosa (now called Ansedonia), one of the earliest and most extensive colonies, still under excavation. Ruins of patrician villas can be seen on Elba, Giannutri and near Porto Santo Stefano.*

Romanesque (11th–12thC)

The most influential single building was the Duomo at Pisa, with its tiers of open arcades, a mixture of Lombard and Oriental stylistic elements imitated in country churches and at Carrara,

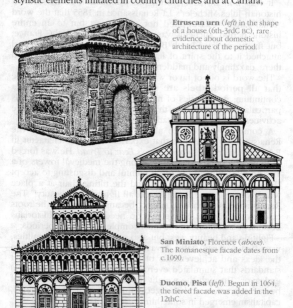

Etruscan urn (*left*) in the shape of a house (6th–3rdC BC), rare evidence about domestic architecture of the period.

San Miniato, Florence (*above*). The Romanesque facade dates from c.1090.

Duomo, Pisa (*left*). Begun in 1064, the tiered facade was added in the 12thC.

Monteriggioni. The 13thC walls (*below*) were built by the Sienese.

Pistoia, Prato and Lucca. Florentine churches — the Baptistry, Santi Apostoli, San Miniato — remained more strictly within the Classical tradition; the Collegiata at Empoli marks the western limit of the Florentine influence. The Benedictine Abbey of Sant'Antimo, built in local alabaster but in a style imported from northern Italy, is one of the most incandescently lovely religious buildings in Italy.

Medieval towns bristled with defense towers; those of San Gimignano and Monteriggioni are the best preserved.

Gothic (13th-14thC)

Gothic architecture was first introduced into Italy by the French Cistercians who built San Galgano around 1218. A native variation of the Burgundian model emerged first in Florence with the preaching churches of Santa Maria Novella and Santa Croce, and reached its noblest expression there with Arnolfo di Cambio's Duomo. The two loveliest Gothic structures in Florence are the Loggia dei Lanzi and the church of Orsanmichele, also originally a loggia. Civic buildings were conceived as fortresses: the Palazzo della Signoria at Florence is the most imposing of these republican strongholds, the Palazzo Pubblico at Siena the most graceful.

Renaissance (15thC)

The innovative genius of Brunelleschi (1377-1446) was nourished first by Florentine Romanesque church architecture, later by

Palazzo Pubblico, Siena. The most graceful Gothic civic building in Tuscany, built from 1297-1342.

Orsanmichele, Florence (*above*). The church was built up from a loggia, enclosed from 1380.

Loggia dei Lanzi, Piazza della Signoria, Florence (*right*). Built from 1376-82.

Innocenti loggia, Piazza SS Annunziata, Florence (*below*). Completed in 1426, an inaugural building of the Renaissance.

23

Culture, history and background

Byzantine and Classical Roman engineering principles. His Innocenti loggia in Florence is the first building of the Renaissance, and his cupola of the city's Duomo its outstanding engineering achievement. Brunelleschi's genius reached its maturity in Florence with the Pazzi Chapel and Santo Spirito.

Of equal caliber but less influential in the Florence of his own day was the Genoese architect Leon Battista Alberti, whose Rucellai Palace and Chapel are elegant and scholarly restatements of Classical themes, and whose facade of S. M. Novella was later imitated all over Italy.

Michelozzo's Medici Palace in Florence remained the prototype for domestic building in Tuscany through the 16thC; there are fine Renaissance palaces at Pienza and Montepulciano. Perhaps the most magnificent of all Medici villas is Giuliano da Sangallo's symmetrical Poggio a Caiano, with its Classical arcaded basement.

High Renaissance and Mannerist (16thC)

The initiative passed to Rome. Michelangelo's first architectural works, the Laurentian Library and New Sacristy at Florence's San Lorenzo, were Medici commissions, built after he had worked for some years in Rome. His dynamic flouting of Classical order and constructional principles provided inspiration for the later Florentine Mannerist architects, Ammannati and Buontalenti.

Santa Maria Novella, Florence (*above*)

Rucellai Palace, Florence (*above*), built from the 1450s.

Medici Riccardi Palace, Florence (*left*), built from 1444-64.

Villa Medici, Poggio a Caiano (1480-85), Giuliano da Sangallo's adaptation of the antique Roman villa type.

The classicizing influence of the Roman High Renaissance style, founded by Bramante, is most evident in Antonio da Sangallo the Elder's domed church of San Biagio at Montepulciano, with a Greek cross plan.

Two 16thC Medici villas near Florence, Artimino and Petraia, were built by Buontalenti for Ferdinand I, and Giuliano di Baccio d'Agnolo's Palazzo Campana at Colle di Val d'Elsa shows Mannerist architecture at its most elegant.

Baroque and Neo-Classical (17th-18thC)

The swirling theatricality of the Baroque was created in Rome, but Florence boasts some fine church facades: G. Silvani's San Gaetano is the most beautiful, and Ferdinando Ruggieri's San Firenze the largest and boldest. The master of Italian Baroque, Bernini, added the Chigi Chapel to the Duomo in Siena. Interesting palaces in Florence include the *trompe l'oeil* Cartelloni in Via S. Antonino, the Capponi in Via G. Capponi, and the Corsini on the Lungarno Corsini.

Modern (19th-20thC)

The sea front at Viareggio is lined with splendid Liberty-style hotels, and in Florence the Villino Broggi, Via Scipione Ammirato 99, is another delightful example of Liberty architecture. The 19thC cast-iron arcades of the Mercato Centrale show the use of new materials, which culminated in the functionalist Florence Station and Nervi's Stadium.

Laurentian Library steps, San Lorenzo, Florence (*left*), by Michelangelo (1550s).

San Biagio, Montepulciano (*above*), designed by Antonio da Sangallo the elder, built 1518-45.

San Gaetano, Florence (*left*), the best Baroque church facade in Florence, built in 1648.

Central Station, Florence (*below*). The first functionalist station in Italy, built in 1935.

Tuscan sculpture

Etruscan

Etruscan sculpture was broadly Greek-based, but more vigorous and less rational in character. The finest examples in Tuscany are in the Florence Archeological Museum, but exceptional pieces do remain at Chiusi, Cortona and Volterra, and the museum at Grosseto is a beautifully organized introduction to the subject.

See *Route 4* in **Planning**.

Roman

Roman humanism led to a new emphasis on portraiture, and the Uffizi possesses one of the most distinguished collections of Roman busts in the world. The sarcophagi in the Pisa Camposanto affected the new sculptural art created by the Pisani in the 13th-14thC, and Roman columns and capitals were often incorporated into Romanesque churches.

Romanesque

Romanesque figure sculpture developed relatively late in Tuscany. In Florence the work is mainly decorative, with Classical or Oriental motifs, as illustrated in San Miniato and the Baptistry.

Pisa emerged as the leading center in the late 12thC and produced the first named Tuscan sculptors: Guglielmo, whose ornate style is demonstrated in the decorations of the Pisa Duomo and Baptistry; and Bonanno, famous for the bronze doors of the Pisa Duomo. Followers of the Lombard Master Antelmi worked in Arezzo, the Casentino, Massa Marittima and Volterra. The wealth of Romanesque sculpture at Pistoia includes the more austere and highly individual work of Gruamonte.

The Pisani and the Gothic

Nicola Pisano and his son Giovanni (active 1258-1314) created a realistic and expressive figure style which looks modern even today. Their four famous pulpits in Tuscany are in the Pisa Duomo and Baptistry, the Siena Duomo and in the church of Sant'Andrea at Pistoia. Giovanni also carved the figures for the facade of the Siena Duomo, which have now been removed to the Museo dell'Duomo, as well as a *Madonna* in the Pisa Duomo and a *Madonna and Child* in the Prato Duomo. They and their immediate successors, Andrea and Nino Pisano, and Tino da Camaiano, established Pisa and Siena as the most active centers, although Andrea is best known for the first doors of the Florence Baptistry. Tino's works are scattered, but well represented in the Duomos of Pisa and Siena and the Bardini Museum, Florence.

The exquisite relief of carvings of another Sienese sculptor, Goro di Gregorio, on the tomb of St Cerbone in the Massa Marittima Duomo, demonstrate the continuing influence of illuminated manuscripts on Gothic sculpture despite the example of the Pisani. The most important Florentine Gothic sculptors were Andrea Orcagna, whose principal works are the relief carvings of the Orsanmichele Tabernacle in Florence, and Nanni di Banco, whose sinuous relief of the *Assumption* over the Porta della Mandorla of the Florence Duomo and the classical *Four Crowned Saints* on the facade of Orsanmichele point gently but firmly toward the dawning Renaissance.

15thC Renaissance

The richest collection of Renaissance sculpture is in the Florence Bargello, where, among many key pieces, are the Donatello and Verrocchio *Davids*, and works by the Della Robbias, Desiderio da Settignano, Antonio Pollaiuolo and Antonio Rossellino, demonstrating the variety of interpretations of the ideals and proportion of Classical sculpture. The two best places in Florence to study the evolution of Florentine sculpture from Gothic to Renaissance are the exteriors of the Baptistry and Orsanmichele. Lorenzo Ghiberti's first set of Baptistry doors, on the N, are still late Gothic; the second set, on the E, are fully of the Renaissance. Ghiberti is represented on the facade of Orsanmichele, as is the transitional work of Nanni di Bianco. Donatello's St George predella, the earliest example of perspective in relief carving, has now followed the St George into the Bargello.

Donatello, who infused feeling and tension into Classical forms, was the dominant genius of 15thC sculpture. To appreciate his full range one must visit the Duomo Museum and the churches of Santa Croce and San Lorenzo as well as the Bargello.

The greatest master outside Florence was the Sienese Jacopo della Quercia whose animated works in Siena include the original carvings from the Fonte Gaia in the Palazzo Pubblico.

16thC Renaissance
The Florentine Michelangelo held that sculpture was the highest art form, and his work in this medium has an unprecedented expressive range. Important works at Florence include his first carvings in the Casa Buonarroti and his last in the Duomo Museum, as well as the *David* and *Slaves* in the Accademia and the Medici Tombs in San Lorenzo. Michelangelo's overpowering genius has caused his contemporaries and Mannerist successors to be seen in an unfair light in the eyes of posterity. A recently arranged room in the Bargello is designed to show his influence on, as well as the individual talents of, Andrea Sansovino, Vincenzo Rossi, Vincenzo Danti, Giambologna and, most impressive, Benvenuto Cellini. Outside Florence, the most exciting works are Domenico Beccafumi's uncharacteristically restrained eight bronze angels in the Siena Duomo.

Baroque and Rococo (17th-18thC)
The ivories in Florence's Argenti Museum express all the inherent fantastication of the Baroque and Rococo spirit, and Ferdinando Tacca's tomb sculptures in the San Lorenzo Cappella dei Principi convey its authoritative courtliness. The greatest Baroque sculpture was created and mostly remains in Rome, although there are some Berninis in the Bargello, Florence and the Siena Duomo. The Florentine Pietro Tacca, sculptor to the grand dukes, produced a number of notable works including the lovable and much-patted Porcellino Fountain in the Florence Mercato Nuovo, and the strange, wicked fountains in Santissima Annunziata. His four Moors at Livorno are strenuous but empty of meaning. G. B. Foggini, one of the most prolific Florentine Baroque artists, both as sculptor and architect, is increasingly admired, especially for his decorative stucco reliefs in the Carmine and Santissima Annunziata.

19th-20thC
There is a revival of interest in early 19thC sculptor Lorenzo Bartolini, whose work has a smoothly accomplished feel. There are works by Marino Marini in his native Pistoia and at Florence in the Alberto della Ragione Collection in the Piazza Signoria and in the new Marini Museum next to the Rucellai Chapel.

Tuscan painting

Etruscan
The only Etruscan tombs now in Tuscany are in the Florence Archeological Museum and at Chiusi.
The Byzantine Manner (12th-13thC)
Each center developed the so-called Byzantine Manner in its own

way, as one can see from the many painted crosses in Tuscan churches. Panel paintings of other subjects are now more usually in museums, although Bonaventura Berlinghieri's *St Francis* has been left in San Francesco, Pescia. Other Tuscan masters were Giunta Pisano and the St Martin Master, represented at the Museo Nazionale at Pisa, Margaritone d'Arezzo, at the Galleria, Arezzo, and Guido da Siena, on show at the Pinacoteca Nazionale, Siena.

Toward the end of the 13thC iconic stylization began to yield to the more vigorous monumentality of Cimabue and the Gothic grace and humanity of the Sienese master Duccio. Cimabue's famous *Crucifixion* is in the S. Croce Museum, Florence; he is also represented in the Uffizi and at S. Domenico, Arezzo, and the mosaics he worked on are in the Florence Baptistry and Pisa Duomo. Duccio is on show in his home town in the Museo dell'Opera Duomo and Pinacoteca Nazionale, and at S. Francesco in Grosseto and the Uffizi.

Giottesque Realism and the International Gothic (14thC)

At the turn of the 13thC Giotto introduced a new kind of painting, representing solid forms placed in three-dimensional space and conveying the humanity of its subjects. His example determined the course of Florentine painting through the High Renaissance. His principal works in Florence are in the Bardi and Peruzzi Chapels of S. Croce and in the Uffizi.

Two schools dominated Tuscan painting: Giottesque Realism from Florence, and the International Gothic from Siena. Giotto's successors include Taddeo Gaddi, Bernardo Daddi, Giottino, Agnolo Gaddi and Spinello Aretino: they refined his settings, but never quite matched his psychological power. Two Florentine painters who rejected Giotto's example and worked within the graceful but two-dimensional Gothic tradition were Andrea Orcagna and Lorenzo Monaco. In Florence, 14thC painting is best represented in the churches of S. Croce and S.M. Novella.

The great Tuscan interpreter of the International Gothic was the Sienese master Simone Martini, whose major works are in the Palazzo Pubblico and Pinacoteca Nazionale at Siena, the Museo Nazionale in Pisa, and the Uffizi. Along with the Horne Museum, Florence, these galleries also house works of the Sienese Lorenzetti brothers, Pietro and Ambrogio, who combined elements from both styles.

The Renaissance (15thC)

The astonishing story of Florentine *quattrocento* painting is best told in the Uffizi, where portable works from the Medici collections and Tuscan churches are arranged chronologically, enabling one to follow the various innovations, preoccupations and influences: perspective, light, anatomy, Neo-Platonic and Christian symbolism, and the first contact with Flemish Realism.

Fortunately, more masterpieces have remained outside this didactic sanctuary than can be listed here. They include, in Florence, the Carmine Masaccios, the Medici Palace Gozzoli cycle, the S. Apollonia Castagnos, the S. Marco Angelicos, the S.M. Novella Uccellos, and the Ghirlandaios in Ognissanti, S.M. Novella and S. Trìnita.

The greatest masterpieces outside Florence are the Piero della Francescas at San Francesco, Arezzo, in the little church at Monterchi, and, at Sansepolcro, the *Misericordia* altarpiece and *Resurrection*. Filippo Lippi's outstanding works are the lovely frescoes in the Prato Duomo. The Museo Diocesano in Cortona possesses one major Angelico and a number of Signorellis. There are delightful narrative cycles at San Gimignano by Ghirlandaio in the Collegiata and Gozzoli in San Agostino.

High Renaissance and Mannerist (16thC)

Florence lost its artistic supremacy. The two greatest Tuscan geniuses, Michelangelo and Leonardo, left Tuscany after the first few years of the century. Only one painting by Michelangelo and three by Leonardo remain in Tuscany, all in the Uffizi, where there are also fine works by other 16thC masters including Andrea del Sarto and the early Mannerists.

The disturbing, highly intellectual style later called Mannerism was the last original Florentine contribution to mainstream Italian painting. The leading Tuscan Mannerist painters were Rosso Fiorentino, Pontormo, Bronzino, Salviati, Sodoma and Beccafumi.

The richest collection of 16thC paintings in Tuscany is at Florence in the Pitti's Palatine Gallery, where Cristofano Allori's ravishing *Judith* sums up many of the achievements of the century, and where masters from other Italian centers compete for attention with Florentines, including Andrea del Sarto, Fra Bartolommeo and the Mannerists.

At Arezzo, Vasari decorated his own house with allegorical frescoes, which have a freshness and charm lacking in his official work. The great Pontormos outside Florence can be seen within a day. They are in S. Michele at Carmignano, at the Certosa Pinacoteca, Galluzzo, and at Poggio a Caiano. The Rossos are farther flung and are to be found at the Galleria, Arezzo; at S. Lorenzo, Sansepolcro; and one of his most stirring works, the *Deposition*, is housed in the Galleria Pittorica at Volterra.

Baroque and Rococo (17th-18thC)

The Baroque, like the Gothic, was a style Florentine artists never embraced wholeheartedly. The most splendid Baroque decorations are in the Pitti Palace, where the first rooms of the Palatine Gallery were frescoed by Pietro da Cortona, and in the ground-floor rooms of the Argenti Museum by A. M. Colonna and Giovanni da S. Giovanni.

The Florentine Rococo painters were not original but cannot be ignored. Their decorations, mainly frescoes, can be seen in many churches, notably San Firenze, the Badia and Ognissanti.

19th-20thC

The Pitti Gallery of Modern Art displays a vast collection of 19thC academic paintings. Several rooms there are devoted to the Tuscan school, known as the "Macchiaioli" after their Impressionistic "blotted" paintings, which reacted against the academic style. Also in Florence, the Alberto della Ragione Collection in the Piazza Signoria contains some interesting 20thC figurative pictures by Tuscan artists.

At Livorno, the Museo Civico possesses several works by Modigliani, who was born here, and by the Macchiaioli, for whom the town was a major center. The Futurist Gino Severini was born in Cortona, where a room in the Museo dell'Accademia Etrusca is devoted to his life and work.

Tuscany and literature

The great period of Tuscan literature began prodigiously, with three writers whose words have since been the chief shaping influence on the Italian language. Dante (1265-1321) was hounded out of his native Florence in 1302 into an exile during which he wrote the greatest work in the language, the *Divine Comedy*, a comprehensive vision of this and the next world. He signed himself "Dante Alighieri, a Florentine by birth but not by character," and his love-hate feelings for the beautiful city which ejected him are especially pungent in the first two parts of the poem, *Inferno* and *Purgatorio*. Spiritualized love is represented by the figure of Dante's Beatrice. Laura was the love of Italy's second greatest poet, Petrarch, born in Arezzo in 1304 to a father who had been exiled in the same purge as Dante. A good translation conveys the meticulous delicacy of his vastly influential love sonnets. His close friend Boccaccio, born in Certaldo in 1313, is the third of the 14thC Tuscan triumvirate. The hundred tales of his *Decameron* start with a description of Florence during the Black Death of 1348.

The next burst of Tuscan vernacular literary talent came late in the 15thC with the subtle, polished poetry of Pulci, Poliziano and Lorenzo de' Medici; little has been worthily translated. Thereafter it was chiefly in prose that Tuscans of genius expressed themselves. Machiavelli's brief *The Prince* (written 1513) still retains the incandescence of its conviction that politics is not about morals but about getting things done, and the *Maxims* of his friend Guicciardini (1483-1540) conveys the realistic appraisal of human affairs Tuscans have prided themselves on ever since. *Storia d'Italia*, Guicciardini's account of the wars and crises of 1492-1534, has been called the most important work to have issued from an Italian mind.

The poems of Michelangelo, unusually troubled and ecstatic for the period, offer a balancing vision not only of his work but also of his times, as does the marvelously picaresque and direct self-revelation of Cellini's *Autobiography* (1558).

It was a scientist, Galileo (1564-1642), who was to be the last great writer of Tuscan prose. Since his *Dialogue Concerning the Two Chief World Systems* and *The Two New Sciences*, Tuscany has contributed little to the mainstream of Italian literature apart from two exceptional 20thC Florentine novels: Aldo Palazzeschi's *Sorelle Materassi* (1934), about genteel poverty in a Florentine suburb, and Vasco Pratolini's *Cronache di Poveri Amanti* (1947), a picture of working-class life in Santa Croce.

In the early 19thC Tuscany began to play a different literary role. Florence, the city which had exiled its own greatest geniuses, was now capital of a region which Shelley, in his famous letter to Medwin of 1820, described as the "paradise of exiles." Dostoevsky (1821-81) was one of these literary exiles, but mostly they were British or American, often taking refuge in Tuscany because the living was cheap, the climate healthy and the peace and order of its landscape and depth of its history cast a spell on the foreign imagination.

Many writers discovered in Tuscany their ideal working environment. Mark Twain, working on *Pudd'nhead Wilson* in Settignano in the 1890s, claimed he had written more in four months than he could in two years at home. Henry James pronounced the atmosphere of Florence better for mental concentration than Venice. D. H. Lawrence wrote *Lady Chatterley's Lover* (1928) sitting on the grass outside his villa at Scandicci, inspired, so his friends said, by contact with a sympathetic alien culture. Shelley, Nathaniel Hawthorne, James Fenimore Cooper and Arnold Bennett all enjoyed productive visits to Florence.

Yet the many foreign poets and novelists who have attempted to write *about* Tuscany have generally failed. Elizabeth Barrett Browning's long verse polemics about the Risorgimento (1847-61) and George Eliot's novel *Romola* (1863) about Renaissance Florence are among the most ambitious and most unreadable efforts. William Dean Howells' *Indian Summer* (1886) is one of the more delightful of novels set in Tuscany; Anatole France's satire *Le Lys Rouge* (1894) is perhaps the sharpest and funniest; E.M. Forster's

Where Angels Fear to Tread (1905) and *A Room with a View* (1908) are the ones that are still widely read. John Mortimer's *A Summer's Lease* (1988) is amusing about life in modern Chiantishire.

Much of this fiction takes place within the foreign community, a large various group of cultivated aliens given to making crucial excursions into a landscape where the senses and intellects of the repressed Northern European may open and flower. Italians, when they appear at all, are often lazy opportunists or forces of nature. Stendhal (1783-1842) was unusual as a foreigner who really did want to understand how Tuscans of all classes lived and thought. The others, even those passionate "Italophiles" the Brownings, didn't often meet real Italians, and their fictional treatments of Tuscany suffer from what Charles Greville, writing about Florentine society in 1830, described as "no foundation of natives."

The only novelist who turned the Florentine foreign community into the subject of truly great literature was Henry James (1843-1916). Although *Portrait of a Lady* is partly set in Florence, usually James did not wish to be regarded as one of the crowd of "local" novelists, and disguised or sublimated his source material. Nevertheless, there is something of Florence in most of his Italian novels, and many of his characters are based in whole or part on Florentine acquaintances. *The Aspern Papers* is a good example — although set in Venice, it was inspired by the story of Jane Clairmont, mother of Byron's daughter Allegra and step-sister of Mary Shelley, who spent her old age in voluntary exile in Florence in possession of many of Shelley's papers. James' concern with the experience of exile and the meeting of cultures gives us perhaps the truest impression of Florence as a paradise of exiles.

Suggestions for further reading
Guidebooks

The *Blue Guide to Florence* is art-historically reliable and updated regularly. Eve Borsook's *Companion Guide to Florence* is readable, learned and full of fascinating detail, but awkward for on-the-spot use. The Touring Club Italiano *Firenze e Dintorni* (1974) and *Toscana* (1974) are the most detailed of all guides; new editions are due in the 1990s. Jonathan Keates' *Tuscany* (1988) is stylishly written, by an experienced and enthusiastic Italophile.

History and art history

Giorgio Vasari's *Lives of the Painters, Sculptors and Architects* (1550) is still the essential basis of the art history; the best selective edition, comprising two volumes, is in Penguin, edited by George Bull. Numerous books about the inscrutable Etruscans include George Dennis' *Cities and Cemeteries of Etruria*, written in the 19thC and now out of print, and Michael Grant's *The Etruscans* (1980). Gene Adam Brucker's *Florence 1138-1737* (1983) is authoritative as well as beautifully written and illustrated. Iris Origo's classic *The Merchant of Prato* (1957) is about a businessman who lived on the eve of the Renaissance; J.R. Hale's *Florence and the Medici* (1977) is the clearest account of how and why the Medici took control; Harold Acton's *The Last Medici* closes the story. Judith Hook's *Siena* is the best short account of the history and the art.

Memoirs and impressions

Books about the Anglo-American passion for Tuscany include Paul R. Baker's *The Fortunate Pilgrims: Americans in Italy 1800-1860* (1964), Olive Hamilton's *Paradise of Exiles: Tuscany and the British* (1974) and Giuliana Artom Treves' *The Golden Ring: The Anglo-Florentines 1847-1862* (1956).

Accounts of Florence and Tuscany as it was earlier in this century can make fascinating reading. E.H. Hutton's books explore the area before and after World War I. Iris Origo's *War in Val d'Orcia* is a rivetting account of World War II, as is Eric Newby's *Love and War in the Apennines*. Read also Iris Origo's autobiography *Images and Shadows*. Alan Moorehead's *The Villa Diana* and Mary McCarthy's *The Stones of Florence* are about Tuscany in the late 1940s and 1950s. If you read Italian you will be uncomfortably amused by Curzio Malaparte's brilliant analysis of the Tuscan character, *Maladetti Toscani* (1964).

Orientation map

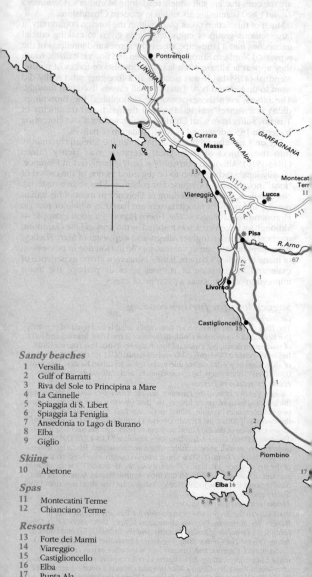

Sandy beaches

1 Versilia
2 Gulf of Barratti
3 Riva del Sole to Principina a Mare
4 La Cannelle
5 Spiaggia di S. Libert
6 Spiaggia La Feniglia
7 Ansedonia to Lago di Burano
8 Elba
9 Giglio

Skiing

10 Abetone

Spas

11 Montecatini Terme
12 Chianciano Terme

Resorts

13 Forte dei Marmi
14 Viareggio
15 Castiglioncello
16 Elba
17 Punta Ala
18 Castiglione della Pescaia
19 Monte Argentario
20 Giglio
21 Ansedonia
* Towns of major artistic/scenic interest

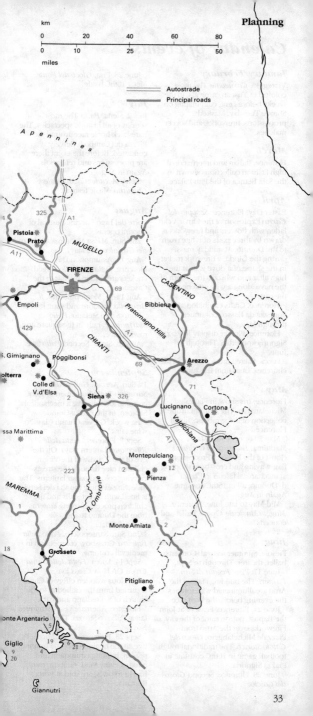

km

| 0 | 20 | 40 | 60 | 80 |

| 0 | 10 | 25 | 50 |

miles

Autostrade

Principal roads

Apennines

Pistoia

Prato

MUGELLO

A11

FIRENZE

A1

CASENTINO

Empoli

325

Bibbiena

Pratomagno Hills

A1

69

CHIANTI

S. Gimignano

Poggibonsi

Arezzo

Volterra

Colle di
V. d'Elsa

69

71

Siena

326

Lucignano

Cortona

2

Vajdichiana

ssa Marittima

A1

Montepulciano

12

MAREMMA

R. Ombrone

223

Pienza

2

Monte Amiata

2

Grosseto

18

Pitigliano

1

nte Argentario

5

Giglio

9
20

4

19

6 21 7

Giannutri

33

Planning

Calendar of events

January/February

Viareggio. *Carnevale.* The most colorful of Tuscan carnivals, in the weeks before Lent, culminating on Shrove Tuesday. Masked processions, fireworks, and soccer matches.

March

Florence, Italian and international high fashion collections shown in the Sala Bianca of the Pitti Palace.

April

Easter Day. Florence. *Scoppio del Carro* (Explosion of the Cart). A cart laden with flowers and fireworks is drawn by three pairs of white oxen to the Duomo. At midday mass, during the Gloria, a firework rocket in the shape of a dove is lit at the high altar and whizzes the length of the nave along a wire attached to the cart.

Florence. Crafts exhibition at the Fortezza da Basso. Continues through May.

Florence. Flower display in Piazza Signoria and Uffizi. Through to June.

Lucca. Sacred music festival in the churches. Lasts until late June.

May

Florence. Iris show in Piazzale Michelangelo. The largest European collection of the symbolic "lily of Florence."

May 20 or next Sun. Massa Marittima. *Balestro del Girifalco* (Joust of the Falcon). Procession, flag-waving and crossbow shooting at mechanical falcon in Piazza d. Duomo, all in 15thC costume. Again in Aug.

Mid-May to late June. Florence. *Maggio Musicale.* Opera, ballet and concerts.

June

Fiesole. Summer festival. Concerts, ballet, theater. Through to Sept.

June 17. Pisa. *Regata di San Ranieri.* The buildings facing the Arno are illuminated with torches the evening before the boat race.

June 24. Florence. Feast of St John the Baptist, patron saint of the city. Fireworks over the Arno from Piazzale Michelangelo. *Gioco del Calcio Storico.* The traditional rough football game in 16thC costume in Piazza Signoria.

June 28. Florence. Second *Gioco del Calcio.*

June 28. Pisa. *Gioco del Ponte.* Mock 16thC battle.

July

July 2. Siena. *Palio.* The most serious of all historic spectacles. The bare-back horse race around the Piazza del Campo is fiercely contested. Before the event there are processions and rehearsals. Again in Aug.

Siena. *Accademia Musicale Chigiana.* Music festival.

August

Torre del Lago Puccini. Festival of Puccini operas.

2nd Sun. Massa Marittima. *Balestro del Girifalco* (see May).

Aug 15, Assumption Day. Florence. *Festa del Grillo.* Caged crickets are sold in the fair in the Cascine.

Aug 15-16. Montepulciano. *Il Bruscello.* Folklore and song festival.

Porto Santo Stefano. *Palio Marinaro.* Parade in the square and rowing race.

Aug 16. Siena. Second *Palio* (see July).

September

1st Sun. Arezzo. *Giostra del Saracino.* Eight horsemen in 13thC costume joust against a mechanical Saracen, in the Piazza Grande.

1st week. Greve. Chianti Classico wine fair.

Sept 7. Florence. *Festa delle Rificolone* (Lantern Day). On the eve of the Nativity of the Virgin children race through the streets carrying colored paper lanterns. The following evening the Via dei Servi is lined with sweet stalls and the children process carrying lanterns from the Duomo to SS. Annunziata.

2nd Sun. Sansepolcro. *Palio della Balestra.* Crossbow competition in medieval costume.

Sept 14. Lucca. *Festa della Santa Croce.* On Holy Cross Eve, a miraculous wooden effigy of Christ is carried from the cathedral to the church of S. Frediano and back.

Florence. Alternate years. Antiques fair at Palazzo Strozzi. Through to Nov.

Sept 28. Florence. On St Michael's Eve, at the beginning of the hunting season, hunting equipment and birds of every kind, ranging from hawks to owls, are sold at Porta Romana.

October
Prato. Season opens at Teatro Metastasio. The home company is one of the liveliest experimental theater groups in Italy. Until April.

Florence. Winter fashion collections shown in Pitti.

Mid-Oct. Impruneta. Agricultural fair of St Luke.

Last Sun. Montalcino. *Sagra del Tordo.* Traditional shooting and eating of thrushes.

November
Florence. Opening of main concert season at Teatro Comunale. Through to mid-Dec.

December
Florence. Opening of opera season at Teatro Comunale. Through to mid-Jan.

See also *Public holidays* in **Basic information**.

When and where to go

May and Sept are the ideal months to visit Florence: cool enough for vigorous sightseeing, summery enough for leisurely day trips into the hills. The countryside in May is radiant with wild flowers, scented with blossom and young grasses. For the grand tourists of the 18th and 19thC, Sept was the start of the Florence season, and a very sensible time it still is, a little warmer and drier than May, and less crowded than Aug, which is in every way the most uncomfortable month.

In fact, those who do not wish to share their vacation with what seems like half the world should avoid Florence, a city ill-suited to mass tourism, in the week before and including Easter and from June through to the end of Aug. Overcrowding, as regular visitors know, can render the narrow medieval streets barely tolerable. However, if you must go in the high season, be sure to reserve a hotel in advance.

Whatever the season, the day will come when Florence seems too much: too much art, too much noise in the narrow streets, a stony maze from which one longs to escape. This is the day to go to Siena, gently dreaming on its landlocked hills, or to Lucca, proud and independent in its star of intact fortifications. These are the two most likeable provincial capitals.

Pisa should be visited for its churches and pictures as well as for the famous Duomo complex. There is pre-Renaissance sculpture in Pisa, Prato and Pistoia, and Renaissance churches in Prato and near Cortona and Montepulciano as fine and important as anything in Florence. The Renaissance paintings which stir the modern soul most profoundly are the Piero della Francescas in and near Arezzo.

Then there are the smaller hill towns, each with its own distinctive shape and character: San Gimignano still bristling with medieval watch-towers; windy Volterra; Romanesque-Gothic Massa Marittima; Pienza and Montepulciano like miniature Renaissance cities. In fact, there is hardly a town or village in Tuscany that is not worth visiting.

The Tuscan countryside is as elusive to the would-be categorizer as it is inspiring to native and visitor alike. Geographically there is no such thing as one Tuscany. Each of the valleys, mountains, plains and stretches of coast has its own beauty, and, as often as not, its own micro-climate. The best-laid plan for visiting Tuscany is the one that leaves room for spontaneous exploration and personal discovery.

Area planners and tours

Historically, Tuscany has been dominated by Florence since the late Middle Ages, but the region's constituent areas have in no way surrendered their individuality to their presiding sovereign. The names of these areas can often baffle foreigners because they have no administrative significance and no precisely defined geographical boundaries. For Tuscans they sum up everything, from the climate and landscape to the character of the native population and the local food and wine. Six of the most enticing are described here.

The Casentino   The remote upper valley of the Arno, to the N of Arezzo, enclosed by wooded mountains. The magnificent specimen forests of beech, fir and chestnut, and the green pastures where white oxen can still occasionally be seen, are loveliest in spring and remain cool even in high summer. The monastic sanctuaries of Camaldoli and La Verna are good bases for walking, picnicking, and gathering wild strawberries and mushrooms. Hotels are few and simple.

The Chianti   The heart of Tuscany and the landscape that matches many people's ideal of the way Italy ought to look. The area that originally gave its name to the wine has expanded over the centuries to include everywhere the wine is produced, which is now from a little to the N of Florence down to Siena. May is the best time, but in high summer, when Florence is hot and full of tourists and the Tuscan coast is crowded with Florentines, there is much to be said for basing a vacation on the Chianti. Alternatively, you could spend a long winter weekend riding or walking along the Etruscan roads which crest the hills, tasting and shopping for wine. Many villas, castles, abbeys and farmhouses have been converted into hotels or residences.

The Garfagnana   The landscape of the upper valley of the fast-flowing Serchio and the valleys of its tributaries is one of the most fascinating in Tuscany for the variety of climate and vegetation. The chilly marble peaks of the Apuan Alps contrast with the lower slopes of the Apennines, wooded with magnificent chestnuts and luxuriant vegetation, and the mild, humid air lower down. Lucca is just to the S, and Barga is the prettiest hill village.

The Maremma   The word means coastal plain, but it is now most often associated with the province of Grosseto, including the coast known as the Costa d'Argento (between Alberese and Ansedonia), the promontory of Monte Argentario and, inland, the foothills of Monte Amiata. The Etruscan-red soil is wonderfully fertile, producing vegetables, fruit, grain, flowers and vines in colorful abundance. The many Etruscan sites remind one that the Maremma was probably more densely populated in the pre-Christian era than it is now. The natives, physically tough and independent-minded, regard themselves as the Wild Westerners of Tuscany; the local cowboys, less often seen than they were, are known as *butteri*. Apart from the Etruscan and Roman sites, you should at least visit Massa Marittima, Pitigliano and the nature reserve of Monti dell'Uccellina. There are very few hotels except on the coast, but some excellent country restaurants.

The Mugello   In the early Renaissance the river basin of the Sieve, the homeland of Giotto and the Medici, was considered to be the healthiest and most beautiful of the rural areas near the city of Florence. Protected by the Apennines to the N and well-watered by mountain springs, the climate of this lovely gentle green valley is more temperate than that of the Arno.

The Versilia   This coastal strip in northern Tuscany boasts the region's longest uninterrupted stretch of white sandy beach, and has an even, balmy climate with mild winters and light rainfall. Forte dei Marmi is fashionable with Italians; Viareggio's prime is past, but it still has a certain decaying period charm. Some of the other resorts are squalid. There are a staggering 690 hotels, some excellent, and plenty of good fish restaurants.

Route 1: Pisa to Florence

Uninitiated visitors to Tuscany, automatically whisked from Pisa Airport to Florence, are often left with a dim impression of the intervening country, which does not reveal its treasures from the autostrada. Apart from three of the most artistically important Tuscan cities — Lucca, Pistoia and Prato — this slower, more interesting itinerary embraces Romanesque churches, Medici villas, radiant mountain landscape, and some of the best restaurants in Tuscany. It is well worth the luxury of a rented car. Anyone unfamiliar with the highlights of the trip could allow two or three days. Otherwise, a selective or partial section of the route could be followed as a day excursion from Florence by taking the autostrada as far as Pisa, Lucca or Pistoia and then returning along the suggested roads.

Leave *Pisa* by the SS12 for *Lucca*, via S. Giuliano Terme and S. Maria del Giudice, where there are two Romanesque churches. From Lucca's Porta Elisa follow the SS435 for *Pescia*, diverging from the Romanesque church of S. Gennaro and for *Collodi*, on the left. After Pescia the road descends alongside River Pescia to *Montecatini Terme*. Heading now for *Pistoia*, one passes the remains of medieval fortifications at Serravalle. Take the *Empoli* road from Pistoia's Porta Leonardo da Vinci; it winds over Monte Albano, commanding ravishing views of the Arno valley as it approaches *Vinci* through woodland and olive groves. From Vinci, fork left onto the pretty *Carmignano* road, which runs for 16km (10 miles) along the s flank of the Albano mountains through pine woods, olives and the vineyards that produce some of the finest Tuscan wines, and past the Romanesque church of S. Giusto. There is a tempting view of Florence from Carmignano, but don't miss the opportunity to visit the Etruscan tombs near Comeana, the village and Medici villa of *Artimino*, and another Medici villa at *Poggio a Caiano*, all within 10km (6 miles) of Carmignano. *Prato* is 8km (5 miles) N of Poggio a Caiano. Aiming now for Florence, eschew the autostrada and choose instead the Roman road along the base of the Calvana and Morello mountains, for *Sesto Fiorentino* and *Castello*.

Route 2: The Chianti

In May, when the landscape of the Chianti is at its loveliest, this short journey into the heart of Tuscany is one of the essential

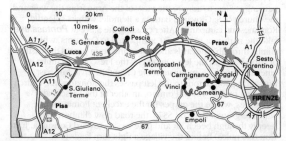

pleasures of a Florentine vacation; all year round, it is a uniquely Tuscan delight. There are excellent restaurants at *Colle di Val d'Elsa, Gaiole, Greve, Monteriggioni, San Casciano, San Gimignano* and N of *Siena*. Blue signs point to the wine growers who will be happy to let you taste their produce and will sell wine, beautifully packaged, by the bottle or cellarful. Since there are some 250 producers in the Chianti Classico zone selling wine under their own labels, it can be difficult to select the best; see *Tuscan wines* for suggestions.

Visitors who want only one leisurely day's outing from Florence can simplify the itinerary by taking the Chiantigiana to Siena and returning to Florence on the SS2 or the autostrada. The whole circular tour can be made to fit into a busy day.

The starting point from Florence is Piazza F. Ferrucci. Take the 18thC wine road, the Strada Chiantigiana, SS222, the classic route into the Chianti, which it bisects lengthwise. After Grassina the vista opens onto a hilly landscape punctuated by medieval towers. Shortly after passing the splendid Baroque Villa Ugolino, you are ushered by a large notice into the Chianti Classico wine zone. The road now descends to *Greve*. To the S, on the road for Lamole to the left, you can see in the distance the privately owned Renaissance Villa Vignamaggio, which appears in the background of an early drawing by Leonardo and where some romantics like to imagine the *Mona Lisa* was painted. At *Castellina* you can turn left onto SS429 into the historic center of the Chianti for *Radda* and *Gaiole*, and then approach *Siena* by the old Chiantigiana, SS408. Otherwise, continue S, via Fonterutoli toward Siena, which you will enter close to the station. If you do not intend to visit Siena, turn right N of the city onto the SS2 for *Monteriggioni*, taking care to avoid the autostrada entrance. After Monteriggioni, turn left for *Colle di Val d'Elsa, San Gimignano* and *Certaldo*, each rising up one after another like medieval mirages. From Certaldo the road carries you NE across the Elsa and Pesa valleys for 23km (14 miles), past the castles of S. Maria Novella and Lucardo to *San Casciano*, at the end NW limit of the Classico zone. Admirers of Machiavelli will want to rejoin the approach road to Florence by way of S. Andrea in Percussina (see *San Casciano*). After a stop at *Galluzzo*, one re-enters Florence by the *Porta Romana.*

Route 3: Florence to Arezzo by the Pratomagno and Casentino

The drive to *Vallombrosa*, less than an hour from Florence, is a favorite Florentine family day outing. By allowing two days for this route to Arezzo you would have time also to visit the remoter monastic retreats of *Camaldoli* and *La Verna*.

From Florence, follow the SS67 along the N bank of the Arno, pausing at Sieci to admire the view of the Arno from the weir and the church of S. Giovanni Battista a Remole, with its splendid Romanesque campanile. After crossing the Sieve at *Pontassieve*, take the narrower road, SS70, signposted to Consuma, which climbs through vineyards and olives and soon passes the castle of Nipozzano on the left. Owned by the Frescobaldi family, its vineyards produce an outstanding Chianti Riserva. Just past Borselli, a short detour to the left passes the Romanesque church of Tosina on the way to Pomino, another of the Frescobaldi properties, where the grapes for the excellent Pomino white wine are grown. Back on SS70, the road now climbs more steeply through beech, fir and pine woods toward Consuma. Just 1km (0.6 miles) before the village a right turn leads to

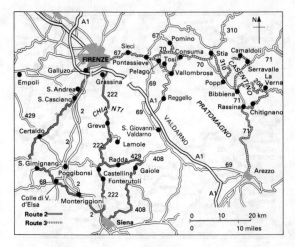

Vallombrosa, secluded in its dense beechwood on the eastern
slope of Monte Secchieta.

Those who wish to return to Florence may vary the route by
returning to Pontassieve via Tosi and Pelago. Otherwise, return
to the SS70 and turn right toward Poppi, crossing the Pratomagno
range through the Consuma pass. Descending into the Casentino
you can see Monte Falterona, where the Arno has its source, on
the left, and ahead the castle of *Poppi*, like a transplanted
Palazzo Vecchio. Fork left 10km (6 miles) after Consuma for the
castle of Romena, the Romanesque church of Romena on a
parallel road, and *Stia*.

From there turn right onto the SS310 via Pratovecchio, where
Paolo Uccello was born in 1397, and along the E bank of the
Arno, past Campaldino, where Dante fought in the battle of 1289
against Arezzo, to *Poppi*. The road for the monastery and then
the hermitage of *Camaldoli* is on the left just beyond Poppi.
Then descend via Serravalle onto SS71 to *Bibbiena*, where a left
turn onto the SS208 leads to the famous Franciscan sanctuary of
La Verna high up in the mountains that separate the Arno and
Tiber valleys. The road from La Verna via Chitignano, which
rejoins the SS71 for Arezzo at Rassina, is rough in places but
worth choosing for the views of the Pratomagno hills ahead as
you descend. After Giovi, where the Arno curves away toward
the W, you emerge from the Casentino into the suburbs of
Arezzo.

An alternative route to Arezzo would be through the Valdarno
by the autostrada A1, exiting at *San Giovanni Valdarno* to
explore the hill villages and Romanesque churches in the
foothills of the Pratomagno.

Route 4: Tracking down the Etruscans

Traces of elusive and intriguing Etruscans remain all over
Tuscany. The tourist who enjoys walking or riding, or who takes
shortcuts along unpaved byroads, will sometimes discover tombs
and trails that are not necessarily signposted or identified. But to
appreciate the Etruscans' achievements in the arts and crafts one
must also visit museums; there are some outstanding objects in
the local museums on the following itineraries.

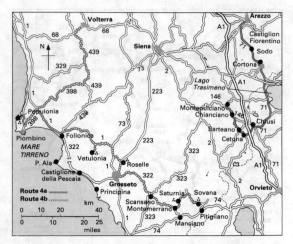

If you wish to test your interest in Etruscan sites before
embarking on a longer journey, begin with *Fiesole*, Comeana
(see *Artimino*) and *Sesto Fiorentino*, all within easy reach of
Florence.

Alternatively, if you are making an excursion to San
Gimignano, go on to *Volterra*, a lovely drive only 27km (17
miles) to the SW. The two densest concentrations of the major
centers are in the Valdichiana and the Grosseto Maremma, most
conveniently visited separately.

a) The Etruscan sites of eastern Tuscany
In the pre-Christian era when the River Chiana was navigable,
the Etruscan cities of the Valdichiana were both prosperous and
artistically sophisticated thanks to fertile farmlands and trade with
other civilizations.

Start at *Arezzo*, the city Livy called the capital of the Etruscan
people. Then take the SS71 for *Cortona*, stopping just to the N of
the city for the tombs at Sodo. Have a look at the extraordinary
bronze lamp in the Etruscan Academy in Cortona and, on the
way S, visit the tomb near the station at Camucia. The quickest
way to *Chiusi*, which has one of the most important Etruscan
museums outside Florence, is by autostrada. Alternatively, take
the SS71 along the shore of Lake Trasimeno. From Chiusi station,
loop S and then NW to visit the minor rural centers of Cetona,
Sarteano, *Chianciano* and *Montepulciano*, all of which
preserve interesting Etruscan fragments. Perugia and Orvieto,
outside Tuscany, are nearby.

b) The Etruscan sites of southwestern Tuscany
This is a much longer journey, requiring about three days, and it
differs in that many of the major sites were abandoned by later
civilizations. The necropoli are often in dense woods or
cultivated fields, so wear stout shoes and be prepared to take the
car over unpaved roads.

Start at *Volterra*, allowing at least half a day for the walls, gate,
necropoli and the museum, with its 600 funerary urns and
miniature votive bronzes. After perhaps spending the night here,
Populonia, on the coast, is a 1½hr drive to the SW, and
Vetulonia another hour farther on. The second night could be
spent on the coast at *Punta Ala*, *Castiglione della Pescaia* or

Principina a Mare. From Vetulonia continue along the Aurelia
(SS1) — but watch out, this is the most dangerous road in
Tuscany — and turn left after 15km (9 miles) for **Roselle**,
following the "*ruderi*" signs for the access road. **Grosseto** is
10km (6 miles) to the S and worth visiting for the material
excavated from Roselle, Vetulonia and other local Etruscan sites,
featured in the Archeological Museum. Now travel inland by the
SS322 via Scansano to Montemerano, where you turn left for
Saturnia, and then **Sovana**; you might spend the third night in
either. To complete a tour of the major sites, journey S into Lazio,
for Vulci, Tarquinia, Cerveteri and Veio.

Route 5: From Siena to the Valdichiana

This itinerary SE from Siena could be accomplished in one long
day, but the variety and unfaltering beauty of the landscape of
the *crete*, the Val d'Orcia and the Valdichiana, and the
importance of the churches and hill towns, which include some
of the finest examples of Renaissance architecture and town
planning outside Florence, justify at least one overnight stop.
Food and wine produced in this radiant countryside and served
in the best of the restaurants is of exceptional quality.

One day   Leaving Siena by the Porta Romana, the Via Cassia,
SS2, follows the River Arbia through a strange, furrowed
landscape of infertile clay hummocks known as the *crete*. After
Buonconvento the Cassia begins to twist dramatically, and the
view becomes more spacious, with **Montalcino** and **Monte
Amiata** visible on the right. From **San Quirico d'Orcia**, on its
high plain overlooking the valleys of the Orcia and the Asso, take
the SS146, which travels E to the Renaissance hill towns of
Pienza and **Montepulciano**. The superb High Renaissance
church of S. Biagio is on the left 2km (1.25 miles) before
Montepulciano. Those who are returning to Siena should leave
Montepulciano by the Porta al Prato, stopping briefly after 1km
(0.6 miles) to admire the simple Mannerist facade of the church

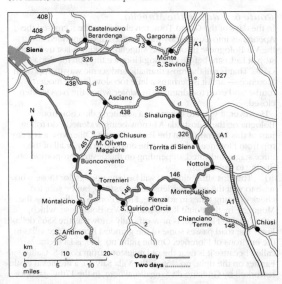

of S. Maria delle Grazie on the left, then proceeding N to Nottola, where you join the SS326 for Siena via Torrita di Siena and *Sinalunga*.

Two days   Follow the route described above, and then make diversions to take in at least some if not all of the following excursions.

a)   At Buonconvento turn left on the SS451 for *Monte Oliveto Maggiore*. Then continue for another 2km (1.25 miles) on the road for S. Giovanni d'Asso as far as lofty Chiusure, for the magnificent panorama of the moon-like landscape below. On the return drive to Buonconvento there are fine views of the *crete*, the Ombrone valley and *Monte Amiata*.

b)   10km (6 miles) S of Buonconvento, at Torrenieri, turn right for *Montalcino*. Then continue S into the Val d'Orcia for Sant'Antimo, set in an enchanted landscape of wheat fields, flickering olives and dark cypresses.

c)   At *Montepulciano* turn right and follow the SS146 for *Chianciano Terme*; the old city can be seen high on the left as one approaches the modern spa. *Chiusi* is a further 11km (7 miles) to the SE, by way of a beautiful undulating road running into the Valdichiana with the tributary of the River Chiana, the Astrone, with glimpses to the left of the lakes of Chiusi and Montepulciano.

d)   Returning to Siena from Chiusi take the autostrada A1 as far as the Valdichiana exit for *Sinalunga*. Stay on the SS326 for 14km (9 miles), diverging for *Asciano* and then returning to Siena on the SS438 through the *crete*, entering the city by the Porta Pispini.

e)   Alternatively, leave the A1 at the Monte S. Savino exit, following the SS73 to *Monte S. Savino*, diverging briefly for *Gargonza* on the right, then for Castelnuovo Berardenga on the eastern edge of the Chianti near the source of the Ombrone. Return to Siena either by the SS326 or by the old Chiantigiana road, SS408.

Route 6: A day in the Mugello

In the days of the Grand Tour, travelers from the N crossed the Apennines into Tuscany by the Futa Pass and continued along the Via Bolognese through the Mugello, making a last overnight stop at La Lastra before entering Florence through the Porta S. Gallo. That is still the most dramatic and scenic way to approach Florence — and it is perhaps a little too slow for the modern tourist, and even too dramatic in winter, when the pass is often closed.

However, if you are driving in a southerly direction from Bologna on the autostrada A1 (now being widened), do follow part of this itinerary from the Barberino exit. Otherwise it is a day trip from Florence, which may be enjoyed in any or all of the three stages indicated, depending on the desired proportion of driving to sightseeing.

a)   This first short itinerary will be long enough for those who wish to visit the great gardens near *Castello*; but be sure to check opening times in advance. From Porta S. Gallo, cross the Mugnone by the Ponte Rosso into the Via Bolognese, which, once outside Florence, is now officially known as the SS65 della Futa. The road passes some of the grandest Renaissance villas in the environs of Florence. On the right, no. 120, is La Pietra, so called because it is near the old milestone from Porta S. Gallo. Farther on the right, no. 156, is the Villa Salviati, a medieval castle reworked by Giuliano da Sangallo, where, in the 17thC, Jacopo

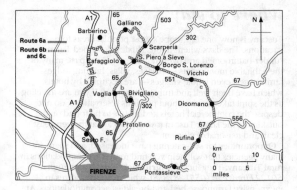

Salviati was given the severed head of his mistress as a New Year's present from his wife. Past Montorsoli at Fontesecca, diverge to the left onto the panoramic road of the Colli Alti (high hills), which twists for 15km (9 miles) along the slopes of Monte Morello, passing Piazzale Leonardo da Vinci, which commands magnificent views of the Arno valley stretching out as far as the Chianti Mountains, to *Sesto Fiorentino*, whence you could return to Florence.

b)   Complete only the first 6km (4 miles) of the Colli Alti, as far as Piazzale Leonardo da Vinci. Returning to the SS65, continue N to *Pratolino*. For the convent of Monte Senario, a 13thC foundation remade in the late 16thC and worth visiting for its lofty situation, fork right from Pratolino. From Montesenario descend into the basin of the Mugello valley via *Bivigliano,* rejoining the SS65 at Vaglia. Taking the left fork at the Novoli intersection, you pass on the left two of the earliest Medici villas, both of which were once fortified castles made into hunting lodges by Michelozzo for Cosimo il Vecchio: first Trebbio, now only occasionally open to the public; then Cafaggiolo, now a hospital, where Poliziano spent the rainy winter of 1478-9 instructing Lorenzo de'Medici's children.

To return to Florence rejoin the autostrada at Barberino. See also *Borgo San Lorenzo*.

c)   Otherwise, take another route and leave the SS65 N of Cafaggiolo, turning right across the Sieve for Galliano, looping right for Sant'Agata and *Scarperia*, then following the SS503 s toward San Piero a Sieve. Just before reaching San Piero a Sieve, turn right for the medieval Franciscan monastery Bosco ai Frati, rebuilt in the Renaissance by Michelozzo, where there is a wooden crucifix in the church attributed by some scholars to Donatello.

Take the SS551 from San Piero to *Borgo San Lorenzo*. The landscape visible from the road along this stretch is disfigured by industrial sprawl as far as Vicchio and Vespignano, after which the road follows the broad curve of the Sieve through gentle, cultivated country to Dicomano, Rufina, center of the smallest and choicest of the Chianti Putto zones, and *Pontassieve*, where the Sieve joins the Arno. Turn w on the SS67 for Florence. The road follows the N bank of the Arno through industrial vineyards controlled by the Ruffino firm, and passes many interesting country churches of which the most notable are S. Giovanni Battista a Remole at Sieci and S. Andrea at Rovezzano, situated on the outskirts of Florence.

Where to stay

Tuscany is now one of Europe's most popular areas for vacations. The days when Aldous Huxley described Tuscany as "under-bathroomed and over-monumented" are past: many of the habitable monuments — palaces, villas, hunting lodges, farmhouses, even whole villages — are occupied by hotels, which have been well and truly bathroomed. If you are traveling as the spirit takes you, without previous reservations, do not despise the commercial hotels and motels to be found on the outskirts of the larger Tuscan towns. Most are at the very least clean and reasonably efficient.

Opportunities for self-catering have increased, and there are many agencies that will help you find rented accommodations in rural Tuscany. They include **Agriturist** (*Piazza San Firenze 3, 50122 Firenze* ☎ *(055) 287838*), which also specializes in inexpensive farmhouse bed-and-breakfast accommodations; **At Home Abroad** (*405 East 56th St., Suite 6H, New York, NY 10022* ☎ *(212) 421-9165*), with a choice of family houses on the Tuscan riviera, apartments in castles, converted farmhouses, and accommodations in a 15thC villa near Florence; and **Italian Villa Rentals** (*P.O. Box 1145, Bellevue, Washington 98009* ☎ *(206) 827-3694*), which has a few rural properties in Tuscany, but specializes in homes and apartments along the Marina di Pietrasanta coast.

There are five official categories of hotel indicated by one to five stars. Standards and prices are strictly controlled by the Regional Tourist Board.

For information about camping see *Sports, leisure, ideas for children*. See also *Staying in Florence* (in *Hotels*).

Where to eat

Two words Tuscans often use to describe good food are *genuino* and *sano* (healthy). Although the 20thC plague of international junk food has inevitably spread along with mass tourism to Tuscan cities, the majority of *trattorie* still serve wholesome, robust, traditional food that is indeed genuine, as to the ingredients and cooking methods, and healthy, according to modern dietary principles. Thick vegetable soups, simply cooked meat or fish, chewy unsalted bread and only one cheese, *pecorino*, may sound a monotonous regime. But when prepared to ancient recipes, flavored with herbs and aromatic wood smoke and accompanied by a bottle of local wine, these dishes add up to one of the most satisfying cuisines in Europe.

It is basically a peasant cuisine. The best Tuscan restaurants are generally outside cities, often in deeply rural areas, behind doors that may not even be signed. You won't necessarily be offered a menu; the proprietor will tell you what has been prepared that day. This is the kind of restaurant that this book tries to single out. There are, of course, many others, and one way of recognizing them is by their unpretentious appearance.

The culinary glory of Tuscany is, in Elizabeth David's words, "that remarkable *bistecca alla Fiorentina*, a vast steak, grilled over a wood fire, which, tender and aromatic, is a dish worth going some way to eat." The best Tuscan beef is from a steer less than two years old. The citified way of presenting it is as a *gran' pezzo*, a roast sirloin.

Pasta is widely available but is not a Tuscan specialty. The farinaceous staple is bread, used to make the bread salad, *panzanella*, and to thicken the excellent peasant soups, which vary by area. There are some 100 varieties of *pecorino*, which is eaten with *fave* (broad beans) as an antipasto.

The *autogrills* that serve the autostrade offer acceptable and sometimes superior meals. Some also sell wine at bargain prices.

See the list of Tuscan restaurants on page 223.

Florence (Firenze) A to Z

Map 2-7. 50100 Firenze. Population: 422,000 i Via Tornabuoni 15 ☎ (055) 216544/5. See "Basic information."

Florence is the most densely packed urban treasure house in Europe. If you were not detained by the profusion of artistic masterpieces it contains, you could walk across its historic center in half an hour. Only two of the sights recommended are beyond pleasant walking distance of the Piazza della Signoria. It is, then, a city that can be explored according to the taste of the individual visitor.

To make the most of this freedom, however, one must adjust to the rhythm of the city, which rises early and closes down at noon for a long siesta. Churches close for three or sometimes four hours in the middle of the day, but they are often open from 7am and open again in the evening until 7 or 8pm. As in the rest of Italy, museum opening hours are too short and subject to change. A law that would rationalize opening hours is under discussion. Meanwhile, most museums are open in the mornings only, closing at 2pm on weekdays, 1pm on Sun and remaining closed on Mon. Inevitably in a city that possesses so much precious art that is fragile with age, there will always be some works that are withdrawn from the public gaze for restoration and some buildings that are temporarily closed. Strikes and inadequate staffing can also lead to unexpected closure.

Fortunately for the independent-minded visitor, mass tourism does not often penetrate beyond the Uffizi, Palatine Gallery, Bargello and Accademia, the four most visited sights in that order. The churches, chapels, painted refectories and small museums are usually peaceful even in high summer. Although no one will be able to take in all the city has to offer in one short visit — and it would be an exhausting waste of time to try — Florence does reveal its essential urban character to the visitor very quickly. Its narrow streets flanked by medieval and Renaissance palaces are, with very few exceptions, unspoiled as yet by modern intrusions. Since the last building boom under the Medici grand dukes, the fabric of Florence has suffered only four drastic changes.

The first happened in the mid-19thC when Florence disastrously prepared itself for its brief period as Italy's capital by demolishing its old walls and part of its center to make way for the Viale and the Piazza della Repubblica. The second was the destruction toward the end of World War II of Ponte Santa Trìnita (subsequently reconstructed) and the areas to the N and S of the Ponte Vecchio. The third was the flood of 1966, the worst in the city's history. The fourth was the traffic, which from the early 1970s dominated Florence more cruelly than any of its hated tyrant-rulers, turning its beautiful squares into parking lots and roaring through its medieval streets.

Now, although inessential motor-traffic is theoretically banned for most of the day from the center (the so-called *zona blu*) and parking is restricted, motor cycles, taxis, buses and those private cars prepared to risk breaking the law continue to roar through the narrow streets. Florence remains the most densely motorized city in Italy, with a car owned by every two inhabitants; and removing the traffic from the center has had the effect of shifting the crush of cars, and the pollution, to the outskirts.

Fortunately there is probably no other major city in the world from which escape is so easy and so delightful. Despite the expansion of *Firenze nuova*, the new Florence to the west of the historic center, much of the lovely Tuscan countryside immediately outside Florence has been consciously and courageously defended from the worst ravages of modern development, and can be reached either on foot or by a short bus ride.

Finding your way about by street numbers

Street numbers in Florence are organized in two separate systems. **Black numbers** indicate **residential addresses**, and **commercial establishments** are given **red numbers**.

Sights and places of interest

Florence is so richly endowed with artistic treasures that the following guide is inevitably highly selective, and the use of stars (★ ☆) has been limited to the greatest and most famous only. This does not mean that they are all that is worth seeing. The city is packed with lesser-known museums, galleries, churches and private collections, which are essential to the specialist and which may charm and fascinate many independent-minded tourists. The *Azienda Autonoma* (see p. 15) provides a complete list of the sights and their current opening hours.

Accademia *(Galleria dell'Accademia)* ★
Via Ricasoli 60 ☎ 214375. Map 3B4 ⊠ ⚐ *Open Tues-Sat 9am-2pm, Sun and hols 9am-1pm. Closed Mon.*

In 1563, 70 leading Florentine artists founded the first Academy of Art in Europe. The organizing members were Vasari, Bronzino and Ammannati, and the president was Cosimo I. Thus academic art, like so many modern institutions, was a Florentine invention. First located at *Santissima Annunziata*, the Accademia was moved to Via Ricasoli 66 in 1764. This building, with its spacious 14thC loggia, is now the Florentine Art School and College.

The Accademia gallery nearby at no. 60 was founded in 1784 by Peter Leopold I, who donated a collection which was greatly enriched by works brought here from the suppressed religious orders in 1786 and 1808-10. Until World War I the Accademia possessed an outstanding collection of early Tuscan masterpieces, the best of which were transferred in 1913 to the *Uffizi*. During the 1970s the display was reorganized and enlarged in order to emphasize the link with the original Academy of Art, and new rooms housing 18th and 19thC academic paintings and sculptures, including hitherto neglected works by Lorenzo Bartolini, were opened in 1982.

Meanwhile, most visitors will come here, as they have for over a century, to gaze up at Michelangelo's *David*.

Rm I, Sala del Colosso Dominated by Giambologna's model (c.1582) for the *Rape of the Sabines* in the Loggia dei Lanzi (see *Signoria*). On the walls are 16thC paintings by Fra Bartolommeo, Perugino, Granacci, and others.

Rm II, Salone di Michelangelo Against the walls, which are hung with magnificent 16thC tapestries, are four of Michelangelo's unfinished *Slaves* (★) of c.1519-36, first meant for Pope Julius II's unrealized mausoleum in St Peter's in Rome (the Louvre possesses two other slaves). The figures may represent the liberal arts enslaved by the death of their patron, Julius II. On the right wall are also the deeply expressive, unfinished *St Matthew* (before 1505), and the Palestrina *Pietà*, no longer attributed to Michelangelo. It was saved from export in 1940 and brought here from the Church of S. Rosalia di Palestrina in Rome. At the far end of the room, Michelangelo's *David* (★) dwarfs and astonishes the perpetual crowds. This tribune was specially built to receive the *David* when it was brought here from the Signoria in 1873. The statue was carved (1501-4) from a block of Carrara marble known as "the giant," which had been spoiled by Agostino di Duccio and abandoned in the courtyard of the Opera del Duomo. The *David* established Michelangelo's reputation as the leading sculptor of his day, and has remained the most potent of all symbols of Florentine republicanism. But it has not always been admired: William Hazlitt, one of the many early 19thC travelers who were irritated by Michelangelo's style, described it as looking "like an awkward overgrown actor at one of our minor theatres, without his clothes."

The *David*... standing forward stripped and exposed and eternally half-shrinking, half-wishing to expose himself, he is the genius of Florence.

D.H. Lawrence, *Aaron's Rod* (1922)

The other rooms are devoted to a study collection of 13th-18thC Florentine paintings, including, in the second of the three rooms to the right of the Salone di Michelangelo, Baldovinetti's important but ruined *Trinity with Saints*.

Anthropological Museum *(Museo Nazionale di Antropologia ed Etnologia)* 🏛

Via del Proconsolo 12 ☎ 296449. Map 5C5 🔲 Open every Thurs-Sat and third Sun of each month 9am-1pm. Closed July-Sept.

Opened in 1869, this was the first anthropological museum in Italy. The collection is displayed on the ground floor of the Palazzo Nonfinito (see *Walk 2* in *Walks in Florence*) and is a fascinating documentation of ethnic custom and costume.

Antica Casa Fiorentina, Museo dell' The house museum of Florence in the *Davanzati Palace*.

Arcetri and Pian dei Giullari

Map 7E4. Bus no. 38.

Florence may be hot and crowded, but half an hour's walk s from the Ponte Vecchio will lift you into the cool, high heart of Tuscany. At no. 2 Pian dei Giullari is the **Astrophysical Observatory of Arcetri** with the first solar tower built in Europe (1872). Opposite the entrance is the Villa Capponi, with famous but private gardens. The **Torre del Gallo** is just to the E: this 19thC reconstruction was once owned by the antiquarian robber baron Stefano Bardini (see *Bardini Museum*). In the adjacent **Villa la Gallina** are Antonio del Pollaiuolo's **frescoes of nude dancers**: persistent or specialist visitors have been known to gain access by appointment.

Pian dei Giullari takes its name from the minstrels who entertained Florentine patricians here from the 12thC. Galileo died in the **Villa il Gioiello** (no. 42). On no. 48 a plaque sentences to imprisonment anyone who dares to play any ball game within 200yds of the monastery of S. Matteo in Arcetri.

In the Via S. Margherita a Montici, at the Villa Ravà, no. 75, Francesco Guicciardini wrote his histories of Italy between 1537-40. Farther on is the church of S. Margherita a Montici commanding stupendous views of the Arno and Ema valleys. Inside are two 14thC panels by the Master of St Cecilia.

(See also *Walk 4* in *Walks in Florence*.)

Archeological Museum *(Museo Archeologico)* ☆
Via della Colonna 36 ☎ 2478641. Map 3B5 ⌧ ✴ Open Tues-Sat 9am-2pm, Sun and hols 9am-1pm. Closed Mon.

To say that the Archeological Museum is of outstanding international importance may sound forbidding to the nonspecialist. In fact, every tourist will find much more here to delight the eye, stimulate the imagination and enrich further sightseeing in Florence and Tuscany. The Etruscan sculptures are an essential and fascinating grounding for those who intend to visit the sites; the Greek and Roman collections will deepen one's understanding of the Renaissance art they helped inspire.

Having suffered appalling damage from the 1966 flood, the museum still has an air of post-crisis impermanence. Many rooms are closed, others badly labeled, and all displays are subject to change, but the finest objects, of which only the highlights are mentioned here, have been brilliantly restored and are on public display.

Ground floor, Rm I   François Vase (c.570BC), the earliest known Attic volute-krater, discovered in 1845 by Alexander François at Chiusi. Smashed by a member of staff of the museum into 638 pieces in 1900, the vase was restored in 1972.

Rm II   Etruscan tomb sculpture (6th-5thC BC), from Chianciano and Chiusi.

First floor   The **Egyptian Collection** is in Rms I-VIII to the left of the stairs. It consists mainly of objects discovered in 1828-9 during a Franco-Tuscan expedition directed by Ippolito Rossellini and Jean François Champollion. The prize piece is the large **chariot** in Rm VIII, found by Rossellini in a 14thC BC tomb at Thebes.

The **Etruscan, Greek and Roman Collection** is in the rooms to the right of the stairs and continues on the second floor.

Rm X   Etruscan tomb sculpture, including *Urn in the Shape of an Etruscan House* (6th-3rdC BC), no. 5539, from Chiusi, a rare piece of evidence about Etruscan architecture, worth bearing in mind when looking at 15thC Tuscan palaces. *Sarcophagus of the Fat Etruscan* (3rd-2ndC BC), no. 5482, from Chiusi, mentioned by Catullus.

Rm XIV   The greatest Etruscan bronzes, including *Wounded Chimera* (5thC BC), discovered at Arezzo in 1553 (the two left legs were restored by Cellini), and *The Orator* (c.7th-2ndC BC), a funereal sculpture found near Trasimeno in 1566.

A small section of the ground floor, entered from Piazza SS. Annunziata, is reserved for special exhibitions. The garden and topographical display charting the evolution of Etruscan culture have been closed.

Argenti Museum   Collection of *objets d'art* in the *Pitti Palace*.

Badia Fiorentina ▥ ☆
Map 5C4.

The old Benedictine Abbey of Florence is the only church besides the Baptistry and S. Miniato mentioned by Dante, who tells us that he saw Beatrice at mass here and that the bell tower of the Badia gave Florence the hours. According to Vasari, the abbey, founded in 978, was enlarged by Arnolfo di Cambio, c.1285. This 13thC building was reoriented and radically rebuilt in the 17thC, but the original apse can still be seen from the outside. The hexagonal Romanesque-Gothic **campanile** was completed in 1330.

The **interior** is best lit in the morning. The **portal** (1495) and **vestibule** leading to Via Dante Alighieri were designed by Benedetto da Rovezzano. The noble Baroque **ceiling** is by Matteo Segaloni, architect of the 17thC church. Immediately to the left of the entrance is Filippino Lippi's restless masterpiece, *St Bernard's Vision of the Madonna* (c.1485). In the left transept is the **monument to Count Ugo**, benefactor of the 10thC foundation (1469-81), the masterpiece of Mino da Fiesole. Two more Minos in the church are the *Madonna and Child with Sts Leonard and Laurence* (1464-70) to the right of the entrance, and the *Monument to Bernardo Giugni* (after 1466) in the right transept. Off the Renaissance Pandolfini Chapel, is the little chapel occupying the site of the church of S. Stefano, where Boccaccio delivered the first literary lecture, on the *Divine Comedy.*

Oranges were cultivated in the center of the large 15thC cloister, designed by Bernardo Rossellino. The tombs date from the 13thC onward. There is a nice view of the three towers of the Badia, *Bargello* and *Signoria* from the upper loggia.

Baptistry *(Battistero)*   The city's oldest building, and once its cathedral. See *Duomo.*

Bardini Museum ▥
Piazza de' Mozzi 1 ☎ 2342427. Map 5F5 ▨ ✿ Open Mon-Tues, Thurs-Sat 9am-2pm, Sun and hols 8am-1pm. Closed Wed.

Stefano Bardini (1836-1922) was the leading Italian art dealer of his day, and by 1883 he had amassed a fortune more than large enough to build this palace. He tore down a 13thC church to create the site and, like the American robber barons of the period, incorporated architectural members from older buildings.

The first-floor windows are framed with the altars from a church in Pistoia. The cool, spacious **interior** is embellished throughout with ceilings, door surrounds and chimney pieces from other earlier buildings. Bardini's taste was almost boundlessly eclectic, and the collection includes, on the ground floor, sculptures and architectural decorations from the Etruscan period to the Baroque.

On the second floor there are pictures, furniture, ceramics, tapestries, musical instruments, arms and armor. The Corsi Gallery is closed pending possible relocation.

Bargello, National Sculpture Museum *(Museo Nazionale)* ▥ ★
Via del Proconsolo ☎ 210801. Map 5C5 ▨ Open Tues-Sat 9am-2pm, Sun and hols 9am-1pm. Closed Mon.

There are a fair number of murderers in the National Sculpture Museum, of which the best known are Donatello's *David,*

Verrocchio's *David*, Michelangelo's *Brutus* and Cellini's model for the *Perseus*. Thus Florentine Renaissance sculpture reflected the Florentine obsession with tyranny.

It is an ironic coincidence that during the turbulent period when these sculptures were created the Bargello was the place where real murderers were tried and sentenced; and the message that crime doesn't pay even if committed in the name of freedom was advertised on the tower walls, frescoed with representations of the mutilated corpses of the condemned. The body of one of the Pazzi Conspirators was hung from a window, where Leonardo made a careful drawing of him, paying special attention to his clothes.

The Bargello was built around an earlier tower in 1255, 5yrs after the establishment of the new Florentine Republic, as its first town hall or Palazzo del Podestà. In 1261 it became the official residence of the Chief Magistrate (*bargello*), and it was used also as a law court and prison. The Sculpture Museum, the most important in Italy, has been here since 1859, and was enriched in 1888 by the Carrand Collection of small bronzes, ivories, enamels, goldsmiths' work and ceramics.

The **courtyard** is the most picturesque part of the palace. Its loggia and staircase are 14thC. Among the sculptures are Ammannati's figures from the fountain in the Boboli gardens. To the right of the entrance is the new **sculpture gallery (★)** opened in 1975. Moving clockwise from the entrance one encounters, most notably: Michelangelo's *Bacchus* (c.1497), his first large free-standing sculpture, *Pitti Tondo* (c.1504) and *Brutus* (c.1540), which possibly celebrates the assassination of Alessandro de' Medici; and Sansovino's *Bacchus*. There are also terra-cotta sketches by Michelangelo's followers and contemporaries. Works by Cellini include the **four bronze statues** and the relief panel of *Perseus Liberating Andromeda*, now brought here for safekeeping from the Loggia dei Lanzi; also his model for the *Perseus* — he boasts in his autobiography that Cosimo I doubted that anyone had the skill to enlarge it. Of the *Narcissus*, he tells us that a defective block of marble dictated the form. His larger-than-life portrait bust of *Cosimo I* (1557) was made, while he was perfecting his bronze technique for the *Perseus*, for the fortress Cosimo built at Portoferraio. You cannot very well ignore Giambologna's enormous, violent *Victory of Florence over Pisa* (1570), or the splendid *Honor Conquering Shame* (1561) and **bronze reliefs** by Vincenzo Danti.

Beyond the courtyard are 14thC sculptural fragments, of which the finest piece is Tino da Camaino's *Madonna and Child*.

First floor   The open staircase leads to the **loggia**, with Giambologna's *Mercury* (c.1564) and bronze animals (c.1570) made for the Medici Villa at **Castello**. On the right is the large **Salone del Consiglio Generale (★)**. On the walls, notice especially the Madonnas by Luca della Robbia, Michelozzo and Agostino di Duccio; on the far wall, Donatello's *St George* (1416) with its original predella, from the facade of **Orsanmichele**; and the two panels of *The Sacrifice of Isaac* by Brunelleschi and Ghiberti, which were competition entries for the second Baptistry doors.

Among the free-standing sculptures by Donatello are the *Marzocco* (1420), the heraldic lion of Florence; *Cupid* (c.1430-40), described by Vasari as "dressed in a rather bizarre fashion"; and the polychrome terra-cotta *Bust of a Man*, probably Niccolò da Uzzano. Compare the swaying elegance of Donatello's early marble *David* (1408) with the late bronze *David* (c.1430), his most famous and titiliating boy and the first free-standing nude of the Renaissance. Note also two sensitive busts by Desiderio da Settignano.

The 15th-17thC **majolicas** from the Carrand and Medici grand-ducal collections are of outstanding interest. The next rooms on this floor contain a large and heterogeneous collection of European and Islamic applied art, most of it from the **Carrand bequest** of 1888.

Salone del Podestà   This was the law court, frescoed during the brief reign of the Duke of Athens. Off the far end is the frescoed **Chapel of the Condemned** with fine intarsiate choir stalls (1493) and lectern (1490). Next is a room of metalwork, with Cellini's *Ganymede*, and another room devoted to 15th-16thC Italian majolicas.

Second floor   At the top of the stairs is the Sala di Giovanni della Robbia where Giovanni Rustici's huge terra-cotta relief panel of *Christ and the Magdalen* demonstrates his superiority to Giovanni della Robbia. Bernini's bust of *Constanza Bonarelli* is usually displayed in this room. Off one end of the room is a display of arms and armor. Off the other, the Sala di Andrea della Robbia leads to the **Sala di Verrocchio** (★). In the center are Verrocchio's *David* (before 1476) and Antonio Pollaiuolo's small bronze masterpiece *Hercules and Anteus*. Among the works displayed on the walls are, clockwise from the entrance, the marble bust of *Battista Sforza, Duchess of Urbino* (1474-7) by Francesco Laurana, Verrocchio's *Bust of a Woman* and *Madonna and Child* (c.1480), and the bust of *Piero Mellini* (1474) by Benedetto da Maiano. Portrait busts and relief carvings by Mino da Fiesole include the tondo of the *Madonna and Child* (1481). Across the Sala di Andrea della Robbia is the **Sala dei Bronzetti** (★), containing the most important collection of bronzes in Italy. The magnificent 16thC chimneypiece is by Benedetto da Rovezzano.

Bellosguardo
Map 6D3. No bus connection.

Bellosguardo is one of the nearest of the hill villages s of Florence. You can walk it in half an hour either from **Porta Romana** or **San Frediano**, and will be rewarded for your stiff climb by views as ravishing as the word *bellosguardo* (fine view) suggests. Via Bellosguardo forks to either side of the piazza. On the w side is the Villa Belvedere al Saracino (1502) by Baccio d'Agnolo, and farther along the Via San Carlo is the Torre Montauto, where Hawthorne stayed. On the E side of the piazza is the park of Villa Ombrellino, where Alice Keppel, Edward VII's last mistress, lived from 1925 to her death in 1947. Her daughter, Violet Trefusis, also died at the Ombrellino.

The best views are from the garden of the Hotel Torre di Bellosguardo in Via Roti Michelozzi (see *Hotels*).

In the piazza a plaque records the most famous of the numerous foreign visitors who have lived in and around Bellosguardo. Aldous Huxley's short story, *The Rest Cure*, is about a neurotic Englishwoman staying here.

Belvedere *(Forte di Belvedere)* ▥
☎ 287055. *Map 3E4* ▣ *Main entrance from Via del Forte di S. Giorgio.*

Crowning the hill of S. Giorgio is the ruthlessly practical Belvedere fortress surrounding its elegant shoe-box-shaped Mannerist palace, both built by Buontalenti in 1590-5 for Grand

Duke Ferdinand I. The terraces are now used for modern **sculpture exhibitions** (🖾) that are only occasionally worthy of a setting commanding some of the most magnificent views of Florence and the surrounding hills and valleys. At the top of the Costa di S. Giorgio is the S. Giorgio gate (c.1260), reduced to about half its original height, embellished with a fresco of the *Madonna and Saints* by Bicci di Lorenzo. The relief carving of St George is a copy of the original now in the *Signoria*.

Two interesting buildings in the Costa di S. Giorgio are the splendid Baroque church of S. Giorgio, lately restored, modernized by G. B. Foggini in 1707, with a boudoir-like oval ceiling frescoed by Alessandro Gherardini, and the house (no. 19) where Galileo was visited by Ferdinand I.

Boboli Gardens *(Giardino di Boboli)* ☆

☎ 213440. Map 4F3 🔟 ▣ ✱ *Open 9am-before sunset. Main gate to left of Pitti: others not always open.*

"The most important if not the most pleasing of Tuscan pleasure gardens .... because the Boboli is a court garden, and not designed for private use." Thus Edith Wharton explained the curiously lowering effect the Boboli can have on one's spirits. At certain seasons, when roses rumble through the somber plantations of holly and cypress or when Florence is gilded with slanted autumn light, the Boboli would be a fine place for a gentle evening stroll. But as another American novelist, Mary McCarthy, has pointed out, this is just the time when the gates close.

Eleanor of Toledo ordered gardens to be laid out behind the Pitti as soon as she and Cosimo I took possession in 1549. The original designer was Tribolo, who died before accomplishing the extraordinary technical feat of taming this wedge of steep quarry. Later alterations by Ammannati, Buontalenti and the Parigi gave the gardens their playful, grandiose complexity.

If you wander freely in the Boboli, the late Mannerist jokes will take you by surprise as they were intended to do. A more purposeful tour should include the following interests.

1. Statue of *Pietro Barbino Riding a Tortoise*, Cosimo I's favorite dwarf immortalized by Valerio Cioli. **2. Buontalenti Grotto** (1583-88), a serious joke about nature; the casts of Michelangelo's *Slaves* replace the originals, now in the *Accademia*, which were installed here for a time in the 16thC. Giambologna's *Venus* is in the third recess, not always open. **3**. The **Kaffeehaus** (1776), for a drink and fine views. **4**. The **Amphitheater**, "One of the triumphs of Italian garden architecture" (Edith Wharton). Built from 1618 by the Parigi for spectacular grand-ducal entertainments. **5. Neptune Fountain** (1565) by Stoldo Lorenzi. **6. Porcelain Museum** (Museo delle Porcellane) (☎ *212557, open Tues-Sat 9am-2pm, Sun 9am-1pm, closed Mon*), a small but choice collection of French, Italian, Viennese and German porcelains, formerly exhibited in the Argenti Museum, has now been installed in the airy Casino del Cavaliere. Panoramic views to the s from the terrace. **7. Cypress Alley** (Viottolone), lined with statues of various periods, the most famous of which, toward the bottom, are the knowingly rustic 17thC groups of games. **8. The Isolotto** (1618) by A. Parigi. The shallow pool, the tall box hedges and the pots of oranges and entwined trees on the island provide cooling relief. Rising from the fountain is a copy of Giambologna's *Oceanus* (the original is in the *Bargello*).

(See also *Pitti Palace*.)

Botanical Garden *(Orto Botanico, Giardino dei Semplici)*
Via Micheli 3 ☎ 284696. Map 3B4 ▢❋ Open Mon, Wed, Fri 9am-noon.

In a stony city where most gardens are hidden behind high walls, this scholarly display of the vegetable heritage of Tuscany makes a refreshing change from art galleries and churches. It is also an excellent preparation for those who plan to visit rural Tuscany and would like to be able to identify the native trees and flowers.

The Giardino dei Semplici, as it was originally called because its first function was the cultivation of medicinal plants, was founded in 1545 by Cosimo I. The natural history museums in the Via la Pira are rarely open, but will eventually be moved to a new science museum, the largest of its kind in Italy, in Via Circondaria.

Brancacci Chapel   A chapel in the *Carmine*, containing Masaccio's influential frescoes.

Carmine *(Santa Maria dei Carmine)* †
Piazza del Carmine. Map 2D2 ☎ 212331. Open Mon-Sat 9am-noon, 4-5pm, Sun 4-5pm.

If Renaissance painting was born in Giotto's Arena Chapel at Padua and reached its fullest maturity in Michelangelo's Sistine Chapel, it was in the **Brancacci Chapel** (★) of the Carmine (right transept, best seen on a clear evening without electric light) that it made its most innovatory and lasting impact. Here, a century after Giotto, the young Masaccio "rivaled nature" and revolutionized Western art. Most Renaissance painters, from Fra Angelico to Raphael, studied these frescoes, but perhaps none understood them as well as Michelangelo (whose nose was broken by Pietro Torrigiano on the steps of the Carmine). Many of the greatest 20thC artists continue to draw inspiration from Masaccio's bold, rigorous, uncluttered technique. A prolonged restoration of the frescoes was completed in 1989.

The frescoes were begun around 1425 by Masolino, who was joined a little later by his protégé Masaccio and so influenced by the young genius that it is not always easy to distinguish their work. The decoration of the chapel was interrupted when they departed for Rome in 1428 and was completed in 1485 by Filippino Lippi. The 18thC **ceiling** is by Vincenzo Meucci and Carlo Sacconi.

There are seven sections by Masaccio. Facing the altar and starting from the near left wall, the outstanding frescoes are the first two in the upper tier: *Expulsion from the Garden* (★), one of the most tragic images in religious art, and the *Tribute Money* (★). Once you have seen these faces with their quick, watching eyes, you will see them again and again in Florence. Below the *Tribute Money* is Masaccio's last work in this chapel, *St Peter Enthroned*; the left portion of this fresco was finished by Filippino Lippi. On the altar wall, bottom left, is *St Peter Heals with his Shadow*; top right, *St Peter Baptizes the Neophytes*; bottom right, *St Peter and St John Distribute Alms*. On the right wall, upper tier, first section of the left, is found *St Peter Heals the Lame Man*; the *Resurrection of Tabitha* on the right section of this fresco is by Masolino. The Florentine houses in the center background are thought to have been Masaccio's starting point.

The **Corsini Chapel** in the left transept was built in 1675-83 by P. F. Silvani. The splendid relief sculptures (1675-91) on the walls and altar are by G. B. Foggini, and the cupola fresco of the *Apotheosis of S. Andrea Corsini* (1682) by Luca Giordano.

The rest of the church is late 18thC, the original building having been destroyed in 1771 by a fire that spared the Brancacci and Corsini chapels. In a **museum** off the cloister are a number of detached frescoes including fragments by Starnina.

Casa Buonarroti   Built by Michelangelo's family after the artist's death; now the *Michelangelo Museum.*

Le Cascine
Map 6D3. Bus 17.
Surprisingly few tourists make use of Le Cascine, the shady park that runs for 3km (1.75 miles) along the N bank of the Arno W from Piazza Vittorio Veneto. Yet it is one of the few places in the city where you can take the air undistracted by traffic and artistic masterpieces; and the private tennis club and swimming pool are open to foreign nonmembers.

Originally a dairy farm belonging to the Medici, the Cascine became the grand-ducal chase in the 17thC. Shelley composed his *Ode to the West Wind* while striding through the Cascine. Later in the 19thC the park was so full of fashionable carriages that Charles Lever described it as being to the world of society "what the Bourse is to the world of trade."

(See also *Shopping* for markets and *Sports, leisure, ideas for children.*)

Corridoio   Vasari's aerial link between the *Pitti Palace* and the *Uffizi*, offering superb views as it crosses the Arno. Tours Tues-Sun mornings; reserve the previous day at the Uffizi.

Corsini Gallery ▥
Palazzo Corsini, Via del Parione 11 ☎ 218994. Map 4C2.
Open by previous appointment on Mon, Wed, Fri 2.30-5.30pm.
The most important private collection in Florence, with works by Signorelli, Pontormo, Raphael, Rigaud and other Italian and European artists of the 15th-18thC.

The palace (1648-56) that gives its name to this stretch of the lungarno is by Pier Francesco Silvani and Antonio Ferri.

Davanzati Palace and Antica Casa Fiorentina, Museo dell' *(Florentine House Museum)* ▥ ☆
Piazza Davanzati, Via Porta Rossa ☎ 216518. Map 4D3 ▨ ✽
Open Tues-Sat 9am-2pm, Sun 9am-1pm. Closed Mon.
The exterior of the Davanzati is the best-preserved of any mid-14thC palace in Florence. Inside, the House Museum offers a rare opportunity to explore an early palace interior and to learn about domestic life in 14th-16thC Florence. If George Eliot had known the Davanzati as it is today, *Romola* would have been a livelier novel. The house was built by the Davizzi family who lived here for over a century before selling to the historian Bernardo Davanzati in 1578. The interior was badly mishandled in the 19thC after the suicide by defenestration of the last Davanzati, but was rescued and accurately restored by Elia Volpi just after the turn of this century.

Architecturally the building is midway between a medieval defense tower and a Renaissance palace. Apart from the 16thC roof loggia, a replacement of the original battlements, and the Davanzati coat of arms placed here in the 16thC, the facade looks very much like the one you can see in the Masolino-Masaccio fresco of the *Resurrection of Tabitha* in the *Carmine.*

The entrance loggia, initially used for important family celebrations, was converted into three wool shops by the end of the 15thC. The horizontal perches running across the windows were used, as shown in the Carmine fresco, for hanging out washing, or birdcages, and for festive drapes.

The interior is largely a reconstruction, and a very good one, by Volpi. The **courtyard staircase** is particularly worth noting as the only one of its type left in Florence. The well is an unusual luxury for a palace of this date; all five floors were served by a shaft carrying buckets of water by rope and pulley. Kitchens, as always in medieval palaces, are on the top floor. The sanitary arrangements include rest rooms, which you can see next to the bedrooms on the three upper floors. The house is unusual in having two *piani nobili*, on the second as well as the first floor.

Of the wall decorations, the most attractive and most complete is in the second-floor bedroom where a fresco cycle illustrates the medieval French poem *The Châtelaine of Vergi*.

Duomo 🏛 ✝ ★
☎ 294514. Map **5**B4. Open Mon-Sat 10am-5pm, Sun 2.30-5pm.

The Piazza del Duomo is the intersection of the city's busiest streets, the headquarters of its ancient voluntary ambulance service (the *Misericordia*, an original Red Cross) and a magnet for the modern tourist industry; but it is no place for a meditative cup of coffee. To appreciate the grandeur and significance of the Duomo and its attendant buildings you must first go away from it, glimpse its flagrant burst of color from the dark narrow city streets and take your coffee overlooking it from a rooftop or from the hills above, where you will see how disproportionately large the cathedral is in a small city.

The cathedral and its belfry suggested the grotesque similitude of a huge architectural zebra and its keeper — the former with a coating or skin, consisting of alternate stripes of black and white marble, the latter exhibiting, on its exterior, all the colours of the rainbow, all the chequers of a gigantic harlequin! Is there no mitigation of the penalty due to this gothic and tasteless idea?
James Johnson MD (1831)

The cathedral (Santa Maria del Fiore), clad in white marble from Carrara, green from Prato and pink from the Maremma, could hardly be more of a contrast with the plain brown understated city around it. Like the two sides of the Florentine character, one is measured, conservative, puritanical, the other

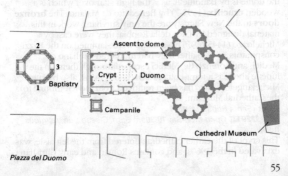

Piazza del Duomo

excessive, innovating, festive; and both are dominated by the great cranium-shaped intelligence of Brunelleschi's dome.

Arnolfo di Cambio was commissioned in 1296 to build a cathedral that would surpass anything produced by the ancient Romans and Greeks or by Florence's rivals the Pisans and Sienese. Work was interrupted by Arnolfo's death, began again in 1331, and after another pause resumed under the direction of Francesco Talenti from 1357-64. The nave was completed in 1380, the tribunes and the drum of the dome finished by 1418.

The problem then was how to raise a dome over a space 42m (138ft) across and 55m (180ft) above the ground. No dome of this size had been built since antiquity, and various unlikely solutions were proposed before Brunelleschi, who had studied Classical building techniques in Rome, provided the answer. His dome, realized in 1436, was the supreme engineering feat of the Renaissance. The lantern was completed in 1461, after Brunelleschi's death; the gallery, on only one of the eight sides of the drum of the dome, was begun by Baccio d'Agnolo in 1506 but abandoned after Michelangelo called it "a cage for crickets."

The Neo-Gothic facade of the cathedral is a late 19thC interpretation of the original one. The apse is best viewed from the corner of Via Proconsolo and Via dell'Oriuolo. The s flank is the earliest section of the exterior, but the most beautiful of the doors, the **Porta della Mandorla**, is on the N nave. Above it is Nanni di Banco's lovely relief of the *Assumption of the Madonna* (1414-21).

The cathedral interior, the fourth largest in the world, is all the more imposing for the sparseness of detailed decoration. There are only a few major works of art to distract from the sense of echoing space. In the left aisle of the nave are the two famous monuments to *condottieri* (mercenary commanders), which have been cited as examples of Florentine meanness because they imitate marble in *trompe l'oeil* fresco. Both have long since been transferred to canvas: the first, **Monument to Niccolò da Tolentino** (1456) by Castagno; the second, **Monument to Sir John Hawkwood** (1436) by Uccello. Just before the crossing is an interesting panel painting of *Dante Explaining the Divine Comedy* (1465) by Domenico di Michelino.

Access to the vast octagonal **crossing** and the three polygonal tribunes of the apse will be barred until the 1990s while the dome is under restoration. Meanwhile, the question is whether the late 16thC frescoes of the *Last Judgment* on the interior dome by Vasari and F. Zuccari, now covered by netting, should be removed to reveal more clearly Brunelleschi's structure.

The noble octagonal marble **choir enclosure** (1555) beneath the dome is by Bandinelli, as is the high altar over which is a wooden **crucifix** (1495-7) by Benedetto da Maiano. The **bronze doors** to the New Sacristy are the only surviving work in this material designed by Luca della Robbia; they were cast by Michelozzo (1445-69). These doors were slammed on the Pazzi conspirators in 1478 after they had murdered Giuliano de' Medici, and Lorenzo de' Medici escaped through them. In the lunette above is a terra-cotta *Resurrection* (1444), also by Luca. Michelangelo's *Pietà* has been removed from the left tribune to the Cathedral Museum.

Crypt *(Santa Reparata)* ▥ ✝
☎ 213229 ▤ *Open Mon-Sat 10.30am-5pm. Closed Sun, religious hols.*

This crypt of the earlier cathedral, entered from the left aisle, was excavated in the 1960s, and contains Roman and early Christian sculptural fragments, 13th and 14thC tombs, and the remains of 14thC frescoes.

Ascent to dome lantern
☎ and opening hours as for Crypt ▨

The ascent should not be attempted by anyone who suffers from vertigo, claustrophobia or weak legs; but those who can manage the stiff climb will be rewarded by a panoramic view and an increased understanding of Brunelleschi's constructional method, which involved the erection of two shells, one inside the other, with these maintenance stairs between.

Baptistry ▥ ✝ ★
⬛ Open 1-6pm.

Dante's "bel S. Giovanni," the Baptistry is the oldest building in Florence, although it is not as old as Brunelleschi and his contemporaries liked to believe. In the early 15thC it was thought to have been the Roman temple of Mars, and it was a deeper influence on Tuscan Renaissance architecture than any real Classical building. Its date is still uncertain, but historians agree that it is not earlier than the 4th-5thC AD, and that it was probably built on the site of the old Roman praetorium. The green and white marble cladding belongs to the 11th-13thC, and the rectangular tribune was added in 1202. The Baptistry was the cathedral of Florence for a century before the completion of S. Reparata.

The gilded bronze Baptistry **doors** (★) chart the progress of sculptural style from Gothic to the Renaissance. The original reliefs are now being removed, after restoration, into the Cathedral Museum. They will be replaced here by reproductions.

The chronological order of the doors is: **1. South gate**, from a wax model prepared in 1330 by Andrea Pisano. The 20 highest panels relate the story of John the Baptist; the eight below depict the cardinal and theological virtues. The Renaissance door surround is by Vittorio Ghiberti. Above the doors is the *Baptist and Salome* (1571), by Vincenzo Danti. **2. North gate** (1403-24) by Lorenzo Ghiberti and assistants. These are the doors resulting from the competition set in 1401. Brunelleschi's losing entry and Ghiberti's winner can be seen in the *Bargello*. The 20 highest panels illustrate scenes from the New Testament; below are the four *Evangelists* and four *Church Doctors*. Above the doors is *The Baptist between a Pharisee and a Levite* (1506-11), by G. F. Rustici, with advice from Leonardo. **3. East gate** (1425-52) by Lorenzo Ghiberti. Michelangelo called these doors "the gates of paradise." They opened a new artistic era when sculptural perspective replaced Gothic stylization. The doors are divided into ten panels with Old Testament scenes. The antique porphyry side columns were presented to Florence by Pisa in 1117 in gratitude for help in the conquest of the Balearic Islands. Above is the *Baptism of Christ*, started by A. Sansovino in 1502 and finished by V. Danti in 1564.

The exquisite Baptistry **interior** is more apparently Classical than the exterior and incorporates Roman columns and capitals. The 13thC mosaics in the vault, the *Last Judgment*, the *Creation*, the *Story of Joseph* and the *Baptist*, have never lost their magic despite five centuries of periodic restoration. The 13thC tessellated marble **pavement** around the font, representing the Zodiac, is unmatched in Florence except by a similar example in *San Miniato*. 14thC Pisan reliefs have been applied to the 16thC font. To the right of the tribune is the **tomb of Cardinal Baldassare Coscia** (1421-7), the schismatic Pope John XXIII, by Donatello and Michelozzo.

Ascent of Campanile
🖼 ✦ *Open summer 9am-7pm, winter 9am-5pm. Closed Easter, Christmas.*

The Campanile (★), built 1334-59, is known as "Giotto's Tower" although Giotto was responsible only for the first story. It was carried on after his death by Andrea Pisano until 1348 and completed by Francesco Talenti. The originals of the sculptural decorations are in the Cathedral Museum. The climb up to the bell tower is relatively easy and the views are spectacular.

Cathedral Museum *(Museo dell' Opera del Duomo)* ★
Piazza Duomo 9 ☎ 213229. Open Mon-Sat summer 9am-8pm, winter 9am-6pm, Sun and hols 10am-1pm. Closed Easter, Christmas, Jan 1.

The Cathedral Museum contains an accumulation of important works brought in over the last century from the Duomo, Baptistry and Campanile. The palace has been the administrative headquarters of the Duomo since the early 15thC. Michelangelo carved the *David* in the courtyard.

Ground floor Sculptures from the 14thC cathedral facade, 16thC drawings of the unfinished facade, and 16th and 17thC models for a cathedral facade, Brunelleschi's death mask, the wooden model for his dome made for the 1418 competition, and tools which were used for its construction. On the mezzanine is Michelangelo's *Pietà* (★), here for the duration of the restoration of the cathedral dome. Perhaps his most tragic religious sculpture, it was made (1550-c.53) for what he planned would be his own tomb. Vasari says the head of Nicodemus is a self-portrait. Dissatisfied with his unfinished work, he broke it up and gave parts away. They were pieced together in the 18thC.

First floor: Sala delle Cantorie Sit down and decide which of the two **choral galleries** (★) makes your heart sing more joyously. They were removed from the cathedral in the 17thC, stored away and forgotten until the 19thC. On the entrance wall is Luca della Robbia's (1431-8) with the original panels displayed below; opposite is Donatello's (1433-9). Underneath that is Donatello's stark, expressionistically penitent *Magdalen* (★), from 1435-55. The 16 statues by Donatello and others are from the bell tower's niches. The most startlingly realistic is Donatello's *Abakuk* (1434-6), known as "Lo Zuccone" ("Big Head").

Sala delle Formelle (★) The **relief panels** were brought here from the Campanile in the 1960s. The earliest are by Andrea Pisano, based on designs by Giotto. The series depicts man's spiritual progress by way of labor, art and the sacraments. "Read but once these inlaid jewels," wrote Ruskin, "and your hour's study will give you strength for all your life."

Sala dell' Altare Panels from the **Baptistry doors** (★) are displayed here after restoration. The **silver altar** from the Baptistry was begun in 1366, then labored over for a century by craftsmen and artists including Verrocchio and A. del Pollaiuolo.

English Cemetery *(Cimitero Protestante)*
Piazzale Donatello. Map 3B5 🖾 Open Mon-Sat, Apr-Sept 9am-noon, 3-6pm; Oct-Mar 9am-noon, 3-5pm; Sun and hols 9am-noon. Closed Jan 1, May 1, Aug 15. Ring for admission: tip expected.

In this oval cemetery lie the remains of Protestants who died in Florence in the late 19thC. Many, like Elizabeth Barrett Browning, had come here from the chilly north to convalesce. Walter Savage Landor, Frances Trollope and Jean Vieusseux are among the famous foreigners buried here.

"Firenze com'era" *(Topographical Museum of Florence as it was)*
Via dell' Oriuolo 24 ☎ 298483. Map 5C5 ▨ Open Mon-Wed, Fri-Sat 9am-2pm, Sun and hols 8am-1pm. Closed Thurs.

The urban development of Florence from the 15th-19thC is traced in this fascinating museum with maps, topographical prints, plans, paintings and photographs. Among the maps of the 15thC city in the first room is an 18thC reproduction of the 1470 "Chain Map" (Carta della Catena); the original is in Berlin. In the following rooms the delightful lunettes painted by Giusto Utens for the Villa Artimino record the appearance of grand-ducal villas and gardens at the end of the 16thC; and 18thC Florence comes alive in Giuseppe Zocchi's prints of churches, palaces and villas. Last comes the shameful story of the destruction of the old center and the building of that monument to 19thC insensitivity, the Piazza della Repubblica.

Fortezza da Basso ▥
Viale Filippo Strozzi. Map 2B3 ▨ ♣ Open for crafts exhibitions only.

The largest historical monument in Florence and the most signposted, the Fortezza da Basso is now a traffic island ringed by the Viale Filippo Strozzi. The fortress was built in 1534-5 for Alessandro de' Medici, the first Duke of Florence. Supported by Charles V, Alessandro's chief purpose was to cow the people of Florence into unquestioning obedience with a citadel, as one contemporary historian described it, "whereby the citizens lost all hope of ever living in freedom." The design is by Antonio da Sangallo the Younger; the carved stones around the entrance depict the Medici emblem.

Within are a school, a restoration center, a barracks, and, since 1978, the **Crafts Exhibition and Merchandising Pavilion**, where some 30 exhibitions are held each year.

Foundling Hospital *(Spedale degli Innocenti)*
One of the inaugural buildings of the Renaissance. (See *Santissima Annunziata*.)

Fra Angelico Museum *(Museo dell' Angelico)*
Collection of Fra Angelico's work, housed in *San Marco*.

Horne Museum ▥
Via de' Benci 6 ☎ 244661. Map 5D5 ▨ Open Mon-Sat 9am-1pm. Closed Sun.

The two enduring achievements of the English art historian Herbert Percy Horne (1864-1916) were his pioneering work on Botticelli, then a still undervalued artist, and the collection he installed in this palace where he lived during the last few years of his life.

The palace was built in 1489 for the Corsi family, and the architect was probably Cronaca, whose Guadagni palace in *Santo Spirito* it resembles. The Corsi were cloth merchants, and the design of their palace answered the requirements of their trade: a large cellar for dyeing vats, a sunny gallery over the courtyard portico for drying wool. The stone capitals, carved in the workshop of Andrea Sansovino, are among the finest in Florence.

The **museum** contains no major masterpieces. Horne was not a rich man, but he collected at a time when a keen and educated eye could spot real bargains, and there are many small treasures throughout the museum. There are pictures by Daddi, Pietro Lorenzetti, Filippo Lippi, Beccafumi, Dosso Dossi, and others; Renaissance furniture and majolica; and the preindustrial domestic utensils which were among Horne's special interests.

Laurentian Library *(Biblioteca Medici-Laurenziana)*
Library designed by Michelangelo in **San Lorenzo**, epitomizing Mannerist architecture.

Medici Chapels *(Cappelle Medicee)*   The Medici
commissioned some superb works of art for their own glorification in these famous chapels in **San Lorenzo**.

Medici Riccardi Palace 🏛 ★
Via Cavour ☎ 217601. Map 5B4 🔟 Open Mon-Tues, Thurs-Sat 9am-12.30pm, 3-5pm, Sun and hols 9am-noon. Closed Wed.

The palace building boom in 15thC Florence was made possible by the financial and fiscal policies of Cosimo il Vecchio, and his palace, built between 1444-64, was a prototype from which Florentine palace architecture rarely departed until the 16thC. The exterior of the palace is best seen from the corner of Via Cavour.

According to one story, Brunelleschi made a model for the Medici Palace which Cosimo rejected as being too elaborate. Brunelleschi flew into a rage and either smashed the model or sold it to Luca Pitti (see **Pitti Palace**). Certainly Cosimo would not have wanted to build a family house that was too ostentatious; he was, after all, the unofficial leader of a supposedly republican government.

In the event it was Michelozzo, the loyal friend who had accompanied Cosimo into exile, who built the Medici Palace, a transitional mixture of medieval and Brunelleschian elements: biforate windows as in the Palazzo Vecchio, arranged symmetrically; graduated rustication, very heavy on the ground floor, entirely smooth at the top; the first *all' antica* palace cornice in Florence, but unsupported by architrave, frieze or columns. The crenelated garden wall carries the design back, with a jerk, into the Middle Ages. These walled side gardens were attached to most new palaces in this area, but this is one of the few to have survived.

The ground-floor windows, enclosing what was originally a loggia, were designed by Michelangelo, and are the first appearance in Florence of the so-called "kneeling windows" that became such a common feature of 16thC palaces. The proportions of the palace were radically altered when the Riccardi, who brought it in 1659, added the seven northernmost windows on the Via Cavour.

The interior, much altered over the centuries, now houses the offices of the Prefecture. Vasari described the Medici Palace as the first to be built for domestic convenience but, inevitably, some of the great symbolic events of Florentine history took place in these rooms. It was here that Lorenzo the Magnificent, when only 21, accepted control of the government, "for in Florence one lives ill in the presence of wealth without power." Emperor Charles VIII was entertained here in 1494 and Charles V of France in 1536.

Uccello's *Battle of San Romano* hung in Lorenzo's bedroom. Donatello's *David* and *Judith* were both originally placed in the courtyard. *Judith*, the tyrant-slayer, was taken away to the **Signoria** after the Medici were expelled in 1494, and was followed there 46yrs later by Cosimo I the tyrant in person. When Cosimo I moved out of the Medici's private palace and into the Palazzo della Signoria, republican government in Florence was irrevocably finished. Gradually, the old family palace was stripped of many Medici-commissioned works of art that are today among the greatest treasures of the city's museums and galleries.

Medici Chapel *(Cappella di Benozzo Gozzoli)* ★
🖼 *Open Mon-Tues, Thurs-Sat 9am-noon, 3-5pm, Sun and hols 9am-noon. Closed Wed.*

The Medici Chapel (★) retained its treasures. Gozzoli's *Journey of the Magi* frescoes (1459), the artist's most popular and imaginative works, were commissioned by Piero de' Medici to commemorate his membership of the religious confraternity of the *Three Magi*. Around the walls members of the Medici family process on horseback through a fairytale Tuscan landscape reminiscent of the Fiesolan hill of Vincigliata (see **Fiesole** in **Tuscany**).

In the first-floor **gallery**, reached by the second staircase on the right of the courtyard, is one of the most exhilarating and ridiculous sights in all Florence. It is Luca Giordano's ceiling fresco, the *Apotheosis of the Medici* (1683), commissioned by the Marchese Riccardi as a gesture of gratitude to the Medici whose palace his family had lately bought.

Michelangelo Museum *(Casa Buonarroti)* ★
Via Ghibellina 70 ☎ 241752. Map 5C5 🖼 *Open Mon, Wed-Sun 9.30am-1.30pm. Closed Tues.*

Michelangelo never actually lived here. The house was built on a plot of land he bought for his nephew and was later partly decorated in Michelangelo's honor by his grand-nephew Michelangelo the Younger.

Ground floor   The drawings are reproductions; the originals are sometimes shown on special occasions. The unfinished *Venus* and *Prisoner* statues are probably not by Michelangelo.

First floor   In the room to the left of the stairs are the two most interesting pieces in this museum. The *Madonna della Scala* (1490-2), Michelangelo's earliest known work, is extraordinarily prophetic in style, and like so many of his later works it is unfinished. Poliziano suggested the subject for the *Battle of the Centaurs* (1492), made while Michelangelo was attached to the Medici household; the artist's preoccupation with interlocking male figures began here. In the next room to the left are architectural sketches and the **wooden model for the facade of San Lorenzo** (1517), never carried out; the plain architecture, typical of his early period, was meant to be a setting for elaborate sculpture. Running along the left of the courtyard is the gallery frescoed in homage to Michelangelo by Baroque artists. In a room to the right of the stairs is the **wooden crucifix** from S. Spirito, first attributed to Michelangelo in 1962, although not all art historians agree on this point. In the next room is a **large model of a river god**, the only full-scale model by Michelangelo in existence.

Ognissanti 🏛 †
Piazza d'Ognissanti. Map 4C1. Refectory open Mon, Tues, Sat 9am-noon. Offering expected.

The church of Ognissanti was founded in the late 13thC by the

Umiliati, the wool-weaving order who taught Florence the skill that was to be the basis of its prosperity. The building was made over completely in 1627 by the Franciscans. A complete restoration was carried out after the 1966 flood. The facade (1637) by Matteo Nigetti is one of the earliest appearances in Florence of the Baroque style. The slender campanile, very like that of *Santa Maria Novella*, is simpler, is 13th-14thC.

The interior is decorated in best-boudoir 17th-18thC Baroque. On the ceiling, *St Francis in Glory* (1770) was frescoed by Giuseppe Romei. Over the second altar on the right are the restored remains of Dom. Ghirlandaio's fresco, the *Madonna of Mercy Sheltering the Vespucci Family* (c. 1472), which gives the only authentic portrait of Simonetta Vespucci (whose funeral was held in this church in 1476), and a probable portrait of Amerigo Vespucci as a young boy. In the sacristy, entered from the left transept, is a large School-of-Giotto *Crucifixion*, a *Crucifixion* by Taddeo Gaddi, and a fresco of the *Resurrection* attributed to Agnolo Gaddi (its sinopia can be seen in the refectory).

The entrance to the **refectory museum** is to the left of the church and through the 15thC cloister. At the far end of the refectory is Dom. Ghirlandaio's fresco of the *Last Supper* (1480).

The two frescoes of saints in their studies (both dating from 1480), Ghirlandaio's *St Jerome* (★) on the left wall, and Botticelli's more mystic *St Augustine* (★) on the right wall, were originally in the choir of the church; the realistic detail of both was inspired by a *St Jerome in his Study* by the Flemish Jan van Eyck owned by Lorenzo de' Medici.

Oltrarno

Although Florence is well served with bridges, any one of which is crossed in a minute, Florentines persist in referring to everything s of the Arno as the Oltrarno, or as the *Arno di là* (over there), as thought it were still the suburb it used to be in the Middle Ages. The Oltrarno certainly has a very distinctive character, a far richer urban mix than you will find anywhere N of the Arno in that part of the city Florentines call the *Arno di quà* (over here).

It is a working-class neighborhood amid which some of the oldest and wealthiest Florentine families have maintained palaces for centuries. Thus, some of the most fashionable restaurants and food stores are in and around San Jacopo, but you can just as easily choose your lunch from a market stall in Piazza *Santo Spirito* or eat with students and craftsmen in any one of many cheap family-run trattorias. You can buy chic boutique clothes or antiques, or you can have your old shoes repaired in a hole-in-the-wall workshop.

It was a place of refuge for early Christians, and even after the 14thC walls embraced the Oltrarno and it became the S. Spirito Quarter of the enlarged city, it remained a place favored by outsiders and subversives. The nobles took their last stand here in 1343; here the signal was given for the Ciompi Uprising. Luca Pitti, a leading opponent of the Medici, chose to build his palace on this, or rather "that," side of the Arno.

In the 16thC, after Cosimo I chose to make the *Pitti* the official ducal palace, the Oltrarno became the most fashionable address in Florence. Its most exclusive street, and still the most interesting for those who like palaces of the grand-ducal period, was Via Maggio, linked to the Via Tornabuoni by Ammannati's beautiful bridge of *Santa Trinita*.

(See also *Walk 3* in *Walks in Florence*.)

Orsanmichele ▥ † ★
Via dei Calzaiuoli. Map 5C4.

The name Orsanmichele refers to an oratory, San Michele in Orto, which stood here in the 8thC. Later the site was occupied by a loggia and grain market, famous for a miraculous image of the virgin painted on one of its pillars. The grain market burned down and was replaced by a grander loggia used as an oratory and as a trading center by the guilds of Florence. This loggia, which is the basis of the present structure, was erected from 1337 by Francesco Talenti, Neri di Fioraventi and Benci di Cione.

From 1380 the loggia was enclosed by Simone Talenti and used exclusively for religious worship. The two upper stories were added as warehouses for emergency supplies of grain. The decoration of the church was supervised by the nearby Guelf organization, which delegated responsibility for each of the outside niches to a guild. Happily this decorative program, which was planned from 1339, did not actually get under way until the early 15thC when Florentine sculpture, after a dullish period, leaped forward into the age of Donatello and Ghiberti.

The original statues are gradually being removed, after restoration, into museums and replaced here by reproductions. Donatello's *St George*, made for the smiths and armorers guild, is now in the *Bargello*, and his *St Louis*, made for the Guelf organization, is in the *Santa Croce* Museum.

E side (Via dei Calzaiuoli): Ghiberti's still-Gothic *John the Baptist* (1414-16); Verrocchio's *Doubting Thomas* (1466-83) and above it the ceramic medallion by Luca della Robbia (1463).
S side (Via dei Lamberti): Donatello's *St Mark* (1411-12); the *Madonna of the Rose*, attributed to Piero di Giovanni Tedesco.
W side (Via dell' Arte della Lana): Ghiberti's *St Matthew* (1419-22) and *St Stephen* (1428); Nanni di Banco's Gothic *St Eligius*. **N side (Via Orsanmichele)**: Nanni di Banco's *Four Crowned Saints*; bronze copy of Donatello's marble *St George*, with the original predella of *St George and the Dragon* (1417), the first relief carving to achieve perspective.

Interior: The odd but satisfying shape recalls the original secular function of the church. The pillars are frescoed with damaged and restored images of patron saints of the guilds. Orcagna's **tabernacle** (★), from 1348-59, one of the most beautiful Gothic aedicules in Italy, houses the miraculous image of the *Virgin* (1347), painted by Daddi.

The upper stories of the church, the **Saloni di Orsanmichele**, are entered through the restored 14thC palace of the Arte della Lana (Wool Guild) across a connecting bridge. There are splendid views from these imposing rooms, restored in the 1960s.

Palatine Gallery   Gallery in the *Pitti Palace* with an outstanding collection of 16thC Italian paintings.

Palazzo del Podestà   Built as Florence's first town hall, the building now known as the *Bargello*.

Palazzo Vecchio   See *Signoria*.

Pazzi Chapel   Brunelleschi's chapel in the cloister of *Santa Croce*.

Piazzale Michelangelo
Map 3E5.

Piazzale Michelangelo is the traditional orientation point for a vacation in Florence. The outlook over the city embraces some of the most celebrated and photographed views in the world. The **monument to Michelangelo** (1875) in the center of the piazzale is dominated by one of the city's two reproductions of Michelangelo's *David* (the original is in the *Accademia*).

If you place yourself at the center of the balustrade facing the Arno and above the tower of *San Niccolò*, you will see, looking left to right across Florence, the bell tower of the *Signoria*; the top of the tower of *Santa Maria Novella*; the *Badia* tower and immediately to its right the cupola of the *San Lorenzo* Cappella dei Principi; the white marble tower of the *Duomo*; Brunelleschi's dome; and, farther right, the minaret-like tower of *Santa Croce*; the green dome of the Synagogue; and the concrete tower of Nervi's stadium complex. In the distance, left to right, are the hills and valleys of northern Tuscany: see *Tuscany A to Z* for hills behind *Pistoia* and *Prato*; the tower of Petraia at *Sesto Fiorentino*; the three peaks of Monte Morello; and *Fiesole*, with the hill of S. Francesco and the Mugnone valley to its left and Monte Céceri, Vincigliato, and *Settignano* to its right. Farther right, on a clear spring day, you can see as far as *Vallombrosa* in the E. Back to Florence and moving to the far corner of the left balustrade and facing W, looking from the Arno southward, one can see the dome of *San Frediano*, the tower of *Santo Spirito*, the silhouetted *Belvedere* and, dominating the view from the S, the Victorian crenelations of the restored Torre del Gallo on the hill of *Arcetri*.

A staircase to the right of the restaurant La Loggia (see *Restaurants*) leads to **San Salvatore al Monte**, begun in 1499 to a design by Cronaca.

Pitti Palace 🏛 ★
Piazza Pitti.

Luca Pitti's motive for erecting a building so unusually bold for mid-15thC Florence was partly a bid to outdo his political rival Cosimo de' Medici. When work began on the Pitti in the late 1450s, the more simply conceived *Medici Palace* was nearing completion. The design of the Pitti is traditionally, but without evidence, attributed to Brunelleschi, and it is possible that the plans carried out by Luca Fancelli could have been those Brunelleschi supposedly submitted to Cosimo who rejected them as too ostentatious.

Although the palace as left unfinished at Pitti's death in 1472 consisted of only the seven central bays of the present structure, both Machiavelli and Vasari commented on the unique size and splendor of the Pitti. Even now that the palace has been enlarged and altered, one can imagine the original impact of these lofty proportions dramatically clad like an Etruscan building in huge, rough-hewn stone blocks. Nevertheless, the Pitti Palace, only one room deep and carved into the steep slope of its own quarry, must have been an uncomfortable living space for Pitti's impoverished heirs.

In 1549 the Pittis sold their palace to Eleanor of Toledo, Cosimo I's wife, and in May of the following year the Medici entourage moved in. Five years later Vasari's **Corridoio** was thrown across the Arno to connect the old palace, the Palazzo Vecchio (see *Signoria*), with the new palace that was to be the grand-ducal and eventually royal residence for the next three centuries. Ammannati's extensions, the superb **courtyard** (★) and the wings toward the Boboli Gardens, were carried out between 1558-70.

Palatine Gallery *(Galleria Palatina)* ★

☎ 210323 ▨ *Open Tues-Sat 9am-2pm, Sun 9am-1pm. Closed Mon.*

Try to allow the full morning for these two most important sections of the Pitti, the Palatine and Argenti. To reach the Palatine you must climb Ammannati's long, steep staircase to the first floor. The Palatine is famous for its great grand-ducal collection of 16thC paintings of which the supreme treasures are the Raphaels and Titians, mostly portraits; also of outstanding quality are the frescoes by Pietro da Cortona. The tiered arrangement, in keeping with the period of the rooms, is that of a 17thC princely collection; the works are thus placed for decorative effect and not, as in the Uffizi, according to date and school. Thanks to the splendid lighting, the good condition of the pictures and the impeccable taste and knowledge with which they are hung, it doesn't take long to accustom oneself to the lack of didactic guidance. Indeed, after the Palatine, the Uffizi seems dismayingly like a textbook.

From the vestibule one passes through two Neo-Classical rooms to the Sala di Venere, where the gallery proper begins. On the ceiling, the bold **fresco allegory** (★) by Pietro da Cortona, which was commissioned by Ferdinand II and executed in 1641-2 with the help of Ciro Ferri, begins with the *Ideal Prince Being Torn from the Arms of Venus*; the cycle continues through the next four rooms. In the center of the room is Canova's statue of *Venus*, sent to Florence by Napoleon as a replacement for the looted Uffizi *Venus de Medici*.

Paintings/Titian *The Concert* (★) is an early work (c.1510-13), which passed as a Giorgione for 250yrs after its purchase in 1654 by Cardinal Leopold; *Portrait of Pietro Aretino* (1545) (★), a talented, roistering Venetian intellectual who thought so highly of this likeness that he presented it to Cosimo I; and *Portrait of a Lady, "La Bella"* (1536) (★), with perhaps the same model as the *Venus* in the **Uffizi**. Of the two glowing landscapes by Rubens, *Peasants Returning from the Fields* (c.1637) (★) is the finer. The *Portrait of Julius II* is a contemporary copy of Raphael's original, now in the National Gallery in London.

Sala di Apollo On the ceiling (1647-60): *The Young Prince Converses with Apollo*, protector of the Arts and Sciences. Paintings: Guido Reni's late masterpiece *Cleopatra; Sacred Family and Deposition* by Andrea del Sarto; Rosso Fiorentino's *Madonna Enthroned with Saints* (1522), enlarged to its present size when it was bought from the church of S. Spirito. Titian: the intensely romantic *Portrait of a Man* (c.1540) (★) was called "The Englishman" because the subject was thought to be the Duke of Norfolk; and *The Magdalen* (c.1531) (★), more ripe than repentant.

Sala di Marte Ceiling (1645-7): the Medici arms surmounted by the grand-ducal crown dominate the composition. Paintings: Tintoretto's finest work in the gallery, *Portrait of Luigi Cornaro*; Van Dyck's *Cardinal Bentivoglio* (c.1623), Papal Ambassador to Flanders and France; Titian's *Ippolito de' Medici* (1532), dressed as a grandee of Hungary and painted 3yrs before he was poisoned at Gaeta; Rubens' *Consequences of War* (1638), an allegory of the Thirty Years' War. Mars, escaped from the arms of Venus, destroys Harmony, The Arts, and Family Life. Rubens himself explained "that grief-stricken woman in black" as "the unfortunate Europe, who, for so many years now, has suffered plunder, outrage, and misery." Also by Rubens, *The Four Philosophers*, a self-portrait with his brother and two scholars.

Sala di Giove   This was formerly the grand-ducal throne room. The frescoes (1643-6) portray the eponymous god in the center and other gods in the lunettes. Paintings: Raphael's portrait of a woman, *La Velata* (c.1516) (★), whose virtuoso handling of the sleeve contrasts with the purity of outline which was to influence Ingres; Bronzino's very early *Portrait of Guidobaldo della Rovere*; Andrea del Sarto's graceful *St John the Baptist as a Boy* (1523) (★), which once belonged to Cosimo I and hung in the Uffizi Tribuna (the background has been damaged by early restoration); Fra Bartolommeo's monumental *St Mark* (1514-16), and *Deposition* (c.1516) (★), which was his last and greatest work, left partly unfinished; and Perugino's *Madonna Adoring the Christ Child*, known as the "Madonna del Sacco" after the bolster on which the child is seated.

Sala di Saturno   The last of Pietro da Cortona's fresco sequence (1663-5) was executed by Ciro Ferri. From c.1515, Raphael's *Madonna della Seggiola* (of the chair) (★) is now, as always, the most popular picture in the Palatine. In the 19thC the waiting list for permission to copy her was 5yrs. The legend is that the circular panel was taken from the end of a wine cask, but the more plausible explanation for the tondo is Raphael's wish to master a traditional Florentine compositional challenge. Also by Raphael are portraits of *Agnolo* (★) and of *Maddalena Doni* (c.1505-6) (★), which were painted a few years after their marriage (an occasion celebrated also by Michelangelo's *Doni Tondo* in the *Uffizi*). Leonardo's *Mona Lisa* suggested Maddalena's pose. *Portrait of Tommaso Inghirami* (c.1515) (★), an important figure at the court of Leo X — Raphael reveals his character through the treatment of his hands as well as of the face; and the *Grand-ducal Madonna* (c.1504-5), so-called because the Grand Duke Ferdinand III, who bought it in 1799, took it with him wherever he traveled. The beauty of Perugino's *Deposition* (1495) (★) has been revealed by cleaning.

Sala dell'Iliade   Neo-Classical decorations. Paintings: Justus Sustermans' *Portrait of Waldemar Christian, Prince of Denmark* (c.1662), the artist's best-known work; Andrea del Sarto's *Assumption of The Virgin* (c.1527), based on the similar, earlier composition on the opposite wall; Artemisia Gentileschi's dramatic *Judith*; Raphael's portrait of a pregnant woman, *La Gravida* (c.1504-8) (★); and Velàzquez' *Philip IV on Horseback*, a studio work sent to Florence as a model for an equestrian statue. In center of room, *Charity* (1824) by L. Bartolini.

Sala dell'Educazione di Giove   Paintings: Caravaggio's *Sleeping Cupid* (c.1608); and Cristofano Allori's *Judith* (★), one of the most universally admired 17thC Florentine paintings for its technical perfection and ravishing use of color.

Sala della Stufa   Formerly a bathroom, the **frescoes** (1637-41) (★) represent the Four Ages of Man and are among Pietro da Cortona's minor masterpieces.

Sala di Bagno   An early 19thC bathroom.

Sala di Ulisse   Paintings: Moroni's *Portrait of a Woman*, intensely human; Raphael's *Madonna of the Impannata* (1514), the *impannate* being the waxpaper-paned windows in the background; and Cigoli's expressive *Ecce Homo*.

Sala di Prometeo   Paintings: Filippo Lippi's *Madonna and Child* (c.1452), the quintessential Early Renaissance picture; Signorelli's *Holy Family*; D. Beccafumi's *Holy Family*. Off the Sala di Prometeo are four rooms decorated in the 1830s. Paintings include landscapes by C. von Poelenburg; Titian's portrait of *Tommaso Mosti* (1526); A. del Sarto's *Stories of Joseph* (1520-23);

G. Schalken's *Girl with a Candle*; and fruit paintings by Rachele Ruysch.

Sala del Poccetti   The room is named for the artist whose frescoes glorifying the House of Medici decorate the ceiling. Paintings: Rubens' *Portrait of a Woman*, probably Catherine Manners, Duchess of Buckingham; D. Fetti's two genre-like parables; F. Furini's exuberant *Hylas and the Nymphs*.

Volterrano Wing   Pictures by 17th and 18thC artists, notably Furini, Giovanni da S. Giovanni, Cigoli, Bilivert and Salvator Rosa. First room: Volterrano's *A Trick of the Parish Priest Arlotto* (c.1650) illustrates an anecdote about Arlotto, a jokester priest who lived in the Mugello in the 1440s. Last room: the most complete collection in existence of fruit paintings by 17thC Neapolitan woman artist Giovanna Garzoni.

Argenti Museum ✩
Entrance near left corner of courtyard ☎ 212557 ▪ Open Tues-Sat 9am-2pm, Sun 9am-1pm. Closed Mon. Ticket good also for Costume Gallery and Porcelain Museum in Boboli Gardens.
Despite its name, this is not primarily a museum of silverware. The exquisite treasures bought or commissioned by the Medici and Lorraine dynasties which it contains form one of the richest displays of luxury craftsmanship in the world. There is no better place to follow the changing taste of Florence's rulers, from the sublime collection of Lorenzo's antique vases to the ridiculous, ingenious opulence that appealed in later centuries. The exhilarating Baroque frescoes of the ground-floor apartments, used as reception rooms for important visitors by Ferdinand II, are rare in Florence for their sense of fun.

Sala di S. Giovanni   Frescoed by S. Giovanni (1634-36), Furini (1638-42) and others for the marriage of Ferdinand II and Vittoria delle Rovere, this room is one of the final, most exuberant tributes the Medici were to pay to Lorenzo the Magnificent.

Sala Buia   Lorenzo's collection of **antique vases (★)** is the glory of the museum. That a sensitive, discriminating poet-diplomat would have his initials carved on such objects shows the confidence of Renaissance man. Grotticina: Carved wooden relief by Grinling Gibbons given to Cosimo II by Charles II of England. The next three rooms are frescoed with stupendous illusionist architecture and historical or allegorical subjects by A. M. Colonna (1638-44). Sala degli Avori: Baroque ivory fantasies, some beautiful, some bizarre jokes.

First floor   Three rooms left of the stairs contain the silver treasure of the Archbishop of Salzburg, brought to Florence in 1815 by Ferdinand III. In the fourth are examples of the not altogether healthy grand-ducal interest in anthropology. Sala dei Cammei: A wonderful collection of cameos, with a *pietradura* mosaic of the Piazza Signoria (1598). Sala dei Gioielli: **Pietradura exvoto** (1617-24) of Cosimo II, a portrait in precious stones, the ultimate in grand-ducal decadence; and a fine collection of Baroque pearls and engraved classical gems mounted on rings.

Returning to the ground floor, the exit is through the former grand-ducal bedroom.

Gallery of Modern Art *(Galleria d'Arte Moderna)*
☎ 287096 ▪ Open Tues-Sat 9am-2pm, Sun 9am-1pm. Closed Mon.
In the 19thC when tourists, even more singlemindedly than today, came to Florence to study the work of artists long dead, this is what living Tuscan artists were producing: stuffy, academic paintings, orgasmic nudes and elaborate furniture. In the middle

of the 19thC Italian painters reacted with their own Impressionist Movement. They are known as the Macchiaioli and their work is to be found in Rms XXIII-XXVI, which also afford rare views of the Oltrarno and the nave of *Santo Spirito*. The gallery has recently been reorganized and houses some 2,000 works in its 30 rooms.

Appartamenti Monumentali (☎ *216673*)   Occupying the right half of the first floor and nowadays usually closed to the public, this apartment, which includes the Savoy throne room, contains no major work of art but is notable for some very fine late Neo-Classical decoration. Most elegant are the oval Queen Margherita's Dressing Room (late 18thC) and the Neo-Classical Sala Bianca, where fashion shows now take place beneath superb stuccowork by G. Albertolli (1776-80).

Meridiana Palace   Behind the right wing of the Pitti, this subpalace was the preferred residence of Victor Emmanuel. It houses a **Costume Gallery** (*ticket and hours as for Argenti Museum*) and the fine **Contini-Bonacossi Collection** of Italian and Spanish paintings (*open by appointment* ☎ *218341*).

Coach Museum (Museo delle Carrozze)   Although advertised, the official word is that this is closed for some years.

Ponte Vecchio ★
Map 4D3.

The Ponte Vecchio spans the Arno at its narrowest point and is very likely the site of the Roman bridge that carried the N-S traffic of the Via Cassia. The present structure dates from 1345, when an earlier bridge was rebuilt so solidly that it has withstood all subsequent floods. The jewelers of the Ponte Vecchio were among the first to be notified of the impending flood of 1966. Their stock was saved but their shops and Vasari's corridor, which crosses the river above the E side of the bridge, were severely damaged. It has also survived the other dangers. The oldest bridge in Florence was the only one spared in August 1944, but the retreating German army blocked access to it, mining Por S. Maria to the N and Borgo S. Jacopo to the S.

The Ponte Vecchio was the Sarajevo of medieval Italy. At its N end, where an equestrian statue of Mars then stood, Buondelmonte dei Buondelmonti was assassinated on the Easter morning of 1215, and a smoldering personal vendetta erupted into the Guelf-Ghibelline civil wars.

There have been shops on the Ponte Vecchio since the 13thC, occupied first by tanners, then butchers, linen merchants, greengrocers and blacksmiths. In 1593 Ferdinand I decided that these "vile arts" were inappropriate to a passage linking the two grand-ducal palaces. The shops were cleared and rented at twice the price to 41 goldsmiths and eight jewelers. The present jewelers may not be able to trace their occupancy back that far, but most have been here for many generations.

(See also *Shopping*.)

Porta Romana
Map 2E2.

Porta Romana is the southernmost of the old city gates and one of the modern city's busiest exits. Erected in 1326, the tower has been cropped but the doors are original, as is the 14thC fresco of the Madonna. A stretch of preserved walls runs N along Viale Petrarca to Piazza T. Tasso. To the S is the old Siena road and the new road to Poggio Imperiale and Impruneta. The Viale dei Colli Alti winds eastward from Porta Romana to Piazza F. Ferrucci, and it is now sometimes possible to walk along the city walls as far as the *Belvedere*. In the villa in Via Colombaia, Florence Nightingale was born in 1820.

Rucellai Palace ▥ ★
Via della Vigna Nuova 18. Map 4C2. Only open to special group tours.

Probably the most beautiful and certainly the most carefully considered of all Florentine palaces, Alberti's Palazzo Rucellai was the first in Florence to conform to the Classical Orders. It was built in the 1450s for Giovanni Rucellai who, after an early retirement from business, devoted himself to scholarship.

Bernardo Rossellino supervised construction, the cost of which in labor alone must have been exorbitant. Alberti's complex and subtle design is chiseled onto a flat stone surface. If you look closely you can see where the stone blocks meet across the drawn rustication.

Contemporary documents leave unanswered many crucial questions about the Rucellai. Even the attribution to Alberti, although generally accepted on stylistic grounds, is undocumented. But examination of the stone work during the most recent restoration confirms the theory that Alberti's plan suggested only the five bays on the left (as you face the palace); the left door would thus have been the central and only entrance. It was very likely Giovanni Rucellai himself who supervised the extension of the module to the right, until he was interrupted by a financial crisis caused by the loss at sea of two ships. Along the entablature, Fortune's Sail, the Rucellai heraldic device, alternates with the Medici Diamond Ring — a reminder of the political alliance of the two families.

The **Rucellai Loggia**, opposite the palace, was probably made for the wedding celebrations of Giovanni's son to a grand-daughter of Cosimo il Vecchio. It belongs to the 1460s, and if the design was suggested by Alberti, the execution was oddly clumsy, as you can see from the inside (the Loggia is often used for art exhibitions). This was the last of the Florentine family loggias, which became impracticable due to the rising cost of land, and therefore unfashionable. It could only have been built for a person as rich and as conservative as Giovanni Rucellai, who acquired over half a dozen properties to create the site.

Behind the palace is the **Marino Marini Museum** (*Piazza S. Pancrazio* ☎ *219432* ▥ *open Sun, Mon, Wed-Sat 10am-6pm, closed Tues*), handsomely installed in the former church of S. Pancrazio.

The adjacent **Rucellai Chapel** (★ *Cappello del Santo Spirito, open Sat 5-7.30pm*) is entered from the Via della Spada. Alberti designed this chapel, the first barrel-vaulted building in the city, in 1467 to house Giovanni Rucellai's funerary monument, the **Aedicule of the Church of the Holy Sepulcher**. An imitation in miniature of the original antique church in Jerusalem, this aedicule is Alberti's most fascinating work, epitomizing everything he stood for as an artist. Inside the aedicule is a damaged fresco of the *Resurrection* by Baldovinetti. The wall opposite the entrance separating the chapel from the church was built in the 19thC.

Santissima Annunziata ▥ † ★
Map 3B4.

The **Via dei Servi**, which links SS. Annunziata to the Duomo, was built as a processional street between the two most important of the Florentine churches dedicated to the Virgin. It is named after the Servite Order, of which SS. Annunziata is the mother church. On the Feast of the Virgin's Nativity the Via dei Servi is lined with candy stalls, and children carry paper lanterns from the Duomo to SS. Annunziata.

As you walk from the Duomo, notice among the 16thC palaces three on the left: the **Pucci** palace (entrance in Via de' Pucci), with an imposing but battered carved emblem of Leo X on the corner; the **Niccolini** palace (no. 15), built in 1550 to a design by Baccio d'Agnolo; and, on the corner of Piazza SS. Annunziata, the **Grifoni** (1557-63), one of the few brick palaces in Florence, built by Ammannati for one of Cosimo's courtiers, and now the Riccardi Mannelli, used as the regional government headquarters.

Although Piazza SS. Annunziata is architecturally the most harmonious open space in Florence, the apparently unified design was achieved over a period of nearly two centuries. The square had assumed its present size by the 14thC, but the first attempt to regularize it was Brunelleschi's loggia of the **Innocenti Hospital** (Spedale degli Innocenti) (1419-26). The central arch of the church portico was built in the mid-15thC, probably by Antonio da Sangallo the Elder. Next, chronologically, came the **loggia of the Servite Confraternity** (1516-25), by Antonio da Sangallo the Younger and Baccio d'Agnolo, deliberately mimicking the Innocenti across the square. Finally, in the early 17thC, the church portico was extended into a loggia.

The equestrian **statue of Ferdinand I** in the center of the square is Giambologna's last work, finished in 1608 by his pupil P. Tacca. It is the subject of Browning's poem *The Statue and the Bust*. Also by Tacca are the two small, fantastic, poison-green fountains (1629).

The Spedale degli Innocenti was the first foundling hospital in the world, and Brunelleschi's **loggia (★)** is the first building in Florence to apply Classical ideas to the Tuscan Romanesque style. The original loggia consists of the central nine bays. Ten of the ceramic tondos of swaddled babies (c.1487) are by Andrea della Robbia; the two at either end, however, are imitations.

Innocenti Gallery *(Galleria dell'Instituto degli Innocenti)* 🏛 *Piazza SS. Annunziata 12* ☎ *243670. Map 5A5* ▨ *Open Mon, Tues, Thurs-Sat: summer 9am-7pm; winter 9am-2pm; Sun and hols 9am-1pm. Closed Wed.*
This gallery on the first floor contains works by, among others, Luca della Robbia, Piero di Cosimo and Domenico Ghirlandaio, including his *Adoration of the Magi* (1488).

The **Church (★)** of SS. Annunziata was founded in 1234 by seven aristocratic families. It became an important shrine, visited by pilgrims from all over Europe, after it was dedicated in the 14thC to a miraculous image of the Virgin Annunciate. Michelozzo, who was the brother of the Servite Prior, rebuilt the church between 1444-81.

The central door under the portico leads to Michelozzo's atrium, known as the **Chiostro dei Voti** after the life-sized wax effigies the pilgrims left of themselves. By the 17thC there were some 600 of these ex-votos in the church; all have disappeared. The **frescoes (★)** have recently been returned after restoration. Illumination is poor, so go in daylight or bring a flashlight. **Right portico wall:** the *Assumption* (1517) by Rosso Fiorentino; the *Visitation* (1516) by Pontormo. **Right wall, far corner:** the *Birth of the Virgin* (1514) by Andrea del Sarto. **Nave wall:** right of nave entrance, the *Arrival of the Magi* (1511) by Andrea del

Sarto. **Left of nave entrance:** *The Nativity* (1460-2), which is Baldovinetti's masterpiece, badly eroded by time and damp, but still showing one of the loveliest landscapes in Tuscan art. **Left of the entrance from the portico, on the left wall:** *Miracles of S. Filippo Benizzi* (1509-10), five of Andrea del Sarto's earliest frescoes.

The extravagantly stuccoed and gilded **nave** and side chapels, decorated in the 16th-19thC when SS. Annunziata was, as indeed it still is, the fashionable church of Florence, are in striking contrast to the strict harmony of the square. Immediately to the left of the nave entrance is the **tempietto** designed by Michelozzo for Piero di Cosimo to house the *Miraculous Image of the Virgin*, whose head is traditionally said to have been painted by an angel, but which has been repainted so often that it is now of no artistic importance. The *tempietto* bears an inscription, which will interest students of the Florentine character, that reads: "The marble alone cost 4,000 florins."

Many of the nave chapels contain splendid Baroque and Neo-Classical decorations. One of the best is the first on the left, the **Feroni Chapel** (1692) by G. B. Foggini. Over the altar, in an ornate, twisting frame, is the *Vision of St Julian* (★) by Castagno (c.1455). The fresco was whitewashed 100yrs after the artist's death as the result of an untrue story told by Vasari that Castagno had murdered Domenico Veneziano. In the second chapel on the left is Castagno's powerful fresco (1454-5) depicting the *Trinity* (★), with St. Jerome between the Madonna and St. Mary Cleofe; and in the chapel to the right of the presbytery, a marble *Pietà* by Bandinelli, who is buried here with his wife.

The **presbytery**, known as the Tribune or Rotonda, was begun by Michelozzo in 1451, finished by Manetti in 1477 according to advice given by Alberti, but much altered by the 18thC decorations. The chapel opposite the nave entrance was decorated by Giambologna for his own grave and those of other Flemish artists working in Florence; the frescoes are by Poccetti. In the next chapel to its left is a *Resurrection* (c.1550) by Bronzino.

The **Chiostro dei Morti** is entered from the left door under the facade portico. Over the door in the far right corner is one of Andrea del Sarto's most loved and famous works, the *Madonna del Sacco* (1525) (★).

Sant'Apollonia, Castagno Museum ▥ ★

Via XXVII Aprile 1 ☎ *287074. Map 3B4* ▨ *Open Tues-Sat 9am-2pm, Sun 9am-1pm. Closed Mon.*

Shortly after his return from Venice in 1444, Andrea del Castagno painted his *Last Supper* (★) for the nuns of S. Apollonia. The refectory of their former convent is now a museum centered around this fresco, which is probably the best known and most influential of all *Last Suppers*, apart from Leonardo's in Milan. The scene is set in a fantastic marbled niche. Christ has not yet revealed the mystery of the sacrament. The sculptured peasant faces of the disciples are calm. On this side of the table the brooding figure of Judas prepares us for the announcement, "One of you shall betray me." Vasari said Castagno looked and behaved like a Judas, and there is certainly something sinister about much of his work.

Above the *Last Supper*, and of at least the same powerful quality, are Castagno's three *Scenes from the Passion*, which have tragically deteriorated. Their sinopie, uncovered when the frescoes were detached for restoration, are displayed on the opposite wall. Castagno's *Famous Men and Women*, painted for the Villa Pandolfini at Legnaia and at one time hung in this museum, are now on view in the *Uffizi*.

Santi Apostoli ⌂ †
Map 4D3.

Charlemagne did not found SS. Apostoli, as the inscription on the otherwise modest facade boasts; nevertheless, this beautiful little church in the center of medieval Florence is very old.

The portal is 16thC, probably by Benedetto da Rovezzano, but the **interior** (★), apart from the 15th-16thC side chapels, is the earliest on this side of the Arno except for the Baptistry (*Duomo*), with which it is roughly contemporary. Vasari confirms what will be obvious to anyone who knows the churches of *Santo Spirito* and *San Lorenzo* when he tells us that Brunelleschi was profoundly influenced by SS. Apostoli. Looking at the nave and aisles from the altar end one might almost believe that Brunelleschi designed this interior. In the right aisle, second altar, is Vasari's *Immaculate Conception* (1541), one of his best and most reproduced paintings, historically important as the most scholarly pictorial representation of a popular belief. At the top of the left aisle is a large terra-cotta tabernacle by Giovanni della Robbia, which is of better quality than many of his works. Next to it is Benedetto da Rovezzano's **tomb of Oddo Altoviti** (1507), whose palace, also by Benedetto, stands on the s side of the square.

The tiny Piazza del Limbo takes it name from the unbaptized babies who were once buried here. To the left of the church is a relief of the *Madonna and Child* by Benedetto da Maiano on the flank of the Rosselli del Turco palace, the facade of which, by Baccio d'Agnolo (1517), is in Borgo SS. Apostoli.

Santa Croce ★ ⌂ †
☎ 244619. *Map 5D4. Open 7.30am-12.30pm, 3-6.30pm.*
"Wait then for an entirely bright morning; rise with the sun, and go to Santa Croce, with a good opera-glass in your pocket."

If you are going to Santa Croce to study the numerous and instructive *trecento* frescoes you should follow Ruskin's advice. But do leave plenty of time. Ruskin scorned the Renaissance, but no modern tourist would want to rush in and out of the Pazzi Chapel and miss some of the finest Renaissance sculptures in Florence.

Santa Croce is not a particularly cheerful quarter. Before the 1966 flood, which caused terrible damage in this low-lying area, it was densely populated with working-class families and craftsmen's workshops. Many of these people have now moved elsewhere and the craftsmen have been replaced by the so-called leather factories, which sell to tourists. But it is still a neighborhood that stretches one's sense of history. This was the center of the dyeing trade, one of the foundations of Florentine mercantile prosperity in the 14th-16thC. One of its main streets is still called Corse dei Tintori, and some of the palaces were built to accommodate the dyeing vats (see *Horne Museum*). The imagination is carried back much further by three streets which trace the semicircular outline of the Roman amphitheater immediately to the w of the Piazza S. Croce.

The great Franciscan preaching church was began in 1294, possibly by Arnolfo di Cambio, "with Giotto at his side and Dante looking on" — or so Ruskin liked to imagine. The Franciscans, as he says, wanted a church for "preaching, prayer, sacrifice,

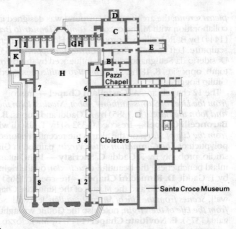

Santa Croce

burial," not for "self-glorification or town-glorification." Be that as it may, consecration was delayed by a schism in the order until the 15thC, when the Renaissance artists who worked here were evidently indifferent to Franciscan ideals of self-abnegation.

Because Michelangelo and Galileo, among other great Italians, are buried here, S. Croce can be regarded as a kind of pantheon of Italian genius. 19thC romanticism found this idea irresistible and must take the blame for the hideous facade, which was paid for by an Englishman, as well as the unfortunate statue of Dante in the square and the minaret-like Gothic bell tower.

Apart from these anachronisms the square looks much as it did in the 16th and 17thC when football matches and other spectacles were staged here by the grand dukes. A disc, dated February 10, 1565 on the ground floor of the frescoed Palazzo dell'Antella (no. 21) marks the center line. The palace (1619), by Giulio Parigi, was frescoed in 20 days by 12 assistants of Giovanni da S. Giovanni. Less picturesque but architecturally more strenuous is the Serristori-Cocchi palace (no. 1, opposite the church) attributed to Baccio d'Agnolo.

During the period of puritanical hysteria induced by Savonarola, heretics were burned in this square, and book burnings continued until 1580. Earlier, in the prime years of the Medicean Republic, S. Croce was the setting for elaborate pageants in honor of Lorenzo the Magnificent's betrothal to Clarice Orsini and of Giuliano's love for Simonetta Vespucci.

The immense, barn-like **church interior** (★ *see plan above*) is T-shaped: a broad nave crossed at the bottom by a straight row of 12 chapels. The nave side chapels were added in 1560 by Vasari; the floor is paved with some 276 tombstones (14th-19thC).

The most outstanding monuments in the nave are as follows, starting with the right nave. **1.** Relief carving of the *Madonna and Child* (1478) by A. Rossellino. **2.** *Tomb of Michelangelo* (1570) by Vasari; there is a sad irony about this tomb made by the servant-artist to Cosimo I for the artist who always refused to work for the tyrannical duke. **3.** Pentagonal marble pulpit (1472-6) by B. da Maiano. **4.** *Monument to Vittorio Alfieri* (1810) by Canova. **5.** Donatello's *Annunciation* (c.1435) (★) in gilded *pietra serena*; the architectural surround was designed in collaboration with Michelozzo. **6.** *Tomb of Leonardo Bruni* (1444) by B. Rossellino, a prototype for Florentine funerary sculpture. Left nave: **7.** *Tomb of Carlo Marsuppini* (1453) by Desiderio da Settignano, directly influenced by the *Bruni* tomb, opposite. **8.** 18thC *Monument to Galileo* designed by Giulio Foggini.

The 12 chapels are: **A. Castellani Chapel** — frescoes of *Scenes from the Lives of Saints Anthony Abbot, Nicolas, John the Divine and John the Baptist* (c.1385) by A. Gaddi and pupils. **B. Baroncelli Chapel** — frescoed (1332-8) by T. Gaddi with *Scenes from the Life of Mary*; on the altar is the recently restored polyptich of *The Coronation of the Virgin*, painted in Giotto's studio, probably by T. Gaddi. **C. Sacristy** — 16thC intarsiaed and inlaid bench chest; the beautiful *Crucifixion* on the right wall is by T. Gaddi. **D. Rinuccini Chapel** — frescoes (c.1365) by Giovanni da Milano and the Master of the Rinuccini Chapel: right wall, *Scenes from the Life of Mary Magdalen*; left wall, *Scenes from the Life of the Virgin*; note also the Gothic wrought-iron gate (1373). **E. Novitiate Chapel** (1445) by Michelozzo, commissioned by Cosimo il Vecchio — on the altar, terra-cotta tabernacle of the *Madonna and Child with Angels and Saints* (c.1480) by Andrea della Robbia or a close follower; Galileo is buried in this chapel.

The two chapels to the right of the chancel, the Peruzzi (**F.**) and the Bardi (**G.**), were frescoed by Giotto and pupils at the height of his mature powers. An overwhelming influence on Masaccio and thus on the whole of *quattrocento* Florentine painting, they were covered with whitewash in the 18thC. Rediscovered in the 19thC, they were subjected to heavy overpainting. When these accretions were removed in this century the Bardi Chapel emerged in much better condition than the Peruzzi. Enough is left to help one solve the puzzle but not quite enough to give instant esthetic pleasure. **F. Peruzzi Chapel** (★) — frescoes (c.1326-30) on the right wall show *Scenes from the Life of St John the Divine*; on the left wall, *Scenes from the Life of St John the Baptist*. **G. Bardi Chapel** (★) — Ruskin compared this chapel to "a large, beautiful, coloured Etruscan vase inverted over your heads like a diving-bell." Above the arch outside the chapel notice the moving *St Francis Receiving the Stigmata*. Frescoes (c.1315-20) of *Scenes from the Life of St Francis*; altarpiece on panel (c. 1250-60) by the Master of the Bardi Chapel.

H. Chancel — frescoes and stained glass (c.1380) of the *Legend of the True Cross* by A. Gaddi; the *Crucifix* over the altar is by the Master of the Fogg Pietà. **I. Bardi di Vernio Chapel** — frescoes (1335-8) show *Scenes from the Life of St Sylvester* by Maso di Banco; ask the sacristan to open the gates to the Niccolini and K. Bardi chapels. **J. Niccolini Chapel** — a remarkable anticipation of the 17thC Baroque style built in 1579-85 by Antonio Dosio. **K. Bardi Chapel** — the wooden **crucifix** by Donatello is supposed to be the one Brunelleschi criticized for looking like a peasant on a cross. To the right of the church is the entrance to the **cloisters**, the **Pazzi Chapel** and the **Santa Croce Museum**.

Santa Croce Museum and Pazzi Chapel ★

Piazza Santa Croce 16 ☎ 244619. Map 5D4 ▨ Open summer 9am-12.30pm, 2.30-6.30pm; winter 9am-12.30pm, 3-5pm. Closed Wed.

Brunelleschi planned the Pazzi Chapel around 1430. Building began in 1443, and the upper part of the facade was completed after his death. The **interior** (★) was more successful even than the *San Lorenzo* Old Sacristy, and probably sums up the modern ideal of the early Renaissance more completely than any other single monument in Florence; there is no other place that has such a calming and restorative effect on the spirits. But it is not quite perfect. As one can see in the corners where fragmentary pilasters are awkwardly squeezed, Brunelleschi did not fully solve the structural problem he set himself here. The blue and white terra-cotta **tondos** of the *Apostles* in the chapel are by Luca della Robbia; the polychrome tondos of the *Evangelists* in the pendentives have been attributed to Brunelleschi.

Museum The most important works are in the refectory. Cimabue's *Crucifixion* (★) is one of the most tragic victims of the 1966 flood. Donatello's St Louis of Toulouse (★) was originally made in 1423 for **Orsanmichele**. The detached fresco of *The Last Supper* on the far wall is Taddeo Gaddi's best work. On the long walls are fragments of frescoes by Orcagna, recovered from the church where they were found beneath Vasari's altars. Bronzino's *Christ in Limbo* (1552), in room 4, was painted as an altarpiece but considered too hedonistic to place in the church.

The **second cloister** is entered from the far right-hand corner of the first cloister, past a very fine portal by Benedetto da Maiano. Finished in 1453 by a close follower of Brunelleschi, this is one of the most beautiful cloisters in Florence.

San Felice ▥

Map 4E2.

This church, in its busy little triangular piazza a few steps from the Pitti, has an attractive Renaissance facade attributed to Michelozzo. The interior is calm, spacious and much restored with a good Giottesque crucifix over the right side door.

I heard last night a little child go singing.
'Neath Casa Guidi windows, by the church,
O bella libertà, O bella!

Elizabeth Barrett Browning, *Casa Guidi Windows*

This may have been the first battered wives' center. In the Renaissance its Dominican nuns offered refuge to women who fled from their husbands. The Brownings lived at **Casa Guidi** (*Piazza S. Felice 8*) for 15yrs until Elizabeth's death in 1861. A passionate supporter of the Risorgimento, Elizabeth's existence was marred by a loathing for her neighbor, Leopold II.

Santa Felìcita ▥

Map 4E3.

There has been a church on this site for nearly 2,000yrs, the first being a hiding place and burial ground for early Christians. In the Renaissance the Benedictine nuns of S. Felicita ran a successful quarry in their properties behind the church, but the building was much altered in the 16thC when it was used as a private chapel by the Medici dukes. In 1736 it was thoroughly remodeled by Ferdinand Ruggieri, who did not, however, disturb the facade portico built by Vasari in 1564 to support his aerial corridor, which passes through the church on its way from the Uffizi to the Pitti. Today the oldest monument in the square is the granite column erected in 1381.

Interior To the right of the entrance is the Brunelleschian **Capponi Chapel** decorated by Pontormo from 1525-8. The *Deposition* (★) over the altar is really a meditation on the beautiful, weightless body of the dead Christ. It is probably Pontormo's most intensely felt and emotionally affecting masterpiece — the figure in brown on the right may be a self-portrait. On the right wall is his *Annunciation*, revealed as another masterpiece by cleaning in the 1960s. In the pendentives of the cupola are four **tondos of the Evangelists** (the *St Mark* is by Bronzino). The grand-ducal tribunes are on either side of the nave w of the transepts. The charming choir (1610-20) is by Cigoli.

Around the corner from the square in Via Guicciardini is Palazzo Guicciardini (no. 15), birthplace of the historian Francesco Guicciardini and still occupied by his descendants.

San Firenze 🏛 †
Map 5D5.

The facade of S. Firenze, which unites three separate earlier buildings, is the biggest and best 18thC Baroque spectacle in Florence. On the left side is the **facade of the church of S. Filippo Neri** designed by Ferdinando Ruggieri in 1715. The central and right-hand section (1772-5), formerly the church and convent of S. Apollinare, now the Tribunal, is by Zanobi del Rosso. Opposite is the elegant **Gondi** palace (1490-1501) by Giuliano da Sangallo. Ring for the porter to see the courtyard.

San Frediano
Map 2C2. Bus 13 to Piazza T. Tasso.

The S. Frediano gate at the sw corner of the city was erected in 1332-4, and is the one through which Charles VIII entered Florence from the old Pisa road in 1494. Filippino Lippi painted the gate in the background of his Nerli altarpiece in *Santo Spirito*. Nearby is the 17thC church of S. Frediano in Cestello, and on the lungarno end of its piazza is the handsome granary made for Cosimo III.

You can climb to *Bellosguardo* from the gate in 30mins.

San Gaetano 🏛 †
Via Tornabuoni. Map 4C3. Rarely open except for services.

The best Baroque church facade in Florence, built by Gherardo Silvani in 1648.

A plaque on the corner of Via de' Corsi and the Tornabuoni commemorates the production in 1594 of the first opera, *La Dafne*, by Jacopo Peri and Jacopo Corsi, the owner of the original palace on this site.

San Lorenzo 🏛 † ★
Map 4B3.

To build their parish church the Medici hired Brunelleschi for the first and only time. Begun in 1419 on the site of a much older church, S. Lorenzo was built, embellished and extended by some of the greatest artists and most skillful craftsmen of the 15th-17thC. Most of this work was initiated, supervised and paid for by the successive members of the Medici family who are buried here.

Seen from its busy market square, S. Lorenzo is an impressive if not harmonious complex. The taller of the two domes at the chancel end covers the Cappella dei Principi; the shallower cupola completes Michelangelo's New Sacristy. The bell tower is 18thC and the unexciting statue of Giovanni delle Bande Nere (1540) is by Bandinelli. Michelangelo's model for a proposed facade, commissioned in 1516 but judged unacceptable by his

Medici patrons, can be seen in the *Casa Buonarroti*.

The **interior** (★) is one of the most understatedly powerful in Italy, designed by Brunelleschi in 1420 but completed after his death by A. Manetti in 1460. The delay was caused by financial crises in the Medici banks, but it is evident that money was not stinted on the final construction. Even the *pietra serena* capitals and the arches that define the space were carved by leading sculptors of the day, including A. and M. Rossellino.

Highlights are as follows: **1.** The *Marriage of the Virgin* (1523), an elegant and vivid picture by Rosso Fiorentino. **2.** A fine and in its day influential **marble tabernacle** (c.1460) by Desiderio da Settignano. **3.** and **4. Bronze pulpits** by Donatello (c. 1460), his last works, finished by pupils; the **Deposition panel** and **Resurrection panel** are by Donatello's own hand. **5.** Bronzino's sadly faded fresco of the *Martyrdom of San Lorenzo* (1565-69). **6.** Martelli Chapel. *The Annunciation* (c.1440) by Filippo Lippi, a masterpiece of perspective, clumsily restored.

The **Old Sacristy** (Sagrestia Vecchia) (★) is entered from the left transept. Brunelleschi's early masterpiece (1421-8) was completed before the church itself; Vasari says Cosimo il Vecchio was constantly present throughout building. This is one of the first mathematically conceived architectural spaces of the Renaissance: a perfect cube completed by a hemispherical umbrella dome. Donatello's **sculptural decorations**, carried out in the 1430s, consist of: the four polychrome medallions illustrating *Scenes from the Life of St John the Evangelist* in the pendentives; the four polychrome **tondos of the Evangelist** in the lunettes; and the **bronze doors** flanking the apse. Donatello was responsible for the architecture of the doors as well as the bronze relief panels: the right door is the *Door of the Martyrs*; the left is known as the *Door of the Apostles* despite its 20 figures. Left of the entrance is Verrocchio's elegant *Monument to Piero and Giovanni de' Medici* (1472).

Laurentian Library *(Biblioteca Medici-Laurenziana)* 🏛 ★
Piazza S. Lorenzo ☎ *210760* 🖪 🖾 *Open, by appointment only, Mon-Sat 9am-1pm. Closed Sun.*

This library was designed by Michelangelo in 1524-34, to house the collection of classical and humanist manuscripts founded by Cosimo il Vecchio, later removed to Rome by Leo X and finally

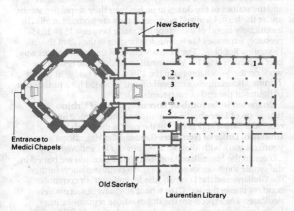

New Sacristy

Entrance to
Medici Chapels

Old Sacristy

Laurentian Library

returned to Florence by Clement VII, who commissioned this building.

Vestibule   An early, dramatic, sophisticated break with the rational, classical principles of 15thC Florentine architecture. The staircase, which fills nearly the entire room, was left unfinished by Michelangelo and completed in the 1550s by Vasari and Ammannati.

Library   The comparatively simple rectangular space is in deliberate contrast to the vestibule. The marble intarsia floor, designed by Tribolo, repeats the ceiling's Medici motifs of the ram's skull and the motto "Semper." Among the codices is the Medici *Virgil.*

Medici Chapels *(Cappelle Medicee)* ★
☎ 213206 ▨ *Open Tues-Sat 9am-2pm, Sun and hols 9am-1pm. Closed Mon. Entrance from Piazza di Madonna degli Aldobrandini.*
On the way to the chapels you pass through the lofty crypt paved with tombstones of the Medici and Lorraine grand dukes. The tomb of Cosimo il Vecchio is in a room below. A staircase on the right leads to the **Chapel of the Princes** (Cappella dei Principi). Designed by Don Giovanni de' Medici and Buontalenti and built by Nigetti from 1602, this portentous, claustrophobic grand-ducal shrine, clad entirely in *pietradura*, is really a monument to Ferdinand I, who ordered it. It was the most expensive of all Medici building projects and the one that posterity, until recently, was to judge as being in the worst taste. The ground plan is based on that of the Baptistry *(Duomo).* A room in the **Opificio delle Pietre dure** (*Via degli Alfani 78* ☎ *210102, open Mon-Sat 9am-2pm, closed Sun*) is devoted to the design and construction of this chapel.

The **New Sacristy** (Sagrestia Nuova) (★) was Michelangelo's first realized architectural creation, begun in 1520 and left unfinished, after interruptions, in 1534. It is an answer, half respectful and half rebellious, to Brunelleschi's Old Sacristy. Imitating the Old Sacristy, it makes a totally different impression because, as Vasari tells us, Michelangelo would not conform to the "measure, order and rule" that were the essence of Brunelleschi's style. It was intended to be seen from the altar.

Leo X and Clement VII, who paid for the New Sacristy, were less concerned to glorify the two Medici dukes entombed here than to strengthen the authority of these dukes' bastard heirs, and the statues of the dukes in niches over their respective tombs are, at the least, idealized portraits, if they are portraits at all. The melancholy mood of the sculptures made between 1524-1533 probably expresses Michelangelo's despair at the fall of the Florentine Republic. The catenary curve of the tomb volutes was later copied exactly by Ammannati (who did some restorative work on the New Sacristy) in the 1550s, for his bridge at *Santa Trìnita.* Michelangelo's original design provided for a further pair of figures at the end of each tomb.

On the left is the **tomb of Lorenzo, Duke of Urbino** (grandson of Lorenzo the Magnificent); the reclining figures represent *Dawn* and *Dusk.* On the right is the **tomb of Giuliano, Duke of Nemours** (Lorenzo the Magnificent's youngest son), with allegorical figures of *Day* and *Night.*

Lorenzo the Magnificent and his brother Giuliano are buried in the simple tomb opposite the altar. To confuse matters further, the Giuliano and the Lorenzo "the Magnificent" (a common courtesy title in the 16thC) to whom Machiavelli successively dedicated *The Prince* are the dukes whose remains lie in Michelangelo's tombs and not the more famous 15thC Medici buried here in near anonymity. On this tomb is Michelangelo's deeply moving *Madonna and Child* (1521), which is flanked by *S. Cosma* by Montorsoli, and by *S. Damiano* by Raffaele da Montelupo.

In a room below, fresco drawings by Michelangelo and his pupils have recently been uncovered, and are often on display in the choir.

San Marco, Fra Angelico Museum *(Museo dell' Angelico)* ★

Piazza San Marco ☎ *210741. Map 3B4* 🔟 *Open Tues-Sat 9am-2pm, Sun and hols 9am-1pm. Closed Mon.*

The **convent and cloisters** of S. Marco were Cosimo il Vecchio's greatest gift to Florence. Cosimo acquired the convent for the Dominican friars of Fiesole. The architect Michelozzo's only work of genius was transmuted by the painter Fra Angelico into a supremely noble expression of balanced Christianity: sincere, compassionate, mystic, learned.

S. Marco witnessed one of the turning points in Florence's history. By the end of the 15thC Florentines had been swung off center into a hectic, puritanical religiosity incited by Savonarola, who became Prior of S. Marco in 1491. The Medici were expelled in 1494, and Jesus Christ was proclaimed King of Florence, with Savonarola acting as political leader. In 1498 the crowds who had fervently responded to his charisma turned against him. S. Marco was besieged, and Savonarola was captured, tried and burned at the stake in the Piazza Signoria.

In 1869 the suppressed convent of S. Marco became a museum honoring Fra Angelico. Today it is a nearly complete one-man show of his *oeuvre*. Most of his greatest panel paintings have been assembled here, brought in from churches, guilds, and other galleries including the *Uffizi*, which now retains only two Angelicos.

During the 1980s new sections of the convent will be opened as a museum housing fragments salvaged from the old parts of the city demolished in the 1860s.

From the vestibule one enters Michelozzo's **Cloister of S. Antonino**. Most of the frescoes are 16th C, but some of the lunettes and the *Crucifixion with St Dominic* in the far left corner are by Angelico. To the right of the entrance is the **Ospizio dei Pellegrini** (★), which is the room where pilgrims were offered hospitality, now housing 20 panel paintings by Angelico, well labeled as to date and provenance. The cult of Angelico as a naive painter stops here — if his spirit was still medieval, his technique was fully informed by the Early Renaissance. Some outstanding works in this room are the *Deposition* (c.1435) from S. Trìnita; the *San Marco Altarpiece* (1438-43) with the Medici patron saints Cosma and Damian; the *Virgin Enthroned* (c.1433), painted for the linen drapers guild, the Linaiuoli; and the 35 *Scenes from the Life of Christ*, completed by Baldovinetti.

Across the courtyard, in the **Sala Capitolare** (the Chapter House), is Angelico's grand, mystic vision of the *Crucifixion* (★) (c.1442). Nearby in the cloister is the bell of S. Marco, the *Piagnona*, which gave the signal for the siege of the convent that led to the imprisonment of Savonarola. In the refectory, to the left of the stairs, is Dom. Ghirlandaio's clear, descriptive *Last Supper*, a variation on the one in the *Ognissanti* refectory.

On the first floor, the 44 **dormitory cells** (★) were frescoed by Angelico and assistants from 1439-45. At the top of the stairs is Angelico's justly famous *Annunciation*. If time is short, visit at least: cell 1. *Noli Me Tangere*, 3. *Annunciation*, 6. *Transfiguration*, 7. the *Crowning with Thorns*, and 9. the *Coronation of Mary*. The **library**, between cells 42 and 43, is Michelozzo's most inspired interior. This was the first public library in Europe, thanks to Cosimo il Vecchio, who donated the manuscripts. Cells 38 and 39 at the bottom of this corridor were reserved for Cosimo's retreats. Cell 11 was the prior's quarters, occupied by Savonarola, whose **portrait** by Fra Bartolommeo is in the vestibule, cell 12.

The adjacent church of S. Marco (1437-52) was built by Michelozzo, but subsequently updated by Giambologna in 1585, by P.F. Silvani in 1678 and by various 18thC decorators. In the center of the wooden ceiling is a canvas of the *Madonna in Glory* (1725) by G.A. Pucci. Poliziano and Pico della Mirandola are buried near the third altar on the left.

The administrative offices of the University of Florence, the various faculties of which are scattered all over the city, are on the E side of the square at no. 4, in the building where Cosimo I kept lions and which was used in later years as the grand-ducal stables.

Santa Maria Maddalena dei Pazzi † ☆
Borgo Pinti 58. Map 3C5.

Santa Maria Maddalena dei Pazzi was a Carmelite nun and member of the banking family who died in 1609 and was canonized in 1685. This church, originally built by Giuliano da Sangallo, was renamed and redesigned in her honor in 1628 by Luigi Arrigucci, who retained Giuliano's side chapels. The frescoes in the nave (1677) are by Jacopo Chiavistelli. The chancel was extended and richly decorated in the year of her canonization by P.F. Silvani, C. Ferri and P. Dandini, with two canvases by Luca Giordano. In the sacristy, off the bottom of the right aisle, is some good late Baroque stuccowork (1767).

The rest of the church complex is something of a box of surprises: frescoes by Poccetti in the Cappella del Giglio; an elegant **courtyard** (1492) by Giuliano da Sangallo, important as the first building project to carry out Alberti's instruction that arches must be supported on square pillars. But the compelling reason to visit S. Maria Maddalena dei Pazzi is in the old chapter room of the convent (☎ *2478420, open 9am-noon, 5-7pm, offering expected*), where Perugino's **fresco of the Crucifixion** (1493-6) (★) covers one wall. This lovely composition, set in a severe illusionistic architectural frame, echoes the peace of the landscape bathed in early morning light.

Nearby, in Borgo Pinti 68, is the large **Panciatichi Ximenes palace**, c.1499, built by Giuliano and Antonio da Sangallo as their own palace and enlarged by Gherardo Silvani in 1620. Napoleon stayed here in June 1796.

Santa Maria Maggiore ⌂ †
Via de' Cerretani. Map 4B3.

The interior is a pleasing mixture of 13thC Gothic as reinterpreted by an early 20thC restoration, with 17th-18thC Baroque decoration. The side altars are by Gherardo Silvani with frescoes and canvases by Giuseppe Pinzani, Pier Dandini, Volterrano, Onorio Marinari and Vincenzo Meucci.

The prize possession of the church is in the chapel left of the high altar. This 13thC polyptych of the *Madonna and Child* was attributed to Andrea di Cione by Berenson, but is now thought to be by Coppo di Marcovaldo.

Santa Maria Novella 🏛 ✝ ★
☎ 210113. Map **4**B2. Open Mon-Sat 7-11.30am, 3.30-6pm,
Sun 3.30-5pm.

Next to the station and only 5mins from the Duomo, S.M. Novella
nevertheless seems remote from the rest of Florence, as indeed it
was before the final ring of walls embraced the area and the
Mugnone, which once flowed here through vineyards, was
diverted N of the Fortezza da Basso. The feeling that one might
almost be in a different city is emphasized by the only Florentine
church facade completed in the 15thC and by the high
proportion of comfortable but undistinguished 19thC buildings,
which fill gaps left in the 16thC when the population of Florence
had not yet expanded as rapidly as expected. In the 19thC S.M.
Novella was known as the "Mecca of Foreigners." Henry James,
William Dean Howells, Emerson, Longfellow and Shelley were
among the literary visitors who chose to stay just a little to one
side of the inspiring but noisy city.

The church of S.M. Novella was built from 1246 by the
Dominicans, successful protagonists at that time of a puritanical
movement similar in its aims to the 16thC Reformation, and far
stricter than the doctrine propounded by the Franciscans, whose
rival preaching church was begun 48yrs later at **Santa Croce**.
The Dominicans had taken possession in 1221 of an old church
which occupied the transept of the present building, and in 1245
the piazza was opened out to receive the crowds attracted by the
Dominican preacher St Peter Martyr. The new church buildings,
supervised by a succession of Dominican architects, were
completed by 1360. A compromise between contemporary
French and native Italian styles, S.M. Novella was the first Gothic
church in Italy to break away from the imported Cistercian mold.

It was in S. Maria Novella that Boccaccio described the
protagonists of the *Decameron*, talking of plague, and it was the
fear and consequences of the plague of 1348 which occasioned
the building of many of the chapels and cloisters. But there is no
hint of these gloomy associations with dogmatism and death in
Alberti's brilliant rationalization of the 14thC facade. Honoring
the Gothic forms of the existing facade, and retaining the lower
arcade and the round window, he raised it into a mathematically
organized space containable within a perfect square. The volutes,
an invention much copied by later architects, conceal the two
aisles. His **facade** (★) was begun in 1456. As one can see from

1 Strozzi Chapel
2 Gondi Chapel
3 Filippo Strozzi Chapel
4 Sacristy
5 Rucellai Chapel
6 Spanish Chapel

Chiostro Grande

Chiostro
Verde

Refectory

Santa Maria Novella

the Rucellai device which sails across the center and from the inscription under the pediment, the patron was Giovanni Rucellai and the date of completion 1470. The two astronomical instruments were placed here in 1572.

The **interior** was updated in 1565-71 by Vasari, who deprived the nave of color and light by whitewashing frescoes and shortening the aisle windows to allow for his side chapels.

The **nave** appears longer than it is thanks to a trick of perspective played by the Gothic architects, who placed the supporting pillars at diminishing intervals. There are several distinguished monuments in the nave, but the outstanding work, halfway down the left wall, is Masaccio's *Trinity* (c.1427) (★), with Mary and St John flanked by the donors, members of the Lenzi family. The central figures are set in an illusionist Holy Sepulcher, which may have been suggested by Brunelleschi, who designed the marble **pulpit** on the nearest pillar.

Left transept The Strozzi Chapel occupies the raised presbytery of the original Romanesque church. The **altarpiece** (1354-7) shows *Christ Giving the Keys to Peter and the Book of Knowledge to St Thomas*, by Orcagna. The frescoes (c.1351-7), by Nardo di Cione, have deteriorated: left wall, *Paradise*, altar wall, the *Last Judgment*, with Dante among the blessed; right wall, the *Inferno*. In the Sacristy is the *Crucifix* from the interior facade by Giotto. The Gondi Chapel, with striking **decorations in marble** (c.1503), by Giuliano da Sangallo, contains Brunelleschi's famous *Crucifix*, his only surviving wooden sculpture, made, according to Vasari, in answer to Donatello's *Crucifix* in **Santa Croce**, which Brunelleschi judged too crudely realistic. In 1485-90 the chancel was decorated behind the high altar by Dom. Ghirlandaio with his most popular **frescoes** (★), commissioned by Giovanni Tornabuoni, Lorenzo de' Medici's uncle. Serious art historians used to dismiss this pretty narrative work as merely journalistic; Ruskin described them as not nice enough for nice people and not vulgar enough for vulgar people, and Henry James as "for the wicked, amusing world." But they are among the valuable pictorial documents we have of their period, and most modern visitors will be fascinated and charmed by them. Left wall: *Scenes from the Life of the Virgin*. Right wall: *Scenes from the Life of the Baptist*.

Right transept The Filippo Strozzi Chapel is frescoed (c.1487-1502) by Filippino Lippi in a strange obsessive style steeped in Roman archeology and anticipating the Baroque: right wall, *Story of St Philip* (★) and left wall, *Story of St John the Divine* (★). Behind the altar is the **tomb of Filippo Strozzi** (1491-3) by Benedetto da Maiano. The Rucellai Chapel was raised in the 15thC. Duccio's Rucellai *Madonna*, now in the **Uffizi**, has been replaced at the altar by Nino Pisano's marble *Madonna and Child* (after 1348). In the pavement is Ghiberti's bronze **tomb of Leonardo Dati** (1425).

Cloisters ★

🕿 282187 ◼ *Open Mon-Thurs, Sat 9am-2pm, Sun 8am-1pm. Closed Fri. Entrance to left of church facade.*

The **Chiostro Verde** (c.1350) is so called because of the green tint of Uccello's **frescoes of the Old Testament**, executed in *terra verde*. They are detached and usually exhibited in the Refectory. Uccello's *Universal Deluge* (★) of c.1445 was restored in the 1950s and again after the most recent deluge of 1966. Tragically deteriorated, it is recognizable as his masterpiece.

The **Spanish Chapel** (★) was an old chapter room of the convent, built c.1350 by Jacopo Talenti, and used for worship in the 16thC by Eleanor of Toledo's Spanish courtiers. The monumental didactic **fresco cycle** (1365-7) by Andrea da Firenze and assistants is a schematic depiction of the Catholic way of life, which is determined by the scenes in the vault and over the altar. Left wall: theology, civilization and intellectual culture revealed by St Thomas Aquinas; right wall: the practical way of life, with the church militant represented by an unrealized plan for the Duomo, the actual dome of which was of course not finished for another 80yrs. Ruskin guessed, probably correctly, that the average tourist would spend 15mins in the Spanish Chapel, studying "its vaulted book, the most noble piece of pictorial philosophy in Italy," whereas he had "taken five weeks to see the quarter of this picture."

In the piazza, the large obelisks, resting on bronze tortoises, mark the limits of the chariot race established here by Cosimo I in 1563. At the far end is the graceful, post-Brunelleschian **Loggia di S. Paolo** (1489-96), with a terra-cotta lunette over the doorway by Andrea della Robbia. In the Via della Scala is a perfectly preserved 17thC pharmacy (see *Shopping*), and immediately to the NW of the piazza is the central **station** (1935), the first functionalist station building in Italy. Although admired by many, a joke made by a rival architect has stuck to the station: "I can see the box the station came in," he said, "but where is the station?"

San Miniato 🏛 ✝ ★

☎ 2342768. Map 3E5. Open winter 9am-noon, 2-5.30pm, summer 9am-noon, 3-7pm.

The sight of S. Miniato invariably makes people smile. A small, venerable green and white jewel, it stands above the city on the highest of the hills immediately to the SE. Apart from the Baptistry (*Duomo*), it is the oldest and most loved church in Florence.

According to a medieval legend, S. Miniato, persecuted by the Emperor Decius and decapitated in the amphitheater, carried his head across the river and up the hill to this place. The commemorative church was built in the 11thC. It was here that the miraculous *Crucifix*, now in *Santa Trinita*, spoke to S. Giovanni Gualberto who went on to found the reforming Benedictine order of Vallombrosa. After the last expulsion of the Medici in 1527 the hill was fortified by Michelangelo and used during the siege as a key defense post against the army of Charles V (see Vasari's fresco in the *Signoria*, Sala dei Cinquecento). Thirty years later the fortified church that had briefly been a symbol of Florentine love of freedom was occupied by the soldiers of the dictator Duke Cosimo I.

The facade dates from c.1090, except for the 13thC mosaic, restored in the 19thC when the Florentines loved S. Miniato perhaps a little too well; and the copper eagle over the pediment, emblem of the Guild of Calimala, which administered the church, dates from 1288. The crenelated **Bishop's Palace** to the right was built in 1295 by Andrea dei Mozzi, Bishop of Florence, as a summer residence. During the 1529 siege Baccio d'Agnolo's squat bell tower, then only just completed, was shielded by mattresses against the Spanish cannonballs. The lovely Romanesque **interior** (★) is marred only by the heavy hand of the 19thC restorer, who coated the stone column shafts with *scagliola* and brightened the polychrome ceiling. The smaller of the Corinthian capitals are Roman. The tapestry-like strip of **pavement**, inspired by Sicilian fabrics and one of the finest of its kind in Italy, is dated 1207 in the zodiac panel.

Nave The giant St Christopher frescoed on the right wall is by an unknown 14thC artist. At the bottom of the nave is Michelozzo's **Crucifix Chapel** (1448). The glazed terra-cotta vault is by Luca della Robbia. Off the left nave the **Cardinal of Portugal's Chapel** (★), dating from 1461-6, is a model of collaborative Renaissance art (*ask the sacristan to open the gate*). Commissioned by Alfonso V of Portugal to house the tomb of his nephew Cardinal James of Lusitania, who died in Florence in 1459, this exquisite chapel was built into the side of the basilica by A. Manetti. The **cardinal's tomb** on the right wall is by A. Rossellino. On the opposite wall, above the Bishop's throne, is Baldovinetti's *Annunciation*, on panel, carefully restored. The glazed terra-cotta **vault and tondos of the Holy Ghost and four Cardinal Virtues** are by Luca della Robbia. In the lunette facing the entrance are two *Angels in Flight*, frescoed by A. and P. del Pollaiuolo.

Sacristy   This is to the right of the raised presbytery. Frescoes by Spinello Aretino (1385-7) represent *Scenes from the Life of St Benedict*.

Presbytery   The delightful marble **pulpit** (1209) is justly famous for its carving and intarsiaed fantasy animals. The 13thC mosaic in the apse was restored by Baldovinetti. Over the altar, left, is *S. Miniato* by Jacopo del Casentino.

Crypt   The 36 columns are of various provenance. Frescoes in the vault show *Saints and Prophets* by Taddeo Gaddi.

Emerging from the church one can wander for half an hour or so among the sweet, nostalgic 19thC and early 20thC tombs in the cemetery, planned in 1839 by Niccolò Matas. The whole church complex retains examples from nearly a thousand years of funerary tradition.

San Niccolò 🏛 ✝
Map 3D5.

The defense **tower of S. Niccolò** in Piazza Giuseppe Poggi was erected in 1324 and has been maintained at it original height by frequent restorations. The steps behind lead up to *Piazzale Michelangelo*. To the sw, Via Belvedere runs along the old walls and the 16thC bastion to Porta S. Giorgio and the *Belvedere* fortress. Or you could walk w along Via S. Niccolò and Via dei Bardi, two of the best-preserved (and noisiest) medieval streets in Florence, to the *Ponte Vecchio*. The medieval road to *San Miniato* from Porta S. Miniato is the way described by Dante in *Purgatorio XII*.

Opposite Porta S. Miniato is the church of **S. Niccolò Sopr' Arno**, with a 15thC interior made over in the 16thC. A recent restoration has emphasized the difference in taste between the two centuries by uncovering the 15thC frescoes but leaving the 16thC tabernacle frames. Sinopie of the restored frescoes are also displayed.

San Salvi ✝ ☆
Via S. Salvi 16 ☎ *677570. Map 7D5* 🚌 *Open Tues-Sat 9am-2pm, Sun 9am-1pm. Closed Mon.*

The work of Andrea del Sarto, Browning's "faultless painter," can sometimes seem boringly academic to modern eyes. But his masterpiece in fresco, the *Last Supper* (★), which was commissioned in 1519 for the refectory of the S. Salvi monastery, is one of the most sumptuous visual treats in Florence. This is the perfect normative High Renaissance painting, in a near-perfect state of preservation. Its beauty saved it during the siege of Florence, when workmen, instructed to tear down any building near the city that might be used by the enemy, refused to destroy this picture.

Closed to the public after the 1966 flood, the refectory was reopened in October 1981. The monastery is now an asylum. A visit to S. Salvi could be combined with lunch at Pepolino (see *Restaurants*) or a day in *Settignano* (see *Tuscany A to Z*). On the way from the center, notice Nervi's admirable **Stadium** (1932).

Santo Spirito 🏛 † ★
Map 4E2.

When Florence was partitioned into four administrative sections in the 14thC, the city s of the Arno became the S. Spirito quarter. Piazza S. Spirito is still the heart of the *Oltrarno*, and it is the square connoisseurs of Florence often say they love most, the place where daily life seems least disturbed by tourists.

The most strikingly lovely of the palaces on the piazza is the **Guadagni** (1503-6) at no. 10, attributed to Baccio d'Agnolo and with a fine courtyard in the manner of Giuliano da Sangallo. In the palace next door, no. 9, is an elegant staircase leading to the Pensione Bandini.

The **church of S. Spirito** was built on the site of an earlier Augustinian monastery to a design by Brunelleschi. The foundation stone was laid in 1436 but the church was not completed until 1487, long after Brunelleschi's death. The delay was caused by financial difficulties, fire, and controversy over the interpretation of the master's design, which was fundamentally respected in the interior.

The modest voluted facade was applied in the 17thC. The slender bell tower (1503-17) is by Baccio d'Agnolo.

Brunelleschi's calm, rational **interior** (★) with its soaring forest of columns is spoiled only by the 17thC *baldacchino* in the chancel. The plan is a more subtle and complex variation on that of *San Lorenzo*. Around the perimeter are 40 semicircular chapels. Those in the transepts and apse give the clearest impression one can find in modern Florence of how 15thC religious art looked in its original context; some of the chapels have inevitably been altered, but more than enough have been left as they were to help one imagine the paintings one sees in galleries back in their proper setting.

Don't miss: right transept, Filippino Lippi's **Nerli altarpiece** (c.1490) (★); and left transept, which is the most perfectly preserved part of the church, the **Corbinelli Chapel** (1492), with architecture and the sculptures by the young A. Sansovino. From the left nave, the door under the organ leads through a noble vaulted vestibule (1492-6), built by Cronaca to a design by Giuliano da Sangallo, into the octagonal **sacristy** (1489-92), also designed by Sangallo.

Refectory *(Cenacolo di Santo Spirito)*
Piazza S. Spirito 29 ☎ 287043 ▨ Open Tues-Sat 9am-2pm, Sun 8am-1pm. Closed Mon.

This is the only part of the Gothic monastery to have survived the fire of 1471. The **frescoes**, badly damaged but of the greatest importance, were attributed by Ghiberti to Orcagna, an opinion not generally supported by modern scholarship.

Santo Stefano al Ponte 🏛 †
Map 4D3.

The lower half of the facade and the attractive doorway are 13thC. The shoe of Buondelmonte dei Buondelmonti's horse is supposed to have been hung here after his assassination (see *Ponte Vecchio*).

The remarkable **interior** (1649-55) by Ferdinando Tacca is unfortunately rarely open except for exhibitions. The raised chancel is an imaginary reconstruction of a Roman theater. Leading up to it is an extraordinary lasagna-like marble flight of stairs (1574) by Buontalenti, formerly in Santa Trìnita.

Santa Trìnita ▥ † ★
Map 4D2.

Piazza S. Trìnita is more a crossroads than a square. The central column, a gift from the Baths of Caracalla given by Pius IV to Cosima I in commemoration of the victory of Montemurlo in 1537, doesn't really focus one's attention, which is pulled to the N along **Via Tornabuoni**, the fashionable shopping street and the widest in Florence, built on the filled-in moat of the 12thC city walls and now lined with 13th-16thC palaces.

Spanning the Arno to the s is Ammannati's **Ponte S. Trìnita** (★) of 1567-70, which is the most graceful bridge in Europe. Michelangelo advised on the design, and the curve of the volutes is borrowed from his Medici tombs in *San Lorenzo*. The bridge was destroyed by bombing in 1944 and rebuilt after the war exactly as it had been before. One-sixth of the original stone was retrieved from the Arno; the rest was supplied by the quarries in the Boboli Gardens, which were specially reopened. The head of the *Primavera* statue was recovered only in 1961.

On the NE corner of the square (no. 1) is the **Palazzo Bartolini Salimbeni**. The building was finished in 1521 just after Raphael's Pandolfini palace (see *Walk 2* in *Walks in Florence*), which greatly influenced Baccio d'Agnolo's design for this, his most original palace. It was the first in central Florence to adopt the Roman tabernacle windows, and contemporary Florentines treated it as a huge joke, pinning notices on the facade saying that it looked more like a church. Baccio's reply is inscribed in Latin over the door: "It is easier to carp than to imitate." Michelangelo thought the cornice made the palace look comically like a man wearing a hat too big for his body. The palace is also known as the *Per Non Dormire* after the family motto inscribed over the windows. The courtyard is decorated with elegant *sgraffiti*.

The first **church of S. Trìnita** was built on this site by S. Giovanni Gualberto, founder of the Vallombrosan Order, in the late 11thC. The original Romanesque facade, depicted by Dom. Ghirlandaio in the Sassetti Chapel inside the church, was replaced by Buontalenti's uncharacteristically clumsy effort in 1594. The Gothic **interior** assumed its present appearance from c.1250 when Nicola Pisano is supposed to have begun the program of enlargement that continued through the 14thC.

Right nave, fourth chapel Compare Lorenzo Monaco's pretty but heavily restored frescoes (c.1420-25) with his altarpiece on the panel of the *Annunciation*. The predella panels are especially fine. The gate is early 15thC.

Right transept In the sacristy, the **tomb of Onofrio Strozzi** (1421), to the left of the altar, is an early example of Renaissance funerary sculpture. The second chapel to the right of the chancel is the **Sassetti Chapel** (★), frescoed by Dom. Ghirlandaio (1482-6) with *Scenes from the Life of St Francis* against a Florentine background: the Signoria, Piazza S. Trìnita, the old Ponte S. Trìnita. In the upper tier of the altar wall are portraits of, among other contemporary Florentines, *Francesco*

Sassetti, who commissioned this chapel, *Lorenzo the Magnificent*, his adoring protégé *Poliziano* and his sons *Piero, Giovanni* and *Giuliano*. Over the altar is Ghirlandaio's *Adoration of the Shepherds* (1485), set in a Tuscan landscape. *Francesco Sassetti* and *Nera Corsi*, his wife, are portrayed on either side of the altar and are buried in the black marble **sarcophagi**, attributed to Giuliano da Sangallo, on the side walls.

Left transept, second chapel   On the left wall, the **tomb of Bishop Benozzo Federighi** (✰), from 1455, is considered one of Luca della Robbia's masterworks for the intense humanity of the crucified Christ in the central panel and the finely modeled face of the Bishop, a rare portrait by Luca. In the fifth chapel, the wooden statue of the *Magdalen* (c.1464), by Desiderio da Settignano and Benedetto da Maiano, invites comparison with Donatello's more tragic figure in the Cathedral Museum (see **Duomo**). In the third chapel is an *Annunciation* by Neri di Bicci, with a sweet, inept Adam and Eve, borrowed from Masaccio's Brancacci Chapel (see **Carmine**).

Lo Scalzo 🏛 † ✰
Via Cavour 69 ☎ 472812. Map 3B4 🔲 Open Tues-Sat 9am-2pm, Sun 9am-1pm. Closed Mon.
The Brotherhood of St John was known as *lo Scalzo* because its members went barefoot in obedience to the rule of poverty.

In 1511 Andrea del Sarto, then 25, began to decorate their cloister in *terra verde* with scenes in austere *grisaille*, from the life of John the Baptist. He worked here on and off for a period of 12yrs, developing the fresco technique which can also be admired in color at **Santissima Annunziata** and **San Salvi**.

The earliest of the Scalzo frescoes is the *Baptism of Christ*; the last to be painted was the *Birth of St John the Baptist*. Notice also especially the *Visitation* (1524), *Charity* (1520) and *Justice* (1515).

The frescoes, badly injured by damp, have been detached for restoration and replaced in their original positions.

Science Museum *(Museo di Storia della Scienza)* 🏛
Piazza dei Giudici 1 ☎ 293493. Map 5E4 🔲 ✳ Open winter 9.30am-1pm and Mon, Wed, Fri 2-5pm, summer 9.30am-1.30pm and Mon, Fri 3.30-7pm. Closed Sun.
The medieval Castellani palace now houses the Science Museum. At one time it was the seat of the Civil Tribune or Giudici di Ruota, which gave its name to the piazza from which one enters the museum.

For nearly three centuries after Florence had lost its artistic supremacy the more intelligent members of the Medici-Lorraine grand-ducal families retained a passionate interest in all branches of science. In 1657 an Academy of Experiment, the Accademia del Cimento, was founded in the Pitti by Grand Duke Ferdinand II and his brother Cardinal Leopold, both pupils of Galileo. This is the historic nucleus of the museum, which is very large, carefully organized and clearly labeled. Printed guides are loaned to visitors on each floor.

Ground floor   An alchemist's laboratory; early scales, music boxes, bicycles, fire extinguishers, and more.

First floor   Rm IV is hardly large enough for the giant **armillary sphere** made in 1593 for Ferdinand I by Antonio Santucci. The sphere demonstrates the theologically acceptable Ptolemaic theory in defiance of the sun-centered system evolved by Copernicus 50yrs earlier. Rm V: in the case opposite the entrance is the lens with which Galileo discovered the four satellites of Jupiter, known as the Medici planets. Wonderfully delicate glass instruments from the Accademia del Cimento are displayed in the other two cases.

Second floor   This floor, opened in 1975, was formerly the headquarters of the Accademia della Crusca, the scholarly body that sits in judgment on the purity of the Italian language. In Rm II is the **large burning lens** made for Cosimo III by Benedict Bregans of Dresden and later used by Sir Humphrey Davy and Michael Faraday to accomplish the combustion of a diamond. In Rm IV is the great lodestone (*Calamita*) given by Galileo to Ferdinand II. In Rms V-VII are anatomical wax models and 18thC surgical implements.

Third floor   Minerals and crystals collected in the 18thC.

Signoria
Map 5D4.

People who dislike Florence often object most to its main square, with its asymmetrical fortress palace, its rows of statues symbolizing conflicting ideologies, and its dull 19thC buildings. Lacking the gaiety and architectural unity of the central squares of Venice or Siena, the Piazza della Signoria will always tend to appeal more to the historical imagination than to the sense of pleasure.

The Signoria is still the political and commercial center of the city, as it has been for nearly seven centuries. The Palazzo Vecchio is still the city hall, and politicians still harangue the public from the *ringhiera*. Farmers still talk business outside the old commercial tribunal, now the agricultural center, in Via de' Gondi, and businessmen and bankers make deals over lunch at Cavallino. The only concessions to mass tourism are the postcard stalls, the high prices at the café Rivoire and the annual historic football game played in costume each year on June 24.

In the late 1980s the decision to repave the Piazza led to archeological excavations of the Roman and medieval remains below ground. There is a plan, which may or may not be realized, to turn the site into an underground museum, with the new sidewalk as its ceiling. Savonarola was hanged and then burned in the piazza on May 23, 1498.

Palazzo della Signoria *(Palazzo Vecchio)* 🏛 ★
Piazza Signoria ☎ *27681* 🔳 *for upstairs rooms, open Mon-Fri 9am-7pm, Sun and hols 8am-1pm. Closed Sat.*

The foundation stone of the Palazzo della Signoria was laid in 1299. The design is traditionally attributed to Arnolfo di Cambio, but the building was not finished until at least a decade after his death. The Signoria was the highest magistracy of the republican government established in 1293. Elected by the guilds, the Signori served for a period of only two months during which they lived virtually as prisoners inside the palace. The palace, like the constitution, was designed to prevent the government from being passed by extremists — subversive activity in the streets of such a small city could be easily searched out from the tall watch tower, where the great bell cast in 1322 tolled danger warnings and summoned the populace to "parliaments," or general assemblies.

The irregular shape of the palace and the off-center position of its tower were not, as is often thought, the result of Gothic whim. The trapezoidal plan derives from the reluctance of the then Guelf government to build on land previously owned by a Ghibelline family. The tower was thriftily erected on the foundations of an earlier family tower close to the church of

S. Piero Scheraggio, incorporated into the *Uffizi* in the 16thC. But the earliest entrance, on the N flank of the palace, was originally placed symmetrically. This side, facing Via de' Gondi, was extended in the late 15thC when the Sala Consiglio Maggiore was built over the customs hall.

The w side, facing the piazza, looks very much as it did in the 14thC, apart from the mezzanine windows enlarged by Michelozzo and the absence of the 14thC *ringhiera*, or tribune, which was destroyed in the early 19thC. Almost nothing, however, remains of the original interior, which was remodeled from the mid-15thC to the late 16thC according to the needs of violently shifting styles of government, from the Medici-controlled republic to the revivals of true republicanism in 1494-1512 and 1527-30, to the hereditary duchy finally established in 1537.

A key date to remember when visiting the palace is 1540, when Cosimo I took the unprecedented step of moving his household from the ancestral *Medici Palace* to the Palazzo della Signoria, which was converted into a ducal palace by his court architect Battista del Tasso. Ten years later, in 1550, Cosimo was persuaded by his wife Eleanor of Toledo to change the official residence to the *Pitti*. The Signoria palace was henceforth known as the Palazzo Vecchio (the Old Palace). Vasari, who succeeded Battista as court architect in 1555, was instructed to decorate the courtyard and Sala del Consiglio in time for the wedding of Francesco de' Medici to Joanna of Austria in 1565. He labored on until his death in 1574, covering the walls of the old palace with carefully programed frescoes glorifying the achievements, ancestors, virtues and mythological counterparts of Cosimo I. Since few modern tourists share this single-minded adoration of Cosimo I, a tour of the palace can become a dispiriting experience. A brief visit, however, should certainly include the following sights.

The two gilded lions and Christ's emblem were placed over the entrance in 1528, but an inscription of the same date, inspired by Savonarola's teachings, which originally read "Jesus Christ, King of Florence Elected by Popular Decree," was replaced with the present words by order of Cosimo I. The courtyard was remodeled by Michelozzo in the middle of the 15thC. Stuccowork and frescoes of views of Austrian cities were added under Vasari for the wedding of Francesco de' Medici to Joanna of Austria in 1565. The porphyry fountain replaced the original

well in c.1555; the original of Verrocchio's bronze putto, made in the previous century for the Medici villa at Careggi, is now upstairs in the Cancelleria.

State Apartments *(Quartieri Monumentali)* ■■

Vasari's **staircase** (1560-3) leads to the **Salone dei Cinquecento** (1495-6), known also as the Sala del Consiglio Maggiore, originally built by Cronaca to house the enlarged representative government of the penultimate republic, but later modified and decorated under Vasari's direction. It is the largest room of its kind in existence and one of the most unpleasant, out of square and frescoed with Vasari's frantic frescoes commemorating the Florentine victories over Pisa and Siena; the fresco program relates to Cosimo I, who is seen in glory on the ceiling.

Some of the statues, especially Vincenzo de' Rossi's *Hercules and Diomedes*, provide welcome comic relief. But the only beautiful thing in the room is Michelangelo's *Victory*(★), which was made for the tomb of Julius II some time between 1506-34 and presented to Cosimo I by the sculptor's nephew. Off this room is the windowless **Studiolo of Francesco I** (★), which is a treasure-trove of late Mannerist art, built as a retreat for Cosimo's solitary, gloomy son, who kept his most precious small possessions in the cabinets, decorated from 1569-73 by more than 30 artists according to an allegorical system dictated by Vincenzo Borghini to Vasari. Each wall represents one of the elements, earth, air, fire and water.

From the **Quartiere di Leone X** (1556-62), rebuilt and decorated by Vasari and others, a staircase leads to the Sala degli Elementi on the second floor. The Terrazza di Saturno, to the right of the stairs, commands a wonderful view to the SE and leads on to the **private apartments of Eleanor of Toledo**. The **chapel** (1540-5) (★) is frescoed by Bronzino.

At the end of the long Salotta di Eleanora, where the detached fresco of the *Expulsion of the Duke of Athens* (c.1343) shows the palace as it was in the 14thC, is the **Sala dei Gigli** (★), built 1476-80 by Benedetto da Maiano, one of the few beautiful rooms in the palace, with **frescoes** (1481-5) by Dom. and Dav. Ghirlandaio. The intarsiate **doors**, with carved marble surround, and the figure of the *Baptist* (1476-81) above are by B. and G. da Maiano.

Off this room in the small **Cancelleria** is the original of Verrocchio's bronze **putto** (1476) from the courtyard fountain, and the famous 16thC *Portrait of Machiavelli*, attributed to Santi di Tito; also the original relief carving of *St. George and the Dragon* (c.1270) from the Porta S. Giorgio.

The Sala dell'Udienza, entered from the Sala dei Gigli through the intarsiate doors, was also built by B. da Maiano; the figure of *Justice* (1476-8) over the door is by the two Maiano. The **frescoes** (1550-60) are by Cecchino Salviati at his best. Donatello's *Judith and Holofernes* (★), made c.1456-60 as a fountain for the courtyard of the Medici Palace and dragged to the Piazza della Signoria after the expulsion of the Medici in 1494 as a symbol of the new republic, was brought inside from the piazza in 1980.

Returning through the Sala dei Gigli, the stairs lead up, past the euphemistically named **Alberghettino** where Cosimo il Vecchio and Savonarola were imprisoned, to the **tower** (★), which commands what is probably the best view of all. Down this flight of stairs is the **Mezzanine**, where pictures and sculptures left to the city in 1934 by the American Charles Loeser (**Collezione**

Loeser) are displayed in three rooms. The treasures of the collection are Bronzino's *Portrait of Laura Battiferri* (★), who was Ammannati's poetess wife, and a marble *Angel* by Tino di Camaino.

In the piazza, the row of statues, which runs from the northern part of the square parallel with the facade of the palace, was deliberately aligned in the 16thC to point in perspective diminution toward the *Uffizi*.

From N to S they are: **1.** Giambologna's equestrian statue of *Cosimo I* (1594). **2.** Ammannati's *Neptune Fountain* (1563-75), a reference to Cosimo's maritime victories — the embarrassed figure of Neptune, "Il Biancone," the "White Giant," caused a 16thC critic to coin the rhyme, "*Ammannato, Ammannato, che bel marmo ha rovinato*" ("what beautiful marble you have ruined"). The nymphs and satyrs, which Ammannati came to regret as provocation of sinful thoughts when he fell under the influence of the Counter-Reformation, were made with the collaboration of Giambologna and other younger artists. **3.** Copy of Donatello's *Marzocco* on an elegant 15thC base; the original is in the *Bargello*. **4.** Copy of Michelangelo's *David*; the original was moved to the *Accademia* in 1873. **5.** Bandinelli's infelicitous *Hercules and Cacus* (1553); Hercules was another of Cosimo's symbols. Flanking the entrance to the palace are two marble herms by Vincenzo de' Rossi and Bandinelli.

The **Loggia dei Lanzi** (★), as it has been called since the 16thC when German halberdiers (*landsknechte*) stood on guard here, was built in 1376-82 for important public ceremonies by Benci di Cione and Simone di Francesco Talenti, probably to a design by Orcagna. Michelangelo once advised that the arcaded module should be repeated all round the perimeter of the piazza, a plan that would have saved the square esthetically. The present arrangement of the statues was settled on in the 19thC.

At front, left to right: **6.** Cellini's *Perseus* (★), the casting of which (1545-54) is described in detail in his autobiography; the originals of the relief panels and small statues around the base are now in the *Bargello*. **7.** Two lions flanking the stairs; the one on the right-hand side is Classical, the other is a 16thC copy. **8.** Giambologna's *Rape of the Sabines* (1583).

Middle row, left to right: **9.** *Rape of Polyxena* (1866) by Pio Fedi. **10.** *Ajax* (or *Menelaus*) *Supporting the Body of Patroclus*, Roman copy of a 4thC BC Greek original. **11.** Giambologna's *Hercules Fighting the Centaur Nessus* (1599).

Against the back wall are six Roman statues of matrons or empresses. On the NE side of the square is the three-bay **Uguccioni** palace (c.1550); the design for the palace is generally thought to have been sent from Rome by Michelangelo. From the balcony a bust of Cosimo I looks out at a statue of himself mounted on horseback.

Raccolta d'Arte Moderna Alberto della Ragione

Piazza Signoria 5 ☎ *283078* ✉ *Open Mon, Wed-Sat 9am-2pm, Sun and hols 8am-1pm. Closed Tues.*

This collection of modern art, given to the city by the Genoese Alberto della Ragione and installed on two floors of the Casa di Risparmio, and provides a comprehensive overview of the mainstream figurative, landscape and still-life traditions in Italian painting from the 1930s to 1960s. Sculptures by Marini, Manzù and others; paintings by, among others, De Pisis, Mafai, Morandi. Of local interest are the views of and from Via S. Leonardo (see *Walk 4* in *Walks in Florence*), which are by Ottone Rosai.

Stibbert *(Museo Stibbert)*
*Via Stibbert 26 ☎ 475520. Map 7C4 ▦ ✜ ✗ compulsory ✱
Open weekdays 9am-2pm, Sun 9am-1pm. Closed Thurs.
Guided tours on the hour.*

The Villa Stibbert is a house worthy of Citizen Kane. The private museum Frederick Stibbert created here in the late 19thC is not quite as large as Hearst's Californian monster mansion, but it is scarcely less amazing. Of Italian-Scottish parentage, Stibbert was an obsessive collector of everything — from buttons to arms and armor. The armor collection, one of the most important in the world, is displayed on model phalanxes which one can imagine marching against one another through the innumerable, vast, gloomy rooms.

Nearby in the Via Bolognese is the **Villa La Pietra**, with one of the most beautiful Italian gardens in Tuscany, re-created at the turn of this century by an Englishman (*open to guided parties by arrangement*).

Strozzi Palace ▦ ☆
Map 4C3.

Of the 100 or so palaces built in 15thC Florence, the Strozzi was the largest. Filippo Strozzi acquired more than a dozen properties to create his site, and the building took 44yrs, from 1489 to 1536. Strozzi watched his palace being built from his small house, to the left (facing the palace from the piazza), which he built as temporary accommodations.

The design of the Strozzi is based on G. da Sangallo's wooden model (see **Piccolo Museo**, below), but Cronaca, who supervised the building, made significant alterations; it was he who added the massive cornice, a reproduction of an ancient Roman cornice.

The palace is faced on three sides with huge blocks of *pietra forte*, supplied by four quarries including two in the *Boboli*. Apart from this sheer quantity of stone and the scrupulously Classical cornice, the exterior, which still conforms to the type of the *Medici Palace*, was not architecturally innovatory. The fine **lamp brackets** by Niccolò Grosso on the corners, flanking the main entrance, are rare surviving examples of Renaissance ironwork.

The interior of the palace is the first of the Renaissance to be made completely symmetrical.

Piccolo Museo di Palazzo Strozzi
☎ 215990 ▣ Open Mon, Wed, Fri 4-7pm.

On the left side of Cronaca's splendid interior courtyard is the entrance to this small museum, which explains how the Strozzi was built. Here you can see the differences between G. da Sangallo's original model and the actual palace.

Vieusseux Library *(Gabinetto Vieusseux)*
▣ Open Tues-Fri 9.15am-12.45pm, 3.15-6.45pm, Sat 9.15am-12.45pm. Closed Sun, Mon.

At the right of the courtyard, this lending library has always been a favorite meeting place for literary foreign residents, especially in pre-Risorgimento Florence when it was a center of liberal activity. Any member of the public can borrow for a nominal fee. About a third of the collection is in English.

The first-floor rooms of the palace are used for temporary exhibitions.

Topographical Museum   A pictorial history of the
city's growth, known as *Firenze com'era.*

Uffizi 🏛 ★

Piazzale degli Uffizi 6 ☎ 218341. Map 5D4 ▨▨ ▣ Open Tues-Sat 9am-7pm, Sun and hols 9am-1pm. Closed Mon. Tours of the Corridoio Tues-Sat mornings must be reserved the previous day.

The painters of 15thC Florence trained in one another's workshops and watched each other's progress with jealous eyes, each sparking off the other's genius and contributing to a chain of innovatory masterpieces which is one of the wonders of Western civilization. The largest and finest collection in the world of paintings from this period is to be found in Rms 7-15 of the Uffizi. First-time visitors on a very tight schedule are advised to take the elevator straight to the picture galleries on the second floor and explore these rooms first. But there is, of course, a great deal more. Nearly all of some 1,700 works of art displayed here are of at least outstanding interest.

The building which parades in solemn double file from the Piazza della Signoria to the Arno was designed by Vasari in 1560 as a suite of offices for Cosimo I: hence the name Uffizi, which means offices, and the official mood of the handsome architecture. Buontalenti carried on the project after Vasari's death, continuing to make modifications and additions until 1586. In 1581 Francesco I had the upper loggias glazed and made into a museum, where he could escape from state duties.

The remains of the Zecca, where the famous florin was minted, were incorporated into the fabric of the building and explain the absence of colonnades at the base of the W wing where it joins the Loggia dei Lanzi. The former church, S. Piero Scheraggio, was absorbed into the N end of the opposite wing; the gloomy statues in niches are the work of 19thC hacks.

In 1743 the Uffizi and its contents were bequeathed to the people of Florence by the Palatine Electress Anna Maria Lodovica, widow of the last Medici grand duke, Gian Gastone. The enlightened Lorraine dynasty continued to add to the extraordinary collection assembled by the Medici over the previous 300yrs. In this century the threat of vandalism, theft and damp has driven more and more masterpieces out of the churches and into this relatively soulless sanctuary. Florentines complain about the Uffizi with some justification. It is too crowded, with an attendance of over 1.5 million people a year (the highest of any Italian gallery), most of whom come to photograph Botticelli's *Primavera*. Too many sections are subject to unannounced and prolonged closure; and too many paintings are protected by clumsy glazing.

Do remember that this is not only a picture gallery. The superb Classical statues lining the stairs and corridors were regarded as the chief glories of the Uffizi until hardly more than 100yrs ago (nobody looked at Botticelli with much interest until the 1880s). Shelley visited the Uffizi every day during his stay in Florence, but took notes only on the sculptures, and Gibbon toured the gallery 12 times before looking at a picture.

Now that the State Archives have been moved to Piazza Beccaria, shops and a restaurant will be installed on the first floor.

Beyond the ticket desk is a room containing the remains of S. Piero Scheraggio and Castagno's *frescoes* (★) of famous men and women (c.1450).

The elevator is for the picture galleries only. Opposite, at the end of the corridor, is Botticelli's damaged *Annunciation* fresco (1481), still recognizably one of his best works. Vasari's great staircase leads to the first floor. Exhibitions from the **prints**

and drawings collection — otherwise closed to the general public — are frequently held in rooms to the left and are highly recommended. The staircase carries on to the picture galleries.

The collection is arranged chronologically through the gallery's two wings. The Florentine pictures are deliberately displayed in order to illustrate the impact made by one master upon another, from Giotto through to Michelangelo and the early Mannerists.

East corridor

Rm 1   Usually closed. Antique carvings.

Rm 2   Three huge **altarpieces of the Maestà (★)** offer a unique opportunity to examine the roots of Florentine and Sienese painting as they were to flower over the next 200yrs. On the right, Cimabue's severe and massive image (c.1280) marks the epitome of the Byzantine Middle Ages. On the left, Duccio's composition (c.1285) is similar, but notice the lighter construction of the throne, the more human relationship between Madonna and Child, and the treatment of the Madonna's hem, a virtuoso passage that anticipates the linear style of Simone Martini and Botticelli. In the center, Giotto's less cluttered altarpiece (c.1310) achieves a new sense of realistic space by the use of *chiaroscuro* and the placing of the angels' heads at varying angles.

Rm 3   In the second quarter of the *trecento* Duccio's successors brought Sienese Gothic painting to a peak of sophistication. In Simone Martini's *Annunciation* (1333) (★) the exquisite, poetic vision and fluttering line are in marked contrast to Giotto's measured abstraction, but the psychological and spatial realism shows his influence. The saints are by Simone's brother-in-law Lippo Memmi. Pietro Lorenzetti's altarpiece *Scenes from the Life of the Blessed Humility* (1341) is more interesting for the charming small panels than for the prosaic central figure. A. Lorenzetti's *Stories of St. Nicholas of Bari* (c.1330) was painted in Florence, but the last panel, in which St. Nicholas obtains miraculous supplies of grain for the starving population of Myra, is poetic and detailed in a way that Florentine painting rarely was.

Rm 4   The painters of the Florentine *trecento* worked more successfully in fresco (see **Santa Croce, Santa Maria Novella**) than on panel, and they are not especially well represented in the Uffizi. Here one can see the work of Bernardo Daddi, Taddeo Gaddi, Giottino and Orcagna.

Rms 5 and 6   In the early *quattrocento*, nearly 100yrs later than Siena and the rest of Europe, Florence produced its only great Gothic painter, Lorenzo Monaco, whose *Coronation of the*

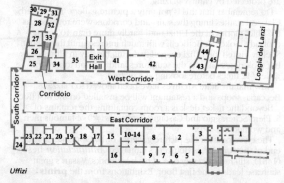

Uffizi

Virgin (1413) dominates the room. But his *Adoration of the Magi* (c.1420) is a far more contemplative, less elaborate picture than the visiting Gentile da Fabriano's contemporary treatment of the same subject on the far wall. Gentile's fairytale extravaganza *Adoration* (★) brings the International Gothic in this gallery to a resounding climax. Credit for the delightful *Life of the Anchorites in the Thebaid*, now attributed to Gherardo Starnina and dated c.1400-10, has in the past been given to artists as disparate as Pietro Lorenzetti, Fra Angelico and Uccello. This is by no means the naïve work it appears at first. The little figures are executed in the naturalistic manner of Giotto, and the sky, for the first time in this gallery and perhaps in the Renaissance, is blue, not gold.

Rm 7   The earliest pictures in this important room are by artists whose full genius is better appreciated elsewhere in Florence. Masaccio and Masolino are represented here by a *Virgin and Child with St. Anne* (1424). Fra Angelico's one-man show is in the Monastery of **San Marco**, where one can compare this *Coronation of the Virgin* (1430) with a later fresco of the same subject. There are only two other pictures by Domenico Veneziano in Florence, neither currently on view (there are only 12 in the world). This *Sacra Conversazione* (1445-8) (★) is one of the supreme achievements of the Early Renaissance master of light. Its limpid colors and precisely described architecture give it the atmosphere of a perfect silence. Domenico must have been deeply affected by the even greater genius of his pupil Piero della Francesca, whose diptych of *Federico da Montefeltro and Battista Sforza* (c.1460) (★) was painted in Urbino. The allegorical **triumphs** on the backs represent the cardinal virtues for Duke Frederico and the theological virtues for his duchess. The deep backgrounds evoke Piero's native landscape near Arezzo. Piero wrote a treatise about perspective, the new science which fascinated Paolo Uccello to the point of near insanity. This obsession is the real subject of the *Battle of San Romano* (★), painted 24hrs after the event in 1456 and hung in a room in the Medici palace. Two flanking panels were sold in the late 18thC and are now in the Louvre and the London National Gallery. The Uffizi piece is the least impressive of the three because of its inferior condition and relatively confusing composition.

Rm 8   Filippo Lippi, a disciple of Masaccio, was much imitated in his own time. The latest and loveliest of the Uffizi Filippos is the *Madonna with Angels* (c.1465) (★), which scholars take as evidence of Botticelli's apprenticeship to the older master. For Filippo's major achievement in Tuscany, see **Prato** (in *Tuscany A to Z*). Filippo's Sienese contemporary Vecchietta is represented by a *Madonna Enthroned* (1457). Notice also Baldovinetti's appealing works.

Rm 9   The Pollaiuolo brothers, Antonio and Piero, were sculptors, engravers and goldsmiths as well as painters. Piero is usually judged the less talented, mainly on the evidence of these *Six Virtues* (1469), ordered by the Merchants' Tribunal. The seventh, *Strength*, was Botticelli's first public commission. The virtues do indeed seem crude and static when compared to Antonio's tiny but vividly dramatic panels of *The Feats of Hercules* in the case between the windows. Antonio's interest in anatomy drove him to undertake human dissections. He was, above all, one of the most gifted draftsmen of the Renaissance, an innovator in the use of line to convey muscular action. In the same case are two exhilarating scenes from the grisly *Story of Judith*, painted by the young Botticelli when he was still under the influence of Pollaiuolo.

Rms 10-14   The great Medici Botticellis hang in this room,
converted into one large area. The design of the room and the
gray lighting are controversial. Botticelli was the greatest linear
painter before Matisse, and the powerful melodic line and lyrical
nostalgia of his art can touch the heart even of those who fail to
grasp his meaning. The *Primavera* (★) (c.1480 — beautifully
restored in 1983) was painted for an adolescent cousin of
Lorenzo de' Medici. Until recently scholars disagreed about just
what it depicts. Many now accept a revealing new gloss which
relates the subject matter to the conventions of early Renaissance
Italian love poetry. The central figure is the ideal woman; a
man who sees her will be conquered and forever changed by Cupid's
arrow. The picture "reads" from right to left, possibly because,
like Petrarch's poetry, it conveys a memory. In comes the Wind
God Zephyr. At his touch, flowers grow from the lips of Chloe,
the happily married nymph, who becomes Flora, goddess of
spring. On the other side of the woman are her "companion"
qualities (beauty and generosity, represented by the three graces)
and Mercury, god of eloquence, conciliation and reason,
pointing upward to heaven.

The *Birth of Venus* (c.1485) (★) was commissioned after
Botticelli's return from Rome and later hung next to the
Primavera. The Adoration of the Magi (c.1475) (★) is one of a
series of *Adorations* from the 1470s; others are in Washington
and London. This one is of special interest because members of the
Medici family appear among the adoring Magi. Lorenzo de'
Medici is at the left foreground, Botticelli himself is in yellow on
the extreme right. The *Man with a Medallion of Cosimo il
Vecchio* (c.1475-80) may be another self-portrait. The *Madonna
of the Magnificat* (c.1482) (★) is perhaps the loveliest of his
religious paintings, and all the more so now that it has been
cleaned; its elaborate curving design has been compared to a
section cut through a rose. The *Calumny of Apelles* (c.1495-1500)
is one of the few late Botticellis in the Uffizi. The frenzied,
dazzlingly stylized execution reflects the political and moral
earnestness that afflicted many sensitive Florentines at the end of
the century under the influence of Savonarola.

Set out from the walls on a screen is a large *Adoration of the
Shepherds* (c.1475) known as the *Portinari Altarpiece* (★) by the
Flemish master Hugo van der Goes. Commissioned in Bruges by
a Medici bank agent, Tommaso Portinari, this marvelous feat of
naturalistic painting had a profound effect on all artists who saw
it after its arrival in Florence in 1488. Behind it is another Flemish
work, Roger van der Weyden's *Entombment of Christ* (c.1450),
painted in Florence. Dom. Ghirlandaio, Filippino Lippi, Botticelli
and Lorenzo di Credi, all influenced by the van der Goes, are
represented in this section of the room. For Ghirlandaio and
Filippino see **Santa Maria Novella** and **Santa Trinita**.

Rm 15   There is no complete or completely accepted
Leonardo in the Uffizi, but no other gallery possesses such
fascinating evidence of his early development. His earliest
known piece of work, done when he was still in his teens
working in Verrocchio's studio, is the profiled angel in the
Baptism of Christ (begun c.1470). Vasari tells us that Verrocchio,
recognizing that this angel was beyond his own very
considerable capabilities, abandoned the painting. Vasari does
not mention the *Annunciation* (c.1475) (★), and its attribution
has been debated by opposing teams of distinguished art
historians since it was brought into the gallery in 1867. The
unfinished *Adoration of the Magi* (1481) (★) is really a drawing

rather than a painting, the preparatory scaffolding he left behind when Leonardo moved to Milan in 1482. To appreciate how startlingly in advance of its time this conception was one need only compare it with Lorenzo di Credi's small *Annunciation* (1485), a faultlessly graceful piece typical of its period. Piero di Cosimo's *Perseus Liberating Andromeda* (1515-20) and *Immaculate Conception* (c.1505-10) shows this idiosyncratic artist more at home with the mythological subject. Note also Signorelli's *Crucifixion with Mary Magdalen* and the Umbrian Perugino's *Pietà*.

Rm 18   The Tribune (★) was designed in 1584 by Buontalenti as an inner temple of the arts and restored in 1970 to something like its original appearance. When Zoffany painted the Tribune in 1775 for Queen Charlotte of England this windowless octagonal room was one of the high points of the Grand Tour. The best works of art in the gallery were displayed here, but nothing in Florence had such drawing power as the *Medici Venus* (★), which was a Roman copy of a Praxitelean figure of the 4thC BC, brought into this inner sanctum in the 17thC by Cosimo III, who is said to have feared that she might corrupt the morals of art students in Rome. For nearly 200yrs she remained a potent sex symbol for educated Europeans, inducing a cultural-erotic trance which men struggled to describe in prose and poetry. Engravings, drawings and reproductions of all sizes flooded across the Alps. Louis XIV had her copied in bronze. She was the only statue in Florence called to Paris by Napoleon. In the puritanical 19thC, a plaster cast in Philadelphia was kept under lock and key. Nathaniel Hawthorne found himself panting as he approached her along the Uffizi corridors. We cannot easily share such raptures today; but it is as well to be reminded of the vagaries of taste when in an art gallery.

All Florentine work of the finest kind...is absolutely pure Etruscan, merely changing its subjects, and representing the Virgin instead of Athena, and Christ instead of Jupiter.

Ruskin, *Mornings in Florence*

Among the many fine 16thC portraits in the Tribune are Vasari's *Lorenzo de' Medici* and Pontormo's *Cosimo il Vecchio* (both posthumous); Bronzino's *Lucrezia* and *Bartolomeo Panciatichi*; and *Eleanor of Toledo with her Son Giovanni I*. Two famous charmers are Rosso Fiorentino's *Musical Angel* and Bronzino's *Don Giovanni de' Medici*.

Rm 17   Entrance (from the Tribune only) is often barred. The room of the Hermaphrodite takes its name from a Hellenistic copy (2ndC BC) of an extraordinarily sensual bisexual figure.

Rm 19   Signorelli's *Holy Family* (c.1491) anticipates Michelangelo's *Doni Tondo* in Rm 25. By Perugino are *Madonna and Child with Saints* (1493) and the fine portrait of *Francesco delle Opere* (1494), a Florentine craftsman.

Rm 20   Dürer's *Portrait of the Artist's Father* (1490) and *Adoration of the Magi* (1504). Lucas Cranach's *Adam* and *Eve* (1528) face Dürer's *Adam* and *Eve*.

Rm 21   Venetian paintings, notably Giovanni Bellini's stupendous *Sacred Allegory* (c.1495) (★), the allegorical significance of which has never been satisfactorily explained. The attributions to Giorgione in this room are questionable.

Rm 22   Holbein's almost tactlessly faithful *Portrait of Sir Richard Southwell* (1536); Altdorfer's *Martyrdom* and *Departure of St. Florian* (c.1525).

Rm 23   Two superb Mantagnas (★), the tiny *Madonna of the Rocks* and the *Adoration of the Magi* (both c.1489); and Correggio's *Rest on the Flight into Egypt.*

South corridor

Fine views and Classical sculptures.

West corridor

This section of the gallery originally housed workshops and laboratories. The 16thC conception of "art" embraced the crafts and sciences. Among the tapestries, note particularly the *Passion of Christ* series, woven in Florence, and the Flemish *Scenes from the Life of Jacob.*

Rm 25   The *Holy Family* (1504), known as the *Doni Tondo* (★), brilliantly restored in 1985, is the only picture in Florence by Michelangelo apart from the drawings in the **Casa Buonarroti** and the recently discovered drawings at **San Lorenzo**. It was commissioned by Angelo Doni on the occasion of his marriage to Maddalena Strozzi during the period when the artist was in Florence working on the *David.* In opposition to Leonardo, Michelangelo held that sculpture was the supreme art, and this tondo aspires to three dimensions. The Classical past, represented by a frieze of nudes in the upper half, is linked to the new Christian era by the figure of John the Baptist. With its emphasis on gesture and deliberately shocking colors, this was a key picture for the 16thC Mannerists. The inventors of Mannerism, Pontormo (see Rm 27) and Rosso Fiorentino, whose astonishing *Moses Defending the Daughters of Jethro* (1523-4) (★) hangs next to the *Doni Tondo*, were both deeply neurotic — agoraphobic, morbid and asocial and, until 50yrs ago, ignored or despised by critics. Today the gratuitous violence of Rosso's *Moses* (the text from *Exodus* says nothing about all this wrenching and pounding) and its jarring, acid colors may seem very modern. In fact it was painted for a patron known for his violent temper.

Rm 26   For Andrea del Sarto see also **Pitti**, **San Salvi** and **Lo Scalzo**. *Madonna of the Harpies* (1517) (★) is a masterpiece of his early maturity. Raphael's *Virgin of the Goldfinch* (1506) shows the influence of his first contact with Florentine artists; his penetrating, scholarly portrait of the first Medici Pope *Leo X with Cardinals Giulio de' Medici and Luigi de' Rossi* (c.1519) (★) is one of his finest late works.

Rm 27   Pontormo began his career as one of Andrea del Sarto's many satellites, but by the time he painted the *Supper at Emmaus* (1525) he had discovered other models; in this case it was a woodcut by Dürer. His masterpieces are elsewhere in and near Florence. See **Santa Felicita**, and **Carmignano**, **Galluzo** and **Poggio a Caiano** in **Tuscany A to Z**.

Rm 28   Titian's euphemistically entitled *Venus of Urbino* (1538) (★) is not a Venus but a pin-up, one of the most intimate, alluring female nudes ever painted. Visitors to Florence have been falling in love with her since she arrived in 1631 as part of the inheritance of Vittoria delle Rovere. For Byron she was "*the* Venus." Other fine Titians include *Flora* (c.1515), *A Knight of Malta* (c.1518), and portraits of *Eleanora* and *Francesco Maria della Rovere*, Duke and Duchess of Urbino (1537).

Rm 29   Parmigianino was the leading central Italian Mannerist. The striking, intricate *Virgin of the Long Neck* (★), left unfinished at his death in 1540, is his best-known work.

Rms 32-34   Veronese, Moroni, Sebastiano del Piombo. Also some rare French 16thC paintings. Note the Clouet *Portrait of Francis I.*

Returning to the corridor via Rm 34, the entrance to Vasari's **Corridoio** (★ ✗ *compulsory: reserve a day in advance, although unfortunately often closed for restoration*) is immediately right. Vasari built this long covered passage for Cosimo I in 1565. It links the Uffizi to the Pitti, crossing the Arno with the Ponte Vecchio and passing through the church of Santa Felìcita. The views are nearly as magnificent as the pictures, the most celebrated of which are the series of self-portraits.

Rm 35   The Umbrian master Federico Barocci's *Madonna of the People* (1575-9); Tintoretto's *Leda* (1570) and portrait of *Jacopo Sansovino* (1566), and *A Venetian Admiral.*

Rm 41   Rubens and Van Dyck.

Rm 42   The large collection of 20thC self-portraits is out of place in this fine Neo-Classical room, which has housed the 4thC Roman sculptures of *Niobe and her Children* (★) since 1790.

Rm 43   Caravaggio's *Sacrifice of Isaac* (c.1590), *Bacchus* (c.1589), and *Medusa* (after 1590). Also, Claude Lorraine's *Seascape* (1677).

Rm 44   17thC Dutch paintings including two self-portraits of Rembrandt as a young (1634) and old (1664) man.

Rm 45   18thC French, Venetian and Spanish paintings by Nattier, Chardin, G. B. Tiepolo, Canaletto, Guardi and Goya.

At the end of this corridor are rest rooms and a pleasant bar, which opens onto a terrace that looks out over the Loggia dei Lanzi.

Exit hall (formerly Rms 34-40)   The famous *Wild Boar* is a Roman copy of a 3rdC BC Hellenistic original and was the model for Pietro Tacca's *Porcellino Fountain* in the Mercato Nuovo. The exit staircase is by Buontalenti.

Zoological Museum *(La Specola)*

Via Romana 17 ☎ 222451. Map 4F2 ⚏ 🖂 Zoological section open Mon-Sat 9am-noon and every second Sun of month. Anatomical models open to individual scholars by appointment only.

The Torrigiani palace, which houses the Zoological Institute, is known as "La Specola" after the astrological observatory set up here in 1775 by Grand Duke Peter Leopold.

The museum, on the second floor, is divided into two sections. The Zoological Museum consists of a collection of specimens arranged in order of organic complexity from molluscs to mammals, including hunting trophies donated by Victor Emmanuel, and ending with a small selection of wax models of human and animal anatomy.

The full collection of some 600 **anatomical wax models** (★) is displayed in the next rooms. They are among the most extraordinary objects in Florence, and remind one just how deep are the roots of the Florentine fascination with human anatomy. The Renaissance artist P. Pollaiuolo dissected corpses in order to improve his understanding of how the human body works. Here, from 1775-1814, an artist, Clemente Susini, and a physiologist, Felice Fontana, collaborated to make these tinted wax reproductions of every part of the human body. The famous *Embryonic Twins* and models of reproductive organs are in a room off Corridor 31.

Next door are the macabre *Plague Victims* by the late 17thC Sicilian Gaetano Zumbo.

The zoological section will eventually be removed to a new science museum in Via Circondaria, which will have all the major Florentine natural history collections.

Walks in Florence

Despite the irritating traffic Florence is best appreciated on foot. The first two walks share a common plan (on the opposite page). A variation on the fourth walk might be along the recently opened stretch of city walls between the **Belvedere** and **Porta Romana**.

Walk 1/Getting to know Florence

On your first evening in Florence, an after-dinner stroll in the center, taking in the **Uffizi**, **Signoria** and **Duomo**, will make you at home in the dense cluster of the city's historic nucleus. Florence is at its best, its most beautiful, after dark when the buses have departed and the floodlighting touches even the most familiar monuments with fresh magic.

Start at Piazza **Santa Trinita** in order to enjoy the floodlit view of **San Miniato** and the **Belvedere** from Ponte S. Trìnita and to admire the recently installed lighting of the **Via Tornabuoni**. If you can resist window shopping, plunge into medieval Florence along Via delle Terme, named for the Roman baths that occupied this site, to the 14thC **Palazzo di Parte Guelfa** on the left. Turn right opposite it under Chiasso delle Misure and left into Borgo **Santi Apostoli**, crossing Por S. Maria into Via Lambertesca, which brings you past Buontalenti's bizarre **Porta delle Suppliche** into Piazzale degli **Uffizi**. A left turn leads straight into Piazza **Signoria**. Turn right around the N corner of the Palazzo Vecchio into Via dei Gondi and Piazza **San Firenze**, where the towers of the **Badia** and **Bargello** rise with dignity beyond the Baroque extravaganza of the S. Firenze facade. Take the Via del Proconsolo, turning left after **Badia** into Via Dante Alighieri. The Casa di Dante is a 19thC fiction made believable by the night lighting. Opposite is the Castegna tower, all that remains of the earliest seat of communal government. Turn right into Via S. Margherita, left at the Corso and immediately right into Via dello Studio, where you will be rewarded with one of those astonishingly sudden views of Brunelleschi's Dome. The cathedral complex — campanile, Baptistry, **Duomo** — reveals itself as you turn left along its S side. Third left is Via de' Calzaiuoli, which brings you past **Orsanmichele** back into the **Signoria**.

Walk 2/A palace walk

This is a walk devoted entirely to those domestic buildings that Italians rather grandly call palaces. It can be divided into three separate walks if you want to go slowly and thoroughly. It will take you, in roughly chronological order, past many of the most important Florentine palaces built for the merchants and bankers of the 14th-16thC.

Florentines being the least pretentious and most ironically humorous of Italians will often refer in conversation to a hut as a palazzo and a palazzo as a little house — which doesn't in the least mean that they are not proud of their palaces. A surprising number are still lived in by the descendants of their first owners; most are used, as flats, restaurants, shops or offices; and your hotel might be in a palace. If you are not with a large party it is always worth ringing the bell and asking to see the courtyard; that is the kind of independently motivated interest Florentines respect. The palaces built in Florence during the 15thC boom provided a model for the rest of Italy. In 15thC Tuscany there was no significant advance on the basic Florentine type except in

-------- **Walk 1**
Allow 30mins-1hr. Maps **4**&**5**.

———— **Walk 2**
Allow 1-2hrs for each of
three sections. Maps **4**&**5**.

Pienza (see *Tuscany A to Z*). Nevertheless, there are certain practical or decorative additions to Florentine palaces that one encounters less often elsewhere.

The stone benches, or *muriccioli*, which run along the base of so many palaces, were a government-imposed condition of building permission. If you decide to rest and gossip on one of these public benches you will be exercising a civic right dear to the republican hearts of Renaissance Florentines. Machiavelli was shocked to find no *muriccioli* in Venice.

The projecting upper stories supported on brackets known as *sporti* were a device to grab more living space in a crowded city. Legislation against them generally failed.

The black and white decoration, or *sgraffiti*, on facades and in courtyards originated in the 15thC and was carried on through the 19thC. Two good 15thC examples not encountered on this walk are the **Coverelli** palace in Via dei Coverelli and the **Lanfredini** palace on Lungarno Guicciardini. The 16thC master of *sgraffiti* was Poccetti.

I. Start in the morning at the *Davanzati*, the best-preserved 14thC merchant's house in Florence. Next, to see what had happened to palace architecture a century later, cross the bottom of the Tornabuoni into Via del Parione; turn first right and immediately left into Via del Purgatorio, which brings you into the little piazza facing Alberti's *Rucellai Palace*. Take the Via della Vigna Nuova back to the Tornabuoni, across which you see the *Strozzi*, later, larger and less refined than the Rucellai. Go down the Tornabuoni to Piazza *Santa Trinita*. On its NE corner is the early 16thC **Bartolini Salimbeni**, the Roman-style palace Florentines thought looked more like a church. Now look up the **Via Tornabuoni** for a minute before strolling up it. The palaces are 13th-16thC. At the top, partly closing the vista, is the

101

Antinori palace, built in the 1460s by the Boni family who received permission to extend their site onto public land to provide this suitably elegant finish to the Tornabuoni.

Once you have reached the Antinori, the **Cantinetta** restaurant is an ideal place to stop for lunch. Otherwise you could have a delicious but expensive snack at **Giacosa** or **Procacci**, before pressing on to the Medici Palace by way of Via Rondinelli, right into Via de' Cerretani, and left along Borgo S. Lorenzo.

II. The *Medici Palace* reopens at 3pm when the **Benozzo Gozzoli Chapel** is often less crowded than in the morning. Walk round the s side of the palace and turn right at the corner of the crenelated garden wall into **Via de' Ginori**, lined with good 13th-16thC palaces. No. 9, the **Barbolani di Montauto**, is an example of a 15thC palace modernized in the 16thC with kneeling windows and herms. No. 19, **Palazzo Taddei**, is a fine and typical early 16thC palace (1503) by Baccio d'Agnolo; Raphael lived here in 1505. After crossing Via Guelfa, Via de' Ginori becomes **Via S. Gallo**. In the 16thC this was a street of churches, monasteries and high garden walls. It has a rather forlorn atmosphere now, but in the 18thC a carriage ride to the S. Gallo gate was *the* fashionable evening outing. On the left, no. 25a, is the severely beautiful portal, possibly designed by Michelangelo, of the **Monastery of S. Apollonia**. Farther along Via S. Gallo on the right, no. 74, is the **Pandolfini** palace (1520), designed by Raphael (who evidently thought the asymmetrical plan suitable for a large suburban site) and built by two members of the Sangallo family. The style of the palace is as Roman as the sympathies of its first owner, Giannozzo Pandolfini, Bishop of Troia, who records his gratitude to the Medici Popes for their help in acquiring the property in the inscription under the magnificent cornice. If you turn right at the corner of the Pandolfini and right again into Via Cavour, you will soon come, on the right, to no. 57, the **Casino di S. Marco** (1574), built on the site of the Medici sculpture gardens by Buontalenti in his most bizarre, satirical vein. Francesco I had his alchemical laboratories here. The Casino is now the Court of Appeals, but, more to the point, if you happen to be thirsty there is a little bar off the inner courtyard to the left.

Turn right out of the Casino, left into **Piazza S. Marco**, and take Via Cesare Battisti into the northern corner of Piazza *Santissima Annunziata*. The rose-brick palace on the corner of Via dei Servi, a cavalier exception to the arcaded harmony of the square, is Ammannati's **Grifoni** palace. Its main entrance is in **Via dei Servi**, lined with grand-ducal palaces., Notice especially two on the right: no. 15, the **Niccolini** (1550), designed by Baccio d'Agnolo with 19thC *sgraffiti*; and on Via Pucci, the **Pucci** palace, ancestral home of the fashion designer, with a fine emblem of Leo X on this corner. Via dei Servi finishes at the *Duomo*.

III. Alternatively, on leaving the Piazza *Santissima Annunziata*, take the first left off Via dei Servi into **Via degli Alfani**. On the right is a 1930s restoration of Brunelleschi's once-important *Rotonda di S. Maria degli Agnoli*. No. 48, on the left, is the **Giugni** palace (c.1577), one of Ammannati's best buildings. The courtyard, usually open, is remarkable for the alarming use of detached Classical elements. The Tuscan order was employed as a patriotic reference to the newly unified grand-ducal Tuscany. Notice the beautiful 16thC wooden gate. Farther along, two simpler palaces on the left, nos. 34 and 32, are also by Ammannati. The green dome you see ahead belongs to

the synagogue. Second right is **Borgo Pinti**, which boasts
14th-16thC palaces. At no. 26, the house with the bust of
Cosimo I over the door, Giambologna lived and died and Pietro
Tacca founded an academy.

At the bottom, as you pass under the Volta di S. Piero — the bar
on the left serves rough wine and good ham sandwiches — you
are crossing the second circle of walls into the 12thC city. Now
turn right into **Borgo degli Albizi**, a street rich in good 16thC
palaces. No. 18 is the **Altoviti**, known as Palazzo dei Visacci after
the herm portraits of famous Florentines. No. 26 is palazzo
Matteucci Ramirez di Montalvi, built by Ammannati for a
favorite of Cosimo I whose emblem as Duke of Siena is over the
door; there are remains of *sgraffiti* by Poccetti. No. 28, the **Vitali**
palace, is also by Ammannati. On the corner of Via del
Proconsolo is the **Nonfinito** palace (now housing the Institute of
Anthropology), begun in 1593 by Buontalenti for Alessandro
Strozzi but left unfinished. A left turn into Via del Proconsolo will
bring you into Piazza *San Firenze*, where Giuliano da Sangallo's
exemplary **Gondi** palace (1490-1520) is on your right opposite
the S. Firenze facade. If you are in luck and have energy enough
left to ring the bell (at no. 2) you will be admitted into one of the
most beautiful courtyards in Florence. You are now a minute's
walk from the *Signoria* and have earned a good dinner. If you
choose to dine at **Cavallino** you will be overlooking the most
famous Florentine palace of all.

Walk 3/The Oltrarno

Allow 1-2hrs. Maps **4**&**5**.

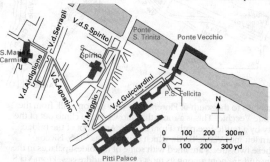

This zigzag route through the *Oltrarno* will take you to its three
important churches and past many of its most interesting palace
facades. You could start with lunch at **Cammillo**, **Celestino** or
Mamma Gina, or a snack at **Cennini** or the **Old Bridge**. Start
off at about 3pm, when the churches begin to reopen, from
Piazza *Santa Felìcita*. The Medici dukes went home to the Pitti
from this church by way of Vasari's aerial corridor, but you must
make do with the Via Guicciardini, where the Machiavelli family
once lived opposite the Guicciardini palace (no. 15). Passing the
Pitti on your left, turn sharp right at Piazza *San Felice* into **Via
Maggio**, so called because it was and still is the widest
(*maggiore*) street on the Oltrarno. Palaces here are 14th-17thC,
but most of the earlier ones were modernized in the grand-ducal
period when Via Maggio was the best address in Florence. No. 26
is **Bianca Cappello's house**, remodeled in 1570-4 by
Buontalenti for the Venetian mistress and future wife of
Francesco I, who paid the bill. The Cappello emblem is over the

rusticated doorway; the *sgraffiti* are by Poccetti. At the bottom of Via Maggio turn left into Via S. Spirito. On the right corner of Via dei Coverelli is **Palazzo Coverelli**, with good restored *sgraffiti*. Turn left into Via dei Coverelli bearing left around the apse and side of the church of **Santo Spirito**. Imagine what the exterior would have looked like if Brunelleschi's unique plan had been carried out; he intended the 40 curved backs of the interior chapels to be expressed on the outside.

Crossing Piazza S. Spirito turn right at its sw corner into Via S. Agostino. Where it crosses Via de' Serragli there is on the right a tabernacle (1427) by Lorenzo di Bicci. Turn left into Via de' Serragli and first right into Via dell' Ardiglione, which soon bends to the right along the side of a walled garden; from its gate there is a view of the apse of the **Carmine** church. This is one of those Florentine streets where the bustle and noise of the city rarely seem to penetrate; it might have been this peaceful when Filippo Lippi was born in 1406 at no. 30. A left turn into Via S. Monaca brings you to the church entrance. If it is now early evening, Masaccio's frescoes might be as he intended them to be seen, lit by the setting sun.

Walk 4/Toward the Chianti via Arcetri or San Miniato

Allow a minimum of 1hr. Map 3E-F4-5.

The hills to the south of Florence are only a short walk from the Ponte Vecchio. This is a route that allows you to climb out of the city by a traffic-free path. From the Oltr'Arno foot of the bridge turn left into Via de'Bardi, which continues as Via S. Niccolò. These two streets are lined with some of the oldest palaces in the city and are now among its most exclusive addresses. From Via S. Niccolò turn right into Via S. Miniato, pausing perhaps for a snack or an ice cream from **Rifrullo** (see *Bars, cafés and ice cream shops*), and through the Porta S. Miniato. Carry on straight up Via Monte alle Croci and take the first right into Via dell'Erta Canina, built for horse-drawn carriages and still mercifully free of road traffic. A stiff, short climb is soon rewarded by a view of the lovely face of **San Miniato** across an olive grove to your left.

When you reach the Viale Galileo Galilei you have three choices. You could turn left for San Miniato; or follow the signs to the right for **Arcetri** and Pian dei Giullari, where you will find the restaurant **Omero**. Otherwise, retrace your steps from the Viale back down the Erta Canina, enjoying the spectacular (and photogenic) views of the flank of **Santa Croce**, the **Duomo**, its campanile and the tower of the Palazzo Vecchio.

(For information about walking in the Tuscan countryside see *Sports, leisure, ideas for children*.)

Staying in Florence

Florence is a thriving commercial city as well as a magnet for mass tourism; and although new hotels are opening all the time to meet the demand it is still wise to reserve rooms well in advance. The Ente Provinciale per il Turismo and Azienda Autonoma di Turismo issue an annual list of all licensed hotels in the city and province as well as information about youth hostels and camping sites.

If you need a hotel at the last minute, try the reservation center at the station, or one of the hotel cooperatives: **COOPAL** (*Via Il Prato 21* ☎ *(055) 219525/292192* ● *571654 Coopal*); **Florence Promhotels** (*Viale A.Volta 72* ☎ *(055) 570481* ● *571605 Flobot*); **Toscana Hotels 80** (*Viale Gransci 9A* ☎ *(055) 2478543* ● *574022 TH 80*).

Hotels are now as expensive as in any other busy European city, but at least you can rest assured that prices and quality of accommodations are strictly controlled within each of the five categories, which are indicated by stars. Be sure to check in advance whether or not breakfast, which is always very expensive (you are paying for the service) and rarely as good as what is offered by the local bar, is included in the price of the room. If breakfast is included and you choose not to take it, it will be deducted from the check, but usually only on request. Other extras, such as telephone calls, laundry and use of the frigobar can add up alarmingly.

Most of the large commercial hotels offer preferential rates for groups of more than 20. Flight/hotel packages, especially off-season, are always an excellent value.

Fewer and fewer hotels maintain their own restaurants. Those that do have improved their food, and half board where available can save money on restaurants.

For a stay of a week or more, and especially if you are traveling with small children, you might prefer a "residence" (service apartment) to a hotel. One of the most attractive is **La Fonte** (*Via S. Felice a Ema 29* ☎ *224421* ▮▮▮), in a handsome Renaissance villa 1.5km (1 mile) s of the center. Other residences include **Alter Ego** (*Via Cavour 102* ☎ *577147*), **Firenze Nova** (*Via Panciatichi 51* ☎ *477851*), **Palazzo Benci** (*Lungarno delle Grazie 28* ☎ *241344*), **Palazzo Ricasoli** (*Via delle Mantellate 2/6* ☎ *352151*) and **Porta al Prato** (*Via Ponte alle Mosse 16* ☎ *354951*).

Although the rough, reliable residential *pensione* is now a thing of the past, it is still possible to find cheerful, clean, inexpensive accommodations, even in the heart of the city. Recommended 1- and 2-star hotels include **Alessandra** (*Borgo SS. Apostoli 17* ☎ *283438*), **Cestelli** (*Borgo SS. Apostoli 25* ☎ *214213*), **Costantini** (*Via de' Calzaiuoli 13* ☎ *215128*), **De Lanzi** (*Via dell'Oche 11* ☎ *296377/268354*), **Donatello** (*Via Alfieri 9* ☎ *245870*) and **Marcella** (*Via Faenza 58* ☎ *213232*).

Despite the recent controls on traffic in the center, Florence is still a noisy city. If you are sensitive to noise, ask for a room on the garden or courtyard.

In summer, when the heat is oppressive, many visitors prefer to stay a little way outside the center. See, for example, *Bagno a Ripoli*, *Fiesole*, *Sesto Fiorentino* and *Settignano* in the *Tuscany A to Z*. The Tuscan countryside is also amply supplied with villas, castles and farmhouses to rent (see *Where to stay* in *Planning*), and there are even villages converted into hotels or residences.

Florence hotels

If you would like to rent a flat in central Florence, try the agency **Florence and Abroad** (*Via S. Zanobi 58, 50129 Firenze* ☎ (055) 490143/487004 ☏570093/570215). They speak English, and will also look for villas in the Tuscan countryside.

Annalena
Via Romana 34, 50125 Firenze
☎ (055) 222402. Map 4F2 ▥ 20
rms ⬚ 20 ▣ ◉ ◉ VISA
Location: Opposite the Boboli Gardens. A comfortably furnished, spacious *pensione* on the first floor of a 15thC palace overlooking the largest private garden in Florence.
⌂ ⎙

Augustus
Piazzetta dell'Oro 5, 50123 Firenze ☎ (055) 283054 ☏570110
☏ (055) 268557. Map 4D3 ▥ 67
rms ⬚ 67 ▤ ☎ ◉ ◉ VISA
Location: Near Ponte Vecchio. A modern building sheltered by its own tiny square.
⌂ ✱ ♿ ▢ ⎙ ⌖ ≪ Ⴘ

Baglioni
Piazza Unit Italiana 6, 50123 Firenze ☎ (055) 218441
☏570225. Map 4B2 ▥ 195 rms
⬚ 195 ▤ ⌂ ⌱ ⊐ ▣ ◉ ◉
VISA
Location: Opposite the station. An enormous, efficient, well-staffed hotel, ideal for business people.
✱ ♿ ▢ ⎙ ⌄ on roof ♨ Ⴘ

Balestri
Piazza Mentana 7, 50122 Firenze
☎ (055) 214743 ☏ (055) 298042.
Map 5E4 ▥ 50 rms ⬚ 50 ▤ ☎
▣ VISA Closed Dec—Feb.
Location: On the Arno, 5mins E of Ponte Vecchio. A 19thC hotel, for four generations in the same family.
✱ ♿ ⎙ ≪ Ⴘ

Bandini
Piazza Santo Spirito 9, 50125 Firenze ☎ (055) 215308. Map
2D3 ⌂ ⊐
Location: In the heart of the Oltr'Arno. This unpretentious and extremely reasonable old *pensione* is a rare survival in Florence and is usually reserved months ahead. The beds and bathrooms are a bit like school, but the furniture and management are charming.

Beacci Tornabuoni
Via Tornabuoni 3, 50123 Firenze
☎ (055) 212645 ☏570215. Map
4C3 ▥ 31 rms ⬚ 26 ▤ ☎ ⊐
⌱ ▣ VISA
Location: N end of Via Tornabuoni. Alinari prints, faded chintzes and rubber plants in big pots give a

dignified old-fashioned feel to this well-known *pensione* on the top three floors of the 14thC Palazzo Minerbetti. Regulars include writers, fashion buyers, actors and ministers of state, mostly from English-speaking countries, who are grateful for the homey but unintrusive atmosphere and comfortable rooms (the good reading lights are an unaccustomed luxury in Florence). A roof terrace for breakfast and drinks; meals can be served in your rooms.
⌂ ✱ ♿ ⎙ ⌄ Ⴘ

Berchielli
Lungarno Acciaioli 14, 50123 Firenze ☎ (055) 264061 ☏575582.
Map 4D3 ▥ 74 rms ⬚ 74 ▤ ▣
CB ◉ ◉ VISA
Location: On the Arno, near Ponte Vecchio. A handsome old hotel modernized in the early 1980s.
♿ ✱ ▢ ⎙ ♨ ≪ ♨

Continental
Lungarno Acciaioli 2, 50123 Firenze ☎ (055) 282392 ☏580525
☏ (055) 268557. Map 4D3 ▥ 63
rms ⬚ 63 ▤ ▣ ◉ ◉ VISA
Location: Near Ponte Vecchio. An efficient hotel in a modern building incorporating the 13thC Torre Guelfa dei Consorti. The best rooms are in the tower — others are neat and functional but noisy.
♿ ✱ ▢ ⎙ ⌄ on roof ≪ Ⴘ ♨

David
Viale Michelangelo 1, 50125 Firenze ☎ (055) 6811696
☏574553. Map 7D4 ▥ 27 rms
⬚ 27 ▤ ☎ ▣ CB ◉ ◉ VISA
Location: Near the Firenze-Sud autostrada junction. A pleasant private hotel in a shady garden; nicely decorated in an unfussy country style. Some rooms are noisy.
✱ ⎙ ♨ ⌄

De La Ville
Piazza Antinori 1, 50123 Firenze
☎ (055) 261805/8 ☏5705/8
☏ (055) 261809. Map 4C3 ▥ 75
rms ⬚ 73 ▤ ☎ ⊐ ⌱ ▣ ◉
◉ VISA
Location: N end of Via Tornabuoni. A modern (1961) hotel next to the Palazzo Antinori. The building is soundproofed and furnished with comfortable good taste.
⌂ ✱ ▢ ⎙

Due Fontane
*Piazza SS. Annunziata 14, 50122
Firenze* ☎ *(055) 280086* ✆ *575550.
Map 5A5* ▥▯ *50 rms* ▭ *50* ▦ AE
VISA
A comfortable, tastefully
modernized hotel facing the most
architecturally harmonious square.
⌂ ✸ □ ▱ 🐾 ◀€ ⟁

Excelsior ▥
*Piazza Ognissanti 3, 50123
Firenze* ☎ *(055) 264201* ✆ *570022*
✆ *(055) 210278. Map 4C1* ▥▥ *205
rms* ▭ *205* ▦ ⌂ ➡ AE CB
◉ ◉ VISA
*Location: 10mins w of Ponte
Vecchio.* The grand old hotel of
Florence retains all the solid,
spacious luxury of the 1920s — but
not, alas, the stylish service. Red
marbled pillars, wooden ceilings,
polished furniture; every comfort
from thick pastel carpets to
enormous bathrooms.
✸ ⌖ □ ▱ ◀€ ♞ ⟁

Grand ▥
*Piazza Ognissanti 1, 50123
Firenze* ☎ *(055) 278781* ✆ *570055.
Map 4C1* ▥▥ *103 rms* ▭ *103* ▦
➡ ➡ AE CB ◉ ◉ VISA
The other old-fashioned luxury
hotel, beautifully restored and
reopened in 1986. All the elegance
of a Swiss-run spa hotel in the
1920s; expansive spaces and
luxurious bedrooms.
✸ ⌖ ▱ ◀€ ♞ ⟁

Helvetia & Bristol ▥
Via dei Pescioni 2, 50123 Firenze
☎ *(055) 287814* ✆ *614552. Map
4C3* ▥▥ *52 rms and suites* ▭ *52*
▦ ➡ ➡ AE CB ◉ ◉ VISA
*Location: Just off n end of Via
Tornabuoni.* A venerable 19thC
hotel restored and reopened in 1989
by the Charming Hotel chain, which
aims to make it the most exclusive,
comfortable and elegantly intimate
of the centrally located luxury
hotels, a veritable home away from
home for those who can afford it.
Courteous and professional
personal service matches the
carefully re-created period
decorations. Bedrooms are
spacious; marble-tiled bathrooms
are equipped with Jacuzzis.
✸ ⌖ □ ▱ ⚘ on roof ◀€ ⟁ ♞

Hermitage
*Vicolo Marzio 1, Piazza del
Pesce, 50122 Firenze* ☎ *(055)
287216* ✆ *(055) 212208. Map 4D3*
▥▯ *18 rms* ▭ *16* VISA
Location: Near Ponte Vecchio. A
comfortable, modern *pensione.* The
dining-room and roof garden look
out over tiled roofs onto the historic
center.
⌂ ✸ ▱ 🐾 ⚘ *on roof* ◀€

Jennings-Riccioli
Corso Tintori 7, 50122 Firenze
☎ *(055) 244751* ✆ *575849. Map
5E6* ▥▥ *55 rms* ▭ *55* AE CB ◉
◉ VISA *Closed mid-Nov to
mid-Mar.*
*Location: On the Arno, near
S. Croce.* This famous, formerly
seedy hotel was completely
renovated in 1986. About half the
rooms overlook the Arno. No. 21 is
E.M. Forster's Room with a View.
✸ ▱ ◀€

Kraft
Via Solferino 2, 50123 Firenze
☎ *(055) 284273* ✆ *571523. Map
2C2* ▥▥ *67 rms* ▭ *67* ▦ ➡ ➡
AE CB ◉ ◉ VISA
Location: Near Le Cascine. An
extremely well-managed hotel in a
relatively peaceful part of the city,
owned by the son of the great Swiss
hotelier. Efficient more than
charming. Forgettable food.
⌂ ✸ ⌖ □ ▱ ⚘ ◀€ ≋ *on roof*.

Liana
Via Alfieri 18, 50121 Firenze
☎ *(055) 245303/4. Map 3C5* ▥▯
18 rms ▭ *12* ➡ AE VISA
Location: 15mins e of Duomo. A
pleasant villa in a quiet street on the
edge of the center, which housed
the British Embassy from 1864-70
but is now decorated in dubious
taste. All the rooms face onto the big
garden, planted with mature trees.
⌂ ⌖ ⚘

Loggiato dei Serviti
*Piazza SS. Annunziata 3, 50122
Firenze* ☎ *(055) 219165/298280*
✆ *575808. Map 5A5* ▥▯ *29 rms*
▭ *29* ▦ AE ◉ ◉ VISA
A new hotel installed with unfussy
tact in the vaulted interiors of the
early 16thC loggia of the Servite
Confraternity, which mirrors
Brunelleschi's Innocenti Loggia
across the piazza.
▱ ◀€

Lungarno
*Borgo S. Jacopo 14, 50125
Firenze* ☎ *(055) 264211* ✆ *570129*
✆ *(055) 268437. Map 4D3* ▥▥ *71
rms* ▭ *71* ▦ ➡ AE ◉ ◉ VISA
*Location: Oltrarno, near Ponte
Vecchio.* A modern hotel (1968),
which hangs over the Arno and, at
the back, has been wrapped around
the 13thC Torre Marsili. The most
attractive rooms are the fourteen

overlooking the Arno and the thirteen within the tower. The proprietor's collection of 20thC art is distributed throughout the hotel.
♨ □ ⌂ ⇐ 🍴 🏊

Monna Lisa
Borgo Pinti 27, 50121 Firenze
☎ *(055) 2479751* ☏ *573300*
☏ *(055) 2479755. Map 3C5* 🏨 *20 rms* 🛏 *20* AE ⊡ ⊙ VISA
Location: 5mins E of Duomo. The Renaissance Neri Palace, part of which dates from the 14thC, retains the atmosphere of a proudly maintained private palace, with polished Tuscan brick floors and antique furniture, original vaulted wooden or frescoed ceilings, and an elegant *pietra serena* staircase. By contrast with the reception rooms, many of the bedrooms are disappointing, especially the singles, which are cramped and sometimes overheated. Eighteen rooms overlook the pretty garden or courtyard; others are noisy. Service can be brusque.
⌂ ⌂ ⌣

Morandi alla Crocetta
Via Laura 50-52, 50121 Firenze
☎ *(055) 2344747* ☏ *(055) 2480954. Map 3B5* 🏨 *to* 🏨 *15 rms* 🛏 *15* ▤ CB ⊙ ⊙
A delightful family-run hotel installed with charm and taste in part of the 16thC convent of the Crocetta. Much recommended to those who appreciate character as well as comfort and good value.
⌂ □ ⌂

Pendini
Via Strozzi 2, 50123 Firenze
☎ *(055) 211170* ☏ *580278. Map 4C3* 🏨 *42 rms* 🛏 *40* AE ⊡ ⊙ VISA
Location: Piazza della Repubblica. Busy, carefully managed and dead central, with big, comfortably furnished rooms.
♨ ⌂

Plaza Lucchesi
Lungarno Zecca Vecchia 38, 50122 Firenze ☎ *(055) 264141* ☏ *570302* ☏ *(055) 2480921. Map 3D5* 🏨 *104 rms* 🛏 *104* ▤ ⌂ ⇒ AE ⊡ ⊙ VISA
Location: On the Arno, near S. Croce. An efficient and friendly hotel specializing in high-class packaged groups.
⇐ ♨ □ ⌂ ⇐ 🍴 🏊

Porta Rossa
Via Porta Rossa 19, 50123 Firenze ☎ *(055) 287551* ☏ *570007*

☏ *(055) 282179. Map 4D3* 🏨 *to* 🏨 *80 rms* 🛏 *71* AE ⊡ ⊙ VISA
Location: Off s end of Via Tornabuoni. The Palazzo Torrigiani was a hotel as early as the 14thC, but the present establishment dates from the 19thC and retains a venerable charm that still appeals, especially to French and English travelers. The bedrooms are huge and will accommodate as many as six beds each (groups welcome).
♨ ⇦ ⌂

Principe
Lungarno Amerigo Vespucci 34, 50123 Firenze ☎ *(055) 284848* ☏ *571400* ☏ *(055) 283458. Map 4C1* 🏨 *21 rms* 🛏 *21* ▤ ⇒ AE CB ⊡ ⊙ VISA
Location: On the Arno, near Ognissanti. A loyal American clientele appreciates the character of this elegantly faded small hotel where some bedrooms retain old brocade wall-hangings and marble bathrooms.
♨ □ ⌂ 🏊 ⇐

Quisisana e Pontevecchio
Lungarno Archibusieri 4, 50122 Firenze ☎ *(055) 216692/215046. Map 5D4* 🏨 *36 rms* 🛏 *36* AE ⊡ ⊙ VISA
The magnificent wrought-iron elevator sets the tone, and the atmosphere of the century-old *pensione* has been carefully preserved in all but two respects: the plumbing and the prices. The film of *A Room with a View* was set here.
♨ ⌂ 🏊 ⇐

Regency Umbria 🏨
Piazza M. d'Azeglio 3, 50121 Firenze ☎ *(055) 245247* ☏ *571058. Map 3C5* 🏨 *38 rms* 🛏 *38* ▤ ⇒ ⌂ ⇒ AE ⊡ ⊙ VISA
Location: 15mins E of Duomo. This chic and comfortable small hotel in its tranquil tree-lined square might have been imported direct from Paris. The bedrooms are in dazzling but well-judged color combinations, but some are small for the price.
⌂ ♨ ⇦ □ ⌂ 🏊

Residenza
Via Tornabuoni 8, 50123 Firenze ☎ *(055) 284197/218684* ☏ *570093. Map 4C3* 🏨 *24 rms* 🛏 *22* ⇒ AE ⊡
An exceptionally charming *pensione*, on the top floors of a Renaissance palace, a miniature grand hotel offering everything from a multilingual staff (English, French and German spoken) to an excellent

restaurant. Meals willingly served on the roof garden or your room. Top-floor rooms, some with balconies, are nicest. Family apartments.
⬥ 🖾 ❧ *on roof* 《€

Rigatti
Lungarno Generale Diaz 2, 50122 Firenze ☎ *(055) 213022. Map 5E4* ⬜ *28 rms* 🛏 *15. Location: On the Arno, between the Uffizi and S. Croce.* A superb position on the top two floors of the Palazzo Alberti, with spacious rooms, an elegant drawing room hung with old brocade, and an outstanding view from the terrace.
⬥ 🥘 ❧ *on roof* 《€

Roma
Piazza SM Novella 8, 50123 Firenze ☎ *(055) 210336* ⊙ *575831* ⊙ *(055) 215306. Map 2C2* ▥ *51 rms* 🛏 *51* ▦ ▱ *AE* ⊙ *VISA Location: Near main railroad station.* The Roma reopened in 1988 as an efficiently modernized hotel with immaculate, comfortable, anonymously decorated bedrooms.
⬥ & ☐ 🖾 《€ ♈

Royal
Via delle Ruote 50-54, 50129 Firenze ☎ *(055) 483287. Map 3B4* ▥ *39 rms* 🛏 *39* ◛ *AE* ▥ *Location: Near S. Marco.* Peace and quiet in a handsome 19thC palace overlooking its own garden.
⬥ 🖨 & 🖾 ❧

Savoy
Piazza della Repubblica 7, 50123 Firenze ☎ *-1(055) 283313* ® *284840. Map 5C4* ▦ *101 rms* 🛏 *101* ▦ ▱ ◛ *AE* ⊙ ⊙ *VISA Location: In the heart of the historic center.* The most central of the grand old Florentine hotels. Service is efficient but rather impersonal.
⬥ & ☐ 🖾 ⛟

Silla
Via dei Renai 5, 50125 Firenze ☎ *(055) 234288. Map 5F5* ▥ *32 rms* 🛏 *28* ◛ *AE CB* ⊙ ⊙ *VISA Location: Oltrarno, near Ponte alle Grazie.* An airy, spacious *pensione*, which is especially attractive in summer. There is a large terrace, and the view across the Arno is fringed by trees in the little park.
⬥ 🖾 & 《€

Torre di Bellosguardo
Via Roti Michelozzi 2, 50124 Firenze ☎ *(055) 2298145/227125. Map 6D3* ▦ *17 rms* 🛏 *17* ◛ *AE CB* ⊙ ⊙ *VISA Location: One minute by car or*

7mins' walk by private footpath from Porta Romana. This beautiful and refined private hotel was opened in 1988 in a 16thC villa surrounded by spacious gardens, olive groves and orchards (which supply the fruit for breakfast) and commands the most spectacular of all views of Florence. Each of the large bedrooms is decorated in restrained good taste with well-chosen antiques and adjoined by an efficient bathroom.
🖾 ❧ 《€ ⇝

Villa Azalee
Viale Fratelli Rosselli 44, 50123 Firenze ☎ *214242/284331* ® *(055) 268264. Map 2B2* ▥ *to* ▥ *25 rms* 🛏 *25* ▦ ◛ *AE* ⊙ ⊙ *VISA Location: On the beltway NE of the center; convenient for the station, Perètola airport and Firenze-Mare autostrada.* A private hotel in a 19thC villa set in pleasant gardens. Bedrooms, some of which give directly onto the garden, are decorated with pretty chintzes.
☐ 🖾 ❧ ♈

Villa Belvedere
Via Benedetto Castelli 3, 50124 Firenze ☎ *(055) 222501* ⊙ *575648* ® *(055) 223163. Map 7E4* ▦ *27 rms* 🛏 *27* ▦ ▱ ◛ *AE* ⊙ ⊙ *VISA Location: Poggio Imperiale, 3km (2 miles) s.* Just the hotel for a peaceful family vacation, in a reconstructed Medici villa overlooking Florence.
🖨 ⬥ & 🖾 🥘 ❧ 《€ ⇝ ⚲ ♈

Villa Carlotta
Via Michele di Lando 3, 50125 Firenze ☎ *(055) 220530* ⊙ *573485* ® *(055) 226147. Map 2E2* ▦ *27 rms* 🛏 *27* ◛ ▱ ▱ *AE* ⊙ ⊙ *VISA Location: Near Porta Romana and Boboli Gardens.* On a quiet street lined with privately-owned 19thC villas, this *pensione* has been modernized with a rather heavy hand but to a high standard of comfort. The proprietress is German, as are many of the guests.
🖨 ⬥ & ☐ 🖾 ❧ ♈

Villa Cora 🏛
Viale Machiavelli 18, 50125 Firenze ☎ *(055) 2298451* ⊙ *570604* ® *(055) 229086. Map 2E3* ▦ *48 rms* 🛏 *48* ▦ ◛ ▱ *AE* ⊙ ⊙ *VISA Location: Near Boboli Gardens.* A sumptuous Neo-Classical villa in a large private park, retaining its extravagant mid-19thC Rococo features: elaborate fireplaces, gilded

stucco, frescoed ceilings, Venetian-glass chandeliers. It would still suit the Princess Eugenia, who stayed here in 1876. Today, although it often caters to expensively packaged tourists and businessmen, the service is unusually sympathetic. A car service ferries guests into Florence — or stroll through the Boboli Gardens into the Pitti in 20mins. A restaurant with piano bar, the **Taverna Machiavelli**, is next door.

🏠 ≋ ⚅ ▢ 🖼 🌱 《 ≋ 🏛

Villa Medici 🏨
Via Il Prato 42, 50123 Firenze
☎ (055) 261331 ⊚ 570179. Map

6D3 ▥ *108 rms* 🛏 *108* 🍽 🖼
≋ 🆓 ⊚ ◉

Location: Near Le Cascine. The frontage is that of an 18thC Corsini villa; the rest was built in 1960 in a style that would suit James Bond. In the immaculate apartments, all somber chintzes and dark wood, international businessmen and art dealers conclude deals in private. Most of the rooms have balconies and overlook the gardens.

🏠 ≋ ⚅ ▢ 🖼 🌱 《 ≋ 🏛

☙ Nearby hotels: **Villa la Massa** (see *Bagno a Ripoli*), **Villa le Rondini** (see *Castello*) and **Villa Villoresi** (see *Sesto Fiorentino*) — all in the *Tuscany A to Z*.

Eating in Florence

Visitors to Florence, even natives of other parts of Italy, are often surprised by the stark simplicity of the restaurants in which some of the city's most delicious and honestly-priced food is served. The traditional Florentine trattoria has plain white walls, washed or tiled, red-tiled floors and wooden tables, which are sometimes communal. The service can be brusque if not downright rude: the Florentines are said to like it that way and have named some of their favorite eating places after the rough tongues of their proprietors. The classic example is **Sostanza**. Such restaurants are not necessarily inexpensive; and some, for example **Coco Lezzone**, are locally very fashionable.

The hearty, earthy Tuscan dishes, such as *crostini*, *ribollita*, *bistecca*, *fagioli* or *castagnaccio*, can also be eaten in more comfortable surroundings. But they are not as ubiquitous in Florence as they were, and usually taste even better in the Tuscan countryside. Some of the most gastronomically interesting restaurants — such as **Cibrèo**, **Pepolino** and **San Zanobi** — serve refined modern variations on the old recipes; others, notably the **Enoteca Pinchiorri**, **Da Noi** and the better hotel restaurants, specialize in first-class international food influenced by the *nouvelle cuisine*.

Fish, now generally available, is particularly good at **La Capannina di Sante**, **Cibrèo** and **Pierot**. Game is harder to find in Florence than in the country, but is always well prepared at **La Maremma da Giuliano**.

Al fresco dining in Florence is not, as it is in so many other Italian cities, a normal pleasure of summer life. A minority of restaurants in the center have gardens or put tables outside in fine weather. Some that do are **Il Barone di Porta Romana**, **Bronzino**, **Cavallino**, **Carmine**, **La Capanina di Sante**, **Da Ganino**, the **Enoteca Pinchiorri** and **Zi Rosa**.

For those tourists who seek fast, familiar food, there are now plenty of snack bars in the center serving pizzas, hamburgers, crepes, ice cream and so on. There are also now a number of Chinese restaurants in Florence.

Fiaschetterie, or wine bars, provide excellent and sustaining

Tuscan food at reasonable prices; but the best *fiaschetterie* are often crowded at lunch with hungry Florentines. *Fiaschetterie* and other inexpensive Florentine restaurants can be found around the food markets of San Lorenzo and Sant Ambrogio (see *Shopping*) and the University near San Marco. At the end of this section there is a list of useful wine bars, pizzerie and tourist snack bars.

Although fewer and fewer hotels maintain their own dining rooms, there are three hotel restaurants that are among the best (and most expensive) in Florence. They all remain open on Sunday nights when most other good restaurants close. They are **Il Cestello** in the Excelsior Hotel, which commands marvelous views from the roof terrace in summer; **Relais le Jardin** in the Hotel Regency; and **Il Verrocchio** in the Villa La Massa.

Wherever you decide to eat in Florence, do not fail to do as the Florentines do and treat yourself on a fine afternoon or evening to a meal in the surrounding countryside where the cooking, the ambience and the prices have not yet been corrupted by the pressure of mass tourism.

Some favorite restaurants within easy driving distance (all of them are in the *Tuscany A to Z*) include **Da Delfina** at *Artimino*, **Cent'anni** at *Bagno a Ripoli*, **Lo Strettoio** near *Castello*, the **Badia a Coltibuono** and **Castello di Spaltenna** at *Gaiole in Chianti*, the **Trattoria del Montagliari** near *Greve*, the **Antica Trattoria Sanesi** at *Lastra a Signa*, the **Girrarosto** at *Pontassieve*, **Zocchi** at *Pratolino*, **Antica Posta** and **La Tenda Rossa**, both at *San Casciano in Val di Pesa*, and **Le Cave** at *Settignano*. Two outstanding Tuscan restaurants that are farther afield — allow most of the day for the journey and for the meal itself — are **La Chiusa** at *Montefollonico* and **Arnolfo** at *Colle di Val d'Elsa*.

Reservations for all restaurants are advisable, especially for Sunday lunch and in the spring and summer months. The majority close on Sunday evening and in August.

Restaurants classified by area

Arcetri
Omero▥▢

Cascine/Teatro Comunale
Pierot▥▢

Duomo
Al Campidoglio▥▢
Mosacce▥▢ ✿
Ottorino▥▢

Ognissanti
13 Gobbi▥▢
Harry's Bar▥▥▥
Il Profeta▥▢
Sostanza▥▢

Oltrarno (Pitti, San Spirito, Carmine)
Cammillo▥▢ to ▥▥▥
Carmine▥▢ ✿
Celestino▥▢
Mamma Gina▥▢ to ▥▥▥
Le Quattro Stagioure▥▢

Porta Romano
Ruggero▥▢

Santa Croce
Giuseppe Alessi▥▢ ✿
Cibrèo▥▢ or ▥▥▥ ✿

Dino▥▢
Da Noi▥▥▥
Enoteca Pinchiorri▥▥▥
Il Fagioli▥▢
La Maremma da Giuliano▥▢ to ▥▥▥

San Marco
Bronzino▥▢ to ▥▥▥
San Zanobi▥▢ to ▥▥▥

San Miniato
La Loggia▥▢

Santa Trìnita/Via Tornabuoni
Cantinetta Antinori▥▢
Coco Lezzone▥▢ ✿
Il Latini▥▢

Signoria/Uffizi
Antico Fattore▥▢
Il Cavallino▥▢
Da Ganino▥▢
Paoli▥▢

Station/Santa Maria Novella
Le Fonticine▥▥▥
Otello▥▥▥
Sabatini▥▥▥

111

Florence restaurants

Giuseppe Alessi ♣
Via di Mezzo 26 (near Santa Croce) ☎ (055) 241821. Map *3C5* ⌷

Giuseppe Alessi is one of the most skillful and serious cooks in Tuscany, a scholar of antique recipes and a fanatic about the integrity and freshness of ingredients. This present address, an egregiously simple wine bar and takeout where tourists are not made especially welcome, may prove temporary. But those who share his passion for delicious and healthy food will follow him wherever he goes.

Antico Fattore
Via Lambertesca 1/3 (near Uffizi) ☎ (055) 261215. Map *5D4* ⌷ ⌷ Ⓐ *Closed Sun, Mon (winter), Sat (summer), Aug.*
This was once *the* Florentine rendezvous of Italian writers and artists. The sustaining Tuscan peasant dishes are better than the pastas. Tables are communal and service slipshod.

Bronzino
Via delle Ruote 27 (near S. Marco) ☎ (055) 495220. Map *3B4* ⌷ to ⌷ ⌷ 🍽 🍴 Ⓐ ⓞ ⓞ ⓥ *Closed Sun, Aug.*
A large, welcoming restaurant currently favored by discriminating Florentines. An ambitious menu offers interesting variations on traditional Tuscan dishes. Portions are enormous.

Cammillo
Borgo S. Jacopo 57 (Oltrarno, near Ponte Vecchio) ☎ (055) 212427. Map *4D3* ⌷ to ⌷ ⌷ Ⓐ ⓞ ⓞ ⓥ *Closed Wed, Thurs, Aug.*
A pleasantly bright family-run trattoria with a loyal American clientele.

Al Campidoglio
Via Campidoglio 8 (near Piazza Repubblica) ☎ (055) 287770. Map *4C3* ⌷ ⌷ 🍽 ⌷ Ⓐ ⓞ ⓥ *Closed Thurs.*
A large, immaculate, old-fashioned restaurant with a balanced regional and international menu.

Cantinetta Antinori
Piazza Antinori 3 (N end of Via Tornabuoni) ☎ (055) 292234. Map *4C3* ⌷ ⌷ ⓥ *Closed Sat, Sun, Aug.*
In elegant rooms off the central courtyard of the 15thC Antinori palace, this chic, crowded restaurant serves products from the Antinori estates which you can take as a quick snack at the bar or build into a full dinner. Wines, oil, bread and cheeses are all excellent, as is the *galletto al Chianti*.

Capannina di Sante
Piazza Ravenna ☎ (055) 688345 *(at the S foot of Ponte da Verrazzano).* All ⌷ 🍽 Ⓐ Ⓒ ⓞ ⓞ ⓥ *Closed Sun, Mon lunch, Christmas week, mid-Aug.*
The freshest fish and seafood in Florence is simply prepared and complemented by well-chosen white wines. The restaurant overlooks the Arno, and its interior rooms are romantic in the evening when candles are lit.

Carmine ♣
Piazza del Carmine 18 (Oltrarno) ☎ (055) 218601. Map *2D3-4* ⌷ ⌷ 🍽 🍴 *Closed Sun in winter, Sat and Sun in summer, Aug.*
A rough, reliable old favorite, especially pleasant in summer with tables in the piazza.

Il Cavallino
Via delle Farine 6 (Piazza Signoria) ☎ (055) 215818. Map *5D4* ⌷ 🍴 🍽 Ⓐ Ⓒ ⓞ ⓞ ⓥ *Closed Wed, Aug 1-24.*
Don't be suspicious of the star location — it might have turned Cavallino into a tourist trap, but hasn't. This is the sort of restaurant Florentines treat as a second home. Whether you dine alone with a book or with a party of friends the service is quick and courteous and the food pleasant.

Celestino
Piazza S. Felicita (Oltrarno) ☎ (055) 296574. Map *4E3* ⌷ ⌷ 🍽 Ⓐ *Closed Sun, Mon, Aug, late Dec.*
A small, fashionable, noisy trattoria run with polished professionalism.

Cibrèo ♣
Via de' Macci 118 (near S. Croce) ☎ (055) 2341100. Map *3D5* ⌷ or ⌷ ⌷ Ⓐ ⓞ ⓞ *Closed Sun, Mon, Aug to mid-Sept, Christmas, Easter.*
One of the most original and congenial of the new generation of restaurants, influenced but not overwhelmed by the *nouvelle cuisine.* Don't pass up any of the four courses. Everything is delicious, and the seasonal *passati di verdura* and *sformati* offered in lieu of pastas are outstanding, as are the homemade desserts. You can enjoy

the same food for half the price in the simpler surroundings of the "*vinaria*" on the other side of the kitchen. And around the corner, **Cibrèo Alimentari** (*Via del Verrocchio 4* ☎ *(055) 677298*) sells exotic delicacies to take out.

Coco Lezzone ♣
Via Parioncino 26 (near Via Tornabuoni) ☎ *(055) 287178. Map 4C3* ▥ ▭ *Closed Sun, Tues eve, Aug, late Dec-early Jan.*
A white-tiled trattoria that looks like a public rest room and is always crammed with chic Florentines packed elbow-to-elbow at communal tables. The attraction is the high quality of the uncompromised Tuscan food, especially the simple meat dishes.

Da Noi
Via Fiesolana 46 (near S. Croce) ☎ *(055) 242917. Map 3C5* ▥ ▭ ☰ ⌂ ▤ *Closed Sun, Mon, Aug.*
The owners of this tiny and very successful restaurant worked previously at the **Enoteca Pinchiorri**; their culinary style is a similar blend of Italian and new French. Reserve some days ahead.

Dino
Via Ghibellina 51 (near Michelangelo Museum) ☎ *(055) 241452. Map 5C5* ▥ ▭ ☰ ⌂ ▤ *AE* ⊙ *VISA Closed Sun dinner, Mon, Aug.*
The menu of this coolly handsome "*enogastronomico*" is designed to accompany the Italian wines from the well-stocked cellar. The cheese board is excellent. Specialties include *risotto alla Renza, stracotto del Granduca, filetto di maiale al cartoccio.*

Enoteca Pinchiorri
Via Ghibellina 87 (near S. Croce) ☎ *(055) 242757/77. Map 5C5* ▥ ▭ ☰ ⌂ ▤ *AE* ⊙ *VISA Closed Sun, Mon lunch, Aug, Christmas.*
This establishment, on the ground floor of the 15thC Ciofi-Iacometti Palace, has been voted best restaurant in Italy by the four leading Italian gastronomic guides. It also demands to be judged by the highest European standards. The proprietor, Giorgio Pinchiorri, has built up a cellar (there are enophiles who would call it the finest in the world) of international wines. His French wife is responsible for the elegant and subtle cuisine. If you choose the *menu de degustazione* and allow the waiter to fill your

glass with the appropriate wine for each course, you will be able to sample the glories of the cellar without committing yourself to full bottles. A pilgrimage restaurant, but mainly, alas, for the super-rich and those on expense accounts.

Il Fagioli
Corso Tintori 47 (near S. Croce) ☎ *(055) 244285. Map 5E5* ▥ ▭ *Closed Sat, Sun, Aug.*
This straightforward Tuscan trattoria is a less distinguished, but more comfortable, spin-off from **Coco Lezzone**.

Le Fonticine
Via Nazionale 79 (near the station) ☎ *(055) 282106. Map 4A3* ▥ ▭ ☰ *AE* *VISA Closed Sat, Sun, Aug.*
The excellence of the cuisine, and especially the pasta, must be partly explained by the Emilian origins of the proprietress. Popular with visiting business executives.

Da Ganino
Piazza dei Cimatori 4 (near Piazza Signoria) ☎ *(055) 214125. Map 5C4* ▥ ▭ ☰ ⌂ ▤ *Closed Sun, mid-Aug, late Dec.*
A tiny, welcoming trattoria tucked away in a miniature piazza. First-class, especially the homemade pastas and *torta di formaggio.*

13 Gobbi
Via del Porcellana 9 (off Borgognissanti) ☎ *(055) 298769. Map 4B2* ▥ ▭ *AE* ⊙ *Closed Sun, Mon, Aug.*
Hungarian or Tuscan specialties, good draft beer or Chianti and gently eccentric piano music.

Harry's Bar
Lungarno Vespucci 22 (near Ognissanti) ☎ *(055) 296700. Map 4C1* ▥ ▭ ▤ *AE* *VISA Closed Sun, Dec.*
Modeled on the original in Venice, but with no business connection, this is a haven for English-speaking visitors. Attentive bilingual service, a good selection of American cocktails, an adequate, short menu that hardly ever changes, and the best hamburgers in town.

Il Latini
Via Palchetti 6 (behind Palazzo Rucellai) ☎ *(055) 210916. Map 4C2* ▥ ▭ *Closed Mon, Tues lunch, late July, Dec 22-Jan 6.*
Love it or hate it — and you do have to be in the mood and very hungry — this noisy, crowded

113

restaurant with its open kitchen, communal tables and hanging hams is one of the best places in Florence to enjoy robust Tuscan country cooking.

La Loggia

Piazzale Michelangelo 1 ☎ (055) 2342832/2345288. Map **3E5** ❙❙❙❙ ▭ 《☰ ☰ ☎ AE ⊙ VISA Closed Wed, two weeks in Aug.
The spectacular views over the city from the spacious 19thC palazzina del caffè make this an ideal place for a first or last meal in Florence. The food is excellent, especially the honestly-prepared Tuscan specialties. Try the manzo con rughetta. Also a café.

Mamma Gina

Borgo S. Jacopo 37 (Oltrarno, near Ponte Vecchio) ☎ (055) 296009. Map **4D3** ❙❙❙ to ❙❙❙❙ ▭ ☰ ☰ AE ⊙ VISA Closed Sun, Aug.
Now under the same management as **La Loggia**, this trattoria with its suspiciously inviting atmosphere and long menu is no longer a cynical tourist trap. Nearly all of the hearty Tuscan dishes succeed. The fritti, which can be so stodgy unless properly prepared, are light and crisp; and there are many other simple and satisfying specialties, such as riso e fagioli, which are becoming rarities in Florence.

La Maremma da Giuliano

Via Verdi 16 (near S. Croce) ☎ (055) 244615. Map **5D5** ❙❙❙ to ❙❙❙❙ ▭ ☰ AE CB ⊙ ☎ VISA Closed Wed, two weeks in Aug.
A justly popular, family-run trattoria offering game in season as well as other delicious specialties. Don't miss the prosciutto di cinghiale, hard to find elsewhere.

Mossacce ✿

Via del Proconsolo 55 (between Duomo and Bargello) ☎ (055) 294361. Map **5C5** ❙❙ ▭ ☰ ☰ AE ⊙ VISA Closed Sat, Sun, Aug.
Although mossacce means "discourteous", Mossacce is always full because the meat is so excellent and such good value.

Omero

Via Pian dei Giullari 11 (Arcetri) ☎ (055) 220053. Map **7E4** ❙❙❙ ▭ ☰ AE Closed Tues, Aug.
Such a sympathetic rustic environment in such a splendid location above the city cannot be entirely spoiled by routine, lackluster food and service, which

one encounters too often here. Better for lunch than dinner.

Otello

Via degli Orti Oricellari 28 (near the station) ☎ (055)215819. Map **2C3** ❙❙❙❙ ▭ ☰ ☰ AE ⊙ ☎ VISA Closed Tues.
A large, comfortable, dignified restaurant more appreciated by foreigners than by Florentines. The salad trolley is welcome on hot days.

Ottorino

Via delle Oche 12-16 (near Duomo) ☎ (055) 218747. Map **5C4** ❙❙❙ ▭ ☰ ☰ AE ⊙ ☎ VISA Closed Sun, Aug.
One of the city's oldest restaurants, moved into spacious new premises where the tastefully modernized Tuscan style of the decor is restful on a hot day and the long menu as well balanced as ever.

Paoli

Via Tavolini 12 (near Orsanmichele) ☎ (055) 216215. Map **5C4** ❙❙❙ ▭ ☰ ☰ AE ⊙ VISA Closed Tues, two weeks in July.
Inoffensive food in a spectacular environment: imitation-Gothic frescoes, polished mahogany benches, wrought-iron lamp brackets — all (apart from the Annigoni canvas and a bust of President Wilson) redolent of the early 19thC when Paoli was established in the beautiful storerooms of a 15thC palace.

Pepolino

Via C.F. Ferrucci 16 (near San Salvi) ☎ (055) 608905. Map **7D5** ❙❙❙ to ❙❙❙❙ ▭ ☰ ☰ AE ⊙ VISA Closed Sun, Aug.
This tiny establishment is the most interesting of the new generation of Florentine restaurants and merits the short drive from the center. The atmosphere — clear black and white decor, crisp napery, flowers on each table — is reassuringly serious; service is welcoming and professional. The menu, changed weekly, emphasizes seasonal produce, with inventive, beautifully presented refinements of traditional Tuscan dishes. Reservation essential.

Pierot

Piazza Taddeo Gaddi 25 (across the Arno from the Cascine) ☎ (055) 702100. Map **2C1** ❙❙❙ ▭ AE ⊙ ☎ VISA Closed Sun, late July.
Homey, honest and very popular fish restaurant, which now also serves classic Tuscan meat dishes.

Il Profeta
Borgognissanti 93 (Ognissanti)
☎ (055) 212265. Map **4C1** *III*
⊐ 🖽 AE 📼 Closed Sat eve,
Sun.
A soothingly understated one-room
restaurant where the quality of the
food never seems to fall short of
excellence.

Le Quattro Stagioni
Via Maggio 61 (near the Pitti)
☎ (055) 218906. Map **2D3** ⊐
■■ AE ◆ ◎ 📼 Closed Sun, late
Aug.
Two small rooms, usually crowded
with antique dealers and fashion
people from the Pitti Moda. The
generalized Italian food lacks real
character, but the multilingual
service is graceful.

Ruggero
*Via Senese 89 (near Porta
Romana)* ☎ (055) 220542. Map
2E2 ⊐ Closed Tues, Wed,
July 7-Aug 7.
This no-nonsense everyday trattoria
opposite the old horse-watering
stop on the road to Rome is owned
by a former cook at **Coco Lezzone**.
The hearty country food makes an
ideal Sunday lunch after a walk
along the city walls between

Piazzale Michelangelo and Porta
Romana. They do a good fish soup
on Fridays.

Sabatini
Via Panzani 9a (near the station)
☎ (055) 282802. Map **4B3** *IIII* ⊐
🖽 AE ◆ ◎ 📼 Closed Mon.
Sabatini is no longer the most
famous and fashionable restaurant
in Florence. But it has a pleasant
environment and often one eats
better here than some critics suggest.

San Zanobi
*Via S. Zanobi 33a (near
S. Marco)* ☎ (055) 475286. Map
3B4 *III* to *IIII* ⊐ 🖽 AE CB ◆ ◎
📼 Closed Sun, Aug.
A calm, refined restaurant run by
two women who cater primarily to
the Florentine professional classes.
Inventive food, lovingly prepared.

Sostanza
*Via del Porcellana 25 (near
Ognissanti)* ☎ (055) 212691. Map
4C2 *III* ⊐ Closed Sat, Sun, Aug.
Known as "il Troia," which is
Tuscan slang for "pigsty," this is one
of the oldest working men's *trattorie*
in Florence. The prices have gone
up, but the *bistecca* is still very
good and the service still very rude.

Other recommended restaurants

Angiolino   Via S. Spirito 36 ☎ 298976. Map **4D2** *I⊐* Closed Sun eve, Mon,
July.
Baldini   Via il Prato 96 ☎ 287663. Map **2B2** *III* Closed Sat.
La Baraonda   Via Ghibellina 67 ☎ 2341171. Map **5C5** *III* Closed Sun,
Aug. Open for dinner only.
La Barcacci   Via dei Lavatoi 1-3 ☎ 283958. Map **5D5** *III* Closed Sun.
Il Barone di Porta Romana   Via Romana 123 ☎ 220585. Map **2E2** *III* to
IIII Closed Sun. Has a pleasant rustic atmosphere and romantic garden.
Buca Lapi   Via dei Fossi 12 ☎ 287062. Map **4C2** *III* Closed Sun. Does
very good *bistecca*.
Buca Mario   Piazza Ottaviani 16 ☎ 214179. Map **4C2** *I⊐* to *III* Closed
Wed, Thurs lunch, two weeks in July.
Buca dell'Orafo   Volta de' Girolami 28 ☎ 213619. Map **5D4** *III* Closed
Sun.
Cafaggi   Via Guelfa 35 ☎ 294989. Map **3B4** *I⊐* Closed Sun dinner, Mon,
late July to mid-Aug.
Carabaccia   Via Palazzuolo 190 ☎ 214782. Map **4C2** *III* Closed Sun, Mon
lunch.
Don Chisciotte   Via Ridolfi 4 ☎ 475430. Map **2B3** *III* Closed Sun, Mon
lunch in Aug.
Garga   Via del Moro, 48-52 ☎ 298898. Map **4C2** *I⊐* to *III* Closed Mon.
Leo in Santa Croce   Via Torta 7 ☎ 210829. Map **5D5** *III* Closed Mon,
mid-July to mid-Aug.
La Macelleria   Via S. Zanobi 97 ☎ 486244. Map **3B4** *I⊐* Closed Sun.
L'Orologio   Piazza Ferruci 5 ☎ 6811729. Map **3D-E6** *I⊐* Closed Sun.
Roberto   Via dei Castellani 4 ☎ 218822. Map **5D4** *III* Closed Wed, two
weeks in Nov, two weeks in Aug.
Vittoria   Via della Fonderia 52 ☎ 225657. Map **2C2** *III* Closed Tues, Aug.
Serves fish only.
Zi Rosa   Via dei Fossi 12 ☎ 287062. Map **4C2** *I⊐* to *III* Closed Thurs. Has
a large garden.

115

Fiaschetterie (wine bars)
The following all close on Sun.

Angiolino (*Via dell'Agnolo 107*); **Antica Mescita S. Niccolò** (*Via S. Niccolò 60-62*); **Da Zazà** (*Piazza Mercato Centrale 26*); **Fani** (*Via degli Alfani 70*); **Fiaschetteria Cambi** (*Via S. Onofrio 1*); **Il Vecchio Vinaio** (*Via de' Neri 65*); **La Fiaschetteria** (*Via de' Neri 17*); **Piccolo Vinaio** (*Via dei Castellani 25*); **Vineria** (*Via de' Cimatori 38*).

Useful snack bars and pizzerie

La Bussola (*Via Porta Rossa 58* ☎ *293376, closed Mon*), a useful pizzeria open until 2.30am; **Nuti** (*Via Borgo San Lorenzo 22* ☎ *210145, closed Mon*); **Old Bridge** (*Via de' Bardi 64, Oltrarno* ☎ *212915, closed Mon*), serve-yourself restaurant with a terrace, on the Arno; **Queen Victoria** (*Por S. Maria, Ponte Vecchio*), large *tavola calda*, with garden; **Il Rifrullo** (*Via San Niccolò 57*), see *Bars, cafés and ice cream shops*.

Bars, cafés and ice cream shops

The bar is the nerve center of Italian daily life. If you need a telephone, a bus ticket, a rest room or simply want to ask directions, look for the nearest bar, which will never be far away. In an Italian bar anyone can drink anything at any time of day. Ordinary coffee (*caffè normale*) is a short, potent espresso; if you like it weaker, ask for *caffè lungo*. *Macchiato* is with a dash of milk; *correto* is laced with brandy. The coffee is almost unfailingly excellent, and a *cappuccino* with a sweet roll makes a better and cheaper breakfast than you will find in any hotel. Many larger bars also sell pastries, sandwiches, ice cream, groceries, even light meals. Be aware that if you sit down the price doubles.

Although open-air cafés are not characteristic of Florence, there are four in the unlovely but central Piazza della Repubblica. The **Excelsior** hotel (see *Hotels*) serves a typical English tea in the afternoons.

The best ice creams are from **Old Bridge** (see *Useful snack bars*, above), the *gelateria* next to **Il Rifrullo** and **Vivoli**.

Cennini
Borgo San Jacopo 51. Map 4D3. Closed Mon.
The most delicious coffee and pastries in the Oltr'Arno.

Donnini
Piazza della Repubblica 15 ☎ *(055) 211862. Map 4C3. Closed Mon.*
The smallest bar in the piazza serves the most unusual hot sandwiches.

Giacosa
Via Tornabuoni 83 ☎ *(055) 296226. Map 4C3. Closed Mon.*
This is where the young elite meet for coffee and buy their pastries, *marrons glacés* and hand-made chocolates. The *cappuccino* is the best in town, and there are also sandwiches and hot snacks. The Negroni was invented here in the 1920s by Count Camillo Negroni.

Gilli
Piazza della Repubblica ☎ *(055) 296310. Map 4C3. Closed Tues.*
This *belle-époque* café, where an orchestra plays old favorites in summer, is the most attractive and comfortable (with good rest rooms) in Piazza della Repubblica.

La Loggia
Piazzale Michelangelo 1 ☎ *(055) 287032. Map 3E5. Closed Wed.*
From the 19thC *palazzina del caffè* you can look past the "Not-the-Real-David" over the most famous introductory view of the city.

Paszkowski
Piazza della Repubblica 6
☎ (055) 210236. Map 4C3.
Closed Mon.
One of the few bars in Florence
where you can eat a hearty
American breakfast, Paszkowski is
also fun when live bands play on
summer evenings.

Procacci
Via Tornabuoni 64 ☎ (055)
211656. Map 4C3. Closed Mon.
As a treat, pamper your taste buds
with a plate of Procacci's exquisite
truffle rolls. Cold drinks only.

Il Rifrullo
Via San Niccolò 57 ☎ (055)
213621. Map 5F6. Open until
1am. Closed Wed.
A favorite rendezvous for young
Florentines. Also a brasserie and
creperie. Its *gelateria* around the
corner serves some of the best ice
creams in town.

Rivoire
Piazza Signoria 5 ☎ (055)
214412. Map 5D4. Closed Mon.
Not the exclusive tea room it once
was, but the hot chocolate is superb,
and the view of the Palazzo Vecchio
probably justifies the high prices.

Robiglio
Via dei Servi 112 ☎ (055)
212784. Map 5B5. Also Via dei
Tosinghi 11 ☎ (055) 215013.
Map 5C4. Open 8am-midnight.
Closed Mon.
A large and luscious selection of
pastries. Specialties include
Saint-Honorés, millefeuilles,
meringues and *torta rustica.*

Scudieri
19 Piazza di San Giovanni 19.
Map 5B4. Closed Wed.
Excellent coffee and pastries;
opposite the Baptistry.

Vivoli
Via Isola delle Stinche 7 ☎ (055)
292334. Map 5D5.
Don't be deceived by the humble
premises — Vivoli is one of the
great Italian ice cream makers.
Some two dozen mouth-watering
flavors as well as open sandwiches,
pastries and coffee. The only
gelateria to be found in Florence
that will satisfy the true connoisseur
of ice cream.

Nightlife and performing arts

Florence enjoys a livelier nightlife than many small Italian cities,
thanks partly to its large student population.

Cinema
The **Cinema Astro** (*Piazza San Simone ☎ (055) 222388*)
shows English-language films every evening except Mon.

Discos and piano bars
The largest, most popular discos are **Space Electronic** (*Via
Palazzuolo ☎ (055) 293082*) and **Yab Yum** (*Via Sassetti 5
☎ (055) 282018*). Smaller discos and piano bars include **Full
Up** (*Via della Vigna Vecchia 21 ☎ (055) 293006*) and **Jackie
O'** (*Via Erta Canina 24 ☎ (055) 2342442*).

Music and theater
The *Maggio Musicale*, a festival of concerts, recitals, opera
and ballet, is held in various venues throughout the city
during May-July. It is wise to reserve tickets well in advance
through your travel agent. In Florence tickets are theoretically
available from the rather inefficient box offices of the Teatro
Comunale and Teatro della Pergola. However, it is usually less
complicated to make reservations through hotel porters or
local travel agents.
  The principal theaters in Florence for music, opera, ballet
and plays are the **Teatro della Compagnia** (*Via Cavour 50
☎ (055) 217428*); **Teatro Comunale** (*Corso Italia 16
☎ (055) 2779236*); **Teatro Niccolini** (*Via Ricasoli 5 ☎ (055)*

213282); **Teatro della Pergola** (*Via della Pergola 10-32* ☎ *(055) 2479651/242361*); **Teatro Variety** (*Via del Madonnone 47* ☎ *(055) 663602*); and **Teatro Verdi** (*Via Ghibellina 99* ☎ *(055) 296242*).

Shopping

When shopping in Florence bear in mind the Florentine character, which is unique in Italy and is as remarkable a legacy of the Renaissance as any church or monument. At all social and economic levels Florentines share a profound respect for two skills: craftsmanship and business, the activities which made Florence the richest city in 15thC Europe and which account for its modern prosperity. The Florentine shopkeepers are probably the most powerful political lobby in the city.

Shopping hours
Normally 9am-1pm, 3.30-7pm, with slight variations, but some in the center now stay open in the lunch hours as well. Most stores close on Mon mornings but open all day Sat, except for food stores, which close on Wed. In summer some of the bigger stores close all day Sat but open Mon.

Most large stores will send your purchases abroad if you wish.

Where to shop
The Via Tornabuoni is the Fifth Avenue of Florence. Most of the grandest stores are in this area, near the Duomo, Piazza della Repubblica, Ognissanti, along the Lungarno, and across the Arno around Borgo San Jacopo.

How to shop
The businesslike Florentines understand comparative shopping and bargaining. An aggressive manner will get you nowhere, but even in big, established stores you can try asking for a discount (*sconto* or *gentilezza*) if you buy more than one item.

What to buy
The best buys are anything made locally of leather, silk and straw (bags, hats and novelties). You can still buy the service of craftsmen in Florence, which is one of the few cities left in Western Europe where making and repairing of anything is done quickly and skillfully. Bookbinding, picture framing and reproduction antiques are Florentine specialties.

Antiques
Many of the established antique stores are in Via dei Fossi and Via Maggio, but look also in Borgognissanti, Borgo San Jacopo and Via Santo Spirito. Auctions are held in fall and spring, the two leading houses being **Sotheby's Italia** (*Via Gino Capponi 26* ☎ *(055) 2479021*) and **Casa d'Aste Pitti** (*Via Maggio 15* ☎ *(055) 296382*). An important antiques fair is held every 2yrs in the Strozzi palace.

Fallani Best
Borgognissanti 15 ☎ *(055) 214986. Map 4C1.*
The top Italian dealer in Art Nouveau and Art Deco.

Ugo Camiciotti
Via S. Spirito 9 ☎ *(055) 294837. Map 4D2.*
French Second Empire clocks and mirrors, signed and dated.

Giovanni Pratesi
Via Maggio 13 ☎ *(055) 296568. Map 4E2* [AE] [◇] [◎] [VISA]
A new and respected young dealer with a more eclectic stock of paintings, sculpture and furniture.

Artisans, restoration and reproductions
The narrow back streets of the Oltr'Arno, where the artisans' workshops are concentrated, are alive with the sounds of hammers and saws and the odors of wood, glue and tanning leather. Florentine craftsmen are highly skilled in every branch of restoration, and many a Florentine-made reproduction has been innocently passed by experts and honest dealers.

Bartolozzi & Maioli
Via Vellutini 5 and Via Maggio 13. Map 4E2.
Wood-carvers who will make anything from picture frames to life-sized lions to table legs. They were entrusted with the restoration of Monte Cassino after its destruction during World War II.

Emilio Malenotti
Via del Presto di San Martino 29. Map 4D2.
A leading restorer of fine furniture.

Luciano Ugolini
Via del Presto di San Martino 23. Map 4D2.
Reproductions of antique copper tubs and jugs.

Manetti e Masini
Via Bronzino 125 ☎ *(055) 700445. Map 6D3.*
Began as restorers of antique majolica, and soon found they could produce exact copies. They sell charming fabrications of 18thC

plates, tureens, vases and ceramic stoves, and repair china.

Marino Cappellini
Via del Presto di San Martino 10. Map 4D2.
Specialists in *trompe l'oeil*. Will paint any surface to look like marble, wood or *pietra dura*.

Raffaello Romanelli
Lungarno Acciaioli 72-78 ☎ *(055) 296047* [AE] [◇] [◎] [VISA]
The firm has been making life-size copies of the most famous sculptures since 1860; it will also make period fireplaces, tabletops and chess sets.

Zecchi
Via dello Studio 19 ☎ *(055) 211470. Map 5C4* [AE] [CB] [VISA]
Zecchi stocks a full range of restorers' and artists' materials, many not available elsewhere in Europe. You can buy *lapis lazuli* from Afghanistan, pure gold leaf, powdered pigments for frescoes, natural gums and resins.

Books, prints and endpapers
Italy was the home of printing and all the crafts of book production; and Florence has been catering to the needs of bookish foreigners for centuries. Foreign-language books are generally available. There are also a number of internationally renowned specialty bookstores.

Alinari
Via della Vigna Nuova 46 ☎ *(055) 218975. Map 4C2* [AE]
The famous sepia photos of 19thC Florence; and one of the most complete archives of black-and-white photos of Italian art. The archive, in Palazzo Rucellai, is open Mon-Fri 11am-1pm.

BM
Borgognissanti 4 ☎ *(055) 294575. Map 4C1.*
This is an extremely useful store that sells not only books in English, as well as Italian, on Florentine culture and history, but also maps, guidebooks, fiction and books for children.

Florence shopping

Centro Di
Piazza dei Mozzi 1 ☎ *(055)
2342666/7. Map 5E5* 💳
One of the most important serious
art bookstores and publishers in
Italy, hidden away in a basement.
The fine catalogs the firm produces
for major European exhibitions are
on sale.

Libreria Condotta
Via della Condotta 29 ☎ *(055)
213421. Open 9am-7.30pm. Map
5D4* 💳 💳 💳 💳
A serious and sympathetic
bookstore with a good selection of
foreign-language books, guides,
classics and art books.

Giannini e Figlio
Piazza Pitti 37 ☎ *(055) 212621.
Map 4E2.*
This delectable little shop opposite
the Pitti, founded in 1856, is the
grandfather of all the paper shops.

Paperback Exchange
Via Fiesolana 31 ☎ *(055)
2478154. Map 3C5.*
Over 10,000 English-language titles
in stock, mostly popular fiction. A
recycling system gives you 25-40
percent of the original price of your
old paperbacks toward any you buy
at 75 percent of the cover price.

Il Papiro
Via Cavour 55 ☎ *(055) 215262.*

Map 5B4 💳 💳 💳 💳 💳
Specializes in marbled papers.
(*Branches at Piazza Duomo 24 and
Lungarno degli Acciaiuoli 42.*)

Porcellino
Piazza del Mercato Nuovo 6-8
☎ *(055) 212535. Map 5D4* 💳 💳
💳
The first self-service bookstore in
Florence and the place to look for
the catalogs and guides that are
maddeningly not sold in museums
and galleries.

Salimbeni
Via M. Palmieri 14-16 ☎ *(055)
2340904. Map 5C5.*
One of the most reputable specialty
art and antiquarian bookstores in
Europe.

Seeber
Via Tornabuoni 70 ☎ *(055)
215697. Map 4C3* 💳 💳 💳 💳
💳
Founded in 1865 to serve the
foreign community and now one of
the largest and best known general
bookstores.

Il Viaggio
Via Ghibellina 117 ☎ *(055)
218153. Map 3D5* 💳 💳 💳 💳
💳
Specialists in tourist guides and
maps, including nautical and
aeronautical maps.

Clothes
Despite the commercial importance of the annual Pitti Moda
shows, the creative center of Italian high fashion is still Milan.
But Florentine women continue to dress, as they always have,
with an impeccable chic that is never flamboyant but often
striking. It is a look that depends on quality: the finest printed
cotton jersey or silks, smooth gaberdines and, of course,
beautiful Florentine leather accessories — these are the kind
of clothes that you will see in abundant, if not inexpensive,
supply.

Some of the best-known non-Florentine designers have
outlets in and off the Via Tornabuoni, which is where you will
find **Giorgio Armani, Yves St-Laurent, Roberta di
Camerino**, and **Valentino**. Other fashion streets are Via de'
Calzaiuoli, Via de' Cerretani, Via Roma and Via Calimala; and,
across the Arno, Via Guicciardini and Borgo San Jacopo. See
also *Leather* p123.

Giuliacarla Cecchi
Via della Vigna Nuova 40
☎ *(055) 213350. Map 4C2.*
Delectable hand-made ball gowns
and wedding dresses.

Luisa
Via Roma 19-21 ☎ *(055)*

217826-8 and Via del Corso
☎ *(055) 294374. Both map 5B4*
💳 💳 💳 💳 💳 *Open
9.30am-7.30pm.*
The most fashionable boutique in
Florence and the first to stock
Japanese designers. Also accessories
and men's clothing.

Neuber
Via Strozzi 32 ☎ *(055) 215763.*
Map 4C3 AE ● ● VISA
Clothing for men, women and
children, all of very good quality
and mostly bearing the labels of
foreign houses.

Principe
Via Strozzi 21-29 ☎ *(055) 216821.*
Map 4C3 AE ● ● VISA
One of a Tuscan chain selling
restrained clothes for men, women,
children and babies, at all prices.

Pucci
Via dei Pucci 6 ☎ *(055) 283061.*
Map 5B4 AE
The Marquese Emilio Pucci's famous
designs can be bought from the

atelier on the first floor of his
ancestral palace. Entrance through
the boutique at Via Ricasoli 59.

Valditevere
Lungarno Soderini 1 ☎ *(055)*
282707. Map 2C2 AE ● ● VISA
An exclusive boutique which sells
reticently classical clothes that are
made from its own beautiful
materials. The clothes are also on
sale at **Gems** (*Via de' Bardi 76*
☎ *(055) 210810*).

Ermenegildo Zegna
Piazza Rucellai 4-7 ☎ *(055)*
211098. Map 4C2 AE CB ● ●
VISA
Top-quality — and very
expensive — men's clothes.

Design and gifts

Cassetti
Via Strozzi 7 ☎ *(055) 210273 and*
Via Tornabuoni 72 ☎ *(055)*
282387. Both map 4C3 AE CB ●
● VISA
The widest selection in Florence of
Italian and international porcelain,
glass and silver. This is where
Florentines buy wedding presents.

Edizione &C
Via della Vigna Nuova 82 and 91
☎ *(055) 287839/215165. Map*

4C2. Also Via dei Pucci 22
☎ *(055) 295061. Map 5B4* AE CB
● ● VISA
Hand-woven writing paper,
filofaxes, original diaries.

Viceversa
Via Ricasoli 53 ☎ *(055) 298281.*
Map 5B4.
A reminder that Italians lead the
world in imaginative modern
design: gadgets, lighting, watches,
clocks, executive toys.

Food
The local produce — dried mushrooms, new-season's dried
beans, wild-boar hams, and especially the green Tuscan olive
oil — is so appetizing that you might well be tempted to bring
home some edible gifts or souvenirs. Florentines who like to
eat well do their grocery shopping at the huge, covered
food-markets of **Sant'Ambrogio** and **San Lorenzo** (see
Street markets) where the selection is enormous and the
prices lower than in shops. Two high-class grocery and wine
stores in the center are **Alessi** (*Via delle Oche 27-29*) and
Vera (*Piazza dei Frescobaldi 3* ☎ *(055) 215465*). The **Pucci**
boutique (see *Clothes*) also sells oil, wine and truffles from
the Pucci country estates. **Dino Bartolini** (*Via dei Servi 30*)
has an enormous selection of cooking equipment, including
vessels for pouring olive oil.

Health and beauty
Florentines take their health and their looks seriously.
Pharmacies, which are nearly as ubiquitous in Florence as
bars, often retain their beautiful original fittings, make their
own soaps, creams and specifics and are happy to give advice
about minor ailments and beauty problems. The top
hairdressers are **Luana Beni** (*Lungarno Guicciardini 7*
☎ *(055) 215240/284885*), a hushed, discreet beauty parlor
patronized by the aristocracy; **Mario di Via Della Vigna** (*Via*

della Vigna Nuova 22 ☎ *(055) 294813/298953)*, hairdressers to the Pitti fashion show models; and **Valentino** (*Via Tornabuoni 105* ☎ *(055) 212323)*, the favorite of English and American visitors. For information about gyms and sports see *Sports, leisure, ideas for children*.

Antica Farmacia di San Marco
Via Cavour 146 ☎ *(055) 210604. Map 5B4.*

This beautiful pharmacy, with its vaulted frescoed ceilings and rows of majolica jars, was founded in the 15thC by the Dominican monks of San Marco. Their specifics include an anti-hysteric, which might come in handy if you are visiting Florence in Aug. Excellent rose water and eaux de cologne.

Bizzarri
Via Condotta 32 ☎ *(055) 211580. Map 5D4.*

This serious, unusual — and, you may think, well-named — shop is at least worth a look. Founded in 1842, it sells pure natural chemicals, essences and herbs, and will mix your own perfume if you know the formula.

Mario di Via Della Vigna
Via della Vigna Nuova 22 ☎ *(055) 294813/298953). Map 4C2.*

Hairdressers to glamorous and busy women, including the Pitti fashion show models. The salon offers a range of beauty treatments, plus a well-stocked perfumery.

Officina Profumo-Farmaceutica di Santa Maria Novella
Via della Scala 16 ☎ *(055) 216276. Map 4B2.*

A perfectly preserved grand-ducal pharmacy: superb hand-made soaps, creams, lotions for every skin type and a delectable potpourri, all to original 17thC formulae. Service is notoriously grudging.

Profumeria Aline
Via Calzaiuoli 53 ☎ *(055) 215269. Map 4C4.*

The largest selection of cosmetics and perfumes in town, with ranges such as Clinique and Lauder.

Profumeria Inglese
Via Tornabuoni 97 ☎ *(055) 263748. Map 4C3.*

Founded by an Englishman in 1843. The mahogany shelves are well stocked with cosmetics, soaps and perfumes, but the medicines have been moved down the Via to the Farmacia Inglese.

Valentino
Via Tornabuoni 105 ☎ *(055) 212323. Map 4C3* [AE] [CB] [◉] [◎] [VISA]

For long a favorite hairdresser of English and American visitors.

Jewelry
Brunelleschi, Verrocchio, the Pollaiuolo brothers, Cellini, Ghiberti: some of the greatest Florentine artists trained as goldsmiths. The shops on the Ponte Vecchio have been occupied by jewelers and goldsmiths since 1593. At the **Casa dell'Orafo** (*Vicolo Marzio 2*), in a deconsecrated church near the Ponte Vecchio, there are some 30 jewelers, each one a specialist in repairing, re-setting or making pieces to clients' specifications.

Buccellati
Via Tornabuoni 71 ☎ *(055) 296579. Map 4C3* [AE] [CB] [◉] [◎] [VISA]

The Florentine branch of the famous Milanese family of jewelers makes handsome, heavy pieces, often in chased gold, inspired by the Renaissance.

Gherardi
Ponte Vecchio 8 ☎ *(055) 287211. Map 4D3* [AE] [CB] [◉] [◎] [VISA]

Known in Florence as the "official coral keeper," Gherardi's prices are about twice what you would pay in Naples, the source of most Italian coral, but the quality and design are superb. He also specializes in cultured pearls, jade, turquoise, tortoise-shell and cameos.

Manelli
Ponte Vecchio 14 ☎ *(055) 213759. Map 4D3* [AE] [CB] [◉] [◎] [VISA]

The Manelli family have been dealing in semiprecious and hard stones for four generations. They can be bought loose or they will string them into a necklace in half an hour or make ear-rings in a week.

Melli
Ponte Vecchio 44-46 ☎ (055) 211413. Map 4D3 AE *(●)* VISA

A rarified collection of antique jewelry, antique porcelains, silver and small *objets d'art*.

Piccini
Ponte Vecchio 23 ☎ (055) 294768. Map 4D3 AE CB *(●) (●)* VISA

Jewelers to the jet set, although the designs slightly dated and the prices too high-flown. They also sell antique jewelry and silver, and will re-set heirlooms. A family firm since 1895.

Rajola
Ponte Vecchio 24 ☎ (055) 215335. Map 4D3 AE CB *(●) (●)* VISA

Very chic enamel work and pieces set with colored stones.

Settepassi
Via Tornabuoni 25 ☎ (055)

215506. *Map 4C2* AE *(●)* VISA
The oldest and one of the grandest Italian jewelers, specializing in precious stones and Oriental pearls set to match the incomes and tastes of the wealthiest Italian families, and to adorn crowned heads of Europe. They also sell antique and modern silver.

Tozzi
Ponte Vecchio 19 ☎ (055) 283507. Map 4D3 AE CB *(●) (●)* VISA

A beguiling stock of delicate objects — coral charms, gold-mesh purses, Baroque pearls — some old, some modern, some real bargains if you know your own taste.

Ugo Piccini
Via Por S. Maria 9-11 ☎ (055) 214511. Map 4D3 AE CB *(●) (●)* VISA

More approachable — and affordable — than the grand jewelers of the Ponte Vecchio and Tornabuoni. The prices are fair and service pleasant. The attractive gold chains, priced by the weight, make excellent presents for special occasions.

Leather
Leather is to Florence what glass is to Venice; that is to say there is altogether too much of it, and very little of what is most prominently on display bears the slightest relation to the unrivaled workmanship of the great artisans who are still active, and whose creations are found in the shops below.

Locally produced leather goods can be up to 40 percent cheaper than abroad. If you want to see how it's done, visit the **Peruzzi** leather factory and shop (*Borgo dei Greci 8 ☎ (055) 263039*), which is open all day; or there is the one in the monastery of **S. Croce** (*Piazza S. Croce 16 ☎ (055) 244533*).

Alessandrini
Via Vaccarreccia 17 ☎ (055) 216088. Map 4C3 AE *(●) (●)* VISA

This is the Florence outlet for the delightful soft leather handbags manufactured by the Tuscan firm Enny.

Beltrami
Via Calzaiuoli 31 and 44 ☎ (055) 214030 and (055) 212418. Map 5C4 AE AE *(●) (●)*
Successful Florentine chain selling top quality men's and women's shoes, accessories and clothes.
(*Other branches at Via dei Pecori 16 ☎ (055) 213290; Via Calimala 9 ☎ (055) 212288; Via Tornabuoni 48 ☎ (055) 287779.*)

Bisonte
Via del Parione 35 ☎ (055) 215722. Map 4C2 AE CB *(●) (●)*
Fashionably sporty and youthful canvas and leather bags made in Florence.

Cellerini
Via del Sole 37 ☎ (055) 282533. Map 4C2 AE *(●)* VISA
Silvano Cellerini is the most skilled and stylish independent artisan in making leather, lizard and crocodile handbags in the city.

Ferragamo
Via Tornabuoni 16 ☎ (055) 292123. Map 4C3 AE CB *(●) (●)* VISA

Florence shopping

Salvatore Ferragamo was the first of the internationally renowned Italian shoemakers. He started in Hollywood in 1914, and bought this palace in the Tornabuoni in 1937. The business now has branches all over the world and makes clothes, ties and scarves too — all in the master's stylish mold.

Gucci
Via Tornabuoni 57-59 and 73
☎ *(055) 264011. Map 4C3* 🆎 💿
💿 📠
Home base for the durable and expensive leather status symbols.

Mannina
Via de' Guicciardini 16 ☎ *(055) 282895 and Via de' Barbadori 23* ☎ *(055) 211060. Both map 4E3.*
Extremely attractive and wearable hand-made shoes and handbags at reasonable prices.

Papini
Lungarno Archibusieri 10-14
☎ *(055) 287879. Map 5D4* 🆎 🆑
💿 💿 📠
The Papini family have been making well-crafted bags, briefcases, suitcases and solid leather boxes for 100yrs. They are also agents for Borbonese, Redwall and Basile.

Raspini
Via Roma 25-29 ☎ *(055) 213077. Map 5C4* 🆎 🆑 💿 💿 📠
Raspini is one of the glamorous names in Florentine leatherware, but unlike **Ferragamo** and **Gucci** it has no outlets abroad — only licensed imitators. (*Branches at Via Martelli 5-7 and Via Por S. Maria 72.*)

Taddei
Piazza Pitti 6. Map 4E2.
Leather boxes, frames, desk sets and jewelry cases hand-made on the premises by a family whose members have been working with leather for a century.

Linens and lingerie
You will find a nice selection of embroidered linens in Via Por S. Maria.

Loretta Caponi
Borgognissanti 12 ☎ *(055) 213668. Map 4C1* 🆎 💿 💿 📠
The dreamily girlish nightdresses hand-embroidered exclusively for Loretta Caponi are among the prettiest — and the most expensive — things you will see in Florence.

Il Parnaso
Via delle Caldaie 14. Map 4E2.
Lace and linens are finely hand-embroidered to antique designs in Giorgio Calligaris' atelier on the first floor. Ring for an appointment.

Street markets

Mercato delle Cascine
Map 6D3. Open Tues 7am-1pm.
This weekly market in the Cascine park is like a huge department store laid out under the poplars along the Arno.

Mercato Centrale
Maps 4&5A3-4. Open Mon-Sat 7am-1pm, 4-7.30pm.
Immediately N of Piazza S. Lorenzo, this impressive 19thC cast-iron food market is the central outlet, wholesale and retail, for fresh meat, fish and vegetables, and also for cheeses, oils and countless other foods.

Mercato Nuovo
Map 4D3. Open daily 9am-5pm.
The famous straw market, also known as the Porcellino. As well as straw there are leather goods, ceramics, linens and other handmade goods, and — a tripe seller!

Mercato delle Piante
Piazza della Repubblica. Map 4C3. Open Thurs 7am-1pm.
A weekly flower market is held here under the loggia of the central post office.

Mercato delle Pulci
Piazza dei Ciompi. Map 3C5. Open Tues-Sat 8am-1pm, 3.30-7pm, first Sun of each month 9am-7pm.
The flea market of Florence sells picturesque junk at irritatingly

jumped-up prices, but is good for ex-votos and old postcards.

Mercato di Sant'Ambrogio
Piazza Lorenzo Ghiberti. Map 3C3. Open weekday mornings.
A comprehensive food market with a more intimate atmosphere than the vast Mercato Centrale. There is a useful lunch counter and a coffee bar inside.

Mercato di San Lorenzo
Maps 4&5B3-4. Open daily 8am-8pm.
The biggest and most popular of the street markets sprawls all around the church of S. Lorenzo and into the adjacent streets. Best shoe bargains can be found on the Borgo S. Lorenzo side, where sandals and espadrilles are half shop price.

Textiles and trim

Florence still manufactures some of the most gorgeous furnishing fabrics in the world. It is an industry that dates back to the Middle Ages.

Antico Setificio Fiorentino
Via della Vigna Nuova 97 ☎ (055) 282700. Map 4C2.
Silk furnishing fabrics — taffetas, damasks, brocades, velvets, satins, borders, fringes and *passementerie* — will be made to order (minimum 30m) in any color or style. The factory across the Arno (*Via Bartolini 4 ☎ (055) 282700*) may be visited by appointment — telephone in advance.

Lisio Tessuti d'Arte
Via dei Fossi 45 ☎ (055) 212430. Map 4C2.
This astonishing firm was founded in 1906 by a master weaver who was inspired to reproduce the finest antique woven silk fabrics. Of the many designs taken from Old Master paintings, the Primavera brocade is the most popular. Lisio has made hangings for the Sistine Chapel, costumes for the Palio and for historic movies, and his creations are exhibited in textile museums throughout the world. The most elaborate designs are produced at the rate of only a few centimeters a day and prices, not surprisingly, are high, but you could follow the example of Florentine women who buy just enough for an evening skirt or dress.

Tuscany A to Z

The joy of Tuscany is that almost any corner of its beautiful and varied landscape is likely to harbor some natural or man-made treasure. Within this A to Z section, text and symbols describe highlight attractions. More cursory listings note additional sights and reliable but unremarkable hotels and restaurants.

Abbadia San Salvatore

Map 9I7. 143km (89 miles) s of Florence, 75km (47 miles) s of Siena. 53021. Siena. Population: 8,232 ℹ Via Mentana 97 ☎ (0577) 778608.
This dour little industrial town near the summit of **Monte Amiata** has grown up around the medieval abbey of San Salvatore. Skiing and climbing nearby. The medieval center is near Piazza XX Settembre.

Sights and places of interest
Abbazia di San Salvatore †
The abbey, founded in 743, became the richest and most powerful center of Benedictine feudalism in central Italy. All that remains is the 11thC church, adapted in the late 16thC and, below, the 8thC crypt supported by 36 columns with wonderful capitals.
Borgo Medioeval *(Old Town)*
A rare and fascinating example of a Gothic-Renaissance mountain village that is almost completely intact.

🍴 **Sala Carli** (*Via Pinelli 46* ☎ *(0577) 779444*).

🛏 🍴 Near the summit of **Monte Amiata**, 14km (9 miles) w, **La Capannina** (☎ *(0577) 789713* ▮▮▯ *open Apr-June, Oct-Nov, and on special request in other months*) is a quiet skiers' hotel, with restaurant.

Abetone
*Map **15**C4. 90km (56 miles) NW of Florence. 51021. Pistoia. Population: 859 i Piazza delle Piramidi Abetone ☎ (0573) 60001.*

In the mountains above **Pistoia** near the Tuscan-Emilian border, Abetone is one of the oldest-established ski resorts in the Apennines, with the most difficult and best-equipped runs in Tuscany. There is also a short summer season for walkers and climbers. Fir trees grow in the protected **forest of Abetone**. Nearby resorts include **Cutigliano** and **San Marcello**.

🛏 There are some 35 hotels, which maintain an adequate but not luxurious standard. One with a pleasant garden is **Bellavista** (☎ *(0573) 60028* ▮▯ *open mid-Dec to mid-Apr, mid-June to mid-Sept*).

🍴 **La Capannina** (*Via Brennero 256* ☎ *(0573) 60562, closed Tues dinner, Wed*), with rooms.

🍴 Outside Abetone: **Da Bizzino** (*Via Secchio 104* ☎ *(0573) 606690* ▮▮▯ *closed Mon, Tues*) is worth the 10min drive for fresh-picked mountain mushrooms, fresh pasta and apple tart; at Cutigliano, 12km (7½ miles) to the SE, is **Da Fagiolino** (*Via Carega 1* ☎ *(0573) 68014* ▮▯ *closed Tues dinner, Wed, Nov*).

Anghiari
*Map **13**F8. 105km (65 miles) SE of Florence, 28km (17 miles) NE of Arezzo. 52031. Pistoia. Population: 6,052.*
There are spectacular views of the upper Tiber valley as far as **Sansepolcro** from this attractive walled hill village. The battle of Anghiari (subject of Leonardo's famous cartoon for an unrealized painting) was fought in 1440 between Florence and Milan.

Sights and places of interest
In the 18thC church of **Santa Maria delle Grazie** is a *Last Supper* (1531) by G. A. Sogliani. The Renaissance **Palazzo Taglieschi** (*Piazza Mameli 16; ring for entrance*) houses a museum of local art and custom.

🍴 **Alighiero** ♣ (☎ *(0575) 788040* ▮▯ *closed Thurs*); **Castello di Sorci** ♣ (*Monterbone, 4km (2½ miles) on Arezzo road* ☎ *(0575) 789066* ▮▯ *closed Mon, bols*), where you get five hearty, wholesome courses and as much wine as you can drink at a low fixed price. See also **Sansepolcro**.

Shopping

Busatti Tessitura (*Via Mazzini 12* ☎ *(0575) 788424*). Specializes in linen, cotton, wool and hemp, since 1892.

Ansedonia
*Map **8**J5. 186km (115 miles) SW of Florence, 45km (28 miles) S of Grosseto. 58016. Grosseto. Population: 316.*
The rocky promontory on the S coast of Tuscany was the site of the Roman city of Cosa, founded in 273 BC. Excavations have produced evidence of a large and flourishing commercial and

agricultural colony, and in 1980 an important 1stC BC villa and its attendant farm buildings were uncovered nearby at Sette Finestre. Ansedonia has been developed with vacation villas.

Sights and places of interest
Ruins of Cosa
Entrance through Porta Romana.

After passing through the best preserved of the gates, the Roman main street leads to the forum. Nearby, a recently excavated private house and garden have been partially reconstructed; the domestic objects and decorations can be seen in the small **museum/restoration center** built by the American Academy. Above is the walled Acropolis and, at the highest point, the Capitolium (≼). Below, on the beach beyond the Roman port, long since silted up, is the so-called **Tagliata Etrusca**, a canal cut by the Romans between their port and the Lake of Burano.

Nearby sight
Lake of Burano
Capalbio Scalo ☎ *(0564) 898829* ⊡
A bird sanctuary since 1968.

═ **Il Pescatore** (*Via della Tagliata 13* ☎ *(0564) 881201* ⦀ *closed Tues, mid-Jan, Sept, Oct*), near the Tagliata. See also *Capalbio*, *Orbetello*, *Port'Ercole*, *Porto Santo Stefano*.

Arezzo ★
Map 12F7. 81km (50 miles) SE of Florence. 52100. Arezzo. Population: 92,087 ℹ *Piazza Risorgimento 116* ☎ *(0575) 20839.*

Arezzo today is a busy, prosperous, provincial town at the center of the rich farming country of the Valdichiana and Valdarno. Its factories manufacture agricultural equipment, women's fashions, leather goods and costume jewelry; and its streets buzz with new, imported motorcycles driven by stylish young Aretines with good jobs and a long, proud ancestry.

Etruscan Arezzo was one of the most powerful and sophisticated cities of the federation. Later, under the Romans, it became a key stronghold thanks to its strategic location commanding all the passes of the central Apennines. Aretine craftsmen were famous throughout the Roman world for their metalwork and ceramics. As an independent republic from the late Middle Ages its sympathies were predominantly Ghibelline, and it was in the Guelf-Ghibelline Battle of Campaldino in 1289 that Arezzo suffered its first defeat by the Guelf Florentines. The republic recovered in the early 14thC under the leadership of Bishop Guido Tarlati, when the Duomo, Palazzo del Comune, the Pieve and the church of San Domenico were built, but finally surrendered to Florence in 1384. Petrarch, Spinello Aretino, Pietro Aretino and Vasari were all born in Arezzo. And it was a leading Aretine family, the Bacci, who were responsible for what is surely one of the most inspired commissions in the history of Renaissance patronage: Piero della Francesca's frescoes in the church of San Francesco.

Events An antique market is held in the Piazza Grande, the main square, on the first Sun of every month; the stalls do business from noon on the previous day.

The annual historic spectacle is the Joust of the Saracen (*Giostra del Saracino*), which takes place in the Piazza Grande on the first Sun of Sept.

An international choral festival in June attracts competitors from all over the world.

Sights and places of interest
Casa di Giorgio Vasari ▥ ☆
Via XX Settembre 55.

Vasari lovingly supervised the building of his own house (1540-48), a delightful example of Mannerist domestic architecture. He also executed the frescoes, which count as the most ingenuous and charming of all his creations.

Duomo †

The imposing 13th-14thC cathedral of Arezzo has an early 20thC facade, a 19thC campanile and, on the right flank, an attractive 14thC portico. The interior is illuminated by high stained-glass windows by Guillaume de Marcillat of which the finest is the *Expulsion from the Temple* at the bottom of the right aisle. The 14thC tomb of *S. Donato* in the apse is a collaborative work by Sienese, Florentine and local artists. At the bottom of the left aisle is Piero della Francesca's oddly stiff *Magdalen* (after 1466), his only surviving work in Arezzo apart from the frescoes in San Francesco. To its left is the magnificent tomb of *Bishop Guido Tarlati* (1330) by Agostino di Giovanni and Agnolo di Ventura, possibly to a design by Giotto. In the sacristy, entered from the left aisle, is a striking and strongly personal detached fresco of *St Jerome* by Bartolomeo della Gatta. The late 18thC Chapel of the Madonna of Comfort contains fine terra cottas by the Della Robbias.

Museo Archeologico Mecenate
Via Margaritone 10.

The loggia of the 16thC monastery, which now houses the Archeological Museum, is built round a curve of the 1stC BC Roman amphitheater. The famous **coralline vases** (☆), glazed according to a technique invented by Aretine craftsmen in the 1stC BC and later much copied, are in Rm. VII.

Museo Statale d'Arte Medioevale e Moderna 🏛
Via S. Lorentino 8.
Attractively arranged on three floors of the 15thC **Bruni-Ciocchi Palace**,
which has a fine courtyard possibly designed by B. Rossellino. There are
important paintings by local artists, notably Margaritone d'Arezzo, Parri di
Spinello, Spinello Aretino, Bartolomeo della Gatta and Vasari; and, in Rms.
VI-VIII, a fine **collection of majolicas** (13th-18thC).

Piazza Grande ★
The main square of Arezzo is one of the liveliest and most architecturally
heterogeneous in Tuscany. The NE side is closed by Vasari's handsome
loggia (1573); its shop-fronts retain their original stone counters. On the w
is the apse of the Pieve and the extraordinary layered facade of the
Palazzetto della Fraternità dei Laici; its ground floor is Gothic (1377), the
Renaissance first floor was begun after 1434 by B. Rossellino who made the
sculptures, and the upper loggia was completed in 1460 by Giuliano and
Algozzo da Settignano, who added the balustrade.

Pieve di Santa Maria 🏛 † ★
Corso Italia, Piazza Grande.
The rigorously ornate **facade** of this parish church is the outstanding
example of Pisan-Lucchese Romanesque architecture in eastern Tuscany.
The church was erected between the mid-12thC and early 14thC. Notice the
fine relief carvings (1216) over the central portal. The tall campanile (1330)
is the emblem of Arezzo; pierced by 40 bifore windows, it is known locally
as "the tower of 100 holes." The nave is divided by clustered columns
supporting early Gothic arches. The oldest part of the church is the raised
presbytery where Pietro Lorenzetti's polyptych of the *Madonna and Saints*
hung over the high altar until withdrawn in 1979.

San Domenico †
Piazza Fossombroni.
Built between 1275 and the early 1300s, San Domenico has a Romanesque
portal and a Gothic campanile, which retains two of its original bells. The
interior is like a giant scrapbook of fragmented frescoes (15th-16thC). Over
the high altar is a moving painted *Crucifix* (1260-65) by the young Cimabue.

San Francesco 🏛 †
The Franciscan basilica in the center of Arezzo was built in the 13th-14thC
in the simple Umbrian-Tuscan style; the campanile is 15thC. In the choir is
one of the major artistic masterpieces of Europe: Piero della Francesca's
noble, compelling **frescoes (★)**, painted in the middle of his career; the
subject is the *Legend of the True Cross*. The legend links man's original sin
to his redemption by tracing a series of events whereby the tree from which
Adam ate the forbidden fruit becomes the Cross on which Christ is
crucified. Earlier painted interpretations of the story can be seen in *Santa
Croce* (see *Florence A to Z*) by Agnolo Gaddi and in San Francesco at
Volterra by Cenni di Francesco.

Piero's frescoes are badly decayed, especially on the w wall, and it takes
time to adjust one's eyes to the complex dimensions of the scheme and the
bare patches of plaster left by the latest restoration. Field glasses can be
rented in the church shop. The tonality of the right wall is cooler, and the
quality of the painting is higher; it was painted without assistance, probably
from 1452-59, before Piero's visit to Rome. The series is thought to have
been finished on the left wall after his return, with a good deal of
assistance. The narrative unfolds as follows.

Right wall, apex: In the right section of the frame Adam announces his
impending death; in the left section, the dead Adam is surrounded by his
children and Seth plants a branch of the tree in his father's mouth. **Central
band, left section:** The tree, grown so large that even Solomon cannot use
it for his palace, has been made into a bridge over the River Siloam; the
Queen of Sheba instinctively recognizes its sacred origins and kneels at the
bridge. **Right section:** The Queen of Sheba is received by Solomon and
predicts to him that a man will be nailed to the tree and the Jews will
thereby be disgraced.

Right window wall, center: The beam is buried by Solomon's order; the
scene deliberately prefigures the Carrying of the Cross. **Bottom:**
Constantine is asleep in his tent on the eve of battle; an angel announces
that he will be victorious if he fights for the sign of the Cross. **Right wall,
lowest band:** The victory of Constantine over Maxentius.

Left window, middle section: Judas is tortured and reveals the
whereabouts of the Cross.

Left wall, central band, left section: The Empress Helena discovers the
Cross; in the background a view of Arezzo represents Jerusalem **Right**

129

section: Judas proves the Cross by raising a man from the dead; the church in the background recalls the architectural style of Piero's friend and fellow mathematician, Alberti. **Lowest band:** 30yrs after the discovery of the Cross, the Persian King Chosroes has stolen it from Jerusalem; he is defeated in battle by Heraclius, Emperor of the East. **Apex:** Heraclius returns the Cross to Jerusalem.

Piero had the power of creating forms which immediately satisfy us by their completeness; forms which reconcile the mathematical laws of proportion with the stress and tension of growth, forms which combine the resilience of a tree trunk with the precision of a pre-dynastic jar.

Sir Kenneth Clark, *Piero della Francesca*

The other frescoes in the chapel are outside the main narrative. The most important is the *Annunciation*, on the lowest section of the left window wall, probably painted in 1466 after Piero's visit to Urbino. The prophet to the right of the window's apex is by Piero, the one on the left by an assistant. Returning to the nave, notice in the third chapel on the left the superb late 13thC *Crucifix of St Francis*, and in the second chapel the Pieroesque frescoes of the *Miracles of St Anthony of Padua* by Lorentino d'Arezzo. The glass of the rose window (1524) of the interior facade is by G. de Marcillat.

Other sights

Other points of interest in Arezzo include the Palazzo Comunale; the Fortezza Medicea, which commands splendid views; the churches of S. Maria in Gradi, SS. Annunziata, S. Agostino, and the Badia; and, 1.5km (1 mile) to the s of the Piazza della Repubblica, the church of S. Maria delle Grazie, with a graceful portico by B. da Maiano. In summer it is pleasant to picnic in the **Passeggio del Prato**, the public gardens behind the Duomo.

⟶ ⇌ **Continentale**
Piazza Guido Monaco 7, 52100 Arezzo ☎ *(0575) 20251* ⅢⅢ❑ *75 rms*
▬ *75* ◨ AE Φ ⓒ VISA *Restaurant closed Sun dinner, 2wks in Aug.*
Modern, comfortable and central. The local businessmen's favorite and the most reliable kitchen in Arezzo.
⬆ & ▢ ▱ ♠

⇌ Arezzo is one of the wealthiest cities in Italy. It is also the official birthplace of the now ubiquitous *papardelle a la lepre*. Nevertheless, there is no outstanding restaurant in town. The obvious choice, for its location next to the Church of San Francesco and for its ambience, is the **Buca di San Francesco** (*Piazza Umberto I* ☎ *(0575) 23271, closed Mon dinner, Tues, July* ⅢⅢ *to* ⅢⅢⅢ). Alternatives are **Le Tastevin** (*Via de' Cenci 9* ☎ *(0575) 28304* ⅢⅢ *closed Mon, Aug*) or **Il Torrino** (*Madonna del Torrino, 8km (5 miles) SE on Sansepolcro road* ☎ *(0575) 360264* ⅢⅢ *to* ⅢⅢⅢ *closed Mon*).

Artimino

Map **15E5**. *22km (14 miles) W of Florence. 50042. Firenze. Population: 260.*
An old walled village in a wine-producing zone.

Sights and places of interest
Artimino, Villa dell' ⅢⅢ ☆
This smiling Mannerist villa, known as the "Villa of the Hundred Chimneys," was built by Buontalenti as a hunting lodge for Ferdinand I. The rooms are decorated with good *pietra serena* fireplaces and frescoes attributed to Poccetti and Passignano. The estate has a shop and small restaurant where its own wines are available (see *Tuscan wines*).
San Leonardo ⅢⅢ ✝
This well-preserved Romanesque church was allegedly founded by Countess Matilda in 1107. It was constructed with Etruscan fragments from the nearby necropolis of Pian di Rosello.

Nearby sights

There are two Etruscan tombs near Comeana, 3km (2 miles) N, where signs point to the **Tomba dei Boschetti** (7thC BC) and the monumental **Tomba di Montefortini** (*ring for custodian*).

≈ **Paggeria Medicea** (*Viale Papa Giovanni XIII* ☎ *(055) 8718081*) is a peaceful hotel in a 16thC villa.

≡ Try **Biagio Pignatta** (☎ *(055) 8718086* **IIⅢ** *closed Wed, Thurs lunch*) in the hotel Paggeria Medicea; or **Da Delfina** (*Via della Chiesa* ☎ *(055) 8718074* **IIⅢ** *closed Mon eve, Tues, Aug*), a pleasant restaurant, specializing in game. Reservation essential. See also **Lastra a Signa**.

Asciano

Map 12G6. 91km (57 miles) SE of Florence, 20km (12½ miles) SE of Siena. 53042. Siena. Population: 5,897.

A walled medieval hill village in the upper Ombrone valley. The Corso Matteotti is lined with interesting old houses.

Sights and places of interest
Museo di Arte Sacra
Piazza Sant'Agata.

Left of the Travertine Collegiata di Sant'Agata (11thC but much restored) is this notable collection of 14th-15thC Sienese School painting and sculpture. Of special interest are the **polyptych** by the young Matteo di Giovanni; *St Michael and the Dragon* by A. Lorenzetti; *Birth of the Virgin* by the Master of the Osservanza; *Madonna* by Barna; and two graceful wooden statues of the *Annunciation* by Francesco di Valdambrino.
Museo Etrusco
Corso Matteotti.

In the former church of S. Bernardino, this museum houses material from the Etruscan necropolis of Poggiopinci, 5km (3 miles) E of Asciano.

Bagni di Lucca

Map 15D4. 101km (63 miles) NW of Florence, 27km (16 miles) N of Lucca. 55021. Lucca. Population: 7,991 i Via Umbertol 101 ☎ (0583) 87946/87245 (May-Oct).

The healing properties of the sulfur and saline waters at the Baths of Lucca were recognized from the 13thC, but it was a foreigner, Napoleon's sister Elisa Baciocchi, who gave Bagni di Lucca its Empire tone. Mrs Trollope was scarcely exaggerating when she wrote, "Bagni di Lucca belongs, like so much else in Italy, exclusively to foreigners." The list of distinguished foreign literary visitors includes Montaigne, Heine, Lamartine, Shelley, Byron, Landor, the Brownings and Ouida.

A little seedy now, Bagni di Lucca is nevertheless an inexpensive place to take the waters or merely to savor the somewhat claustrophobic atmosphere created by the mild, humid climate, the mature plane trees, and the weight of nostalgia for the vanished Victorian presence. Those who enjoy hill-climbing will share the pleasure Shelley took here.

In the Piazza del Bagno is a charming early 19thC bath house, now abandoned and crumbling. Just above is the **Palazzo Bonvisi**, where Shelley and Byron stayed and which Montaigne described. The **English Cemetery**, reached by a bridge over the River Lima behind the Circolo dei Forestieri, is sadly neglected.

≈ **Bridge** (*Ponte a Serraglia, 3km (2 miles) W* ☎ *(0583) 87147* **□**); **Svizzera** (*Via Contesa Cesalini 30* ☎ *(0583) 87114*).

≡ **Circolo dei Forestieri** (*Piazza Varraud* ☎ *(0583) 86038* **IIⅢ** *closed Mon, Jan*).

Bagni di Petriolo
Map 11H6. 30km (19 miles) SW of Siena, 43km (27 miles) NE of Grosseto. Grosseto.

"This place is ... in a deep valley made by the Farma River. It is famous for its trout. All around it rise lofty mountains, rocky but wooded and grassy too ... Here for twenty days the Pope had the warm waters poured through a pipe onto the crown of his head; for the physicians said this would be beneficial, since his brain was too moist," wrote Pius II, who took the waters here in 1460.

The little spa town is still surrounded by serenely lovely countryside and encircled by 15thC walls, built, according to the Pope, "that brigands might not lie in wait for the bathers as had sometimes happened in the past."

☞ ⇌ Terme di Petriolo
Civitella Marittima, 58040 Pari, Grosseto ☎ (0564) 908871 |||| 59 rms
🔲 *59 ⇌ Closed Nov-April.*
A well-managed and fully-equipped health spa. The service is unusually pleasant, and the restaurant serves fresh local produce that has been carefully prepared.
🏠 ⚡ 🖼 ≈ 🌶 ✓ 🐎 ♈ 🏊

Bagno a Ripoli
Map 12E6. 7km (4 miles) SE of Florence. 50012. Firenze. Bus no. 33. Population: 25,139.

This suburb of Florence was named after the remains of a Roman bath discovered in the 17thC. There is pretty hill country above, and the 14thC church of S. Pietro a Ripoli.

☞ Villa La Massa
50010 Candeli, Firenze ☎ (055) 630051 ⊕ 573555 ⊛ (055) 632579 ||||
42 rms 🔲 *42* 🈀 🚗 🅰🖬 🕙 🕞 🎥
A 16thC villa on the Arno, now a beautifully run and furnished hotel set in a romantic park. The restaurant, **Il Verrocchio**, is outstanding.
🏠 ⚡ ♿ ▢ 🖼 ♥ ⪪ ≈ 🌶 🏊

⇌ Centanni
Via Centanni 7 ☎ (055) 630122 |||| ▢ 🚗 🈀 ⇌ Closed Sat lunch, Sun, Aug.
In an entrancing location, especially on a hot summer evening.

Barga
Map 14D3. 111km (70 miles) NW of Florence, 37km (23 miles) N of Lucca. 55051. Lucca. Population: 10,952 ℹ Piazza Angelio ☎ (0583) 73499.

The prettiest hill town in the Garfagnana stands above an active industrial new town.
Event An opera festival takes place in summer.

Duomo *(San Cristofano)* ✝
The rectangular, buttermilk-colored Duomo, rebuilt from the 9thC, contains an extraordinarily well-preserved late 12thC **pulpit**, sculpted with all the serious charm of the period with scenes from the *Lives of Christ and Mary*.

In the apse is a huge wooden statue of *St Christopher*. In the chapel to the right are attractive unglazed Robbianesque terra cottas. The **loggetta of the Podestà**, to the left of the Duomo, preserves a rare set of 15thC official measures.

☞ ⇌ La Pergola *(☎ (0583) 711239 ▢ closed Fri in winter, Dec).*

Bibbiena
Map 12E7. 59km (37 miles) SE of Florence, 32km (20 miles)
N of Arezzo. 52011. Arezzo. Population: 10,716 i Via
Cappucci ☎ (0575) 93098.

The chief town of the Casentino, the remote upper valley of the
Arno enclosed by wooded mountains. The great monasteries of
Camaldoli and *La Verna* are reached by road from Bibbiena.
The 16thC **Dovizi Palace** — which once belonged to Benedetto
Dovizi, influential playwright, secretary of Pope Leo X and
patron of Raphael — stands opposite the 15thC church of **San
Lorenzo**.

The main street leads uphill to the delightful Piazza Tarlati,
which commands a view of the Casentino toward *Poppi* and
where there is a clock tower in the remains of the medieval
Tarlati fortress. The church of **SS. Ippolito e Donato**, rebuilt in
the 14thC and 15thC and later given a Baroque facelift, contains a
Madonna and Child (1435) by Bicci di Lorenzo and a panel of
the same subject (c.1420) by a rare artist, Arcangaelo di Cola da
Camerino.

Off the La Verna road is the Renaissance church of **Santa
Maria del Sasso**, with interesting paintings inside.

☞ ⊨ **Amorosi Bel** ✿
Via Dovizi 18, 52011 Bibbiena, Arezzo ☎ (0575) 593046 ⫼ 20 rms
▭ 12 ▥ Restaurant closed Wed; last orders 7.30pm.
This old inn has a solemn turn-of-the-century atmosphere.

Bivigliano
Map 12D6. 18km (11 miles) N of Florence. 50030. Firenze.
Population: 620 i Via delle Scuole 4.

A summer resort on the w slope of Monte Senario. High above
the town is the Convent of Monte Senario, the mother house of
the Servite Order, founded in the 13thC. The buildings date
mostly from the late 16thC. Stupendous views of the Arno and
Sieve valleys.

Nearby sight
9km (5.75 miles) s is the 15thC Servite **Convent of La Maddalena**, with
frescoes by Fra Bartolommeo.

☞ ⊨ **Giotto Park** (☎ (055) 406608 ☎ (055) 8456836 ⫼ to ⫼⫼ closed
Nov-Mar except Christmas; restaurant closed Tues, Wed lunch).

⊨ See *Fiesole*.

Borgo San Lorenzo
Map 12D6. 29km (18 miles) NE of Florence. 50032. Firenze.
Population: 14,724.

The principal center of the Mugello (see *Route 6* in *Planning*),
this town, now an industrial center, was destroyed by an
earthquake in 1919.

Nearby sights
3km (2 miles) N, approached by a fine avenue of cypresses, is the church of
S. Giovanni Maggiore, with an 11thC campanile and, inside, a rare
Romanesque intarsiaed ambo.

5.5km (3½ miles) w is **S. Piero a Sieve**, where the parish church contains
a terra-cotta font in the style of Luca della Robbia; above is Buontalenti's S.
Martino fortress.

To the NE of S. Piero a Sieve a country road leads to the **Convento del**

133

Bosco ai Frati, one of the original Franciscan communities, rebuilt (1420-38) by Michelozzo. In the sacristy is a wooden *Crucifix* attributed to Donatello. Two villas, **Cafaggiolo** (*now a hospital, open by appointment*) and **Trebbio**, both built by Michelozzo for the Medici, are to the w of S Piero a Sieve beyond Novoli.

7km (4 miles) SE is **Vespignano**, birthplace of Giotto. The house designated as Giotto's is N of the road. Farther along is **Vicchio**, where Fra Angelico was born and where Benvenuto Cellini took refuge from 1559-71 in the house next to the Oratory in Corso del Popolo.

3.5km (2 miles) NE of **Scarperia**, an industrial and crafts center with a fine Palazzo Pretorio of 1306, is the village of **Sant'Agata**, with a strikingly unusual Romanesque Pieve. The road to the N climbs through the **mountain pass of Scarperia** at 882m (2,894ft), the "little Switzerland" of the Mugello, known as "*il Giogo.*"

🛏 At San Piero a Sieve there are **Ebe** (*Via Provinciale* ☎ (055) 848019 *IIII* □ *closed Fri*) and **Da Felicina** (☎ (055) 848016 *IIII* □ *closed Sat*), which has rooms. Two useful restaurants at Barberino di Mugello are **Le Capannine** (*Viale Don Minzoni 88, Cavallino Mugello* (*near the autostrada exit*) ☎ (055) 8420078 *IIII* □ *closed Mon*) and **Il Cavallo** (*Viale della Repubblica 7* ☎ (055) 841363, *closed Wed*), which does good cheeses and fresh fish as well as meat. .

Camaldoli

Map 12E7. 71km (44 miles) SE of Florence, 46km (28 miles) N of Arezzo. 52010. Arezzo. Population: 50.
Camaldoli, mother house of a reforming Order of the Benedictines founded in the early 11thC by St Romauld, stands isolated high in the Apennines above the Casentino. Its buildings are mostly of the 17th-18thC, and of little interest apart from the 16thC **pharmacy**.

Eremo
2.5km (1½ miles) above the monastery, at 1,104m (3,622ft), is the **eremo** (hermitage) where the medieval monks lived in absolute isolation in the middle of their magnificent **forest**. The delightful Baroque church of Il Salvatore and the 20 monastic cells, including the one occupied by St Romauld, may be visited.

🛏 Near the monastery is **I Pucini** (☎ (0575) 556017, *open daily in summer, closed Sat and Sun in winter*).

🍽 **Il Cedro**
Moggiona, 5km (3 miles) s on the Poppi road ☎ (0575) 556080 *IIII* □ 🍷 🍴 ◁€ *Closed Mon during Oct-May.*
A serious and popular small restaurant overlooking the mountains.
Specialties: Sformati, tortelli di patate, fritti di verdure.

Capalbio

Map 8J6. 182km (113 miles) SW of Florence, 18km (11 miles) NE of Ansedonia. 58011. Grosseto. Population: 3,950.
This walled medieval village is a center of horse-breeding and near the large **Maremma hunting reserve**, open to the public in season (*inquiries to Riserva Turistica di Caccia dell'Ente Provinciale per il Turismo, Castello Collacchioni* ☎ (0564) 896024). Walk around the 14thC ramparts and through the old, unspoiled streets.

Restaurants
Capalbio is well endowed with attractive, aromatic restaurants, which serve hunters' food, especially wild boar (try the wild boar sausage) and roebuck cooked in unusually appetizing ways. Most light open fires in the winter and spread onto terraces in summer.

≋ **Da Maria** (*Via Comunale 3* ☎ *(0564) 896014* ▮□ *closed Feb, Tues except July and Aug*); **La Torre** (☎ *(0564) 896070* ▮□ *closed Thurs*); near the hunting reserve, 5km (3 miles) NW, **Al Fontanile dei Caprai** (☎ *(0564) 896216* ▮■□ *open Sat, also Sun in winter, eve in July and Aug, lunch on licensed hunting days*).

Caprese Michelangelo
Map 13F8. 123km (76 miles) SE of Florence, 45km (28 miles) NE of Arezzo. 52033. Arezzo. Population: 1,799.
An agricultural hill village where Michelangelo was born on Mar 6, 1475, while his father was the Florentine magistrate (*podestà*). The magistrate's house, the Casa del Podestà, is opposite the entrance to the restored 14thC **Castello**.

✍ ≋ **Fonte della Galletta** ♣ (*6km (4 miles) to W at Alpe Faggeto* ☎ *(0575) 793925* ▮□ *to* ▮▮□ ▲▣ *closed Oct-Apr, restaurant closed Wed*) for game and mushrooms.

Carmignano
Map 15E5. 22km (14 miles) W of Florence. 50042. Firenze. Population: 7,691.
This little town is surrounded by vineyards which produce the venerable Carmignano wines (see *Tuscan wines*).

San Michele ✝
In this Gothic parish church hangs Pontormo's *Visitation* (★), one of his greatest and best-known masterpieces.

≋ See **Artimino, Lastra a Signa**.

Carrara
Map 14D2. 126km (80 miles) NW of Florence, 55km (34 miles) N of Pisa. 54033. Massa-Carrara. Population: 70,213
ℹ *Via Garibaldi* ☎ *(0585) 70668.*
To reach the duomo in what remains of the old center of Carrara, one must penetrate a vast modern boom town still thriving on the quarries which have yielded their famous marble for over 2,000yrs. Today they are one of the major world sources, producing 500,000 tons a year.

Sights and places of interest
Duomo ▥ ✝ ☆
An ornate version of the Pisan-Lucchese style. The lower facade and portal date from the 12thC, and the elaborately carved Gothic upper story, with its rose window, was added in the 14thC. The simple, elegant interior contains a 14thC *Virgin Annunciate* and Gothic-style *Angel*.
   Piazza Alberica boasts some fine Baroque palaces including Pietro Tacca's birth place. In Piazza C. Battisti is the Neo-Classical **Teatro degli Animosi** (1840), admired by Dickens and other 19thC travelers.
Mostra Nazionale Marmi e Macchine
Viale XX Settembre ✸
A permanent exhibition demonstrating techniques of marble quarrying, cutting and carving. The **quarries** themselves, 7km (4 miles) to the E, at Colonnata and Fantiscritti, will admit visitors.

✍ **Michelangelo** (*Via Carlo Rosselli 10* ☎ *(0585) 777161-3* ▮□ *closed late Dec-early Jan*).

≋ **Soldaini** (*Via Mazzini 11* ☎ *(0585) 71459* ▮▮□ *closed Mon, Sun eve*) is cool and pleasant; 7km (4½ miles) toward Marina di Carrara at Avenza is **Il Muraglione** (*Via Fivizzano 13* ☎ *(0585) 58771* ▮▮▮ *closed Sun in winter*), an old country inn.

Cascina

Map 14E4. 75km (47 miles) SW of Florence, 17km (10 miles)
SE of Pisa. 56021. Pisa. Population: 34,701.
In this center of furniture manufacture is the 12thC **Pieve di
Santa Maria**, a remarkably well-preserved example of the Pisan
Romanesque style. The 14thC Oratory of San Giovanni is
frescoed (1398) inside by Martino di Bartolomeo.

Nearby sights
Vicopisano, 6km (3½ miles) to the NE, retains picturesque 14thC
fortifications restored by Brunelleschi. 9km (5½ miles) to the NW is Calci,
with a fine 11thC Pisan-Romanesque **Pieve**. Nearby on the Montemagno
road is the **Certosa di Pisa**, a splendid complex of 17th-18thC Baroque
buildings.

Castellina in Chianti

*Map 12F6. 50km (31 miles) s of Florence, 21km (13 miles) N
of Siena. 53011. Siena. Population: 2,843.*
This small town was the first seat of the medieval Chianti League
and one of the original centers of the Chianti Classico
wine-growing zone. The medieval **Rocca** was extended by the
Florentines in 1400; Etruscan remains include the 4thC BC tomb
of Montecalvario and a well.

⟳ Salivolpi
*Via Fiorentina, 53011 Castellina in Chianti, Siena ☎ (0577) 740484
❙❙ 19 rms.*
A charming family-run hotel.
🏠 🖾 🥾 🚶 ≈

⟳ Tenuta di Ricavo
*53011 Castellina in Chianti, Siena ☎ (0577) 740221 ❙❙❙❙ 25 rms ⬚ 25
━ ⬚ 🗐 Closed Nov-Mar.*
Location: 4km (2½ miles) s, on San Donato road. An isolated medieval
farming village transformed into an excellent Swiss-managed hotel.
🏠 🖾 🥾 ♒ ≈

⟳ Villa Casalecchi
*53011 Castellina in Chianti, Siena ☎ (0577) 740240 ❙❙ to ❙❙❙ 14 rms
⬚ 14 ━ ⬚ 🗐 AE ▣ 🖾 Closed Nov-Mar.*
Location: 1km s, on Siena road. Enfolded in a pine wood in the hills.
🏠 🖾 ♒ ◁ᛦ ≈

⚌ La Torre
*Piazza Umberto ☎ (0577) 740236 ❙❙❙ ☐ ⚌ 🚗 ━ ▣ 🖾 Closed Fri,
one week in Dec.*
A generous choice of perfected rustic dishes.

⟳ ⚌ See also *Greve, Radda in Chianti.*

Castello

*Map 6B3. 6km (3½ miles) NW of Florence. 50019. Firenze.
Bus no. 14 to Careggi from Florence Duomo or station.*
Here, at the base of Monte Morello, are three important Medici
villas within pleasant walking distance of one another. Two more
Medici villas, **Trebbio** and **Cafaggiolo**, are a short drive up the
Via Bolognese (see *Route 6* in *Planning*), and *Artimino* and
Poggio a Caiano are to the w. See *Sesto Fiorentino.*

Sights and places of interest
Villa Medicea della Petraia 🏛
☎ (055) 451208 ▣ ✗ *Villa open Tues-Sun 9am-1.30pm. Gardens*

open 9am-3.30pm in winter, 9am-4.30pm in spring, 9am-6.30pm in summer. Closed Mon.

The old castle, of which the adapted central tower remains, was rebuilt from c.1575-90 by Buontalenti for Cardinal Ferdinand de' Medici. In the courtyard, glassed over by Victor Emmanuel, who used it as a ballroom, is a pleasing fresco cycle glorifying the Medici by Volterrano. On the garden's upper terrace, Tribolo's elegant marble **fountain** is dominated by Giambologna's bronze *Venus*. To the E is a magnificent park.

Villa Medicea di Careggi 血

Viale G. Pieraccini. The villa is now a nurses' home: to visit, apply to the hospital of Santa Maria Nuova in Florence.

Careggi was one of the earliest villas used by the Medici for rest and study. The old castellated house was modified for Cosimo il Vecchio by Michelozzo, who added the loggiaed wing to the left in the 1430s. Cosimo, his son Piero and his grandson Lorenzo the Magnificent all died here. The villa was burned and looted after the expulsion of the Medici, and restored in the 16thC by Pontormo and Bronzino.

Villa Medicea di Castello 血 ☆

☎ *(055)454791* ▣ *Garden only open daily.*

Castello belonged to Lorenzo di Pierfrancesco de' Medici; Cosimo I was brought up here and hired Tribolo in 1537 to redesign the well-preserved **gardens** (★), which were completed in 1592 by Buontalenti, who rebuilt the villa. The **fountain** of *Hercules and Anteus*, with statues by Ammannati, was designed by Tribolo. The **grotto** with fountains and wonderful exotic animals is by Giambologna. The colossal bronze half-figure known as *January* in the terraced park is by Ammannati.

❧ **Villa le Rondini**
Via Bolognese Vecchie 224, 50139 Castello, Firenze ☎ *(055) 400081*
Ⓣ *575679* Ⓕ *(055) 268212* ▮▮▯ to ▮▮▮▮ *35 rms* ▭ *35* ⇔ ▨ ⇆ [AE] ◉ ▣
[VISA]

A peaceful hotel in a 16thC villa on the hill of Monterinaldi.
▱ ▨ ❧ ⦉ ⇜ ℘ ⧖ ▦ ♈

⇶ **Lo Strettoio**
Serpiolle ☎ *(055) 403044* ▮▮▮▮ ▭ ⇴ *Closed Sun, Mon, Aug.*
Honest home cooking in an old mill. Reservation essential.

Castiglion Fiorentino
Map 12G7. 100km (62 miles) SE of Florence, 17km (10½ miles) S of Arezzo. 52043. Arezzo. Population: 11,164
i *Corso Italia 111.*

This walled market town, a major center in the Valdichiana, slopes down a hill above the Arezzo-Cortona road.

Sights and places of interest
The graceful 16thC **Loggia del Vasari** in the central Piazza del Municipio frames a fine view, and from the **castle keep** above it one can see over the Valdichiana as far as *Monte Amiata*.

Palazzo Comunale/Pinacoteca
Piazza del Municipio.

The most notable works in the gallery include a cheering 15thC reliquary bust of *St Ursula* as a shy, happy girl, made in the Rhineland; a 13thC Umbrian painted crucifix; and paintings by Bartolomeo della Gatta. There are also paintings by Bartolomeo della Gatta in the **Collegiata** and, in the adjoining **Pieve**, a *Deposition* (1438) by Signorelli. The late 13thC church of **S. Francesco** has a *St Francis* (1280-90) by Margaritone d'Arezzo.

Nearby sights
On a hilltop 4km (2½ miles) S is the imposing 13thC **Castello di Montecchio Vesponi** (*not open to the public*), given by the Florentines to the English *condottiere* Sir John Hawkwood.

Castiglione della Pescaia
Map 10I4. 162km (101 miles) S of Florence, 22km (14 miles) W of Grosseto. 58043. Grosseto. Population: 8,376.

The main coastal resort of the Maremma is also a busy fishing village, and private and professional craft moor in the lively harbor at the mouth of the River Bruna. Above is the 14th-15thC **Rocca Aragonese** defending the original medieval village, now over-gentrified. To the s stretch sand beaches.

✍ **David** (*at Poggiodoro, 2km (1¼ miles)* N ☎ *(0564) 939030* ⅢⅢ *closed mid-Oct to Easter*) is a quiet hotel with views.

✍ **Riva del Sole**
58043 Castiglione della Pescaia, Grosseto ☎ *(0564) 933625* ⅢⅢ *176 rms* ▭ *176* ▦ ═══ ▬ ⓐ ⓔ ⓒ ⅧⅢ *Closed Oct-Apr.*
A large, modern hotel in a new resort 3km (1.75 miles) up the coast.
▱ ⟨ ⅋ 🖼 🐾 ⚲ ⚲ ⚲ ⚲ ⚲ ✦ ⚲

═ **Da Romolo**
Via della Libertà 10 ☎ *(0564) 933533* ⅢⅢ ▭ *Closed Tues, Nov.*
The best of the fish restaurants. **Specialty:** *Spaghetti con frutti di mare.*

═ Or try **Il Gambero** (*Via Ansedonia 29* ☎ *(0564) 937110* ⅢⅢ).

✍ ═ **Tana del Cinghiale**
At Tirli, 17km (10½ miles) N *of Castiglione* ☎ *(0564) 945810* ⅢⅢ
Closed Wed, mid-Jan to mid-Feb.
A hunting lodge, with rooms, specializing in wild boar.

Certaldo
*Map **11**F5. 40km (25 miles)* SW *of Florence, 40km (25 miles)* NW *of Siena. 50052. Firenze. Population: 15,899.*
Certaldo Alto, the fortified red-brick village where Boccaccio spent much of his life and died in 1375, stands above a modern suburb in the valley of the Elsa. The village was rebuilt in the 15thC and restored, a little too crisply, in the 19thC and again after World War II.

Sights and places of interest
Casa del Boccaccio
Via Boccaccio 18. Ring next door as signposted for entry.
A postwar reconstruction of a house that possibly belonged to Boccaccio's family.
Palazzo Pretorio
Piazzetta del Vicariato.
Rebuilt in the 15thC, this palace has a pretty courtyard with *quattrocento* frescoes by P.F. Fiorentino and, in the adjacent chapel, fresco fragments by Gozzoli and Giusto d'Andrea.
SS. Michele e Jacopo †
Boccaccio's tomb was removed in 1783 by those who disapproved of his work. The modern tomb carries his own epitaph and his portrait bust (1503) by G.F. Rustici.

Excursion
The Franciscan convent of **San Vivaldo** is 20km (12½ miles) SW by a twisting road. The present convent, from the early 16thC, is enfolded in the forest of Boscolazzeroni. The pilgrim chapels, each with a painted terra-cotta scene from the Passion, are unique in Tuscany. There are fine Romanesque churches at Pieve a Chianni, San Pancrazio and San Lazzaro a Lucardo.

═ See *San Gimignano*.

Chianciano Terme
*Map **9**H7. 120km (75 miles)* SE *of Florence, 85km (53 miles)* SE *of Siena. 53042. Siena. Population: 7,294.*

If you are driving from Chiusi you will see two Chiancianos: the old hill town and, below it, the modern spa, one of the most important in Italy. The curative powers of the waters have been valued since the Roman age. There are various types of water for internal consumption or bathing.

A lovely rural road to the s leads to Sarteano, after 7.5km (5 miles), and Cetona, 14km (9 miles), both of them Etruscan villages.

☞ There are some 200 hotels and boarding houses of all categories during the season (Easter-Oct).

La Casanova
Strada della Vittoria 10 ☎ *(0578) 60449* //// ⊡ ≡ ⊕ ⊸ AE ⊙ VISA
Closed Wed, Jan-Feb; Nov-Dec open evenings only.
Set invitingly in a wooded park, this elegant restaurant offers Tuscan cooking with inventive touches.

Chiusi
Map 9H7. 126km (79 miles) SE of Florence, 67km (42 miles) s of Arezzo. 53043. Siena. Population: 9,108 i Via Petrarca 4 ☎ (0578) 20003.

The Etruscan city of Camars, one of the greatest of the lucomonies, is best known to classical scholars and readers of Macaulay's *Horatius* for its king, Lars Porsena, who attacked Rome in 508BC. Today Camars lies buried around and under the little town of Chiusi, whose street plan is that of Clusium, the Roman military colony it became in 296BC.

Sights and places of interest
Duomo †
Beneath the campanile of the Romanesque cathedral, constructed from building fragments of the two earlier civilizations, is a large **cistern**, possibly 1stC BC. To visit, apply to the Museo Etrusco.
Museo Nazionale Etrusco ★
One of the outstanding Etruscan museums in Italy. The material, excavated from the vast necropolis surrounding the city, notably demonstrates the influence of Greece, Mesopotamia, Egypt and Rome on its sophisticated and receptive culture. There is a superb and varied collection of cinerary urns and sarcophagi, of which the most famous is the sarcophagus depicting the battle of the Gauls with a **portrait of Lars Sentinates** on the cover. Also noteworthy are specimens of the heavy black *bucchero* ware, imitating metal, which was made only in Chiusi, and an unusually fine collection of Attic vases.
Necropoli Etrusca
✗ *compulsory. Visits only permitted with guides from the Museo Etrusco.*
The most notable Etruscan tombs are: To the N, along the Via delle Tombe Etrusche: the c.3rd-4thC BC **Tomba della Pellegrina**, with fine sarcophagi; the 5thC BC **Tomba della Scimmia** (Monkey Tomb), which retains rare wall paintings; and the Tomba del Granduca, with cinerary urns. To the E: the 5thC BC **Tomba Bortci Casuccini**, with its original door and frescoes of games; and the 1stC BC **Tomba delle Tassinaie**.

Il Patriarca ✿
Querce al Pino, 53043 Chiusi ☎ *(0578) 274007* //// 22 rms ⊡ 22 ⊸
⌂ ≡ VISA *Restaurant closed Wed.*
The most pleasant of a cluster of hotels serving the autostrada exit.
⌂ ⊡ ⚲ ☂

La Frateria di Padre Eligio
10km (6 miles) s at Cetona in the Convent of San Francesco
☎ *(0578) 238015/238261* //// ≡ *Closed Tues, Jan.*
A first-class restaurant, with good local wines, in the refectory of a converted Franciscan convent. Five rooms.

≈ 2.5km (1½ miles) to the N, on shore of Lake Chiusi, **La Fattoria** (*with rooms* ☎ *(0578) 21407* **▮▮▯** *to* **▮▮▮▮** *closed Mon, Feb*), where tiled floors and beamed ceilings give a farmhouse atmosphere; also **Zaira** (*Via Arunte 12* ☎ *(0578) 20260* **▮▮▯** *closed Mon in winter*), a delightful restaurant in the center serving inventive food.

Colle di Val d'Elsa
*Map **11**F5. 49km (30 miles) s of Florence, 25km (15 miles) NW of Siena. 53034. Siena. Population: 15,618.*

There is an impressive view of this two-tiered town from the *Monteriggioni* road. The upper town has conserved its medieval street plan and some fine architecture.

Colle di Val d'Elsa has been a manufacturing center of fine crystal glass from the mid-14thC. Fiercely contested between Siena and Florence in the 13thC, the town became part of the Florentine dominion in 1333.

The architect and sculptor Arnolfo di Cambio was born here in 1232.

Sights and places of interest
Colle Bassa
The lower town is also known as il Piano, and its hub is the lively Piazza Arnolfo di Cambio. Nearby in Via dei Fossi is the church of **S. Agostino** with an unfinished 13thC facade and beautiful 16thC interior designed by Antonio da Sangallo the Elder.

Colle Alta ☆
The upper town and the remains of its 12th-13thC fortifications are strung along the ridge of the hill. Notice the frescoed palace facades in Via XX Settembre and other streets. The **Porta Nuova**, leading to the Volterra road at the end of Via Gracco del Secco is a fine piece of late 15thC military architecture, probably by Giuliano da Sangallo. The medieval village is reached by a bridge from which there are fine views; straddling the ravine is the splendid unfinished Mannerist **Palazzo Campana** (1539) by Giuliano di Baccio d'Agnolo.

The **Via del Castello** opens into the Piazza del Duomo where the 14thC Palazzo Pretorio houses the **Antiquarium Etrusco** displaying material excavated from a necropolis near Monteriggioni. Inside the Baroque **Duomo** (1619) is a bronze *Crucifix* over the high altar attributed to Giambologna and a bronze lectern by P. Tacca. The **Palazzo Vescovile** (*Via Castello 27*) houses a little **Museo d'Arte Sacra**, where ecclesiastic vestments and objects and a late 14thC Sienese school triptych are displayed in one frescoed room.

In the old Palazzo dei Priori is the **Museo Civico**, with pictures by R. Manetti, P. F. Fiorentino and others; under a loggetta are frescoes by S. Ferri of *David and Goliath* and *Judith and Holofernes.* Toward the bottom of Via Castello, no. 63 is the early 13thC **tower-house of Arnolfo di Cambio**.

≈ Villa Belvedere
53034 Belvedere ☎ (0577) 920966 ☎ 575304 **▮▮▯** *15 rms* 🛏 *15* 🚗 🚪
≈ 🖻 ⬛ 𝑉𝐼𝑆𝐴
This hotel in an 18thC villa, a former residence of Tuscan grand dukes, is set in a park planted with magnificent old trees. Under the same management as the Palazzo Ravizza in Siena.
🏠 🖻 ⚘ 🐎 ⟪ 𝇊 ⛵ 🐎 ☕ 🍽

≈ Arnolfo
Piazza Santa Caterina 2 ☎ (0577) 920549 **▮▮▮▮** ≈ 🍴 *AE* ◧ *Closed Tues, mid-Jan to mid-Feb.*
The atmosphere, of a hushed temple of food, verges on the pretentious. But the professionally prepared seasonal specialties justify the Michelin star, and the wines, served with ceremonious solemnity, are fabulous. Reservations essential.

≈ ≈ **La Vecchia Cartiera** (*Via Oberdan 5-9* ☎ *(0577) 921107* **▮▮▯** *closed Sun eve, Mon, July*); and **Da Viro** (☎ *(0577) 920231, closed Sun*), a new restaurant run by a young couple.

Excursion
A minor road runs s off the Volterra road from S. Maria delle Grazie through beautiful countryside to the old hill towns of **Casole d'Elsa** (14km/9 miles) and **Radicóndoli** (32km/20 miles).

Collodi
Map 15D4. 63km (39 miles) NW of Florence, 17km (10 miles) NE of Lucca. 51014. Pistoia. Population: 2,233.
Just to the w of *Pescia* is the village where Carlo Lorenzini, author of *Pinocchio*, spent his youth and gained his pen name, Carlo Collodi.

Sights and places of interest
Parco di Pinocchio
✷ *Open daily until sunset.*
Games, statues and pavilions on the theme of Pinocchio and his creator.
Villa Garzoni Gardens ☆
▨ *Open daily.*
The most famous of Tuscan Baroque gardens was laid out in the 17thC and further embellished with waterworks, statuary and French parterres in the late 18thC by Ottaviano Diodati.

Gambero Rosso (*Via S. Gennaro 2* ☎ *(0572) 429364* ▯ *to* ▯▯ *closed Mon eve, Tues, Nov*), dull but convenient. See also *Pescia*.

Cortona ☆
Map 13G8. 102km (63 miles) SE of Florence, 32km (20 miles) SE of Arezzo. 52044. Arezzo. Population: 22,561.
The mythical founder of Cortona was Corythus, father of Dardanus, which suggests that Cortona was older than Troy; and certainly the town was already long established when it was occupied by the Etruscans in the 8th-7thC BC. The Romans took over in the 4thC BC; and in 217BC the main Roman army was destroyed nearby at Lake Trasimeno by the Carthaginian general Hannibal. The commune which emerged from the Dark Ages in the 12thC was brutally sacked by Arezzo in 1258, recovered in the 14thC under the steadying rule of the Casali lords, and was eventually sold to Florence in 1411. The new association with Florence and the arrival of Fra Angelico, who spent some 10yrs in the monastery then attached to San Domenico, freed the art of Cortona from the archaizing domination of Siena. In the second half of the 15thC Cortona produced its own great native painter, Luca Signorelli, whose work can be seen in the Diocesan Museum and the church of San Nicolò. The painters Pietro da Cortona and the Futurist Gino Severini were also natives of Cortona.

Modern Cortona, the principal town of the Valdichiana, is a serious place inhabited by farmers and bookish foreigners.

The brown sandstone buildings of the old town are scattered down the steep upper slope of Monte Sant'Egidio and wrapped in medieval walls, which incorporate large sections built by the Etruscans. The main street, Via Nazionale, known locally as Ruga Piana because it is the only level street, leads from Piazza Garibaldi to the medieval nucleus, Piazza Repubblica.
Events Market day is Sat. There is an annual antique fair from Aug 25-Sept 25.

Sights and places of interest
Leave time to explore some of the atmospheric old streets: Vie Benedetti, Maffei, Guelfa, Roma, Dardano and Berretini.

Museo dell'Accademia Etrusca ⅏
Palazzo Pretorio, Piazza Signorelli.

The Palazzo Pretorio, which houses the Etruscan Academy, was built in the 13thC and was later the residence of the Casali rulers; it was extended in the 17thC. In the main hall is the centerpiece, the famous but repulsive 5thC BC **Etruscan Lamp** (★), the largest and most elaborate Etruscan object of its kind. Small Etruscan objects are displayed in the glass cases, and among the pictures are the entrancing Greco-Roman painting on slate of the *Muse Polyhymnia* and a very fine Pietro da Cortona *Madonna and Saints*.

The following rooms are filled with an intriguing, badly-labeled miscellany of Egyptian objects, porcelains, a good coin collection and, at the end, a small room devoted to Gino Severini.

Museo Diocesano ⅏
Piazza Trento Trieste.

This important museum is opposite the Duomo in a former church, which was modified and partly frescoed by Vasari. Its rather gloomy atmosphere is lit up with the glowing spirituality of Fra Angelico's *Annunciation* (1433) (★); the predella is unusually fine, especially the episode of the *Meeting at the Golden Gate*. The other Angelico, a triptych of the *Madonna and Child with Saints*, also has a superb predella depicting *Scenes from the Life of St Dominic*. Most notable among a number of Signorellis are his *Deposition* and *Communion of the Apostles*. Other highlights are the Sassetta *Madonna and Saints*; P. Lorenzetti's *Crucifix* and *Madonna and Angels*; and the Roman **sarcophagus decorated with Amazons and Centaurs**, admired by Brunelleschi and Donatello.

At the far end of Via Dardano is the **Porta Colonia**, the best-preserved section of Etruscan wall, which commands a wonderful view.

Other sights

The most charming of the churches is **San Domenico**, which contains frescoes by Fra Angelico and Signorelli and an altarpiece of the *Assumption* (c.1485) by Bartolomeo delle Gatta. Behind it are public gardens where one may walk and enjoy fine views of the plain below. The **Sanctuary of St Margaret**, farther along Via S. Margherita, is an ugly 19thC church, which conserves the beautiful Gothic **tomb of St Margaret** by Angelo and Francesco di Pietro. From there it is a short climb to the **Fortezza Medicea**, commanding another magnificent view.

Nearby sights

Madonna del Calcinaio ⅏ † ★
3km (2 miles) s, off Camucia road. For entry ask custodian, who lives in adjacent farmhouse.

A masterpiece of church architecture, designed (1485-1513) by the military engineer Francesco di Giorgio, and notable for the springing energy of the interior space, which is organized so that the crossing is lit at all times of day by the round windows above. Vasari's answer, the church of **Santa Maria Nuova** (1554), is above the town.

There are four **Etruscan tombs** in the vicinity. Those at Sodo, to the NW toward Arezzo, and at Camucia, to the s toward Lake Trasimeno, are under huge mounds of earth known as *meloni*, and date from the 7th-6thC BC. The two near the Madonna del Calicinaio, the Grotta di Tanella and the Tanella Angora, may date from the 4thC BC.

3.5km (2 miles) to the NE, in a lovely situation, is the **Convent Le Celle**, founded by St Francis between 1211-21; one may visit St Francis' cell and the little 16thC church.

⚘ **Oasi G. Neuman**
Via Contesse 1, 52044 Cortona ☎ (0575) 603188 ▯▯ 36 rms ▭ 36 ⇌
▭ ⊟ *Closed Oct-Mar.*
Location: Just outside walls to the s. In a former convent.
▱ ⚘ ⚘ ⚘

⚘ **San Michele**
Via Guelfa 15 (0575) 604348 ▯▯▯ 36 rms ▣▣ ▣▣ ▣ ▣ ▣▣
All mod cons, in a medieval street in the center.
⇕ ⚲ ▢ ▱ ⚘

⇛ Local dishes are served in the cool, intimate, brick-vaulted rooms of **La Loggetta** (*Piazza Pescheria ☎ (0575) 603777 ▯▯▯ closed Mon, also Sun in* *winter, Jan)*; **Tonino** *(Piazza Garibaldi 1 ☎ (0575) 603100 IIIII closed Tues)* is a noisy restaurant known for its antipasti.

Elba ★

Map 10l2-3. Province: Livorno. Getting there: By ferry, from Piombino, 1hr by car ferry, 30mins by hovercraft (ferries run frequently through the day, reservation advisable July-Aug), from Livorno, daily boat takes 3hrs direct to Portoferraio or 5hrs with stops at islands of Gorgona and Capraia; by air, summer flights from Pisa. Population: 28,429.

Elba is the largest of the Tuscan islands, at 27km (17 miles) long and 18km (11 miles) across at its widest, E end, with an extremely irregular coastal perimeter measuring nearly 150km (93 miles). The highest point is the summit of the granite Monte Capanne (1,018m/3,340ft.), which dominates the wild western lobe of the island. Around the rest of the coast majestic cliffs alternate with inviting sandy bays backed by evergreens.

The iron ore of Elba has been mined for at least 3,000yrs. The Greek name for the island was Aethalia (Soot Island). The Etruscans transported the iron ore in great quantities to the mainland for smelting at *Piombino*; the main port was named Portoferraio (Port Iron) in the 8thC.

The more recent history of Elba was affected by two of the great modern imperialists, Duke Cosimo I of Florence and Napoleon. In 1548 Cosimo built and fortified Portoferraio and called it Cosmopolis. His ostensible purpose was to police the pirate-infested Tyrrhenian Sea; his more compelling motive was to gain a stronghold against the forces of Spain and France. In the end he was obliged to share control of the island with the Spanish, who built their own fortress at Porto Azzurro.

In 1814 the Congress of Vienna ceded Elba to Napoleon as his dominion in exile. He spent nine restless months here, reforming the administration of the island, furnishing his two villas, and plotting his escape, which took place on Feb 26, 1815.

The island can offer vacationers facilities for sailing, waterskiing, underwater fishing, tennis, golf and riding.

Hotels and restaurants on Elba

The standard of the 140 hotels on the island is extremely variable. Many hotels insist on half-board, which is a pity, because their kitchens can rarely cope with the fresh fish which is the great gastronomic treat of Elba. Nearly every species of Mediterranean fish is caught in the clear waters; which one you order will determine the price of your meal. All the local wines are excellent, with a distinctive flavor from the minerals in the soil.

A-Z of towns

Capoliveri

Map 10l3. 5km (3½ miles) sw of Porto Azzurro. Population: 2,397.

An isolated mining, fishing and wine-producing village on the SE lobe of the island below the iron mountain of Monte Calamita. Stunning views to the W.

☜ **Antares** *(8km (5 miles) N at Lido ☎ (0565) 940131 Iⵏⵏ to IIIⵏ closed Nov-Mar)* is a quiet hotel with good views.

═ **Il Chiasso** *(☎ (0565) 968709 IIIII closed Tues, Nov-Easter).*

Lacona

Map 10l3. 14km (9 miles) s of Portoferraio. Population: 200.

A quiet bathing resort on the s coast at the head of the long promontory that Napoleon made into his hunting estate.

⌑ Capo Sud
Lacona, 57037 Portoferraio, Isola d'Elba ☎ *(0565) 964021* 💳 *to* 💳💳
39 rms 🛏 *39* 🚗 🏠 ⚊ 🍽 *Closed Oct-Apr.*
A quiet and comfortable group of cottages.
🏠 📺 ⚘ 《 ✓

Marciana
Map 10I2. 27km (17 miles) w of Portoferraio. Population: 2,272.
This wine-producing village on the slope of Monte Capanne is
dominated by the ruined castle of Appiano, the hereditary rulers
of Elba in the Middle Ages. The **Antiquarium** (*apply to
custodian in Via della Fonte*) displays prehistoric, Etruscan and
Roman material.

The **summit of Monte Capanne** (★) is reached by funicular
(🚠) in 30mins or by mule in about 2½hrs. A 40min drive to the
NW is the sanctuary of the **Madonna del Monte**, where
Napoleon stayed in 1814.

⌑ At Sant'Andrea, 6km (4 miles) NW, **Cernia** (☎ *(0565) 908194* 💳) and
Piccolo Hotel Barsalini (☎ *(0565) 908013* 💳) are both peaceful hotels
with gardens, closed Nov-Mar.

⚊ **Publius** (*at Poggio* ☎ *(0565) 99208* 💳💳💳 *closed Mon, mid-Nov to late
Mar*), good Tuscan cooking and one of the loveliest views on Elba.

Marciana Marina
Map 10I2. 20km (12½ miles) w of Portoferraio. Population: 1,907.
A relatively unspoiled fishing village in a lovely open position.

⌑ Gabbiano Azzurro
57033 Marciana Marina, Isola d'Elba ☎ *(0565) 99226* 💳 *39 rms*
🛏 *39* 🍽 🚗 💳 💳 🍽 🍽 💳
Modern, straightforward, friendly. No dining-room.

⚊ Two popular medium-priced fish restaurants on the harbor are
Rendez-Vous da Marcello (☎ *(0565) 99251, closed Wed in winter*) and
Teresina (☎ *(0565) 99049, closed Tues, Dec-Jan*).

Marina di Campo
Map 10I2. 17km (10½ miles) SW of Portoferraio. Population: 1,732.
This fishing village and bathing resort commands a wide arc of
sand beach on the Gulf of Campo on the S coast.

⌑ Lo Scirrocco
Loc. Fetovaia Casa 19, 57034 Campo nell'Elba ☎ *(0565) 987060* 💳
16 rms 🛏 *16* 🏠 🚗 ⚊
Location: 9km (6 miles) W at Fetovaia. A handsomely decorated and
comfortable private hotel overlooking a pleasant, isolated sand beach.
🏠 ⚓ 📺 🦆 ⚘ 《 ✓ ♿

⌑ Also at Fetovaia, **Galli** (☎ *(0565) 987965* 💳 *closed Oct-Apr*).

⚊ **Bologna**
Via Firenze 27 ☎ *(0565) 97105* 💳 💳 💳 💳 🍽 💳 💳 *Closed Tues,
mid-Oct to Mar.*
A big, cheerful fish restaurant in an old boat house.

⚊ **Da Gianni** (*at La Pila Airport* ☎ *(0565) 976965* 💳 *to* 💳💳💳 *closed
Nov-Feb*).

Porto Azzurro
Map 10l3. 15km (9 miles) se of Portoferraio. Population: 2,960.

The center of the Spanish protectorate in the 16th-17thC, Porto Azzurro is still a charming sight from the Narengo side of the Gulf of Mola, although the harbor front has been spoiled by timid development.

To the N is the massive Fortezza di Portolongone, built by the Spanish in 1603; soon afterward they built the nearby sanctuary of the **Madonna di Monserrato**, which still stands 1.5km (1 mile) N of the town.

Portoferraio
Map 10l3. Population: 11,135.

The busy main town of Elba is magnificently situated on a promontory which shelters its fine harbor. The old port is guarded by two fortresses that were built by Cosimo I in 1548, the large **Forte del Falcone** and the picturesque **Forte della Stella**.

Sights and places of interest
Palazzina Napoleonica dei Mulini ☆

Napoleon created his residence in exile from two old windmills above the city near Forte della Stella. The furnishings for this delightful little palace were commandeered from his sister Elisa's house at Piombino; the plate and library were brought from Fontainebleau.
Villa Napoleonica di San Martino ☆

6km (4 miles) to w, on Marciana road.

Even in exile, an emperor must have a country estate; Napoleon filled this modest villa with personal symbols.

The long Neo-Classical **Pinacoteca Foresiana** (1851), nearby, houses a large collection of 16th-19thC art.

≈ **Fabrica**
57037 Portoferraio ☎ *(0565) 966181* ✆ *590033* IIII *to* IIIII *75 rms*
🛏 *75* ⇒ ⊞ *AE* ⊡ *Closed Oct-Apr.*
Location: 8km (5 miles) se at Magazzini.
🏠 ⚓ ⁅ ⇌ 🖼 ⚘

≈ **Hermitage**
La Biodola, 57037 Portoferraio ☎ *(0565) 969932* ✆ *500219 (summer)
211116 (winter)* ⊛ *(0565) 969984* IIIII *120 rms* 🛏 *120* ⊞ ⇒ ⇌ 🏠 *AE*
Closed Oct-Apr.
Location: 10km (6 miles) sw at La Biodola. Discreetly set into a hillside overlooking a beautiful bay. **La Biodola** *(*☎ *(0565) 969966* IIII*) is under the same management.*
🏠 ⧺ ☐ 🖼 ⚓ ⁅ ⇌ ⚱/ ⚲ ⛵ ⛾

≈ **Villa Ottone**
57037 Portoferraio ☎ *(0565) 966042* ⊛ *(0565) 966376* IIII ⇒ ⇌ *AE*
CB ⊡ ⊙ *VISA Closed Oct-Mar.*
Location: 11km (7 miles) se at Ottone.
🏠 ⚓ ⁅ ⇌ ⚲ ⧺ ⅊

≈ **Picchiae Residence**
57037 Portoferraio ☎ *(0565) 966072* IIIII *95 rms* 🛏 *95* ⇒ 🏠 ⇌ *AE*
⊡ *Closed Oct-Apr.*
Location: 8km (5 miles) s of Portoferraio, off Porto Azzurro road. A modern, peaceful hotel offering marvelous views.
🏠 ⚘ ⁅ ⇌ ⚲ ⛾

⊐ A restaurant in the town with pleasant outdoor tables is **La Ferrigna** *(Piazza Repubblica* ☎ *(0565) 92129* I *closed Tues in winter).*

⊐ At Casaccia on the road to La Biodola is **Benassi** *(*☎ *(0565) 92628* I *closed Mon, Oct).*

Procchio
Map 10I2. 10km (6 miles) SW of Portoferraio. Population: 532.

One of the chief sand-beach resorts on the N coast.

Desirée
Lido di Spartaia. 57030 Procchio ☎ *(0565) 907502/3* ⊕ *590649* ⊛ *(0565) 907884* ▥□ *to* ▥▥ *72 rms* ▭ *72* ◠ ⥲ ▤ AE CB ⊙ ⊙ WB *Closed Nov-Apr.*

A modern and anonymous but efficiently managed hotel.

▨ ⍟ ⚓ ⋒ ⣿ ✓ ♉ ⏏ ▦

Golfo
57030 Procchio ☎ *(0565) 907565* ⊕ *590690* ▥▥ *to* ▥▥ *94 rms* ▭ *94* ◠ ⥲ ▤ AE ⊙ WB *Closed Nov-Apr.*

A large, modern hotel in a pine wood with an especially attractive beach and an unusually good restaurant.

⌂ □ ⟨⟨ ⋒ ✓ ♉ ◉ ▦ ▦ Y

Rio Marina
Map 10I3. 20km (12 miles) E of Portoferraio. Population: 2,420.

This is the principal mining town of Elba, and on the third floor of the Palazzo Comunale is an interesting little **mineral museum**. The **iron mines** may be visited on Sat in summer by appointment (☎ *(0565) 962001*).

⥲ **La Canocchia** (*Via Palestro 3* ☎ *(0565) 962432* ▥□ *to* ▥▥ *closed Mon in winter*).

Excursions
Island of Capraia

Boats depart from Portoferraio daily in summer, Mon and Wed in winter; the journey takes 2-3hrs each way.

⥲ **Il Saracino** (☎ *(0565) 905018* ▥□ *closed Oct-Mar*).

Island of Montecristo

Hotels and travel agents will arrange party reservations to visit the deserted island, now designated as a nature reserve.

Empoli
Map 15E5. 33km (20 miles) W of Florence. 50053. Firenze. Population: 45,802.

The vast and unlovely sprawl around Empoli, an important center of glass manufacture, disguises exceptional works of art. The painters Jacopo Chimenti, called Empoli, and Pontormo, were born here. The modern composer Ferrucio Busoni was also a native. In fall there is a festival of his work.

Sights and places of interest
Collegiata ▥ †

At the historic center of Empoli is the church that marks the western limit of the influence of the Florentine Romanesque; the lower section of the facade dates from 1093. The upper part is a post-World War II reconstruction of F. Ruggieri's late 18thC "rationalization."

Museo della Collegiata ☆
Piazzetta San Giovanni, to the right of the Collegiata.

The museum incorporates the Baptistry of the Collegiata.

Ground floor A 15thC stone emblem shows the original appearance of the Collegiata facade; there is also a School-of-Donatello baptismal font, and a 16thC English brass lectern.

First floor **Rm. 5** contains Bicci di Lorenzo's *St Nicholas of Tolentino* defends Empoli from the Black Death (1445), interesting for the view of early 15thC Empoli. In **Rm. 6:** Lorenzo Monaco's *Madonna Enthroned with Saints* (1404); Bicci di Lorenzo's *Madonna Enthroned with Saints* (1423); two works by Pontormo, *St John the Evangelist* and *St Michael Archangel;* and a tabernacle of *St Sebastian*, sculpted by A. Rossellino and painted by Francesco Botticini. In **Rm. 7** are two free-standing sculptures of the *Madonna Annunciate* and the *Angel Gabriel* (1447) by B. Rossellino; a *Madonna and Child*, usually attributed to the young Filippo Lippi; and a tabernacle of the *Holy Sacrament* (1484) by Francesco and Raffaello Botticini. Two more images of the Madonna in this room are the relief sculptures by Tino di Camaino (early 14thC) and by Mino da Fiesole (c. 1465-70). **Rm 8:** *Pietà* and other detached frescoes (c. 1425) by Masolino, from the church of Santo Stefano; and frescoes of *St Andrew* and *John the Baptist*, rare works by Gherardo Starnina. **Rm. 9:** Terra cottas from the Della Robbia workshop.

In the 14thC church of **Santo Stefano** in Via S. Stefano there is a *Madonna and Child* (1424) and other frescoes by Masolino.

See *Artimino, Lastra a Signa*.

Fiesole ☆

Map 12E6. 8km (5 miles) NE of Florence. 50014, Firenze. Population: 14,788. Getting there: No. 7 bus from Florence (SM Novella).

When Florence was a mere cluster of buildings on the Arno, Fiesole, on its conical hill overlooking the valleys of the Arno and the Mugnone, was one of the chief cities of Etruria. Some scholars place the Etruscan settlement as early as the 8thC BC, although the town is not recorded until 225BC. Faesulae was an important Roman military colony from 80BC and later the capital city of Roman Etruria. In 1125 Florence sacked and superseded its mother city. *Pietra serena*, the cool gray stone employed so effectively by Florentine architects, comes from the nearby quarries of Monte Ceceri.

Fiesole is slightly cooler than Florence in summer, although the difference is often wishfully exaggerated.

Event The *Estate Fiesolana*, a festival of concerts and films, takes place in the Roman Theater in July-Aug.

Sights and places of interest

The main square, on the site of the Roman forum, is the **Piazza Mino da Fiesole**.

Duomo †
The exterior of the Duomo (San Romolo), enlarged in the 13thC, was made dreary by a 19thC restoration. The **Cappella Salutati**, to the right of the choir, contains two fine works by Mino da Fiesole: the **tomb of Bishop Salutati**, and an altar of the *Madonna and Saints*.

Museo Bandini
Via Dupré.
A miscellany of furniture, majolica, Renaissance pictures and Etruscan fragments.

San Francesco †
Above the public gardens is this 14thC church enlarged in the 15thC but now nearly ruined by ill-considered restoration in the early 20thC. The cloisters are charming, and there are magnificent views.

Below S. Francesco is the ancient basilica of **S. Alessandro**, on the site of the Roman temple of Bacchus. The wonderful marble columns dividing the interior space are Roman.

Teatro Romano ⅏ ☆
Via Marini.
Here there are atmosphere and views as well as the Roman theater (c.80BC), which has a capacity of 3,000; it was rediscovered in 1809 and excavated in 1873. To the right are the baths, discovered in 1891, and to the left the Roman-Etruscan temple, first fully revealed in 1918. Behind is a stretch of **Etruscan wall**.

Nearby sights

Badia Fiesolana ⅢⅢ ✝ ★
Ask at porter's lodge for entry.
300m NW of San Domenico, this was the cathedral of Fiesole until the
11thC, and is now part of the European University. Cosimo il Vecchio
commissioned an unknown architect to rebuild this church in the
mid-15thC. The unfinished facade (1464) incorporates the little green and
white Romanesque facade of the earlier church. The superb cruciform
interior is one of the glories of Renaissance architecture.

San Domenico ⅢⅢ ✝ ☆
In this hamlet, 1.5km (1 mile) sw of Fiesole, is the monastery of S.
Domenico, built for Dominican monks in the early 15thC. Fra Angelico took
religious orders here and was prior from 1449-52. The church portico and
campanile were added in the 17thC by Matteo Nigetti, and the **interior** was
remodeled in the late 15th-early 16thC, when the elegant stone arches to
the nave chapels, some by Giuliano da Sangallo, were added. Over the first
altar on the left is the fascinating **altarpiece** by Fra Angelico (c.1428), with
its background repainted by Lorenzo di Credi (c.1501); it was recently
cleaned.
   In the convent, to the right of the church portico (*ring for admission*), the
Chapter House has a fresco of the *Crucifixion* by Fra Angelico. His fresco
of the *Madonna and Child*, now damaged, was in the church.

Villa Medici
*Via Vecchia Fiesolana. Open on request. Apply to Signora Anna
Mazzini.*
This was one of the first pleasure villas of the Renaissance, built, according
to Vasari, by Michelozzo for the son of Cosimo de' Medici. Parts of the
garden, including the "secret" garden overlooking the Arno valley from
below the villa, date from the late 15thC.

Villa Palmieri
*Via Boccaccio 128. Can be visited with Agriturist (see "Gardens,"
page 207) or on request. Apply to Signora Bellandi.*
This may have been the site of the garden of Boccaccio's *Decameron.* But
the existing house was built in 1697, and the garden much altered in the
19thC. Queen Victoria, who stayed here twice, planted one of the cypresses
in 1888.

⫸ **Villa San Michele** 🏛
Via Doccia 4, 50014 Fiesole ☎ *(055) 59451* ✆*570643* ⅢⅢ *28 rms* 🛏 *28*
🍴 🗠 ⬚ ⬚ 🆑 ⬚ ⬚ ⬚ *Closed mid-Nov to mid-Mar.*
In a 14thC villa enlarged in the 15thC by Santi di Tito, the hotel, now under
the same management as the Cipriani in Venice, is almost too luxurious for
comfort. The stupendous price includes one *à la carte* meal in the
excellent restaurant.
🏠 ⬚ 🖼 🐎 ⚓ ⩓ 🌿 ⛵

⫸ ▱ **Aurora** (*Piazza Mino da Fiesole 39* ☎ *(055) 59100, restaurant
closed Sun dinner, Mon, Nov*), in the central square.

⫸ ▱ At San Domenico, **Bencistà** (*Via B. da Maiano 4* ☎ *(055) 59163* ▱ *to
* ⅢⅢ *closed winter*) is a peaceful old-fashioned *pensione* with an attractive
garden.

⫸ ▱ 9km (6 miles) NE at the Olmo intersection near the Convent of La
Maddalena (see *Bivigliano*) is **Dino** (*Via Faentina 329* ☎ *(055) 548932
* ▱ *closed Jan, restaurant closed Wed*), a cheerful country inn and pizzeria.

▱ **Etrusca** (*Piazza Mino* ☎ *(055) 599484, open until 2am, closed Thurs*);
Le Lance (*Via Mantellini 2b* ☎ *(055) 599090, closed Mon, Jan*) is a
superior pizzeria with a terrace. See also **Pratolino, Settignano.**

Forte dei Marmi
*Map **14**D2. 104km (65 miles) w of Florence, 34km (21
miles) NW of Lucca. 55042. Lucca. Population: 10,193.*
Forte dei Marmi is the quiet, discreet upper-class resort of the
Versilia laid out in neat rows among the pine wood and used
mainly by Italians. The fort (1788) stands in the central piazza.

Hotels

If you have not reserved a hotel, you will find a good selection of all categories in Viale Morin.

Augustus
Viale Morin 169,55042 Forte dei Marmi, Lucca ☎ *(0584) 80202* ☢ *590673* ▥▥ *to* ▥▥ *70 rms* 🛏 *70* ▦ ◂ 🏠 🏠 ᴀᴇ ⊙ ⊙ ▨ *Closed Oct to mid-May*
A modern hotel near the beach.
🏠 ⧦ ☐ ☞ ⛷ 巛 ≋ ✓ ⁒ ⛴ ⛵ 🛥 🐟 ⊙

Augustus Lido
Viale Morin 72 ☎ *(0584) 81442* ▥▤ *to* ▥▥ *19 rms* ◂ ᴀᴇ ᴄʙ ⊙ ⊙ ▨ *Closed Oct-May.*
With a cool garden.
⧦ ☞ 🐟

Hermitage
Via Cesare Battisti ☎ *(0584) 80022* ☢ *590673* ▥▤ *to* ▥▥ *70 rms* 🛏 *65* ▦ ◂ 🏠 ⇋ ᴀᴇ ⊙ ⊙ ▨ *Closed Oct-May.*
A quiet hotel with large pool and restaurant.
🏠 ⧦ ♿ ☐ ☞ 🐟 ≋ ✓ ⁒ ⛴ ⛵ 🛥 ⊙

Tirreno
Viale Morin 7,55042 Forte dei Marmi, Lucca ☎ *(0584) 83333* ▥▤ *59 rms* 🛏 *59* 🏠 ⇋ ᴀᴇ ⊙ ▨ *Closed Oct-Easter.*
An attractive second-category hotel in an old villa.
☞ 🐟 ✓

⟋ Also: **Astoria Garden** (*Via Leonardo da Vinci 16* ☎ *(0584) 80754* ▯▯ *to* ▥▯); **Kyrton** (*Via Raffaelli 14* ☎ *(0584) 81341* ▯▯); **Raffaelli Park** (*Via Mazzini 37* ☎ *(0584) 81494* ▥▯); **Raffaelli-Villa Angela** (*Via Mazzini 64* ☎ *(0584) 80652* ▯▯ *to* ▥▯).

⇋ **Lorenzo**
Via Carducci 61 ☎ *(0584) 84030* ▥▥ ⇋ ▦ ᴀᴇ ᴄʙ ⊙ ⊙ ▨ *Closed Mon in winter and mid-Dec to end Jan.*
The fashionable restaurant of Forte dei Marmi specializes in the freshest fish available on the day. Luxurious pastas, e.g., *fettuccine con aragosta, farfalline al ragu di pesche, ravioli ai funghi.*

⇋ Also: **La Barca** (*Viale Italico 3* ☎ *(0584) 89323* ▥▥ *closed Tues, also Mon eve in winter, Nov*); **Bistrot** (*Via della Repubblica 14* ☎ *(0584) 89897* ▥▥ *closed Mon in winter*); **Madeo** (*3km (2 miles)* sᴇ *at Via Giambattista Vico 75* ☎ *(0584) 84068* ▥▥ *closed Tues in winter*), a very good fish restaurant with garden; **Maito** (*Via della Repubblica 10* ☎ *(0584) 80940* ▥▥ *closed Wed in winter*); **Il Quadrifolglio** (*Via A. Franceschi 6* ☎ *(0584) 85112* ▥▥ *closed Tues in winter*); **Tre Stelle** (*Via Montauti 6* ☎ *(0584) 80220* ▯▯ *to* ▥▥ *closed Mon*), in the center near the fort.

Gaiole in Chianti
Map **12F6**. *69km (43 miles)* sᴇ *of Florence, 28km (17 miles)* ɴᴇ *of Siena. 53013. Siena. Population: 2,627.*
The medieval lord of this market town in the Chianti Classico zone was one of the founders of the original Chianti league. On a hill to the ᴇ, which can be climbed in 15mins on foot, is the medieval village of **Barbischio**. The fortified **Fattoria Meleto** stands in the midst of its vineyards 2.5km (1½ miles) to the s. The ramparts of the castle of **Vertine** rise above the road to *Radda in Chianti*. To the s is **Brolio**, headquarters of the wine-making estate, built by Bettino Ricasoli, who was one of the first heroes of the united Italy.

⟋ ⇋ **Castello di Spaltenna** ᴍ
Just above Gaiole to the w ☎ *(0577) 749483* ▥▯ *to* ▥▥ *15 rms* 🛏 *7*

□ ▬ ⟶ ⟨⟨ AE ⊡ VISA *Closed mid-Jan to Feb.*

This elegant and professionally managed establishment in the monastery of the 13thC Pieve di Spaltenna is all the rage with the Chiantishire set. The restaurant offers a choice between standard Tuscan cuisine and more "creative" dishes, such as coulibac, soufflés, "prego" steak, and the chef's pâté.

⌂ ⛵ ⟨⟨ ≈ ⟩° ✓ ⛵ □ ⚏ ☿

≈ **Badia a Coltibuono** �🏛
Coltibuono, 5km (3 miles) to NE ☎ (0577) 749424 ⅢⅡⅡ □ ▬ ⟨⟨ ⟶ ⟨⟨
AE ⊡ ⊡ VISA ® Pontormo's early Nov to mid-Dec.

The 11thC ex-monastery buildings (which include a Romanesque church) are now part of an active wine estate, where wine and oil are on sale. The proprietor's wife, the magnificently named Lorenza de' Medici, runs a luxurious cooking course in the Badia.

Galluzzo (Certosa del) 🏛 † ☆
Map 6E3. 6km (4 miles) s of Florence ☎ (055) 2049226. Bus no. 36 or 37 from Florence ⊡ ✗ compulsory. Open Tues-Sun summer 9am-noon, 3-6pm; winter 9am-noon, 2.30-5pm. Closed Mon.

The monastery which stands impressively above the Via Cassia was founded by the Florentine Niccolò Acciaiuoli in 1342. The **Pinacoteca** is housed in the Gothic Palazzo degli Studi; the dominating works are Pontormo's damaged **lunettes of the Passion cycle** (1522-25), detached from the *chiostro grande* . They were painted while he was living in the monastery during a plague in Florence and, although deeply influenced by Dürer, are striking examples of the Mannerist style Pontormo helped to invent. There are also paintings by Mariotto di Nardo, Dürer and Ridolfo del Ghirlandaio. The church of **S. Lorenzo**, in its large 16thC courtyard, has a high *pietra serena* facade (1556). The interior is divided into two sections: the Monks' Choir (with good 16thC stalls) and the Lay Brethren's Choir. A staircase leads to the subterranean chapels where members of the Acciaiuoli family are buried. The superb **tomb-slab of Cardinal Agnolo II Acciaiuoli** was attributed to Donatello by Ruskin and others, but is now thought to be 16thC. Notice also especially the Gothic **monument to N. Acciaiuoli**.

The monastic complex includes the *parlatorio*, with 16thC stained glass; the *sala capitolo*, with a frescoed *Crucifixion* by Mariotti Albertinelli; and the *chiostro grande*, embellished with 66 terra-cotta medallions of *Saints and Prophets* by Andrea and Giovanni della Robbia. Off the *chiostro grande* are the cells. The pharmacy sells liqueurs distilled in the monastery.

Gargonza 🏛
Map 12G7. 80km (50 miles) SE of Florence, 28km (17 miles) SW of Arezzo. 52048. Arezzo.

The 13thC houses in this tiny fortified village, where Dante took refuge after learning of his exile from Florence, can be rented by the week or, out of season, by the night. Gargonza is freely open to visitors, complete and unspoiled within its walls.

⌇ ≈ **Castello di Gargonza** 🏛
Info and reservations: Count Roberto Guicciardini, Castello di Gargonza, 52048 Monte San Savino, Arezzo ☎ (0575) 847021 or (055) 296151 ◉ 571466 ® (0575) 847054 ⅢⅡⅡ to ⅢⅢⅢ 35 rms in 20 houses ▭ in each house ▤ ▤ AE ≈ Closed Jan.

The interiors have been attractively modernized, and the high position, surrounded by woodland, is open to cooling breezes and extensive views of the Valdichiana. The restaurant, **Il Castello** (☎ (0575) 847065 ⅢⅡⅡ) *closed*

Mon, late Jan, early Feb), just outside the walls, offers plain Tuscan cooking.
🏠 🖼 ⚓ ⫷ 🛤 �- ⇒ ⚓ 🍷

Giglio
Map 8K4. 14km (9 miles) SE of Monte Argentario. Getting there: By boat, 1hr from Porto Santo Stefano. 58013. Grosseto. Population: 1,706.

The second largest island in the Tuscan archipelago, Giglio is wilder, poorer and much smaller than **Elba**, being only 8.5km (5 miles) long and 5km (3 miles) across at its widest. The three centers — **Giglio Porto**, **Giglio Castello**, a hilltop town, whose maze of steep traffic-free streets is surrounded by anti-pirate walls, and **Campese** — are linked by a hair-raising bus service. Campese is the main sand-beach resort, and there are other sand beaches at Cala dell' Arenella and Cala delle Cannelle. The island is rich in rare species of wildlife. Boats depart for Giannutri (see *Port'Ercole*).

⚓ **Arenella** (☎ *(0564) 809340* 🔲), quiet and adequately comfortable.

🍽 In Giglio Porto, **Il Doria** (☎ *(0564) 809000* 🔳) and **La Vecchia Pergola** (☎ *(0564) 809080* 🔳), both in Via T. de Revel, overlook the harbor.

Greve
Map 12F6. 27km (17 miles) S of Florence, 40km (25 miles) N of Siena. 50022. Firenze. Population: 10,232.

The main market town of the Chianti is graced with a delightful asymmetrical central square, Piazza Matteotti, lined with porticoed 17thC buildings. It is a good place to shop for wine (see *Tuscan wines*).
Events   Market day is Sat, and a wine fair is held in Sept.

⚓ **Villa le Barone**
Via San Leonino 19,50020 Panzano in Chianti, Firenze ☎ *(055) 852383* 🎚 *25 rms* 🔲 *25* ⚓ 🍽 🏠 🅰🅴 *Closed Nov-Mar.*
An exceptionally attractive country villa in an isolated position.
🏠 🐎 ⚓ 🛤

🍽 The calm, pleasant **Giovanni da Verrazzano** (*Piazza Matteotti* ☎ *(055) 853189* 🔳 *closed Sun eve, Mon, Jan and Feb*) has some rooms.

🍽 **Trattoria del Montagliari**
Via di Montagliari 28 (on the SS222), Panzano in Chianti ☎ *(055) 852184* 🍽 🏠 �- ⫷ *Closed Mon, one week in Aug.*
Giovanni Cappelli's trattoria on the Montagliari wine estate is as welcoming in winter when fires are lit as in summer when you can eat outside overlooking the Chianti hills. Specialties include homemade *pappardelle* with game sauces according to the season, and excellent chianina beef.

🍽 **Omero** ✿
Passo dei Pecorai, 5km (3 miles) to N ☎ *(055) 850716* 🔲 🔲 🔳 🍽
🚘 �- ⫷ 🅰🅴 *Closed Wed, Aug.*
A classic family restaurant. **Specialties**: *Homemade pastas and desserts.*

Grosseto
Map 8I5. 141 km (87 miles) S of Florence, 73km (45 miles) S of Siena. 58100. Grosseto. Population: 69,301 i Viale Mongerosa 206 ☎ *(0564) 22534.*

Grosseto is the principal city of the Tuscan Maremma, the coastal plain where the natives regard themselves as a special and separate breed of Tuscans, toughened by centuries of hardship and proud of their land's recently restored fertility.

In the period of the great Etruscan cities that flourished here, the area to the NE of Grosseto was a navigable gulf. By the Middle Ages it was a freshwater lake, which eventually subsided into malaria-infested swamp land.

The history of the Maremma after the fall of the Roman Empire was that of a battlefield contested by Florence, Siena, the Papal States and pirates from the Barbary Coast. When it became part of the Sienese territories in the late Middle Ages it was scantily populated; and in the mid-18thC, two centuries after the Florentine conquest of Siena, the area was nearly deserted. The first effective efforts to reclaim the land and rid the Maremma of malaria were initiated by the Lorraine grand duke Leopold II in 1828; but it was not until the early years of this century that significant progress was made. In 1943-44, Grosseto was the victim of severe bombing raids. The early 1950s saw a systematic program of agricultural incentives and repopulation, and the population of Grosseto has since expanded more than five times.

It is against this violent background that Grosseto today must be read. Its spirit is that of a modern city that has not quite discovered its own character.

Sights and places of interest

The main square is Piazza Rosselli, just to the N of Porta Nuova. What remains of the original urban nucleus is contained within an impressive hexagon of bastioned **brick walls** built by the 16thC Medici. Traffic is prohibited in the center.

Duomo †

Originally built in 1294-1302, but the imitation Romanesque facade dates from 1845; inside is a 15thC font and, in the left transept, an *Assumption* by Matteo di Giovanni.

Museo Archeologico e d'Arte della Maremma ☆
Via Mazzini.

The collection is displayed chronologically beginning with prehistory and ending with 13th-17thC paintings on the second floor.

The ground floor is largely devoted to material excavated from *Roselle*. On the first floor is a topographical explanation of the Etruscan Maremma and material from the sites. On the second floor are 13th-17thC Sienese pictures of which the most noteworthy are Sassetta's *Madonna of the Cherries* and Pietro di Domenico's *Pietà*.

San Francesco †
Piazza della Independenza.

A 13thC Gothic church. Over the high altar is an early Duccio *Crucifixion*.

━━ Near the museum is the sensible, modest **La Maremma** (*Via Fulceri P. dei Calboli 5* ☎ *(0564) 21177* ▯ *closed Mon, Aug*); the **Enoteca Ombrone** (*Viale G. Matteotti 69-71* ☎ *(0564) 22585* ▥ *closed Sun eve, Mon, Jan, 2wks in July*) has an extensive cellar and the most ambitious kitchen; also **Buca di San Lorenzo** (*Via Manetti 1* ☎ *(0564) 25142* ▥ *closed Mon*).

At Istia d'Ombrone, 7km (4½ miles) E, **Terzo Cerchio** (*Piazza del Castello 1* ☎ *(0564) 409235* ▯ *closed Mon, Nov*) is a good place to sample traditional country cooking of the Maremma.

Impruneta

Map 12E6. 14km (9 miles) S of Florence. 50023. Firenze. Population: 14,884.

This large agricultural village is located on a plateau overlooking the Greve and Ema valleys.

Event   The lively agricultural fair of St Luke in mid-Oct.

Sights and places of interest
Santa Maria dell' Impruneta 🏛 ✝

The fine porticoed facade that overlooks the main square was added in 1634; the tall bell tower is 13thC. The design of the handsome **aedicules** (1456) flanking the entrance to the polygonal presbytery is attributed to Michelozzo, and they are embellished with terra-cotta decorations by Luca della Robbia. To the right of the church are two pretty cloisters.

🍽 **I Tre Pini**, 6km (4 miles) N at Pozzolatico (☎ (055) 208065 ▮▮▯ closed Mon, Jan), is pleasant in summer.

Lastra a Signa
Map 15E5. 13km (8 miles) W of Florence. 50055. Firenze. Population: 17,000.

Although unprepossessingly set in an industrial zone and badly damaged during World War II, the historic center retains its 14thC walls. The **Loggia di S. Antonio** (1411) could be an early work by Brunelleschi, and the **Palazzo Pretorio** has terra-cotta coats of arms and a handsome window of 1570.

Antica Trattoria Sanesi
Via Arione 33 ☎ (055) 8720234 ▮▮▯ ⌷ ⌷ Closed Sun dinner, Mon, Aug.

A classic Tuscan restaurant with the welcoming, genuine atmosphere of an old coaching stop. The steaming platters of pasta are irresistible, especially when sauced with truffles or asparagus. *Finocchiona, bistecca fiorentina* and game in season are all exactly as they should be. Reservations are essential.

🍽 See also **Artimino**.

La Verna
Map 13E8. 75km (47 miles) SE of Florence, 58km (36 miles) N of Arezzo. 52010. Arezzo.

Monastery ✝
This monastery, reached by a beautiful twisting road of 26km (16 miles) from *Bibbiena*, was founded in 1214 by St Francis, who received the stigmata here on Sept 14, 1224. The chief artistic attractions are the Andrea della Robbia terra cottas in the churches, of which the loveliest are the *Annunciation* and *Adoration of the Child* in the Chiesa Maggiore.

Above the monastery is a magnificent **forest** of old beeches and firs.

Livorno
Map 10F3. 116km (72 miles) W of Florence, 19km (12 miles) S of Pisa. 57100. Livorno. Population: 177,101 ℹ Piazza Cavour ☎ (0586) 33111; at the port, Palazzo Dogana ☎ (0586) 25320.

The major commercial port of Tuscany and still one of the greatest in the Mediterranean, Livorno was the creation of the Medici grand dukes: their most ambitious and successful project. The transformation of the medieval fishing village into a port that would more than compensate for the silted-up port of Pisa was initiated by Cosimo I in 1571. Six years later, the new "ideal city" of Livorno designed by Buontalenti was founded. In 1593 Ferdinand I declared Livorno an open city, guaranteeing tax exemptions, free trade with all international ports, and freedom of worship for all religions; and in 1621 that remarkable Englishman, Robert Dudley, the marine engineer in the service of the grand dukes, completed the extension of the harbor with his great Medicean mole (harbor wall).

By 1600 Livorno had a population of 5,000, activated, then as now, by a substantial Jewish community. 18thC foreign visitors found it a charming as well as prosperous city with many fine contemporary palaces. These disappeared along with the charm and the historic center during the bombardments of 1943.

The old English name Leghorn, from the early Italian Legorno, is rarely used today except, of course, to describe the type of straw hat first made here in the 19thC.

Sights and places of interest

The old pentagonal center envisaged by Buontalenti is bisected by its main street, Via Grande, which links the huge harbor complex with the Piazza Repubblica. The city is guarded by two fortresses: the Fortezza Nuova (1590) above Piazza Repubblica, and the Fortezza Vecchia (1534) designed by Ant. da Sangallo the Younger, in the harbor.

Monument to Ferdinand I *("Quattro Mori" or "Four Moors")*
Piazza Micheli.

Facing the old harbor, this esthetically controversial monument consists of a statue of *Ferdinand I* (1595) wearing the order of St Stephen by G. Bandini and the **four bronze Moors** added by P. Tacca in 1626. Some admire these straining Michelangeloesque figures; others would say that they combine ineptitude with unfeeling virtuosity. The diarist John Evelyn, who was of the first opinion, described the scene he witnessed in this piazza in 1644 when Livorno was the chief slave port of the northern Mediterranean: "Here...is such a concourse of slaves, Turcs, Moors and other nations, that the number and confusion is prodigious; some buying, others selling, others drinking, others playing, some working, others sleeping, fighting, singing, weeping, all nearly naked, and miserably chained." The **English Cemetery** (*Via Verdi 63*) was the first Protestant cemetery in Italy. Tobias Smollett lies here.

Museo Civico G. Fattori
Villa Fabbricotti.

A collection of paintings by the Macchiaioli, and several Modiglianis.

☞ The **Gran Duca** (*Piazza Micheli 16* ☎ *(0586) 891024* ▯) faces the harbor.

🍽 **La Barcarola** (*Viale Carducci 63* ☎ *(0585) 402367* ▮▮▯ to ▮▮▮▮ 🔲 *closed Sun, Aug*) is the best of the fish restaurants, with a lively atmosphere. Otherwise, try: **L'Antico Moro** (*Via Di Franco 59* ☎ *(0586) 884659* ▯); **L'Aragosta** (*Piazza dell'Arsenale 6* ☎ *(0586) 29377* ▮▮▯ to ▮▮▮▮ *closed Sun, Oct*); **L'Attias** (*Via Ricasoli 127* ☎ *(0586) 899441* ▮▮▯ *closed Thurs, 2wks in May, Aug*); **Alla Chetichella Osteria** (*Via E. Rossi 18* ☎ *(0586) 29029* ▯ to ▮▮▯ *closed Tues, Sat and Sun lunch*); **Il Fanale** (*Scali Novi Lena 15-17* ☎ *(0586) 25346* ▮▮▯ to ▮▮▮▮ *closed Mon, 2wks in July, Aug*); **Da Rosina** (*Via Roma 251* ☎ *(0586) 800200* ▮▮▯ *closed Thurs, 2wks in Aug*).

Lucca ★

*Map **14**E3. 74km (46 miles) w of Florence, 22km (14 miles) NE of Pisa. 55100. Lucca. Population: 91,814* ℹ *Via Vittorio Veneto 40* ☎ *(0583) 43639.*

Alone of all the Tuscan city states, Lucca resisted the thrust of Florentine imperialism and remained independent of united Tuscany until the 19thC. The town is still a separate and special place, its narrow medieval streets, red-brick palaces and tower houses and elaborate Romanesque churches encircled by the best-preserved 16th-17thC walls in Italy.

A Roman colony from 180BC, capital city of Tuscany under the medieval Lombard and Frankish emperors, and a free commune from 1119, Lucca emerged in the early 14thC as the second richest city in Tuscany. Under the forceful leadership of the merchant-soldier Castruccio Castracani, Lucca became a serious threat to Florence; but Castracani's death in 1328 left the government divided and open for short periods to subjection by its enemies.

In 1369 Lucca was granted a charter of independence by the Emperor Charles IV. Representative governments alternated with periods of signorial rule until the mid-16thC when the oligarchy closed ranks against the populace. Thus protected from internal opposition the Republic fortified itself against the threat of Cosimo I's pan-Tuscan policies with its new ring of walls and retained its autonomy until 1799. Napoleon gave Lucca to his sister Elisa Baciocchi in 1805; in 1817 it passed as a duchy to Maria Louisa de Bourbon; and in 1847, Lucca was finally absorbed into the Tuscan grand-duchy.

The Romanesque churches of the Tuscan silk town are in the Pisan style, richly embroidered with polychrome marble insets and relief carvings executed for the most part by visiting Lombard and Pisan sculptors. Another, later visitor, Jacopo della Quercia, carved a number of works for Lucca including his early masterpiece, the tomb of *Ilaria del Carretto* in the Duomo. The most talented local sculptor, hardly represented outside his native city, was Matteo Civitali, active in the 15thC.

In the 16th-18thC the Lucchese nobility built grand summer retreats in the cool hills to the NE. These villas (see *Excursions*) are among the most exhilarating examples of Mannerist and Baroque architecture in Tuscany. The anglicized gardens of many of the villas testify to the long-standing special relationship with Britain.

Events　The birthplace of Luigi Boccherini and Giacomo Puccini is still musically active. In spring and early summer there is a festival of sacred music performed in the churches. Concerts of contemporary and classical music are held throughout the *Estate Musicale* from July-Sept, and in Aug a festival of music and theater takes place in the Villa at Marlia.

The feast of the Holy Cross is celebrated on the previous evening with a procession from S. Frediano to the Duomo.

An itinerant antique market comes to Piazza San Martino on the third Sat and Sun of each month.

Sights and places of interest

Piazza Napoleone is the main square. The Neo-Classical monument to *Maria Louisa de Bourbon* in the center is by L. Bartolini. The Palazzo della Provincia (begun 1578) on the w side is based on designs by Ammannati; its early 19thC interior is by L. Nottolini.

A delightful walk can be taken along the tree-shaded path on the 4.2km (3-mile) ring of **ramparts**. Be sure also to see **Via Guinigi** and **Via Fillungo**, well-preserved medieval streets.

Duomo *(San Martino)* ▥ ✝ ★
Erected in the 11th-13thC, the cathedral's asymmetrical facade (1204) is largely the work of Guidetto da Como. Under the portico are fine relief carvings (begun 1233) by a Lombard master. The interior was Gothicized in the 14th-15thC. Four of Puccini's ancestors served here as organists and choir-masters.

In the left transept is Jacopo della Quercia's **tomb of Ilaria del Carretto** (★), his earliest surviving masterpiece (c.1406) and the first sculptural creation of the Renaissance to use Roman decorative motifs. The statue of *St John the Evangelist* nearby is also by Jacopo. In the adjoining chapel is an exceptionally fine panel of the *Madonna with Sts. Stephen and John the Baptist* by Fra Bartolommeo. In the left nave is the **tempietto** (1484) by Matteo Civitali, which houses the Volto Santo, the 11thC effigy of Christ carried through the city in procession on Holy Cross eve. Other works in the Duomo by Civitali include the pulpit (1498) in the right nave; and, in

155

the right transept, two angels (1477) and the monumental S. Regalo altarpiece. In the sacristy, off the right nave, is a stunning *Madonna with Sts. Peter, Clement, Paul and Sebastian* by Domenico Ghirlandaio.

Museo Nazionale 🏛
Villa Guinigi.

The Villa Guinigi was built in 1418 for Paolo Guinigi, political leader of Lucca from 1400-30.

Ground floor: Etruscan and Roman pieces excavated locally; works by Lucchese sculptors of the 8th-15thC, including M. Civitali.

First floor: 13th-19thC paintings, intarsia work, furniture and textiles. One of the painted crosses in Rm. XI is signed by Berlinghieri. In Rm. XIV are two altarpieces by Fra Bartolommeo.

Pinacoteca Nationale 🏛
Palazzo Mansi, Via Galli Tassi 43.

This collection of Renaissance to 19thC pictures from the Medici collection was given to Lucca by Leopold II. The 17thC palace retains much of its elaborate furniture.

San Frediano 🏛 † ★
Erected from 1112-47 on the site of a 6thC basilica. The mosaic of the *Ascension* on the facade, possibly by Berlinghieri, was heavily restored in the 19thC. Inside, the 12thC font at the top of the right nave is decorated with relief carvings of the story of *Moses*, the *Good Shepherd* and the *Apostles*. In the Trenta Chapel at the bottom of the left aisle are reliefs by Jacopo della Quercia and assistants, notably a Gothic polyptych **altarpiece** (1422) with a superb predella.

Across the Via Fillungo the oval outline of the Roman amphitheater is traced by medieval houses forming the intensely picturesque **Piazza Anfiteatro** (★). Via Cesare Battisti, which twists toward S. Michele in Foro, is flanked by 17th-18thC palaces.

San Michele in Foro 🏛 † ☆
A few steps to the N of Piazza Napoleone, Piazza San Michele occupies the site of the Roman forum. On the corner of Via Vittorio Veneto is the Renaissance **Palazzo Pretorio**, designed by M. Civitali, altered in the 16thC.

Begun in 1143, the church of S. Michele is a typical example of Pisan-Lucchese architecture. The high white marble facade belongs to the 13thC and the Lucchese tradition of rich decoration; the apse is in the Pisan style, possibly by Diotisalvi. Inside is a *Madonna and Child* by Andrea della Robbia and, in the left transept, a panel painting of *Four Saints* by Filippo Lippi.

Among other notable churches in Lucca are **S. Giovanni**, **S. Maria Forisportam**, **S. Giulia** and **S. Alessandro**.

➛ Hotels in the center: **Universo** (*Piazza del Giglio 1* ☎ *(0583) 43678* ▯) and **La Luna** (*Via Fillungo* ☎ *(0583) 43634*).

➛ Villa di Corliano 🏛
10km (6 miles) sw at Rigoli, 56010 San Giuliano Terme ☎ *(050) 818193* ▯ *18 rms* ➛ ᴀᴇ ᴠɪꜱᴀ
A frescoed villa in a fine park managed by descendants of its original patrician owners.

➛ Villa Principessa
5km (3 miles) outside on the SS12R, 55050 Massa Pisana ☎ *(0583) 370037* ◉ *590068* ◎ *(0583) 379019* ▮▮▮▮ *36 rms* ▭ *36* ▦ ➛ ⇥ ᴀᴇ ᴄʙ
◉ ◉ ᴠɪꜱᴀ
A luxuriously converted 18thC villa in a noble park, now a popular center for Italian business conferences.
🏠 🌱 ♨ ♦ ♣ ▯ ▱ ⚡ ♈

▤ Two excellent restaurants within the walls are **Buca di Sant'Antonio** (*Via della Cervia 3* ☎ *(0583) 55881* ▯ *closed Sun eve, Mon, late July*), where regional specialties are served, and the simpler **Da Giulio** (*Via San Tommaso 29* ☎ *(0583) 55948* ▯ *closed Sun, Mon, Aug, Christmas*). In the countryside nearby are **Solferino** (*San Macario in Piano* ☎ *(0583) 59118* ▯ *to* ▯▯ *closed Wed, Thurs lunch, one week in Jan, two weeks in Aug*), which has one of the most ambitious kitchens in rural Tuscany, and the charming **Vipore** (*Pieve Santo Stefano* ☎ *(0583) 59247* ▯▯ *closed Mon, Tues lunch, 10 days in Jan*).

See also *Excursions* on the next page.

Shopping

Many gourmets consider the olive oil of Lucca to be the best produced in Italy — but be careful you are buying real Lucca oil.

Gelateria Veneta di Arnoldo (*Via Vittorio Veneto 74* ☎ *(0583) 47037*) serves the best ice cream in town.

Excursions

1. Villas outside Lucca ★

Head N from Lucca on the *Abetone* road, along the E bank of the River Serchio. After 16km (10 miles) is the 11th-12thC Pieve di Brancoli.

Then make for Marlia, near Fraga.

Villa Imperiale 血

Marlia 🖼 *ℐ compulsory.*

The most famous and imposing of the villas near Lucca, adapted and redecorated in First Empire style when it was the summer residence of Elisa Baciocchi. Magnificent 17thC park.

Take the road for Segromigno Monte.

Villa Mansi 血

3km (1.75 miles) E of Marlia 🖼 🖳

A late 16thC villa transformed in the early 18thC with a charming facade and good Baroque furnishings and pictures on the first floor. There is a restaurant on the ground floor.

Take the road for Camigliano.

Villa Torrigiani 血

1.5km (1 mile) S of Segromigno 🖼 *Closed Thurs.*

Built in the 16thC with a spectacular Mannerist facade. The 17thC park was anglicized in the 19thC except for the sunken garden and the ingenious surprise fountains.

🍴 **La Mora**

Via Sesto Moriano 1748 ☎ *(0583) 57109* �□ 🔲 🔳 ☰ 🛏 🚗 ⋘ 🆎 🆑 ⊡ 🔘 ▥ *Closed Wed eve, Thurs, Oct.*

Near Ponte a Moriano, 9km (6 miles) from Lucca. The shop sells wines and olive oil. Regional specialties include *Gran farro*, *ravioli alle erbe* and *agnello della Garfagnana*.

---

2. Santa Maria del Giudice

Located 8km (5 miles) SW of Lucca are two Romanesque churches in the Pisan-Lucchese style: **San Giovanni Battista** and **Santa Maria Assunta**.

Magliano

Map 8J5. 27km (17 miles) SE of Grosseto. 59051. Grosseto. Population: 4,219.

A magnificently situated hilltop town of Etruscan origin surrounded by well-preserved Renaissance walls. The church of **San Giovanni Battista** is an attractive blend of Romanesque, Gothic and Renaissance; and the church of the **Annunziata** contains a *Madonna and Child* by Neroccio.

A ½hr walk to the SE is the romantic ruin of the Romanesque church of **San Bruzio** and the remains of the Etruscan necropolis.

🍴 **Aurora** (*Piazza Marconi 5* ☎ *(0564) 592030* 🔲 *to* 🎫 *closed Tues in winter*); **Da Sandra** (*Via Garibaldi* ☎ *(0564) 592196* 🔲 *to* 🎫 *closed Thurs*).

Massa

*Map **14**D2, 115km (71 miles) NW of Florence, 45km (28 miles) NW of Pisa. 54100. Massa-Carrara. Population: 65,814.*

A booming, untidy frontier town at the mouth of the Frigido valley below the foothills of the Apuan Alps, Massa did not become part of Tuscany until 1859, and it is still the least "Tuscan" of Tuscan provincial capitals.

Piazza Aranci, the old center, is dominated by the startling 17thC **Palazzo Cybo Malaspina**, which encloses an attractive loggiaed courtyard (1665) by G.F. Bergamini. The **Duomo** has a modern facade and a Baroque interior.

Above the town is the medieval **Rocca** and a Renaissance palace which was the residence of the 16thC Malaspina Dukes.

⇌ Il Bottaccio

5km (3 miles) sw at Montignoso, Via Bottaccio 1 ☎ (0585) 340031 ∭
▰ 🏠 ≈ AE CB ◑ ⊡ VISA

Located in an otherwise not especially distinguished area, this restaurant, which occupies a beautifully converted old watermill, is one of the greatest gastronomic surprises and treats in all Tuscany. Although the menu changes frequently, nothing seems ever to be less than perfect. There are some rooms.

Massa Marittima
*Map **10**H4. 132km (79 miles) sw of Florence, 64km (40 miles) sw of Siena. 58024. Grosseto. Population: 10,297.*
The mineral-rich territory of Massa Marittima was mined by the Etruscans and Romans; the copper and silver mines were the economic base of the independent republic which was constitutionally established in 1225 and flourished proudly until it was conquered by Siena in 1335. The Duomo, one of the most beautiful and richly decorated churches in Tuscany, was erected during the period of communal independence; and the first miners' code in Europe was drawn up in the city in 1310.
Event The *Balestra del Girofalco*, a crossbow competition with a mechanical falcon as target, takes place in medieval costume on May 20 and the second Sun in Aug.

Sights and places of interest
The town is in two distinct parts: the Romanesque lower town or Città Vecchia is linked by Via Moncini to the Gothic upper town or Città Nuova, built after the Sienese conquest.

The center of the old town is Piazza Garibaldi.

Duomo *(San Cerbone)* 🏛 ✝ ★
This lovely cathedral in the Pisan Romanesque-Gothic style was completed between 1287-1304. The **relief carvings** over the portal depict five episodes in the life of San Cerbone, patron saint of the cathedral, with the beguiling beasts who helped him. The campanile rising from the arcaded left flank was largely reconstructed in the 1920s.

At the top of the right aisle is the font, where St Bernardino was baptized in 1380, with relief carvings (1267) by Giraldo da Como and a 15thC tabernacle rising from its center. In the chapel to the left of the high altar is a panel painting of the *Madonna della Grazie* (c.1316), closely influenced by Duccio's *Maestà* in *Siena*.

Ask the sacristan to unlock the access door to the subterranean chapels. In the polygonal undercroft is the exquisite **Arca di San Cerbone** (1324), Saint Cerbonius' tomb, by the Sienese sculptor Coro da Gregorio in a painterly style influenced by illuminated manuscripts.

Opposite the Duomo is the **Palazzo Comunale**, the town hall created from a complex of 14th-15thC tower houses.

Museo/Palazzo del Podestà 🏛
The magistrate's palace, c.1230, now houses a small archeological collection and Sienese pictures; outstanding is A. Lorenzetti's *Maestà*.

Upper town *(Città Nuova)*
The upper town is guarded by the huge **Fortezza dei Senesi**, built by the Sienese after their conquest of Massa Marittima in 1334. Its center is Piazza Matteotti, from where the Corso Diaz leads to the Gothic church of San Agostino (1299-1313), which possesses interesting 16th-17thC pictures by Empoli, Pacchiarotti, Lorenzo Lippi and others.

Nearby sight
Museum of Mining (Museo della Miniera) in Viale Martiri di Niccioleta.

≈ **Roma** (*Via Norma Parenti 17-19* ☎ *(0566) 902644* ☐ *closed Wed*).

Montalcino
Map 8H6. 109km (67 miles) s of Florence, 41km (25 miles) s of Siena. 53024. Siena. Population: 5,702.

Montalcino stands on an olive-clad hill above the Ombrone and Asso valleys. The site was inhabited by the Etruscans and Romans, and in the early Middle Ages belonged to the Benedictine Abbey of **Sant'Antimo** (see below). A period of communal independence came to an end in 1260 when the town was subjected to Sienese rule after the battle of Montaperti. Montalcino provided sanctuary for Sienese aristocrat Republicans who fled their besieged city in 1555. Sienese gratitude is still expressed twice a year when the standard bearers representing Montalcino occupy the place of honor in the procession that precedes the Palio.

Brunello di Montalcino is one of the great Italian wines. See *Tuscan wines* for advice about where to taste it and other local wines.

Sights and places of interest
Piazza del Popolo is the main square; the **Palazzo Comunale** with its high tower dates from the 13th-14thC; the imposing loggia was added in the 14th-15thC. Above, in Piazza Garibaldi, is the church of **Sant'Egidio**, built by the Sienese in 1325. Over the first altar on the left notice the wooden *Crucifixion* (15thC) framed by 16thC inlaid wooden doors.

There are sweeping views from the Neo-Classical **Duomo** (1818-32) and from the church of the **Madonna del Soccorso**.

The **Rocca**, which dominates the town, was built by the Sienese in 1361 and was one of the most crucial defense posts of the Republic. The bastion was added by the Medici after the conquest of Siena. Inside is an *enoteca* of local wines, where you can also sample the local cheeses, oil, hams and other good things that might make up a picnic.
Museo Civico e Diocesano
Via di Ricasoli 29.

Below the Rocca, this museum houses 14th-15thC Sienese pictures, ecclesiastic objects including a 12thC illuminated bible, 15thC polychrome wooden statues, and a separate archeological collection.

In Piazza Cavour is the former pharmacy of the Hospital of Santa Maria, frescoed by V. Tamagni.

Nearby sights
Sant'Antimo ▥ ✝ ★
Near Castelnuovo Abate, 8km (5 miles) to s. Apply for entry to custodian at Via del Centro 12, Castelnuovo Abate.

This radiantly lovely Romanesque church, set in a gentle golden valley, is built of travertine with architectonic decorations in alabaster and translucent onyx quarried locally. It dates mostly from the early 12thC. The monastery was founded, according to tradition, by Charlemagne early in the 9thC. The doorway on the left flank, adorned with geometric carvings in the Lombard style, and the crypt, survive from the earlier building. The beautiful **interior** is embellished with fine capitals. There are frescoed apartments off the clerestory.

≈ **Taverna dei Barbi**
2km (1¼ miles) s of Montalcino, off the Sant'Antimo road ☎ *(0577) 848277* ▥▢ ☐ ≈ ⌂ ⌐ ⟨⟨ *Closed Wed, late Jan, early July.*

Superb Brunello wines complement traditional local dishes made from produce grown on this well-known wine-making estate.

=== La Cucina di Edgardo ✿
Via Saloni 9 ☎ *(0577) 848282* ❚☐ *to* ❚☐❚ AE CB ⬡ ⬡ 📷 *Closed Wed, Jan.*

A tiny (*reservation essential*) and very interesting restaurant where you must follow the advice of the proprietor.

➳ === Il Giglio (*Via Saloni 5* ☎ *(0577) 848167* === *closed Mon, Jan*) is in the center.

Monte Amiata
Map 8H6.

The isolated conical peak of this extinct volcano, 1,738m (5,702ft) high, is visible from Siena and in much of its art.

"Surely here, if anywhere in the world," wrote the Sienese Pope Pius II in his *Commentaries*, "sweet shade and silvery springs and green grass and smiling meadows allure poets." The upper slopes are equipped for skiing and climbing.

The summit is most easily reached from *Abbadia San Salvatore*, the most populous center. Other, more picturesque villages, are Arcidosso, Bagnone, Castel del Piano, Piancastagnaio and Santa Fiora.

Montecatini Terme
Map 15D4. 49km (30 miles) NW of Florence, 49km (30 miles) NE of Pisa. 51016. Pistoia. Population: 21,764.

One of the most famous and fashionable spas in Europe, Montecatini Terme was laid out in the early 20thC around a stately park. The warm saline waters are recommended for liver ailments and skin problems. The **Stabilimento Tettuccio** is the smartest place to take the waters, and its café is the main rendezvous. The season is Apr-Nov.

From Viale A. Diaz, a funicular railroad ascends to the beautifully situated old town, Montecatini Alto. To the N there is lovely walking country in the Valdinievole.

Nearby sight

8km (5 miles) s at Ponte Buggianese is the church frescoed by the modern painter Pietro Annigoni.

➳ Montecatini has some 500 hotels, mainly clustered around the **Parco delle Terme**; most open only during the season. The best known luxury hotel is the **Grand Hotel e la Pace** (*Via della Torretta 1* ☎ *(0572) 75801* ▥▥), which has a good restaurant.

If you find the atmosphere of Montecatini oppressive try a hotel just outside the town: **Grotta Giusti** (*5km (3 miles) SE at Monsummano Terme, Via Grotta Giusti 17* ☎ *(0572) 51165* ▥☐) has spa and sports facilities and is set in a peaceful park; and **Park Hotel Sorgenti** (*2km (1¼ miles) outside at Pieve a Nievole* ☎ *(0572) 831116* ▥☐) is in a pleasant country house furnished with antiques and surrounded by a large park.

=== A very classy restaurant in the center is the **Enoteca da Giovanni** (*Via Garibaldi 27* ☎ *(0572) 71695* ▥▥▥ AE ⬡ 📷 *closed Mon*).

Montefollonico
Map 12H7. 112km (70 miles) SE of Florence, 60km (37 miles) SE of Siena. 53040. Siena. Population: 820.

A walled hill village overlooking the valleys of the Orcia and Chiana. There is also an unpaved road from *Montepulciano* which can be walked in 45mins.

🍽 **La Chiusa**
☎ (0577) 669668 ⅢⅢ *with rooms* ☐ 🛏 🚗 《 AE CB ⊙ ⊙ VISA
Closed Tues (except in Aug-Sept), Jan to mid-Mar, Nov, lunch in July, Aug.
Like so many of the greatest Italian restaurants, La Chiusa specializes in local produce prepared according to the most refined culinary traditions of the area. Before embarking on the feast you would be wise to discuss the menu and ceiling price with the enthusiastic young proprietors.

Monte Oliveto Maggiore
Map 8J6. 104km (65 miles) SE of Florence, 36km (22 miles) SE of Siena. 53020. Siena.

The abbey †
Magnificently situated above the barren clay hills near *Siena*, the red brick buildings of this abbey date from the 14th-18thC; their institutional appearance is the result of a 19thC restoration.

The **chiostro grande** is decorated with important but heavily-restored and over-painted frescoes of *Scenes from the Life of St Benedict.* Nine are by Signorelli (1497-98), the rest by Sodoma (from 1505). In the church the intarsiaed **choir stalls** (1503-05) by Giovanni da Verona are exceptionally sophisticated exercises in perspective.

🍽 **La Torre** (☎ (0577) 707022, *closed Tues* ☐).

Montepulciano ☆
Map 12H7. 119km (74 miles) SE of Florence, 65km (40 miles) SE of Siena. 53045. Siena. Population: 14,297 i Via Ricci 9 ☎ (0578) 757442.

Like *Pienza*, 14km (9 miles) to the w, Montepulciano is neither town nor village, but a miniature Renaissance city. See these two little hill cities one after another and you will have captured the essence of the 15thC urban ideal as realized by some of the most distinguished Italian architects of the period. From the 12thC, Montepulciano modeled itself on Florence and Siena, its political masters. Its fortifications were rebuilt when Montepulciano fell to the Sienese in 1495-1511.

Agnolo Ambrogini, the leading humanist poet and scholar of the 15thC and tutor to Lorenzo de' Medici's children, was born in Montepulciano and called himself Poliziano after the medieval Latin name of his birthplace, Mons Politianus. The Jesuit Cardinal Robert Bellarmine was largely responsible for the flourish of Baroque architecture that followed.

Vino Nobile di Montepulciano is a redoubtable Tuscan wine.
Event   An annual music festival, the *Cantiere Internazionale d'Arte*, takes place here in July-early Aug. Founded in 1975 and run by a distinguished international committee, it emphasizes community involvement in performances of 20thC music.

Sights and places of interest
Follow the Corso from Porta al Prato to the far end of the town and loop back along its western edge.
The Corso
Via Gracciano nel Corso   The Corso is lined with good Renaissance palaces. No. 99, Palazzo Avignonesi, is attributed to Vignola; no. 72, the Cocconi, is attributed to Antonio da Sangallo the Elder. The lower story of no. 81, the Palazzo Bucelli, is faced with a mosaic of Etruscan and Roman tombs and cinerary urns. On the right is Michelozzo's delightful, Gothic-Renaissance church of **Sant'Agostino**; the lovely terra-cotta relief over the portal of the *Madonna and Child with Sts John the Baptist and Augustine* is also by Michelozzo.

Via di Voltaia nel Corso   The palace on the left, the Cervini, no. 21, with graduated rustication and a breaking-wave frieze, was designed by Antonio da Sangallo the Elder but not completed. Farther along on the left is the church of Gesù, which has a charming curved Baroque interior.

The last stretch of the Corso, **Via dell'Opio**, leads to the Via del Poliziano past no. 5, the house where Poliziano was born in 1454, to the Gothic church of **S. Maria dei Servi**, which has a Baroque interior.

The highest point of Montepulciano is its center, the wide and splendidly various **Piazza Grande**.

Duomo †
Designed by Ippolito Scalza and built on the site of the earlier parish church from 1592-1630, the Duomo contains a superb altarpiece of the *Assumption* (1401), possibly Taddeo di Bartolo's best work. Michelozzo's **Tomb of Bartolomeo Aragazzi** was dismantled in the 17thC and is now displayed in fragments placed to the left of the entrance, on the first two pillars of the nave, on either side of the altar and elsewhere. Notice also, in the right nave, the 15thC Sienese school polychrome *Annunciation.*

The **Palazzo Comunale**, next to the Duomo, was begun in the late 14thC, but its facade is later, possibly designed by Michelozzo. From the top of its tower you can see a panorama of southern Tuscany and into Umbria. Opposite are the Tarugi (no. 3) and Contucci (no. 6) palaces by Antonio da Sangallo the Elder.

Museo Civico 🏛
Via Ricci 11.
The Gothic Neri-Orselli Palace houses 13thC-17thC paintings, terra cottas and 15thC illuminated choir-books.

Nearby sight
San Biagio 🏛 † ★
Situated just outside the town to the sw, this church (1518-45) is the masterpiece of Antonio da Sangallo the Elder. The densely classicizing interior, all in the same pale honey travertine, is weighted with loyalty to the architectural principles of Bramante. The **Canon's House** and **well head** were also designed by Sangallo but completed posthumously.

⌘ ⥤ Il Marzocco
Piazza Savonarola ☎ (0578) 757262 ⫼ *18 rms* 🖾 *16* 🛏 ⥤ AE ◉ VISA *Closed late Nov-early Dec.*
Conveniently located inside the walls, this small hotel-restaurant offers clean, cozy rooms and good, simply prepared food.
❧

⥤ See also *Montefollonico.*

Monteriggioni
Map 11F5. 55km (34 miles) s of Florence, 15km (9 miles) NW of Siena. 53035. Siena. Population: 6,573.
A complete medieval village encircled by 13thC walls built by the Sienese against the Florentines: Dante compared the 14 towers to giants (*Inferno XXXI*).

The **Museo del Seminario Arcivescovile** has Vecchietta's moving and remarkable detached fresco of the *Lamentation* (c.1445).

Nearby sight
Abbadia Isola †
Less than 3km (1.75 miles) sw, this tiny village conserves a Romanesque church in the Lombard style from the 11thC Cistercian abbey of S. Salvatore. The church possesses an altarpiece (1471) by Sano di Pietro, a fresco of the *Madonna and Child with Saints* by Taddeo di Bartolo, an early 15thC font and an Etruscan-Roman cinerary urn. In the priest's house is a *Madonna and Child*, possibly by Duccio.

⥤ Il Pozzo
Piazza Roma 2 ☎ (0577) 304127 ⫼ 🖂 AE ◉ *Closed Sun eve, Mon, Aug.*
An elegant and efficient country restaurant.

🐚 🚃 At Strove, 4km (2½ miles) sw, two restaurant-hotels, both closed in mid-winter, are **Casalta** (☎ (0577) 301002 🔲 *restaurant closed Wed*) and the **San Luigi Residence** (☎ (0577) 301055 🔲🔲), in a converted farmhouse surrounded by olive groves.

Monte San Savino
Map 12G7. 86km (53 miles) SE of Florence, 22km (14 miles) SW of Arezzo. 52048. Arezzo. Population: 7,565.
An agricultural hill village, birthplace of the sculptor Andrea Sansovino. The main street is the Corso Sangallo, lined with fine palaces and churches. The little church of **Santa Chiara** (1652) contains terra cottas by Sansovino and other sculptors including Sansovino's earliest important work, an altarpiece of *Sts Laurence, Roch and Sebastian* and the exquisite tabernacle to the left of the high altar, by Sansovino and Andrea della Robbia. Sansovino is thought to have designed the handsome Corinthian **Loggia dei Mercanti** farther along the Corso. The **Palazzo Comunale** opposite is by Ant. da Sangallo the Elder. In Piazza di Monte is the church of **S. Agostino**, with a handsome Gothic portal. Inside, it has early 15thC frescoes and, over the high altar, an *Assumption* (1539) by Vasari.

Lucignano, a short drive to the s, is an exceptionally attractive hill town, which has retained its elliptical medieval plan and commands a panorama of the Valdichiana. The Museo Comunale has a fine collection of mainly Sienese pictures.

🐚 **Sangallo** (*Piazza Vittorio Veneto* ☎ (0575) 843010 🔲🔲).

🚃 At Lucignano, 6km (4 miles) s, **La Rocca** (☎ (0575) 836775 🔲 *closed Wed, Jan*).

🐚 🚃 See also *Gargonza*.

Monte dell'Uccellina, Parco Naturale della Maremma ☆
Map 11I-J5. 157km (98 miles) s of Florence, 17km (10 miles) s of Grosseto. Entrance at Alberese ☎ (0564) 407098 📷 ✗ compulsory, on foot in summer ✱ Open Wed, Sat, Sun, hols.
The extremely varied ecological balance of the coastal terrain is protected in the Maremma Nature Reserve, at its loveliest in early June when the broom flowers. Demonstrations of cattle roping are sometimes given by the local *butteri* (cowboys).

🚃 **Pizza Alberese** (☎ (0564) 407134 🔲) serves fish as well as pizzas and has tables outside. Or try **Da Remo** (☎ (0564) 405014 🔲) at Rispescia Stazione. See also *Talamone*.

Orbetello
Map 8J5. 183km (113 miles) s of Florence, 43km (27 miles) s of Grosseto. 58015. Grosseto. Population: 14,749.
The capital of the Spanish Garrison States, the *Presidii*, from 1557 retains something of the atmosphere (and the faces) of a Spanish colonial town. The fortifications on the mainland side were initiated by the Sienese and extended by the Spanish.

The **Duomo** (1376) has a pretty Gothic facade decorated in the Sienese style. In the first chapel on the right is a rare pre-Romanesque marble **altar-front**. The **Orbetello Oasis**, a sanctuary for migrating birds, is nearby (☎ (0564) 860239).

163

✇ **Presidi** (*Via Mura di Levante* ☎ *(0564) 867601* ▯ *to* ▯▯) is a sensible, friendly hotel on the lagoon.

═ **Il Cantuccio** (*Via Mentana 7* ☎ *(0564) 867587* ▯▯ *closed Mon, two weeks in Nov*); **Da Egisto** (*Corso Italia 190* ☎ *(0564) 867469* ▯ *to* ▯▯ *closed Mon, Nov*); **Osteria del Lupacante** (*Corso Italia 190* ☎ *(0564) 867681* ▯▯ *closed Wed, Nov*).

Laguna Blu does good ice creams.

Two restaurants 7km (4½ miles) NE on the Via Aurelia near Orbetello Scalo, both with rooms, are **Il Cacciatore** (☎ *(0564) 862020* ▯ *closed Wed*) and **La Ruota** (☎ *(0564) 862137* ▯ *closed Thurs, Feb*). See also *Ansedonia, Port'Ercole, Porto Santo Stefano*.

Pescia

Map 15D4. 61km (38 miles) NW of Florence, 19km (12 miles) NE of Lucca. 51017. Pistoia. Population: 18,979.

This horticultural and paper-making center in the Valdinievole is renowned for its carnations and asparagus. The town has been divided into five districts or *quinti* since the 13thC. The civic center, Piazza Mazzini, is on the right bank of the River Pescia; the religious center, Piazza del Duomo, on the left bank.

Sights and places of interest
Piazza Mazzini

The long, narrow square is a lively architectural farrago of 14th-19thC houses, closed at the s end by the 15thC **Oratory of the Madonna di Piè di Piazza**, possibly designed by Brunelleschi's adopted son Buggiano, and at the N end by the 13th-14thC Palazzo dei Viacri.

In the nearby Piazza S. Stefano is the **Museo Civico**, with Tuscan paintings of the 14th-16thC.
Duomo †

The Baroque Duomo (1693) has a late 19thC facade and a sturdy Romanesque-Gothic campanile. Inside are the Renaissance **Turini Chapel** by G. di Baccio d'Agnolo, and the remains of a 13thC ambo.
San Francesco †
Via Battisti.

The restored interior of this Gothic church contains a rare Romanesque painting by Bonaventura Berlinghieri of *St Francis* (1235), executed only 9yrs after the death of the saint. The Brunelleschian **Orlandi-Cardini Chapel** (1451) may have been designed by Buggiano.

Also in Via Battisti is the 11th-14thC Oratory of Sant' Antonio containing a moving wooden group of the *Deposition*.

The huge steel and glass flower market, the **Nuovo Mercato dei Fiori**, occupies a site of 40,000sq.m. on the road to Chiesina Uzzanese.
Nearby sights

3km (1.75 miles) to the E of Pescia is the beautifully situated village of Uzzano. There are good Romanesque churches at or just outside the villages of Castelvecchio, Montecarlo, Villa Basilica and S. Gennaro.

See also *Collodi*.

═ **Cecco** ✿
Viale Forti 84 ☎ *(0572) 477955* ▯▯ ▭ ≡ 🏠 ⬤ AE *Closed Mon, early July.*

Pleasant service and exceptional food. In Apr and May the local *asparagi giganti* should be tried. **Specialties:** *Pastas, pollastrino al mattone.*

✇ ═ **Villa delle Rose** (*51012 Castellare di Pescia* ☎ *(0572) 451301* ▯▯▯ *to* ▯▯▯▯ *restaurant closed Mon, Tues lunch*) has a cool park and ⇖.

Pienza ★

Map 9H7. 120km (75 miles) s of Florence, 52km (33 miles) s of Siena. 53026. Siena. Population: 2,622.

Few men have left such a vivid and complete picture of their period as did Enea Silvio Piccolomini, born in 1405 of an impoverished branch of a noble Sienese family, Pope as Pius II from 1458-64, in his candid autobiography, the *Commentaries.*

Pienza, the Utopian city with which he glorified his humble birth-place, Corsignano, is the first modern example of considered town planning. This joyous little Renaissance New Town is a celebration of the bracing winds of change that blew from every direction through the culture of 15thC Italy. It is a meeting ground of the Gothic and Renaissance styles, of the German church architecture Pius had seen on his travels and the strict Classical principles laid down by Alberti, of Florentine and Sienese art, of the Tuscan countryside and the sophisticated urbanity of the Tuscan *quattrocento* spirit.

As soon as Pius was elected Pope he commissioned Bernardo Rossellino to rebuild Corsignano. Work began in 1459. Three years later the piazza and street grid were complete and the new city was renamed Pienza by Papal bull. Pius left instructions that his cathedral, "the finest in all Italy," should never be altered in the smallest detail.

The remote situation of Pienza has ensured that his order was carried out.

Sights and places of interest

The central **Piazza Pio II** is like an open-air room looking s through the two window spaces on either side of the cathedral, which is flanked by the Palazzo Piccolomini on the right and the Palazzo Vescovile (Bishop's Palace) on the left. The N side is closed by the Palazzo Comunale and a wing of the Ammannati Palace, built by one of Pius' cardinals. The beautifully carved well-head (1462) was designed by Rossellino.

Cattedrale ▥ †
The travertine facade follows Alberti's Classical principles of organization. On the pediment is the papal coat of arms. The interior was inspired by the German *Hallenkirchen* Pius admired.

He specially commissioned the **paintings** by illustrious Sienese artists: Giovanni di Paolo, Matteo di Giovanni, Vecchietta and Sano di Pietro. The Classical frames and the decorative carvings elsewhere in the church were executed by Sienese craftsmen. The Gothic **canons' stalls** (1462) in the central chapel are magnificent. In the crypt, below the apse, is a **baptismal font** by Rossellino.

Museo della Cattedrale
In the Canon's House. Sienese paintings, Flemish tapestries, illuminated choir-books and ecclesiastical vestments including, most notably, the **cope** embroidered for Pius II in England.

Palazzo Piccolomini ▥
Piazza Pio II.
The papal residence is a rougher version of Alberti's and Rossellino's *Rucellai Palace* (see *Florence A to Z*), with one important addition, the three-tiered loggia on the s side. The elegant courtyard gives access to the hanging gardens below the palace.

Palazzo Vescovile
Pius acquired for Rodrigo Borgia, the future Pope Alexander VI, the old Gothic Palazzo Pretorio, which Borgia adapted and later gave to the city.

Pieve di Corsignano †
Below the town, 1km (½ mile) from the Porta al Ciglio. Pius II was baptized in the rough stone font that remains in this endearing little Romanesque church, which now stands alone in a sloping olive grove.

= **Il Prato**
Via Dante Alighieri 25 ☎ *(0578) 748601* ▯▯ ▬ ◄€ ▞▞ ▞▞ ▞▞ *Closed Wed, July.*
Excellent antipasti — and don't fail to sample the vin santo.

= Also **Buca delle Fate** (☎ *(0578) 748448* ▯▯ *closed Mon*) and **Dal Falco** (☎ *(0578) 748551* ▯▯ *to* ▯▯▯ *closed Fri, Nov*).
See also *Montalcino* and *Montefollonico.*

Pietrasanta

Map 14D3. 104km (64 miles) NW of Florence, 35km (22 miles) N of Pisa. 55045. Lucca. Population: 25,722.
The main town of the Versilia and center of marbleworking is 3.5km (2 miles) inland from its coastal resort Marina di Pietrasanta. The imposing 13th-14thC Duomo is much restored.
Event An exhibition of marblework by local artisans is held July-Sept in the Consorzio Artigiani.

 Peralta *(3km (2 miles) SE of Camaiore at Pieve di Camaiore* ☎ *(0584) 951230* ▥ *closed Nov-Mar)* is a small, secluded rural hotel with a mainly English staff. A good base for walking.

 Il Gatto Nero *(Piazza Carducci 32* ☎ *(0584) 70135* ▥ *closed Mon, Oct)* is a family-run restaurant with bohemian personality.
There is a better selection of restaurants at Camaiore, 10km (6 miles) E, including the **Antica Trattoria Bernadone** ♣ *(Via Provinciale* ☎ *(0584) 951118* ▥ *to* ▥ *closed Wed, Oct)*, which serves honest, homemade food. See also *Forte dei Marmi*.

Pisa ★

Map 14E3. 91km (56 miles) W of Florence, 3km (2 miles) N of Galileo Galilei international airport at S. Giusto. 56100. Pisa. Population: 103,849 i Piazza Arcivescovado ☎ *(050) 560464, and Piazza Stazione* ☎ *(050) 42291.*
The golden age of Pisa was the 12thC, when the Duomo was completed and the Baptistry and campanile were begun. Pisa had enjoyed a modest maritime economy even during the Dark Ages, thanks to its natural harbor at the mouth of the Arno, and was favored by successive Emperors who needed the support of its strong navy. In 1162 the Emperor Federico Barbarossa granted the commune control of a large coastal territory stretching to the N and S beyond the modern Tuscan borders.

The Duomo, a mix of the Italian and Oriental styles familiar to Pisan sailor merchants, was widely copied and infused Tuscan Romanesque architecture with new vigor. In sculpture, too, Pisa led the way, producing in Nicola and Giovanni Pisano the first great modern figure sculptors.

After the destruction of its fleet by the Genoese at the battle of Meloria in 1284, the communal government, distracted by internal conflict, neglected the shallow harbor, which began gradually to silt up. The city fell to Florence in 1406, the port in 1421. There was one final bid for independence in 1495 when Pisa, under the protection of Charles VIII, revolted, not to be retaken until 1509.

The Florentines paid special attention to the welfare of their prize conquest, which remained commercially active even after the harbor had finally silted up in the 16thC. The University, which is today one of the most respected in Italy, was revived in 1472 by Lorenzo de' Medici, who temporarily forbade Florentines to study elsewhere, and in 1561 Cosimo I made Pisa headquarters of his new Crusading Order of St Stephen.

Pisa's most illustrious son was Galileo, who taught at the University (which has had a strong science faculty ever since). In the 19thC, when Walter Savage Landor, Shelley, Byron and later the Brownings all made their homes in Pisa for short periods, the city was a brooding backwater shrouded in the mists of its Maremma, where the rich grazing lands had once been a source of its republican prosperity. Elizabeth Barrett Browning found it "very beautiful and full of repose"; but to Shelley's more feverish imagination Pisa sometimes seemed "a desolation of a city, which was the cradle, and is now the grave of an extinguished people." In the last years of World War II some of Pisa's greatest monuments were severely damaged.

Events   The annual *Regatta di San Ranieri*, a race among the city's four historic quarters, is held on the evening of June 17.

The *Gioco del Ponte*, a mock battle in 16thC costume between residents of the Mezzogiorno (s of the Arno) and Tramontana (N of the Arno), takes place on June 28.

Concerts are given in the Palazzo dei Cavalieri, Dec-May.

Sights and places of interest

The center of the modern city is Piazza Garibaldi. Immediately to its s is the **Ponte di Mezzo**, the city's oldest bridge, which gives the best view of the elegant palaces lining the Arno.

Campo dei Miracoli *(Piazza del Duomo)* ★

The buildings of Pisa's religious center are placed on their emerald lawn like carved ivory pieces in a great ecclesiastical game. The complex is enclosed on the w and N sides by sections of the 13thC city walls.

Baptistry ⅲ † ★

Begun in 1152 by Diotisalvi, carried forward from 1260-84 by Nicola and Giovanni Pisano, the Baptistry was completed by its Gothic dome in the 14thC. Of the four portals notice especially the one facing the Duomo. The *Madonna* in the lunette is a copy of Giovanni Pisano's original now in the Museo Nazionale.

Inside, to the left of Guido da Como's octagonal **baptismal font** (1246), is Nicola Pisano's **pulpit** (1260) (★); the style of his relief carvings was affected by the Roman sarcophagi which in the 13thC were used as the tombs of Christian Pisans buried around the Duomo; this pulpit marks the first appearance in Italy of the French Gothic style. The panels illustrate the *Nativity, Epiphany, Presentation at the Temple, Crucifixion* and *Last Judgment*. The statues round the walls, by Nicola and Giovanni Pisano, were originally on the exterior of the Baptistry.

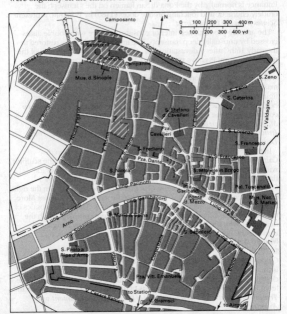

Campanile 🏛 ✝ ★
📷 ✳

The circular bell tower of Pisa is perhaps even more famous for leaning 4.5m (15ft) out of plumb than for its architectural elegance. Begun in 1173, its foundations were tilted by a subsidence of the soil when the third story was half built. After a pause of 100yrs the tower was completed in the mid-14thC. It is, of course, from this tower that Galileo is supposed to have dropped the three metal balls of different masses that disproved Aristotle's theories about the acceleration of falling bodies. A spiral staircase of 294 steps leads to the top.

Camposanto (Cemetery) ☆

The legend has it that earth for the cemetery of Pisa was brought in shiploads from the Holy Land early in the 13thC. This sacred ground was enclosed by a rectangular building begun in 1277 and completed in the 15thC. The walls of the interior portico were frescoed by leading Italian artists including Taddeo Gaddi, Spinello Aretino and Benozzo Gozzoli. Over the centuries, a precious collection of antique sarcophagi was assembled here. What could be salvaged from wartime damage has been painstakingly pieced together; but the ghostly frescoes speak more eloquently through their sinopie, now in the **Museo delle Sinopie**.

The most interesting works are in the N section. In the N portico are the remains of Gozzoli's popular *Grape Harvest* and *Drunkenness of Noah*; and, among other fine sarcophagi, the 2ndC AD sarcophagus depicting *Phaedra and Hyppolitus*, which affected the style of Nicola Pisano's Baptistry pulpit. Off the portico, to the left of the Cappella Ammannati, is the **Salone degli Affreschi**, where the greatest of the Camposanto frescoes, detached and restored, are hung. The most famous is the *Triumph of Death* (*Trionfo della Morte*) by an unknown late 14thC master, which inspired Liszt's *Totentanz*; hence the bust of the composer near the entrance. Among the sculptures are Giovanni Pisano's *Madonna and Child* and five statues from Tino di Camaino's *Tomb of the Emperor Henry VII* in the Duomo.

Duomo 🏛 ✝ ★

The most influential Romanesque building in Tuscany and the first to be dressed in black and white horizontal stripes, the Duomo was begun in 1064 by Buscheto; its tiered facade was added in the 12thC by Rainaldo. Entrance is normally by the Porta di San Ranieri on the S transept; the crudely energetic and touching bronze doors (1180) by Bonanno represent *Scenes from the Life of Christ*.

The grandly proportioned interior consists of a nave with double aisles crossed by unusually deep transepts. The interior was heavily restored in the early 16thC after a devastating fire. At the bottom of the left side of the nave is Giovanni Pisano's **pulpit** (1302-10) (★). It bears an inscription suggesting that this extremely complex work caused the artist considerable worry. The result was one of the most personal and dramatic sculptural masterpieces of its own or indeed any time. The relief panels, divided by figures of prophets and saints, depict scenes from the New Testament beginning with the *Birth of the Baptist*, facing the column. The sequence continues with the *Annunciation, Visitation, Nativity, Adoration of the Magi, Presentation at the Temple, Flight into Egypt, Slaughter of the Innocents, Kiss of Judas* and *Passion, Crucifixion, The Elect*, and *The Damned*.

In the E corner of the right transept is a reconstruction of Tino di Camaino's **tomb of Emperor Henry VII** commissioned when the sculptor was made Head of Works of the Cathedral in 1315. On the balustrade flanking the entrance to the presbytery are two **bronze angels** by Giambologna, who also made the *Crucifix* over the high altar. On the right as one enters the presbytery is Andrea del Sarto's charming *St Agnes*. More paintings by Andrea hang below the choral galleries. The 13thC mosaics of the *Redeemer in Glory* in the vault of the apse were completed with the head of *St John the Evangelist* by Cimabue in 1302. Below hang good canvases by Beccafumi.

Museo delle Sinopie ☆
☎ (050) 22531.

Opposite the S side of the piazza, in the Ospedale Nuovo della Misericordia, is this fascinating display of preparatory drawings, revealed by the destruction of the Camposanto frescoes, a unique opportunity to study the technique of some of the leading artists of the 13th-15thC. They include the *Triumph of Death* and Gozzoli's *Scenes from the Old Testament* and *Annunciation*.

Museo Nazionale di San Matteo ★
Lungarno Mediceo.

Behind the church of San Matteo on the Lungarno Mediceo, the former
convent, once used as a prison, now houses a superb collection of Pisan
sculpture and 12th-15thC Tuscan pictures. Among the many outstanding
pieces, notice especially: **figures from the exteriors of the Duomo and
Baptistry** by Giovanni Pisano; the *Madonna of the Milk* by Andrea Pisano,
formerly in Santa Maria della Spina; two *Crucifixes* by Giunta Pisano; the
Madonna and Child and *Scenes from the Childhood of Christ* by the Master
of San Martino; Simone Martini's polyptych of the *Madonna and Child with
Saints*; Masaccio's *San Paolo*, part of a polyptych, of which the other
sections are now scattered or lost, which was the master's first major work.

Nearby on the Lungarno Mediceo is the **Toscanelli** palace where Byron
lived in 1821-22.

Piazza dei Cavalieri ★

Five minutes' walk from the Duomo is the central square of medieval Pisa
rebuilt in the 16thC by Vasari as headquarters of the Knights on the order of
St Stephen. The **Palazzo dei Cavalieri** (1562) is decorated with splendid
and fantastic *sgraffiti* incorporating the busts of six Medici grand dukes.

To its right is the church of **S. Stefano dei Cavalieri** (1569), also
designed by Vasari but with a later facade. The **Palazzo dell'Orologio**, on
the N of the square, was adapted in 1607; it stands on the site of the tower
where Count Ugolino della Gherardesca and his male heirs were starved to
death by their political rivals in 1288; this episode, grimly described by
Dante in *Inferno, XXXIII*, inspired Shelley's poem *The Tower of Famine*.

Santa Maria della Spina ▥ † ★
Lungarno Gambacorti.

Named after a thorn from Christ's crown brought from the Holy Land by a
Pisan merchant, this beautiful church was the swan-song of the Pisan
Gothic style. The last of the great Pisan churches and perhaps the loveliest,
it assumed its present size in the 1320s. The building originally stood closer
to the Arno; in 1871 it was moved, stone by stone, to its present drier site.

Other sights

Other Pisan churches well worth visiting are S. Caterina, S. Francesco,
S. Michele in Borgo, S. Paolo a Ripa d'Arno, S. Nicola, S. Sepolcro, S. Zeno
and S. Frediano.

❦ Dei Cavalieri
Piazza della Stazione 2 ☎ *(050) 43290* ❶ *590663* ❸ *(050) 502242* ▥
102 rms ▭ 102 ▤ ▣ ▭ ▭ ▣ ▣ ▣
Conveniently located near the station and air terminal, this well-managed
modern hotel has an elegant and tranquil restaurant.
⇕ ▢ ▨ ▲ ☿

❦ Ariston (*Via Maffi 42* ☎ *(050) 561834* ▭), basic, near Duomo.

═ Sergio
Lungarno Pacinotti 1 ☎ *(050) 48245* ▥ ▭ ▰ ▰ ▤ ▣ ▣ ▣ ▣ ▣
Closed Sun, Mon lunch, late Jan-early Feb, one week in July.
The fashionable restaurant of Pisa and one of Tuscany's best offers a large
choice of modern and traditional dishes. Service is attentive and practiced.

═ Vecchi Macelli
Via Volturno 49 ☎ *(050) 20424* ▥ *to* ▥ ▰ ▤ ▣ ▣ *Closed Sun
lunch, Wed, mid-Aug.*
A sympathetic small restaurant (be sure to reserve) which serves
outstanding *pasta fresca* — try the *saccottini di cappesante con salsa di
gamberi* or, in winter, the *ravioli farciti con salsiccia e cavolfiore* — as well
as delicious meat, fish, fresh vegetables and desserts.

═ Also: Da Bruno (*Via Luigi Bianchi 12* ☎ *(050) 560818* ▥ *closed Mon
eve, Tues, early Aug*); Lo Schiacciandoci (*Via Vespucci 104* ☎ *(050)
21024* ▥ *closed Sun eve, also Sun lunch in summer, Mon, Aug, early Jan*).
See also *Excursions*, over.

Excursions
1. S. Piero a Grado †
6km (4 miles) SW of Pisa is a Romanesque basilica of the

mid-11thC built on the site where St Peter is thought to have landed on his way from Antioch to Rome.

🍴 There is a good choice of fish restaurants on the coast near S. Piero. At Marina di Pisa, try **L'Arsella** (*Via Padre Agostino* ☎ *(050) 36615* ▯ *to* ▯ *closed Tues eve, Wed, Jan*).

2. Tenuta di San Rossore
6km (4 miles) W of Pisa is a protected littoral wood of oaks and pines, formerly a royal estate, between the mouths of the Arno and the Serchio.
   See also *Cascina*.

Pistoia ★
Map **15D5**. *37km (23 miles)* NW *of Florence. 51100. Pistoia. Population: 94,637* **i** *Piazza Duomo* ☎ *(0573) 21622.*

In 63BC the Roman revolutionary Catiline was cornered by Roman legions near Pistoia; facing defeat he plunged through the enemy ranks to his death. Dante considered the Pistoiesi to be even more dangerous than Catiline; and certainly their past is deeply scarred by factional conspiracy and violence. It was in Pistoia, as Dante recounts in the *Inferno, XXIV*, that the fierce political contest between Blacks and Whites originated.

   For at least 200yrs after the commune had surrendered to Florence in 1329 its citizens retained their reputation for rude manners and rough justice. Machiavelli described them as "brought up to slaughter and war"; and when the first pistols were made in Germany in the 16thC, they were named after the vicious little daggers worn by Pistoiesi and known as "*pistolese.*" Today Pistoia is a peaceful provincial capital surrounded by the orchards and nursery gardens which are the basis of its economy. Its main attraction for tourists is the wealth of Romanesque sculpture, especially the three pulpits in S. Bartolomeo, S. Giovanni Fuorcivitas, and S. Andrea, which, if seen in that order, will enable one to follow the first "renaissance" of Tuscan sculpture as it evolved from 1250-1300.

Sights and places of interest
The early 14thC walls, still partly intact, were later strengthened with bastions by the Medici. But the main historic monuments of the town lie within the earlier walls, the outline of which is traced in part by Corso Gramsci.
Duomo 🏛 †
The marble porch, which gives the cathedral the appearance of crouching ready to pounce, was added in the mid-14thC to the 12th-13thC Pisan-style facade. The terra cottas (1505) over the central portal and in the vault above are by Andrea della Robbia. The interior walls are decorated with fragments of 13th-14thC frescoes uncovered during a recent restoration. At the top of the right aisle is the 14thC **tomb of Cino da Pistoia**, who was Dante's friend. In the Cappella di San Jacopo, off the right aisle, is the extraordinary silver **St James Altar**, one of the supreme examples of the Italian goldsmiths' art and crowded with many endearing details. It was created from 1287-1456 by a succession of Tuscan sculptors including Brunelleschi, who made the two **figures** on the left side. In the chapel to the left of the high altar is a *Madonna and Saints* (1485) by Lorenzo di Credi, possibly begun by Verrocchio; also the bust of *Archbishop Donato de' Medici* by A. Rossellino or Verrocchio.
Baptistry †
Opposite the cathedral is the tall, hexagonal Gothic Baptistry (1338-1359), by Cellino de Nese to a design by Andrea Pisano. The interior is bare except for the original font, rediscovered during a recent restoration, and the shaming commercial art exhibitions which are, incredibly, permitted to take place here from time to time.

Palazzo del Comune 🏛

The town hall, a very fine example of Gothic civic architecture, was founded in 1294 by the enlightened Florentine governor Giano della Bella, but building was delayed by political upheavals and not completed until 1355. Over the central door and on the corners are the crests of Medici Popes. The aerial corridor from the Sala Maggiore to the Duomo was added in 1637. The **Marino Marini Center** (the sculptor was born in Pistoia in 1901) is off the courtyard; among the works on display are portraits of *Thomas Mann, Henry Miller* and *Chagall*. The **Museo Civico**, opened in 1981, occupies rooms on the first and second floors.

Palazzo del Podestà

This 14thC building is still the city's tribunal. Left of the entrance is the old court, with judge's seat, table of justice and bench of the accused.

Ospedale del Ceppo 🏛

Piazza Giovanni XII. Not open to the public.

The startling frieze over the porch of the hospital looks at first glance like the work of a Russian social realist. It was executed in the early 16thC by members of Andrea della Robbia's workshop and illustrates the *Seven Works of Mercy*, a fascinating picture of poverty and illness in the 16thC. The lovely Verrocchiesque tondas over the columns are probably by Andrea himself. The hospital is still in use.

Sant'Andrea 🏛 †

The 12thC church has an enchanting but unfinished facade. The reliefs (1166) of the *Journey and Adoration of the Magi* over the central portal are by the brothers Gruamonte and Adeodato. The interior is by the city's outstanding work of art, the **pulpit** (★) by Giovanni Pisano (1298-1301). This pulpit was finished a year before Giovanni started work on the pulpit of the **Duomo** in **Pisa**. These carvings are so intensely dynamic that one can scarcely believe they were created two centuries before the age of Michelangelo. Their subject is the *Life of Christ* and the *Last Judgment*. Opposite the pulpit is a wooden *Crucifix*, also by Giovanni, in a fine 15thC tabernacle frame.

San Bartolomeo in Pantano †

Piazza S. Bartolomeo.

A 12thC church, with a reconstructed **pulpit** (1250) by Guido da Como.

San Giovanni Fuorcivitas †

Via Francesco Crispi.

The name refers to the original 8thC church that stood outside the city walls. The building was erected from the mid-12th to 14thC and restored after damage during World War II. The entrance is by the decoratively vivid but scarred N flank. Inside, the **holy water stoup** in the center is notable for the four busts of cardinals by the young Giovanni Pisano. On the right wall is the **pulpit** (1270) by Gugliemo da Pisa, a follower of Nicola Pisano; the reliefs illustrate *Scenes from the New Testament*. On the left wall are the glazed terra-cotta figures of the *Visitation*, a moving work attributed to Luca or Andrea della Robbia. To the left of the altar is a large polyptych (1353-55) by Taddeo Gaddi.

Zoo *(Giardino Zoologico)*

Via Pieve a Celle 160 ☎ *(0573) 571280* 🅿 ♿

The new and attractively planned zoo is 4km (2½ miles) sw of Pistoia.

Other sights

Visitors with leisure should also look at the churches of S. Francesco; S. Domenico; S. Paolo; S. Maria delle Grazie, designed by Michelozzo; and the Cappella Tau, decorated with 14th-15thC frescoes.

❧ **Arcobaleno**

Via Valdi e Collina 37, Sanmommè, 51020 Pistoia ☎ *(0573) 470030* ☏ *(0573) 470147* 💳 *28 rms* 🛏 *28* 🚮 ≕ 🍴 *summer* ▥ 💳 *Closed 10 Jan-10 Feb.*

Location: 15km (9 miles) to N at Sanmommè. A vacation hotel in the mountains popular with children for the sports facilities and disco.

🏠 🖼 💐 ⛷ ♨ ✣ ⛵ 🏖 ⚓ Ƴ ☺ ♉

❧ **Residence il Convento**

Via S. Quirico 33, 51030 Santomato ☎ *(0573) 452651* 💳 *24 rms* 🛏 *24* 🚮 ≕ 💳 ▥ 💳

Location: 5km (3 miles) to NE near Ponte Nuovo. A peaceful retreat in an 18thC ex-convent overlooking Pistoia.

🏠 🖼 🍴 💐 ⛷

♋ Villa Ombrosa
30km (19 miles) NW *at San Marcello Pistoiese, Via M. D'Azeglio,*
51028 San Marcello Pistoiese ☎ *(0573) 630156* ⫾◻ *27 rms* ⫽⫽ ⬥ ⬛
Open July to mid-Sept only.
Atmospherically furnished with antiques and set in a cool, shady garden.
◨ ⬥ ⬛

♋ 10km (6 miles) N at Piteccio, **Villa Vannini** (*Via Villa di Piteccio 6,*
51100 Piteccio ☎ *(0573) 42031* ⫾◻ *to* ⫾⫾◻ *8 rms*), a peaceful and refined
hotel in a Neo-Classical villa.

⫽⫽ There is nothing special in the historic center. Just outside is **Rafanelli**
Sant'Agostino (*Via Sant'Agostino 47* ☎ *(0573) 523046* ⫾⫾◻ *closed Sun*
dinner, Mon, Aug).

⫽⫽ Osteria
Via Provinciale Pratese 58, Agliana ☎ *(0574) 718450* ⫾⫾◻ ◻⫾ ⬛⬛ ⬥
Closed Mon, Tues eve, Wed in Aug.
This rustic, friendly country place, halfway between Pistoia and Prato,
prepares Tuscan home cooking with a daily set menu.

⫽⫽ See also *Montecatini Terme* and *Prato.*

Shopping
The biggest and best of the plant sellers is **Zelari Pianti** (*Via*
Pratese 504 ☎ *(0573) 532121*).

Pitigliano
Map **9**J7. *218km (134 miles)* S *of Florence, 74km (46 miles)*
SE *of Grosseto. 58017. Grosseto. Population: 4,443.*
From a distance Pitigliano is one of the most amazing sights in
Tuscany. Carved out of a rock escarpment above a natural moat
formed by three deep ravines, this was the seat of the Roman
Orsini barons when they took control of the area in 1293. It
retains the dour, impressive stamp of a war lord's headquarters,
remarkably intact, charmless but fascinating.
   The main square, Piazza della Repubblica, is dominated by the
14th-15thC **Palazzo Orsini**, modified in the 16thC by Giuliano
da Sangallo. The strongly atmospheric medieval *borgo* straddles
the escarpment beyond the Duomo.

♋ ⫽⫽ **Guastini** (*Piazza Petruccioli 4* ☎ *(0564) 616065* ◻ *to* ⫾◻ *closed*
Fri, mid-Jan).

Poggibonsi
Map **11**F5. *41km (25 miles)* S *of Florence, 33km (20 miles)*
NW *of Siena. 53036. Siena. Population: 25,784.*
A commercial and industrial center (wine and furniture).

Nearby sights
2km (1¼ miles) S is the 13thC Gothic church of **San Lucchese**, rebuilt after
World War II, containing frescoes by Bartolo di Fredi. 8km (5 miles) SE on
the Siena road is the fortified medieval hamlet of **Staggia**, where the
museum (*apply at sacristan's house*) attached to the parish church
possesses a panel of the *Communion of the Magdalen* by A. del Pollaiuolo.

♋ ⫽⫽ **Alcide** (*Viale Marconi 67a* ☎ *(0577) 937501* ⫾◻ *closed Wed, July*).

Poggio a Caiano
Map **15**E5. *17km (10 miles)* W *of Florence. 50046. Firenze.*
Population: 5,892.

Villa Medicea di Poggio a Caiano 🏛 ★
☎ 877012 📠 *Open Tues-Sun, villa 9am-1.30pm, gardens 9am-4pm in winter, 9am-5pm in spring, 9am-7pm in summer. Closed Mon.*
The most innovative and influential of all Medici country houses, built for Lorenzo de' Medici from 1480-85, and the only important surviving building for which he was personally responsible. The architect was Giuliano da Sangallo, who adapted the antique Roman villa type to the requirements of Renaissance country life.

The arcaded ground floor provides a balcony for the *piano nobile*. The central loggia with its Robbianesque terra-cotta frieze was probably added in the 16thC. The curved staircases were added in the 17thC.

The traditional central courtyard is replaced by a two-story-high **salone** frescoed by Andrea del Sarto (until 1512), Franciabigio (until 1520), Pontormo (until 1532) and completed by A. Allori (1582). The Classical subjects refer to events in Medici history. The high point is Pontormo's fresco in the lunette of the right wall of *Vertumnus and Pomona* (1521), an idyllic and graceful picture of a Tuscan summer's day and a masterpiece of design.

⇌ See *Artimino* and *Lastra a Signa*.

Pontassieve
*Map **16**E6. 18km (11 miles) E of Florence. 50065. Firenze. Population: 19,752.*
A commercial wine town. The Rufina wine zone (see *Tuscan wines*) is just to the N, and there are pretty roads into the Pratomagno hills to the E. The Wed market is good for shoes.

🏰 **Castello di Sammezzano**
50067 Leccio-Rignano Sull'Arno, Firenze ☎ *(055) 867911* 📠 *573078*
▥▥▥ *15 rms* ▭ *15* 🚗 🚪 ⇌ 🔒 🏧 ⬛ 📺
Location: Near the Incisa autostrada exit from Florence. A 17thC castle stupendously decorated in 19thC Moorish style.
🏠 ⇕ 🔲 🖼 🍸 ⚘ ⟨ ♨ ☒

🍴 **Moderno** (*Via Londra 5* ☎ *(055) 8315541* ▥▥▥) is in the town.

⇌ **Archimede** (*N of Regello* ☎ *(055) 869055/868182* ▥▥▥ *with rooms, closed Wed*) is pleasant in summer.

⇌ **Il Girarrosto** ♣ (*Via Garibaldi 27* ☎ *(055) 8302048* ▥▥▥ ▭ ⬛ 🚗 ➡ 📺 *closed Mon, July*), a popular game restaurant.

Pontremoli
*Map **14**B2. 164km (102 miles) NW of Florence. 53km (33 miles) NW of Massa. 54027. Massa-Carrara. Population: 10,335.*
The principal town of the Lunigiana, named after the Etruscan city of Luni (which is now in Liguria).

A 19thC Neo-Classical facade has been added to the Baroque cathedral. The town boasts a pretty oval Rococo church, the Madonna del Ponte (1738).

Other sights
In the **Castello** on the hill of Piagnaro is a museum exhibiting the strange, totemic *stele* statues and other pre-Etruscan material from the area.
1.5km (1 mile) to the SE of the center, the church of SS Annunziata has a fine 16thC interior with a marble *tempietto* (1527) attributed to Jacopo Sansovino.

🍴 ⇌ **Golf** (*Via Pineta* ☎ *(0187) 831573* ▥▥▥ *closed Jan, restaurant closed Mon*).

☷ **Da Bussè** (*Piazza Duomo 9* ☎ *(0187) 831371* ▯ *closed Fri, July*) is an old-fashioned rustic trattoria.

Poppi

Map 12E7. 53km (33 miles) SE of Florence, 38km (24 miles) N of Arezzo. 52014. Arezzo. Population: 5,790.

Poppi is the starting point for the beautiful drive to *Camaldoli*. It is worth pausing here to admire the arcaded old streets.

Sights and places of interest
Palazzo Pretorio ▥

Originally the castle of the Guidi lords, the palace was rebuilt in 1274 and extended in 1291. Its resemblance to the *Palazzo Signoria* (see *Florence A to Z*) suggests that Arnolfo di Cambio may have had a hand in the design.

Primo Parco Zoo

Just outside the town, in a ravishing setting, this is the first zoo in Europe to be devoted exclusively to European animals (▣ ✻).

☷ See *Camaldoli*.

Populonia

Map 10H3. 149km (93 miles) SW of Florence, 89km (55 miles) NW of Grosseto. 57020. Livorno. Population: 122.

The only Etruscan town built on a coastal site, Populonia was inhabited from the 9thC BC and in the 7thC BC became a rich industrial city — the blast furnace of the ancient world. Iron ore imported from *Elba* was smelted here in such quantities that the necropolis was buried in slag and the beaches are still streaked with black. The inhabitants may have been the first Etruscans to mint coins in the 5thC BC. Populonia fell under the influence of Rome in the 3rdC BC, and by the 4thC AD was nearly empty.

The village is dominated by its restored medieval **rocca**. A privately owned **Etruscan museum** in the main street (*apply to custodian at no. 11*) houses an interesting collection of small, sacred and domestic objects from the necropolis.

Necropolis ☆

3km (2 miles) E of village ✗ compulsory (tours roughly on the hour).
This complex comprises tombs of the 9th-3rdC BC.

☷ **Gambero Rosso**

15km (9 miles) N at San Vincenzo, Piazza della Vittoria 13 ☎ *(0565) 701021* ▥▥ ▭ ▰ ☷ ☗ ᴀᴇ ⊙ ᴠɪꜱᴀ *Closed Tues, Nov.*
An elegant seaside restaurant specializing in fish and game.

Port'Ercole

Map 8J5. 190km (118 miles) S of Florence, 50km (31 miles) S of Grosseto. 58018. Grosseto. Population: 3,400.

A fashionable sailing resort on the E coast of Monte Argentario, which has attracted a faithful English summer colony. The Etruscans gave it the name of Port of Hercules. The three fortresses that guard it testify to its strategic importance; there is nowhere outside Malta where one can see Renaissance principles of fortification so well defined.

The Cala Galera, built next to the harbor in 1975, is one of the best-equipped marinas in the Mediterranean.

Sights and places of interest
Forte Filippo ▥

✗ compulsory: tours on Wed.
The best demonstration of late Renaissance fortification in the

Mediterranean. Mathematically and technically flawless, it is in an excellent state of preservation. Now converted into private apartments.

Forte Stella ⊞

South of the harbor, this now abandoned hexagonal fort on a four-sided bastion base was built by the Spanish in the 17thC.

Rocca Spagnola ⊞

Permission necessary from mayor's office (easily obtained).

The Rocca Spagnola is the original nucleus of the medieval fortress, refined and extended in the 15th-16thC, which dominates the historic center of the town, Piazza Santa Barbara. It forms a complete village.

On the Tombolo di Feniglia is a protected pine forest and a sandy beach where Caravaggio died in 1610.

☜ Don Pedro

Via Panoramica 7, 58018 Port'Ercole, Grosseto ☎ *(0564) 833914* Ⅲ▯
44 rms ▭ 44 ▦ ▣ ▱ ▰ *Closed Nov-Easter.*

The most attractive and best managed medium-price hotel in the area.
‡ ▱ ▨ ◐

☜ Il Pellicano ▥

Cala dei Santi, 58018 Port'Ercole, Grosseto ☎ *(0564) 833801*
▣ *500131* ▣ *(0564) 833418* Ⅲ 34 rms ▭ 34 ▦ ▬ ▰ ▥ AE CB ◉ ▥
Ⅲ *Closed Oct-Easter.*

The most attractive luxury hotel on the Argentario. Peace and quiet, attentive service, American country-house decor and a good restaurant.
▱ ▱ ▨ ◐ ▨ ▨ ⅌ ▰ ▰ ▰

☜ Villa Letizia

1km (½ mile) to the N ☎ *(0564) 834181* Ⅱ▯ 23 rms ▰

A simple but comfortable hotel overlooking the Cala Galera Marina.
▱ ▨ ◐ ⅌ ▢ ▱

▰ **La Grotta Pescatore** (☎ *(0564) 833970* ▯) is a popular fish restaurant on the harbor.

There is a better choice of restaurants at *Porto Santo Stefano*.

Excursion
The island of Giannutri

23km (14 miles) to the s, the island is reached from Port'Ercole. Near Cala Maestra is a 1stC AD Roman villa. Good underwater fishing in the clear waters of the Cala dei Grottoni.

Porto Santo Stefano

*Map **8J5**. 193km (121 miles) s of Florence, 53km (33 miles) s of Siena. 58019. Grosseto. Population: 10,100.*

This active fishing port on the N coast of Monte Argentario retains some of its charm. Boats depart frequently for *Giglio*.

▰ **Armando** (*Via Marconi 1/3* ☎ *(0564) 812586* Ⅲ *closed Wed, Nov*), a fish restaurant in the town; **La Fontanina** (*at S. Pietro above the town* ☎ *(0564) 825261* Ⅲ to Ⅲ *closed Wed*), with a vine-covered terrace; **La Formica** (*at Pozzarello* ☎ *(0564) 814205* Ⅲ *closed Wed in winter, Nov*); **Dal Greco** (*Via del Molo 1* ☎ *(0564) 814885* Ⅲ *closed Tues in winter*), a new restaurant with a terrace overlooking the old harbor; **Orlando** (*Via Breschi 3* ☎ *(0564) 812788* Ⅲ *closed Thurs, Nov-Feb*); **Da Siro** (*Corso Umberto I 102* ☎ *(0564) 812538* Ⅲ *closed Mon, Dec*), a peaceful restaurant overlooking the sea, with a wide selection of fish dishes.

Prato ★

*Map **15D5**. 19km (11 miles) NW of Florence. 50047. Firenze. Population: 156,955.*

Florentines say that if you listen closely in Prato late at night when the textile factories are closed you will hear a whirring: it is the sound of the inhabitants spinning in their back parlors, for 75 percent of the manufactured wool exported from Italy comes from Prato, and most of it is produced by small, privately-owned firms. Its population has doubled in 30yrs and is now the fourth largest and possibly the most affluent in central Italy. Florentines also call Prato the tail that tries to wag the dog.

The first cloth mills on the banks of the Bisenzio were in operation in 1108, half a century earlier than the first in Florence. But the prosperous city that grew up around a meadow (*prato*) was no more successful than most Tuscan communes at self-government. Unable to control its political factions, Prato placed itself under the protection of the Anjou rulers of Naples in 1313. In 1351, the Queen of Naples sold her rights to the city to Florence for 17,500 florins. The commercial fortunes of Prato were given an enormous boost later in the 14thC by the business operations of Francesco di Marco Datini, subject of Iris Origo's admirable biography, *The Merchant of Prato*. But although Prato enjoyed a greater economic and political autonomy than many Florentine-dominated cities, it rebelled on several occasions, and in the 16thC Florence punished it by rationing its permitted production of wool.

Apart from its distinctive green and white striped churches, there are two artistic masterpieces, both by Florentines, which compel a visit to Prato: Filippo Lippi's frescoes in the Duomo and Giuliano da Sangallo's church Santa Maria delle Carceri.

Events   The **Teatro Metastasio** (*Via Cairoli 59* ☎ *(0574) 26202*) is the home of one of Italy's most enterprising experimental companies. In spring and summer, concerts are given in the Metastasio and in the Castello.

The *Ostensione del Sacro Cingolo*, the ceremonial display of the Virgin's Holy Girdle from the external pulpit of the Duomo, takes place on May 1, Easter Day, Aug 15, Sept 8 and Dec 25.

Sights and places of interest

The old town sits within a partly intact hexagon of 13thC walls on the sw bank of the River Bisenzio.

Castello dell'Imperatore

For a good orienting view walk around the battlements of this castle, built in the 13thC for the Emperor Frederick II.

Opposite the Castello is **Santa Maria delle Carceri** (see opposite).

Duomo ▥ † ★

The striped facade was applied to the Romanesque building in 1384-1457. The glazed terra-cotta lunette of the *Madonna with Sts. Stephen and Lawrence* (1489) over the portal is by Andrea della Robbia. Projecting from the right corner is the covered **pulpit of the Holy Girdle** (1428-38) by Donatello and Michelozzo. The originals of Donatello's carvings of *Dancing Putti* have been removed to the Cathedral Museum.

The sturdy green and blonde interior conserves remarkable works of art, but the nave is bare except for the pulpit (1473) by Mino da Fiesole and A. Rossellino. Left of the entrance is the **chapel of the Holy Girdle** (1385-95); the legend of the Holy Girdle is illustrated by Agnolo Gaddi's frescoes (1392-95). The Holy Girdle was brought from the Holy Land to Prato in the 12thC, and its story is still popular in Tuscany. Over the altar is a *Madonna and Child* (c.1317) by Giovanni Pisano. Behind the high altar of the cathedral, in the choir, are Filippo Lippi's frescoes (1452-66) (★) of the martyrdom of *St John the Baptist*, on the right wall, and of *St Stephen*, on the left (a coin-operated light switch is on the left of the last chapel in the left transept). Filippo labored over these frescoes for 14yrs during which he was tried for fraud and fathered a child by the nun Lucrezia (who may be the model for the dancing Salome). They are the considered masterpieces of his troubled maturity, and yet they glow with a clear-eyed vivacity and apparently spontaneous grace which make them among the most immediately pleasing of Renaissance paintings.

The chapel to the right of the altar is frescoed with scenes from the *Lives*

of the Virgin and of St Stephen, begun by Paolo Uccello or a disciple and
completed, still in the early 15thC, in a strange quasi-Mannerist style by
Andrea di Giusto. In the right transept is a tabernacle of the *Madonna of the
Olive* (1480) by all three Maiano brothers; also a panel painting of the *Death
of St Jerome* by Filippo Lippi.

Museo dell'Opera del Duomo *(Cathedral Museum)*
In the Bishop's Palace to the left of the Duomo. The main attractions are
Donatello's reliefs of *Dancing Putti* from the exterior pulpit, but they are
less good than the miniature frieze of dancing putti on the exquisite
reliquary of the Holy Girdle (1446) by Maso di Bartolomeo.

Galleria Comunale
Piazza Comune.
The gallery occupies three floors of the 13th-14thC Palazzo Pretorio. The
large collection includes minor 14th-15thC altarpieces in good condition,
two panels by Filippo Lippi, Neapolitan fruit paintings, and plaster models
by L. Bartolini.

Santa Maria delle Carceri 🏛 ✝ ★
Giuliano da Sangallo's harmoniously proportioned cruciform interior,
begun 1485, is a masterpiece of Italian Renaissance architecture, a perfect
restatement of Brunelleschi's principles. The blue and white terra-cotta
decorations and medallions are by Andrea Della Robbia.

Other sights
Palazzo Datini in Via Rinaldesca, which Francesco di Marco Datini had
built for himself in the late 14th-early 15thC; Datini's tomb in the nearby
church of **San Francesco**; and the late 14thC frescoes in the chapter room
off the cloister, which include a picture of *St Matthew as a Money Changer*,
a rare, but in Prato appropriate, genre subject.

🍴 **Il Piraña**
Via Valentini 110 ☎ *(0574) 25746* ⅢⅢ 🗖 ▦ ᴀᴇ CB ◉ ▣ *Closed Sat,
Sun, Aug.*
Do not be deterred by the location of this restaurant, which is 10mins' drive
from the center opposite a string of factories. Even the Florentines will tell
you that this is now one of the best fish restaurants in Italy, although the
decor is an excessively fussy attempt to be ultramodern.

🍴 Also: **Da Bruno** (*Via Verdi 12* ☎ *(0574) 23810* ⅢⅢ *closed Sun, Thurs
dinner, Aug*); **Tonio** (*Piazza Mercatale 161* ☎ *(0574) 21266* ⅢⅢ *to* ⅢⅢ
closed Sun, Mon, Aug), which has good pictures on the walls, a small varied
menu stressing fish, and a loyal business clientele.

Pratolino
*Map 12E6, 7C5. 12km (7½ miles) N of Florence. Firenze.
Gardens open on summer weekends.*
This vast, cool, hauntingly beautiful park was laid out in the
16thC for Grand Duke Francesco I and became the favorite
residence of his second wife Bianca Cappello. Buontalenti's villa
and most of the water-powered mechanical grottoes which were
famous throughout Europe in their day were demolished in the
19thC when the park was redesigned in the informal English style
and planted with specimen trees. A chapel by Buontalenti and
the Grotto of Cupid have survived from the 16thC. But the most
astonishing feature from the original garden is Giambologna's
craggy, colossal *Appennino* (★), a grotto surmounted by a head
in which you can stand upright and survey the park through the
eyes. There is a stupendous view of the valleys of the Mugello
from the **Convent of Monte Senario** above Pratolino.

🍴 **Zocchi** (☎ *(055) 409202* ⅢⅢ *closed Mon*), which overlooks the park, is
a big, sunny restaurant offering a huge array of antipasti and meats from the
charcoal grill.

🍴 **La Botteghina** (*on the Via Bolognese at Montorsoli* ☎ *(055) 401433*) is
a fish restaurant.

Punta Ala

*Map 10I5. 150km (93 miles) SW of Florence, 40km (25
miles) W of Grosseto. 58040. Grosseto. Population: 190.*
This luxurious resort on a headland overlooking the island of
Elba was founded in 1960. It offers golf, sailing, riding, polo,
tennis and sand beaches and is near the Etruscan sites.

Hotels

Cala del Porto
*Via del Porto, 58040 Punta Ala, Grosseto ☎ (0564) 922455 ● 590652
⊗(0564) 920716 ⅢⅡ 42 rms ⌷ 42 ▦ ▣ ⌷ ▭ AE CB ● ● VISA
Closed Oct-Apr.*
Comfortably appointed hotel overlooking the sea.
⌂ ⊟ ▢ ▨ ⛵ ❄ ≋ ❦ ✓ 🚶 ⛳ 🎾 ⊙

Gallia Palace Hotel
*Via delle Sughere, 58040 Punta Ala, Grosseto ☎ (0564) 922022/3/4/5
● 590454 ⅢⅡ 98 rms ⌷ 98 ▦ ⌷ ▭ AE Closed Oct-May.*
The modern luxury hotel of Punta Ala is an architecturally impersonal
building set in a splendid garden. Good service and the best restaurant in
Punta Ala.
⌂ ⊟ ‡ ⊝ ▢ ▨ ⛵ ≋ ❦ ℘ ✓ 🚶 ⛳ 🏌 ⛵

Piccolo Hotel Alleluja
*Via del Porto, 58040 Punta Ala, Grosseto ☎ (0564) 922050 ● 500449
⊗(0564) 920734 ⅢⅡ 42 rms ⌷ 42 ▦ ⌷ ▭ AE ● ● VISA*
The most attractive of the hotels, which preserves something of the mood
of the old Tuscan farmhouse, the nucleus of the original estate.
⌂ ⊟ ‡ ⊝ ▢ ▨ ▨ ⛵ ❄ ≋ ❦ ℘ ✓ 🚶 ⛳ 🏌 🎾 ⊙ ♫

▭ Restaurants on the port include a reasonable serve-yourself. See also
Castiglione della Pescaia.

Radda in Chianti

*Map 12F6. 58km (36 miles) S of Florence, 34km (21 miles) N
of Siena. 53017. Siena. Population: 1,588.*
A little hill village which became headquarters of the Chianti
League in 1415. The medieval street plan and sections of the
fortifications survive. 3km (1.75 miles) N is **Volpaia**, a pretty,
restored medieval village.

⌘ Relais Fattoria Vignale
*Via Pianigiani 15, 53017 Radda in Chianti ☎ (0577) 738300 ⅢⅡ 24
rms ▬ AE ● VISA Closed Jan-late Mar.*
The 18thC manor house of a wine-making estate.
⌂ ⛵ ❄ ≋ ▨ ▨

▭ **Vignale** (☎ (0577) 738094, closed Thurs, Fri lunch, mid-Jan to late
Feb).

Roselle

*Map 11I5. 131km (81 miles) S of Florence, 10km (6 miles)
NE of Grosseto. Grosseto.*
Etruscan Roselle, like *Vetulonia*, was an island dominating the
waters of the gulf that then filled part of the Grosseto Maremma.
Excavations have revealed layers of civilization stretching back to
the Neolithic age. The Etruscan city, one of the federation of 12,
was taken over by Rome early in the 3rdC BC. Portable material
uncovered is now in *Grosseto*.
  The **ruins (★)** are in a remarkably complete state of
conservation, surrounded by a nearly intact ring of Etruscan- and

Roman-built walls. Remains of the Roman city include the forum, a stretch of paved street, basilicas, villas, amphitheater and baths. Etruscan remains include rare artisans' cottages of the 7th-6thC BC.

San Casciano in Val di Pesa

Map 15E5. 17km (10½ miles) s of Florence. 50026. Firenze. Population: 14,522.

A busy agricultural-industrial town graced by the church of the **Misericordia** (which possesses several fine Sienese paintings, including a *Crucifixion* on panel by Simone Martini) and by three of the region's best restaurants.

Nearby sights

3km (1.75 miles) to the N is the one-street hamlet of **Sant'Andrea in Percussina**, where Machiavelli spent 15yrs in exile from Florence during which he wrote his six great works, including *The Prince*. His house is privately owned but sometimes (irregularly) open to the public.

Restaurants

Antica Posta
Piazza Zannoni 1 ☎ (055) 820116 |||| with rooms ☐ ■ ☲ AE ⊙ VISA Closed Mon, Aug.
Lace tablecloths, Rosenthal china, fresh flowers, and seriously good food prepared by the two imaginative young proprietor-chefs of a small restaurant that does a magnificent *bistecca fiorentina* as well as unusually elaborate dishes. Reservation essential.

La Biscondola
5km (3 miles) SE at Mercatale, Via Grevigiana ☎ (055) 821381 |☐ to |||| ⊕ AE ⊙ VISA Closed Mon, Tues lunch.
A pleasant, traditional Tuscan trattoria.

Nello ♧
Via IV Novembre 64 ☎ (055) 820163 ||☐ Closed Wed eve, Thurs, July.
Substantial country cooking, including game in season.

La Tenda Rossa
5km (3 miles) NW at Cerbaia, Piazza del Monumento 9 ☎ (055) 826132 |||| ☲ ▦ Closed Wed, Thurs lunch, 2 weeks in Aug.
An outstanding trattoria that rarely disappoints. Excellent hot antipasti, pastas, home-grown vegetables and herbs, and homemade breads.

San Galgano 🏛 † ★

Map 11G5. 101km (63 miles) SW of Florence, 33km (20 miles) SW of Siena.

The ruined church of San Galgano is one of the most moving sights in Tuscany. Although meadow grass now grows in the roofless nave, the magnificence of the once-powerful Cistercian foundation is still apparent. Built between 1218-80, the church introduced French Gothic architecture to Tuscany.

On a hill above is the little Romanesque church of **San Galgano**, with the 14thC chapel frescoed by A. Lorenzetti.

✍ ☲ See *Bagni di Petriolo*.

San Gimignano ★

Map 11F5. 55km (34 miles) SW of Florence, 38km (24 miles) NW of Siena. 53037. Siena. Population: 7,501.

San Gimignano *"delle belle torri"* (of the beautiful towers) is the best-preserved medieval town in Tuscany. Its defense system once involved more than 70 towers, of which 13 survive. Warring factions dropped rocks and burning pitch on their enemies from these towers, which were also important status symbols. Height meant prestige for medieval Tuscan noblemen, as for 20thC American tycoons, and from a distance San Gimignano bears an eerie resemblance to a tipsy, miniature New York.

Most Italian cities looked very like San Gimignano in the 12th-13thC. The skyline of medieval Siena bristled with more than 50 such towers, and that of Florence with more than 100. E. M. Forster's early novel, *Where Angels Fear to Tread*, is set in San Gimignano, which he calls "Monteriano."

The narrative painter Benozzo Gozzoli was born here. His charming frescoes in the Collegiata and the church of San Agostino are not great art, but are easy to enjoy.

Events Colorful masked processions take place on the first and last Sun of the carnival period before Lent.

Operas are performed in summer in Piazza del Duomo.

Sights and places of interest

Porta San Giovanni (1262), the finest of the town gates, is the main entrance; there is a parking lot nearby. The town is in any case best toured on foot.

There are marvelous views from the 13thC town **walls** and from the **Rocca**, built by the Florentines in 1353.

Piazza della Cisterna

The main square is actually triangular, and retains at its center the original 13thC cistern. The buildings are 13th-14thC, of which the finest is the 14thC Palazzo Tortoli (no. 7), in the Sienese style.

Piazza del Duomo

The monumental buildings and seven towers of the Piazza del Duomo are all pre-1400. On the w of the square is the Collegiata. The Palazzo del Popolo is on the s side and the Palazzo del Podestà on the E.

Collegiata †

The Romanesque facade of the Collegiata was enlarged by Giuliano da Maiano in the 15thC, but has been often restored since. The interior is notable for its 14th-15thC frescoes. On the interior facade the frescoes include the *Martyrdom of St Sebastian* (1465) by Gozzoli; the painted wooden statues of the *Annunciation* (1421) are by Jacopo della Quercia. On the right wall the *New Testament Scenes* (c.mid-14thC) are the greatest identified achievements of Barna da Siena; they were completed by Giovanni d'Asciano.

Off the right nave is the **Cappella di Santa Fina** (★), one of the high points of Renaissance architecture, built in 1468 by Giuliano da Maiano with an altar by Benedetto da Maiano. The beautiful frescoes (1475) by Domenico Ghirlandaio and assistants depict two *Scenes from the Life of Santa Fina*; according to the legend, wallflowers sprang from the towers on the day she died.

In the presbytery, the ciborium over the high altar is by B. da Maiano. The choir stalls in the apse are by Antonio da Colle. On the left nave wall are frescoes of the *Old Testament* (c.1367) by Bartolo di Fredi, and in the 14thC Baptistry loggia, off the left nave, is a fresco of the *Annunciation* by Dom. Ghirlandaio.

Palazzo del Podestà ▥

On the E side of the square, this 13thC building was enlarged in the 14thC. Its imposing Torre del Ragnosa at 51m (167ft) was meant to set the maximum legal height for towers, but tower-building rivalry continued.

Palazzo del Popolo

On the s side of the square, this building houses the Pinacoteca Civica, and offers a spectacular view from the top of its tower, the **Torre Grossa**. Inside, on the first floor, the Sala di Dante, so called as the poet spoke here in 1300 in favor of an alliance with Florence, contains an important *Maestà* (1317) by Lippo Memmo. The **Pinacoteca**, on the next floor, has a collection of 13th-15thC Sienese and Florentine paintings, including a profoundly moving painted *Crucifix* (late 13thC) by Coppo di Marcovaldo.

Sant'Agostino †

A Romanesque-Gothic church (1290-98) of impressive simplicity. In the

Cappella di S. Bartolo, right of the main entrance, is a marble altar (1494) by B. da Maiano. Over the high altar, the *Coronation of the Virgin* (1483) is a major work by Piero del Pollaiuolo. In the choir is Gozzoli's *Life Story of St Augustine* in 17 frescoed scenes (1464). In the left nave is Gozzoli's *St Sebastian* (1464).

Via San Matteo

The main street, with travertine paving and medieval buildings, notably the Romanesque church of San Bartolo and the *casa-torre* Pesciolini at no. 32.

Other sights

Of the many more Romanesque churches within the walls, the most interesting is **San Jacopo**, at the NE corner.

Outside the walls, 4.5km (3 miles) from Porta San Matteo, is the Romanesque **Pieve di Cellole** (1237).

≋ ═ Bel Soggiorno
Via San Giovanni 91, 53037 San Gimignano, Siena ☎ (0577) 940375 ⑧ (0577) 940375 ❙❑ 25 rms ▣ 25 ◪ 🛏 🖭 ▥ ▣ ⑩ ▥ Restaurant closed Mon, mid-Jan to mid-Feb.

Wonderful views of the town from this 13thC house.
✱ ⊡ ⁂ ⽆

≋ ═ La Cisterna 🏛
Piazza della Cisterna 23, 53037 San Gimignano, Siena ☎ (0577) 940328 ⊛575152 ❙❙❙❙ 50 rms ▣ 50 ◪ ═ 🛏 ▥ ▣ ⑩ ▥ Closed mid-Nov to mid-Mar.

Huge rooms in a 13thC palace with an Edwardian atmosphere. The restaurant, **Le Terrazze** (*❙❙❑ closed Tues, Wed lunch*), offers splendid views from spacious rooms with low ceilings with exposed beams. Pastries are especially delicious.
◪ ✱ ⅙ ❑ ⊡ ⽆ ⿹

≋ ═ Le Renaie e Leonetto
6km (4 miles) N at Pancole ☎ (0577) 955044/955072 ❙❑ 26 rms ▣ 26 🛏 ▥ ⑩ ▥ Closed late Nov, restaurant closed Tues.

A pleasant country inn.
◪ ⁂ ⇢

≋ ═ Pescille
4.5km (3 miles) S near San Donato ☎ (0577) 940186 ❙❑ 32 rms ▣ 32 ▬ ▥ ▣ ⑩ ⑩ ▥ Closed Feb.

A modest, peaceful hotel with a restaurant, **I Cinque Gilli** (*closed Wed*).
◪ ⊡ ⁂ ⽆ ⇢ ⋊

San Giovanni Valdarno

*Map **11**F6. 45km (28 miles) SE of Florence, 37km (23 miles) W of Arezzo. 52027. Arezzo. Population: 19,908.*

The birthplace of the painters Masaccio and Giovanni da San Giovanni is now the chief industrial and market town of the Valdarno. The market is held on Sat.

2km (1¼ miles) to the S, in the church of the convent of Montecarlo, is one of Fra Angelico's masterpieces, an *Annunciation* (c.1440), with a fine predella. 13km (8 miles) to the NE, near Loro Ciuffena, is the tiny farming hamlet of Gropina. Its Romanesque church, **S. Pietro**, has unusual capitals and primitive carvings on its pulpit. The area is rich in Etruscan and Roman remains and Romanesque churches, and there are fine views from the foothills of the Pratomagno.

═ Vicolo del Contento ❖
Loc. Mandri 38, 52020 Castelfranco di Sopra, Arezzo ☎ (055) 9149277 ❑ ▦ ⽆ ═ 🛏 ▬ ⇢ ⑩ ▥ Closed Mon, Tues, Aug.

Probably the most interesting and sympathetic restaurant in the Valdarno. Local clients appreciate the refined international cooking. Tuscan meals are also outstanding but must be ordered in advance.

San Miniato

Map 15E4. 44km (27 miles) w of Florence, 39km (24 miles) e of Pisa. 56027. Pisa. Population: 24,701.

Medieval San Miniato was the seat of the Lombard Imperial Vicariate in Tuscany and therefore known as S. Miniato al Tedesco ("of the German"). The fortifications, of which only two towers remain, were rebuilt in 1240 by Frederick II.

Sights and places of interest

The 13thC **Duomo** has been rebuilt and restored many times; its pompous interior decorations are 18th-19thC. Its bell tower, the **Torre di Matilde**, predates the Duomo and was built as a defense tower.

The **Museo Diocesano**, to the left of the Duomo, retains sacred art from the region including works by Filippo Lippi, Neri di Bicci, Fra Bartolommeo, Empoli and Verrocchio.

A short, stiff climb from the Prato del Duomo brings one to the tower which is the last surviving reminder of Frederick II's **Rocca**, a reconstruction of the original that was destroyed during World War II. On a clear day the view embraces the whole of the Arno plain. Below the Prato del Duomo is **Piazza della Repubblica**, the most picturesque in the town. The Seminario retains 14thC shop-fronts and 17thC *sgraffiti*.

☞ ⇌ **Miravalle** (*Piazza Castello 3* ☎ *(0571) 418075* ▢).

San Quirico d'Orcia

Map 8H6. 111km (64 miles) se of Florence, 43km (29 miles) se of Siena. 53027. Siena. Population: 2,231.

A village overlooking the Orcia and Asso valleys.

Collegiata †

The Romanesque-Gothic Collegiata has three magnificent **portals**: on the facade (1080); on the right flank (late 13thC), adorned with lions and caryatids by a follower of Giovanni Pisano; and at the head of the right transept (1298). Inside is an unusually fine triptych by Sano di Pietro and good choir stalls (1502) by Antonio Barili.

Nearby sights

San Giovanni d'Asso, 15km (9 miles) n, dominated by its 12thC Castello; and **Castiglione d'Orcia**, 5km (3 miles) s, home town of the artist Vecchietta, which is near the atmospheric medieval village of **Rocca d'Orcia**. 6km (4 miles) se is the little spa town of **Bagno Vignoni**, now rather run down.

☞ ⇌ **Posta-Marcucci** ❀
53027 Bagno Vignoni, Siena ☎ *(0577) 887112* ◉ *(0577) 887443* ▢ *48 rms* ▭ *43* ⇌ ▭

Location: 6km (4 miles) s, off the Via Cassia. Its thermal baths, used by St Catherine of Siena and Lorenzo the Magnificent, make this simple but comfortable hotel a restful place to take the waters.

⌂ & ⚓ ≈ ⚓ ▱ ▚ ⋙ ⋎°

Sansepolcro

Map 13F8. 114km (71 miles) se of Florence, 39km (24 miles) ne of Arezzo. 52037. Arezzo. Population: 15,695.

In this somewhat mournful town close to the Umbrian border Piero della Francesca was born after 1420 and spent the last 14yrs of his life writing his treatises on *Perspective* and the *Five Regular Bodies*. It was probably in the early 1460s that he executed his masterpiece, the *Resurrection*, in his native town.

Museo Civico
Via Aggiunti 65.

Piero's hypnotic *Resurrection* (★) has been called the greatest picture in the world. Sir Kenneth Clark describes the spell it casts:

"Before Piero's Risen Christ we are suddenly conscious of values for which no rational statement is adequate; we are struck with a feeling of awe, older and less reasonable than that inspired by the Blessed Angelico. This country god, who arises in the grey light while humanity is asleep, has been worshipped ever since man first knew that the seed is not dead in the winter earth, but will force its way upwards through an iron crust. Later He will become a god of rejoicing, but His first emergence is painful and involuntary. He seems to be part of the dream which lies so heavily on the sleeping soldiers..."

Opposite is Piero's early polyptych, the *Madonna della Misericordia* (1446–c.1458) (★). Like the *Madonna del Parto* at **Monterchi** (see below), this Madonna of Mercy is both a pretty, young peasant girl and icy goddess, whose state of spiritual detachment has been likened to that evoked by Buddhist and African sculpture. The whole polyptych is in uneven condition, and other sections were painted by assistants. Also by Piero are the frescoes of *St Julian* and *St Louis of Toulouse*.

Notable among the other works in the museum are a processional flag representing the *Crucifixion* by Signorelli; Pontormo's *St Quentin*; and battered but fine 15thC choir stalls which demonstrate the influence of Piero on perspective intarsia work.

Other sights

In the Romanesque-Gothic **Duomo**, paintings include two panels by Matteo di Giovanni, part of a polyptych of which the central panel, the *Baptism of Christ* by Piero, was purchased for the London National Gallery in 1861 — for £241.

The church of **San Francesco** retains its Gothic high altar (1304) for which Sassetta painted his *St Francis* altarpiece, an early influence on Piero, now scattered, parts being in London and Paris.

In the 16thC church of **San Lorenzo** is a dramatic *Deposition* (c.1528-30) by Rosso Fiorentino.

✑ ⇌ Il Fiorentino ♣ (*Via L. Pacioli 60* ☎ (0575) 76033 ◨ *to* ▥▥◨ *restaurant closed Fri, June 15-July 15*) is a friendly and unpretentious restaurant that serves delicious traditional food of the region.

⇌ Oroscopo
1km (½ mile) NW at Pieve Vecchia, Via Togliatti 66 ☎ *(0575) 734875* ▥▥▥ ▭ ▦ ▣ ◘ *Open dinner only, closed Sun, Tues, Nov.*
Recently opened by a young couple who take their cooking very seriously. If you choose the *menu de degustazione* you can sample a different wine by the glass with each course.

⇌ See also *Anghiari*.

Excursion

17km (11 miles) s of Sansepolcro, in the tiny cemetery chapel on the edge of the village of **Monterchi**, is another masterpiece by Piero, the *Madonna del Parto* (★ *custodian always on duty*). Pointing proudly to her pregnant womb, she is revealed to us by two triumphant angels, reverse images of the same cartoon.

Saturnia

Map 9K7. 215km (134 miles) s of Florence, 57km (35 miles) SE of Grosseto. 58050. Grosseto. Population: 631.

The Etruscan town on this site was called Aurinia. The Romans named it Saturnia because they believed it had been founded by Jupiter's father. The walls built by the Sienese in the 15thC incorporate Etruscan and Roman sections.

The Etruscan necropolis lies to the N of the walls, the most interesting tombs being in the Puntone area.

The spa of **Terme di Saturnia**, where sulfurous water springs at a constant temperature of 37°C (99°F), is 3km (2 miles) to the s. The road N to *Monte Amiata* passes through a beautiful, sparsely populated landscape dotted with medieval castles and villages.

❧ Terme di Saturnia
Strada della Follonata, 58050 Saturnia, Grosseto ☎ *(0564) 601061*
🏧 *500172* 💵 *93 rms* 🖼️ *93* ▦ ▬ 🛏️ ⊨ AE 🔌
A serious first-class spa hotel offering a wide range of treatments.
🏠 ✻ & 🖥️ 🖼️ ⚓ ⋙ ⁂ ✚ ▬ 🛏️ ♈ ❍

❧ Villa Clodia (*Via Italia 43, 58050 Saturnia* ☎ *(0564) 601212*□ *12 rms, closed mid-Jan to mid-Feb*), views of the spas and the beautiful countryside from a turn-of-the-century building.

❧ ⊨ Da Ventura (*Via Aggiunti 30* ☎ *(0575) 76560* 💵□) is cheerful and near the Museo Civico.

⊨ Michele ai due Cippi
In the main square ☎ *(0564) 601074* 💵□ AE *Closed Tues, Jan.*
This excellent restaurant is one of the most popular in the Maremma. Be sure to reserve.

❧ ⊨ Laudomia
9km (6 miles) s at Poderi di Montemerano ☎ *(0564) 620062/620013*
💵□ 🛏️ AE 🔌 🔌 VISA
A welcoming traditional rustic hotel and restaurant.

Sesto Fiorentino
Map 6B2-3. 9km (6 miles) NW of Florence. 50019. Firenze. Bus 28 from Florence station. Population: 44,458.
An important center of the porcelain and ceramics industry. In the central square, Piazza Ginori, is the 15thC Palazzo Pretorio.

To the E of Sesto is **Quinto**, where the imposing 7thC BC Etruscan **tomba della Montagnola** is in the Via Fratelli Rosselli (*custodian at no. 95*).
Museo delle Porcellane di Doccia
Via Pratese.
In a park along the Via Pratese, this modern museum (1965) exhibits a superb collection of 18th-20thC porcelains from the Doccia factory founded in 1737 by Carlo Ginori.
Villa Corsi-Salviati
Via Gramsci. May be visited with Agriturist (see "Gardens," page 207) or on request to the Conti Corsi-Salviati.
A refreshing surprise in an otherwise dreary area. The villa and garden have been altered over four centuries to suit the tastes of succeeding generations. The Smithsonian Institute holds a lecture program here in summer, and the University of Michigan houses its Florence course in the villa.

❧ Villa Villoresi
Via delle Torri 63, 50019 Sesto Fiorentino, Firenze ☎ *(055) 4489032*
💵□ *28 rms* 🖼️ *28* ▬ 🛏️ 🔌 VISA
A beautifully maintained 14thC villa.
🏠 🖼️ ⋙ 《 ⋙

❧ ⊨ Montelagip (*Campo Bisenzio* ☎ *(055) 4211881* 💵□ *to* 💵💵), with a superb restaurant.

⊨ La Terrazza (☎ *(055) 8873302* 💵□ *closed Sun, Mon, Aug*) is in the Castello of Calenzano.

Settignano
Map 7D5. 8km (5 miles) E of Florence. Bus 10 from Piazza San Marco, Florence. 50135. Firenze. Population: 1,563.
A Florentine suburb in the Fiesolan Hills graced by cypresses, olive groves and fine old villas. Renaissance sculptors who were born or made their home for a time in the area near the *pietra serena* quarries of Monte Ceceri include Desiderio, the

Rossellino brothers, the Maiano brothers, Benedetto da Rovezzano and Michelangelo. Boccaccio set the *Decameron* in these hills, and D'Annunzio lived here during his love affair with Eleanora Duse in the Villa Capponcina.

One of the many foreign literary residents was Walter Savage Landor, author of *Imaginary Conversations*, who lived in the 15thC Villa Gherardesca in the 1820s; another was the art historian Bernard Berenson, whose **Villa I Tatti** (☎ *603251, open by appointment Tues pm*), is now run by Harvard University as a center for Renaissance Studies. The English attachment to this countryside reached a peak late in the 19thC when Queen Victoria visited the Castle of **Vincigliata** (see below). The gushing sensibilities of English esthetes were satirized by Anatole France in his novel *Le Lys Rouge*.

See also *Fiesole*.

Sights and places of interest

Approaching from central Florence, the Via G. D'Annunzio leads past Nervi's concrete **Stadium** in the Campo di Marte to Ponte a Mensola, where the church of **S. Martino a Mensola** (*ring for entrance*) has an elegant *quattrocento* interior with a triptych by Taddeo Gaddi. The Via D'Annunzio then climbs to the village of Settignano. There is a good view of Florence from Piazza Desiderio and, in the 16thC church of the Assunta, a pulpit designed by Buontalenti and a Della Robbia *Madonna*.

To the NE is Montebeni, Berenson's favorite walking country and still unexpectedly rural. A left turn off the Montebeni road leads to the Castle of **Vincigliata**, Victorianized in 1855 by John Temple Leader.

Gameraia

Open when owner not in residence.

One of the loveliest of all Tuscan gardens. The villa was destroyed in World War II, but the 1.2ha (3-acre) garden, with its architectural clipped yews planted when it was laid out in the 17thC, is well maintained. "But description faints and fails before the enchanting reality," wrote Harold Acton. "Perhaps the best way to evoke its atmosphere is to listen to Mozart's *Eine Kleine Nachtmusik*."

☞ The **Villa Linda** (*Poggio Gherardo 5* ☎ *(055) 603913*□) is a simple *pensione* run by Benedictine nuns.

≡ **Le Cave**

Via delle Cave 16, Maiano ☎ *(055) 59133* *III*□ □ ■■ ⇔ ⇜ ⟨ε *AE* ◙ **⊙** *Closed Thurs, Sun eve, Aug.*

An old *bottega* that once served the quarry workers. The food is variable; but the situation is magical.

≡ **Osvaldo** (*Via G.D'Annunzio 51* ☎ *(055) 602168* *III*□ □ ⇔ *closed Tues eve, Wed, Aug*) is a favorite with fellows of **I Tatti**.

See also *Fiesole*.

Siena ★

Map **11G6***. 68km (42 miles)* s *of Florence, 53100. Siena. Population: 64,251* i *Via Fiorentina 89* ☎ *(0577) 50044.*

Soft Siena, City of the Virgin, stands on her pedestal of three hills, vain of her beauty, absorbed in her past. She is the other half of Tuscany, feminine counterpart of the hard-headed masculinity of Florence. According to a persistent legend, Siena was founded by Senius, son of Remus; hence the wolf, one of the city's most prominent emblems. But the earliest certain knowledge we have of Siena, apart from evidence of an Etruscan settlement, is of the Roman colony Saena Julia.

During the early Middle Ages Siena enjoyed a privileged relationship with the Hohenstaufen emperors; and as a free republic from the early 12thC she attained a precocious

pre-eminence in banking and trade, and became the leading
Ghibelline center in Tuscany and the natural rival of Guelf
Florence. Although the defeat of Florence at the Battle of
Montaperti in 1260 is still celebrated in Siena as a glorious event,
it was less significant than the Florentine victory 9yrs later at
Colle di Val d'Elsa. Then Siena joined the Guelf alliance and from
1287 was governed as an oligarchy by a Council of Nine "Good
Men" chosen from the middle classes. The Republic flourished
under the balanced, methodical rule of the Nine; the late 13th to
early 14thC was an age of stability, prosperity and artistic
achievement. But the turmoil and discontent following famines
and the Black Death of 1348 led to the overthrow in 1355 of the
Nine by the nobles assisted by the working class.

There is nothing in the world quite like Siena; it is a medieval city
that might be likened to a rare beast, with heart, arteries, tail,
paws and teeth. Only the skeleton is left, intact, and it is enough
to astound us.

                                                    Bernard Berenson

Spiritually Siena was guided through the turbulent post-plague
years by two remarkable religious reformers, later canonized as
St Catherine of Siena (1347-80) and St Bernardino of Siena
(1380-1444). Politically, the next two centuries were marked by
fruitless wars, voluntary submission to foreign control — Charles
IV from 1355, Gian Galeazzo Visconti from 1399, Charles V in
1530 — and periods of unstable independence when the power
of nobility became increasingly stronger.

In 1552 the city rebelled against the Spanish occupation, and
2yrs later the combined forces of Charles V and Duke Cosimo I of
Florence advanced on Siena and laid siege for 18 months during
which the population was halved and the countryside
devastated. In 1557 Charles sold the city outright to Cosimo, and
in 1559 Siena and her territories were officially annexed to the
Tuscan grand duchy by the Peace of Cateau-Cambrésis.

As the unwilling bride of Florence, Siena was treated as a
second-class member of the Tuscan empire. No public banks
were permitted to operate until 1622; the wool industry collapsed
in the mid-17thC and by the mid-18thC most Sienese noble
families were deeply in debt. "Cracking, peeling, fading,
crumbling, rotting," Henry James wrote of the city in 1909.

And yet, visitors to Siena in the late 20thC will find more here
than art to admire and even envy. It seems that the ideal of the
Common Good, practiced by the Nine and revealed to posterity
in Ambrogio Lorenzetti's famous frescoes in the Palazzo
Pubblico, may not have been forgotten.

Sienese art

Siena is a Gothic city. Its greatest buildings — the Duomo and
Palazzo Pubblico — and best-known pictures — Duccio's
Maestà, Simone Martini's *Maestà* and Ambrogio Lorenzetti's
Good and Bad Government — were created in the late
13th-14thC. In the 15thC the Sienese by and large ignored the
Florentine Renaissance. They continued to build ogival palaces;
even their major painters, Giovanni di Paolo and Sassetta, made
decorative, two-dimensional pictures on gold backgrounds. Not
until the 16thC did Renaissance painting arrive with Sodoma and
Domenico Beccafumi, the greatest Sienese Mannerist.

Most important works of art were commissioned by the
government or religious bodies, powerful, conservative groups
who knew exactly what they wanted as to style and subject

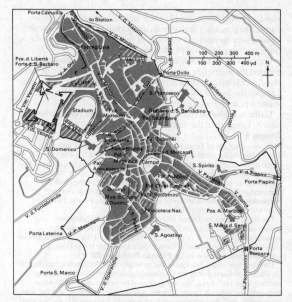

matter. Over half the pictures commissioned between 1350-1550 were of the Virgin, Queen of Siena; collaborative projects were more common than in Florence.

Sienese sculpture advanced earlier and further than its sister arts, thanks partly to the influence of Giovanni Pisano, whose figures for the facade of the Duomo are among the most important examples of Gothic sculpture in Italy. The greatest native Sienese sculptor, Jacopo della Quercia, effected the transition to the Renaissance; his principal works in the city are the Fonte Gaia and the Baptistry font.

Events   The *Palio*, the bare-backed horse race around the Campo on July 2 and Aug 16, is the central event of the Sienese calendar and the focal point of every Sienese citizen's life. It is one of the strangest and most magnificent public spectacles: a mixture of pomp, licensed violence and corruption, skill, courage, luck, history, and fantasy. Ten of the city's 17 *contrade* (wards) are chosen by lot to participate in the race, which is preceded by a spectacular procession. The *palio*, or banner, is the prize. The second and more important *Palio* on Aug 16 is in honor of the Assumption of the Virgin. Tickets are extremely expensive, but the rehearsals on the previous days can be viewed for a more reasonable price from a seat at one of the restaurants in the Campo.

Master classes and a festival of concerts are held in July and Aug under the auspices of the Accademia Musicale Chigiana, 82 Via di Città ☎ (0577) 46152.

A weekly market is held on Wed morning.

Sights and places of interest
Siena is built on three landlocked hills, which form the most westerly spur of the Chiana mountains. Since the early 13thC the city has been divided into three districts, or *terzi*: Città, San Martino and Camollia. The essential civic unit is the *contrada*, or

ward, of which there are 17. Their fantastic names (Caterpillar, Eagle, Dragon, etc.) derive from allegorical carts paraded at the Palio. Every Sienese is a member of the *contrada* in which he is born and remains loyal to it for life.

The old city is surrounded by 7km (4½ miles) of intact walls, entered through eight gates. The main streets are the Via di Città, Banchi di Sotto and Banchi di Sopra, which meet just above the Campo, the hub of the city, at the **Croce del Travaglio**, a good starting point for a tour of the city.

Traffic is excluded from the center; convenient parking lots are near S. Domenico, the Stadium and the Lizza.

Campo ★

The central square of Siena, one of the most magical public spaces in Europe, lies at the confluence of the three hills on which the city is built. Its sloping, semicircular shape often elicits comparisons: to a fan, shell, or amphitheater. For the Sienese it is a cloak — the cloak of the Madonna spread out to protect her favored city. The perimeter of the cloak is trimmed with lacy palaces of which the most striking is the curved **Sansedoni**, originally a group of 13 palaces extended in the 14thC and restructured in the early 18thC.

The brick paving is divided into nine sections symbolizing the government of the Nine Good Men, who were responsible for the systematic development of the Campo from the late 13thC. At the center of the curve is a reproduction of Jacopo della Quercia's Fonte Gaia, the original of which is now in the **Palazzo Pubblico** (🏛 ★).

The structure of the Palazzo — the most graceful Gothic civic building in Tuscany — reflects that of the communal government for which it was erected from 1297-1342. The wings (raised by one story in 1681) were occupied respectively by the Podestà, responsible for justice, and the Nine, responsible for administration, and separated by the central body housing the Biccherna, or treasury, and the General Council. The black and white communal shield, the *balzana*, decorates all the openings of the facade. From the left corner, the bell tower (1325-48), known as the *Mangia* after the nickname ("wastrel") of its first bell-ringer, leaps — in William Dean Howells' vivid words — "like a rocket into the starlit air." The **Cappella di Piazza** at the base of the Mangia was built from 1352-76 and modified in 1468. To its right is the entrance to the Cortile del Podestà, which gives access to the sections of the palace open to the public. For a stunning view climb the 503 steps to the top of the Mangia.

The **Museo Civico** (★) is on the first floor of the Palazzo Pubblico. The following is a description of its rooms.

Sala del Risorgimento   The six frescoes, by the best late 19thC Sienese artists, relate episodes from the life of Victor Emmanuel II.

Sala di Balia   The only room in the palace decorated by non-Sienese artists. The frescoes (1407) by Spinello Aretino and Parri di Spinello depict the life of the Sienese Pope Alexander III.

Sala dei Cardinali   Sculptures by followers of Jacopo della Quercia.

Sala del Concistro   Portal by B. Rossellino; frescoes by Beccafumi of the *Political Virtues* (1529-36).

Antichapel   Frescoes (1414) by Taddeo di Bartolo. The huge *St Christopher* symbolizes the duty of the commune to care for the weak.

Chapel   The elegant iron gate (1437) may have been designed by Jacopo della Quercia. The Gothic **choir stalls** (1428) illustrate the Nicene Creed. Frescoes of *Scenes from the Life of the Virgin* (1407) by Taddeo di Bartolo. Over the altar, the *Sacred Family with St Leonard* by Sodoma.

Sala del Mappamondo   The room where the city council met. The painted map after which the room was named no longer exists, but a recent restoration has revealed the existence of yet another 14thC fresco beneath the equestrian portrait of *Guidoriccio da Fogliano* (★), until recently assumed to be by Simone Martini. Originally part of a cycle running round three walls of the room and illustrating the castles conquered by Siena after 1314, this fresco records the victory over the nobles of Montemassi and Sassoferrato. On the opposite wall is the *Maestà* (1315) (★), signed "Siena had me painted by the hand of Simone [Martini]." The Virgin is represented by the Queen of Heaven and Siena.

Sala della Pace   Sienese dedication to law and order received its most complete and vivid pictorial expression with Ambrogio Lorenzetti's *Allegory of Good and Bad Government* (★), painted in 1338-40 for the council chamber as a reminder of the Augustinian and Thomist teachings that justice and common good are the first aims of good government. On the wall opposite the windows, *Good Government* is represented by a king wearing the colors of the *balzana* and surrounded by symbolic virtues and attributes. On the right wall, we see the *Effects of Good Government in the City and Country*. For all its didactic intricacy, this picture may still be enjoyed in the spirit which St Bernardino described it in the 15thC: "I see merchants buying and selling, I see dancing, the houses being repaired, the workers busy in the vineyards or sowing the fields..." On the left wall is the ruined fresco of *Bad Government and its Effects*.

Sala dei Pilastri   Sienese pictures of the 14th-15thC, including Neroccio di Bartolommeo's diptych of *St Bernardino*.

Loggia   The remains of Jacopo della Quercia's carvings for the **Fonte Gaia** (1409-19) (★). The fountain commemorated the appearance of water in the Campo.

Chigi-Saracini Palace 🏛
Via di Città 89. Visits on request ☎ (0577) 46152.

Built in the 14thC for one of the great Sienese banking families, this lovely stone and brick palace now houses the distinguished Academia Musicale Chigiana, who hold some of their summer concerts here (see *Events*, page 187) and a collection of 14th-17thC Tuscan paintings.

Across the Via di Città, at no. 126, is the **Palazzo Piccolomini delle Papesse** (1460-95), built for Pius II's sister, probably by B. Rossellino, in the Florentine Renaissance style.

Duomo 🏛 ✝ ★
The cathedral of Santa Maria dell'Assunta was the most expensive and carefully considered building project of Siena's golden age. Its construction, which occupied nearly two centuries, was in the beginning supervised by committees of Sienese citizens, and there was no Sienese artist or craftsman of any distinction who did not work at some time on the cathedral. Long after the structure was completed in the late 14thC, they continued to embellish the interior. The result is perhaps less satisfying as a work of architecture than for its individual components.

The site chosen for the building, which began in the late 12thC, was the Castelvecchio, the earliest inhabited part of the city. The basic structure was complete in 1215, the hexagonal cupola in 1264, and the facade was begun in 1284. In 1339 an extraordinary and hopelessly ambitious decision was taken: Siena would build a new and greater cathedral, rivaling those of Florence and Orvieto, for which the old cathedral would serve as transept. This unwieldy, prohibitively expensive scheme was abandoned after the 1348 plague, and the old cathedral was finally completed in 1382.

The skeletal remains of the new cathedral (**Duomo Nuovo**), now housing the Cathedral Museum (see over), stand to the right of the Duomo, behind Buontalenti's Palazzo della Prefettura. Opposite the Duomo is the **Hospital of Santa Maria della Scala** (🏛), the most important institution in medieval and Renaissance Siena after the Duomo and Palazzo Pubblico. The building, which dates from late 13th-14thC, is still in use as a hospital; in the Sala d'Infermeria modern patients are surrounded by frescoes illustrating the care of the sick in the Renaissance. Over the high altar of the adjoining church of **Santa Maria della Scala**, rebuilt in 1466, is Vecchietta's superb bronze *Risen Christ* (1476). To the left of the Duomo is the early 18thC imitation-Gothic Palazzo Arcivescovile (Archbishop's Palace), with Ambrogio Lorenzetti's enchanting, naturalistic *Madonna Lactans*.

The polychrome marble **facade of the Duomo** is best studied from the far right corner of the square. The lower section (1284-96), the first building project in Tuscany to reflect the Gothic influence of *San Galgano*, was designed by Giovanni Pisano. The statues are copies of the originals, by Giovanni or assistants, now in the Cathedral Museum (see over). The central bronze door dates from 1958, and the gabled upper section in the high Gothic style was begun in 1376; the mosaics are 19thC. From the right transept rises the Romanesque **campanile** (1313).

The **interior** is most immediately striking for the giddy optical effect of the black and white stripes. The **floor** (★) is paved in marble with 56 designs produced by over 40 leading Sienese artists, executed by craftsmen in *sgraffiti* or intarsia, a remarkable collaborative work carried out between 1369-1547. Notice especially Beccafumi's *Old Testament Scenes* between the cupola and high altar.

Libreria Piccolimini (★)   Located off the left nave, this is the most brilliantly decorative room in Tuscany. It was built in the 1490s by Francesco Todeschini Piccolomini (Pope Pius III). The vividly charming

Tuscany/Siena

frescoes (1502-05) by Pinturicchio depict ten *Scenes from the Life of Pius II*. In the center of the room is the beautiful and influential *Three Graces*, a 3rdC Roman copy of a Hellenistic statue. Fine illuminated choir-books are displayed on late 15th benches.

To the w of the library is the great **Piccolomini Altar** (1503), designed by Andrea Bregno. The statues of *Sts Peter and Pius and Sts Gregory and Paul* are by the young Michelangelo.

Left transept   The **chapel of St John the Baptist** (1481-98) is entered through an elegant marble portal. Frescoes include Pinturicchio's two portraits of *Alberto Arighieri*, in youth and old age. The vigorous bronze statue of the *Baptist* (1457) is by Donatello; that of *St Catherine of Alexandria* (1487) is by Neroccio. The **pulpit** (1266-68) (★) is by Nicola Pisano, assisted by his son Giovanni and pupils including Arnolfo di Cambio; 6yrs later than the great **Baptistry** pulpit at *Pisa*, this work is freer and more innovatory. The seven panels, separated by figures of prophets and angels, depict *Scenes from the Life of Christ*. The staircase was added by Riccio in 1570.

The **chapel of St Ansano** contains a **monument to Cardinal Petroni** (1317-18) by Tino di Camaino and, in the pavement, the slab **tomb of Bishop Giovanni Pecci** by Donatello.

Presbytery   The **high altar** (1532) by Peruzzi bears a huge **ciborium** (1462-72) by Vecchietta. The two higher flanking *Angels* (1489) are by Giovanni di Stefano, those placed lower down (1499) by Francesco di Giorgio Martini. Eight serenely beautiful **candelabra-angels** (1548-50) on the nave pilasters are by Beccafumi, perhaps his masterpieces as a sculptor. In the apse are 51 finely carved **choir stalls** (14th-16thC). The **window** above (1288) is one of the earliest examples of Italian stained glass, made from cartoons by Duccio.

Right transept   The **Chigi chapel** (1661) was built for the morbidly pious Fabio Chigi, Pope as Alexander VII, to designs by Bernini. *St Jerome* and the *Magdalen* in niches on the entrance wall are by Bernini. The *Madonna del Voto* over the altar is by Guido da Siena or a follower.

Baptistry (★)   Facing its own Piazza San Giovanni, the Baptistry is situated beneath the apse of the cathedral and is reached by a steep flight of steps to the right of the Duomo. The impressive Gothic **facade** (1317-82) is incomplete in the upper section. The **interior** was designed by Camaino and Tino di Camaino and frescoed by, among others, Vecchietta. At its center is Jacopo della Quercia's hexagonal marble **font** (1411-30) (★), a masterpiece of artistic collaboration in the Gothic-Renaissance style. Two of the statues around the basin, *Faith* and *Hope*, are by Donatello. The six gilded bronze relief panels include Jacopo della Quercia's powerful *Zacharias Expelled from the Temple*, Ghiberti's *Baptism of Christ* and Donatello's *Herod's Feast*.

To the E of the Baptistry is the **Palazzo del Magnifico** (1504-08), designed by G. Cozzarelli for Pandolfo Petrucci, autocratic political leader of Siena from 1487-1524. The beautifully wrought bronzes on the handsome facade have been replaced by copies.

Museo dell'Opera del Duomo or Cathedral Museum (★)   This is in the right aisle of the Duomo Nuovo.

Ground floor   Among the carvings from the cathedral facade, the **ten figures** (1284-96) (★) by Giovanni Pisano are among the most important Gothic sculptures in Italy. In the center is a bas-relief of the *Madonna and Child with St Anthony Abbot and Cardinal Antonio Casini*, a late work by Jacopo della Quercia.

First floor   **Sala di Duccio:** Duccio's *Maestà* (1308-11) (★), the inaugural work of the great period of Sienese painting, was carried to the Duomo when complete in a magnificent candlelit procession while the bells of Siena pealed the Gloria and the citizens offered prayers and alms to the poor. It stood over the high altar of the cathedral until removed to a side chapel in 1505. Originally painted on both sides, the panel was split and dismantled in the 18thC. The *Madonna Enthroned* now faces the 26 *Scenes from the Passion*. On the left wall are 19 **panels from the predella and upper section** (others are in London, Washington and New York). On the right wall are P. Lorenzetti's triptych of the *Nativity of the Virgin* (1342) and a *Madonna and Child* (1283) by the young Duccio.

Sala del Tesoro: The finest treasures are Giovanni Pisano's tiny wooden *Crucifix* and F. da Valdambrino's busts of saints.

Second floor   **Sala della Madonna degli Occhi Grossi:** The room is named after the 13thC panel of a large-eyed *Madonna* in the center. The outstanding picture is Simone Martini's *Blessed Agostino Novello with Four*

of his Miracles (c.1330) (★), formerly in Sant' Agostino. **Sala dei
Conversari**: Works by Matteo di Giovanni, Beccafumi, Pomarancio and
Luca Giordano. From the next room one may climb to the rim of the
Duomo Nuovo for spectacular views.

The **Cripta delle Statue** is entered from the steps leading to the Baptistry.
It contains statues from the Duomo and fresco fragments (1270-80), the
earliest known Sienese wall paintings.

Fonte Branda

The most famous and one of the oldest of the many Sienese wells, recorded
from 1081, arched over in 1246.

Fontegiusta †
Via Fontegiusta, off Via Camollia.

The church of the Madonna of Fontegiusta was built in 1482-84 in gratitude
for a Sienese victory over the Florentines. The elegant portico was added in
1489. The unusual square interior contains 16thC Sienese paintings and a
large tabernacle by Marrina.

Via Camollia ends at the **Porta Camollia** (1604), the most northerly of the
Sienese gates opening onto the Florence road. The famous Sienese
welcome *Cor magis tibi Sena pandit* (Siena opens wide its heart to you)
was inscribed when the gate was rebuilt in honor of a visit by Ferdinand I.

Forte di Santa Barbara

Built in 1560 by Duke Cosimo I, this fort now houses the Enoteca Italica
Permanente (see *Tuscan wines*). The views from the ramparts are best at
sunset. To the NE is the **Lizza**, the triangular public park of Siena.

Loggia della Mercanzia

Erected in 1428-44 where the three principal streets of Siena meet above the
Campo, and now housing the Provincial Tourist Board. The statues of saints
are by Vecchietta and A. Federighi. The upper story is 17thC.

Piccolomini Palace ▥ ☆
Via Banchi di Sotto.

The palace, begun in 1469, was very likely designed by B. Rossellino. It
resembles his *Rucellai Palace* (see *Florence A to Z*) and **Piccolimini
Palace** at *Pienza*. With the nearby **Logge del Papa** (1462), designed by A.
Federighi, this constitutes the most important Renaissance building
complex in Siena. The palace houses the State Archives; among the
documents on view are the **covers of the registers of Biccherna**, the
treasury, illuminated by leading Sienese artists from 1258-1659.

The 16thC ex-monastery opposite the palace is the seat of the University
of Siena. Via San Vigilio leads to the picturesque medieval buildings of the
Corte del Castellare degli Ugurgieri.

Pinacoteca Nazionale ▥ ★
Via San Pietro 29.

The outstanding collection of 12th-early 17thC Sienese pictures is housed in
the graceful early 15thC Gothic **Palazzo Buonsignori**. The display is
arranged chronologically beginning on the second floor. The following is
an introductory tour of some of the major works.

Rm. I: Altar frontal of *The Redeemer* with symbols of the Evangelists and
scenes from the Passion (1215), the earliest dated Sienese painting. **Rm. II:**
Works by Guido da Siena (13thC) the first of the great Sienese masters.
Rms. III-IV: Duccio, especially the finely executed but damaged *Madonna
dei Francescani*. **Rm. VI:** Simone Martini's *Madonna and Child*. **Rms.
VII-VIII:** The *Two Views*, attributed to A. Lorenzetti, are the earliest known
examples of pure landscape painting in pre-Renaissance European art. Also
by A. Lorenzetti: *Madonna with Saints and Angels* and *Annunciation*
(1344). P. Lorenzetti: *Madonna and Child* (1328-29), originally in the center
of an altarpiece of which the superb *Stories of the Carmelite Order* formed
the predella. *Birth of the Virgin* (c.1380-90) by Paolo di Giovanni Fei.

Rm. XIII: Giovanni di Paolo's *Last Judgment* and *Madonna of Humility*,
Sassetta's *Last Supper* and *St Anthony Abbot*. **Rm. XIV:** Neroccio's
Madonna and Saints (c.1475); Francesco di Giorgio's *Annunciation* and
Nativity. **Rm. XVIII:** Sano di Pietro's *The Virgin Commending the City of
Siena to Pope Calixtus II* (1456); F. di Giorgio's *Coronation of the Virgin*.

First floor. Rm. XXIII: Pinturicchio's *Holy Family with the Young St
John*. **Rms. XXX-XXXII:** Sodoma's *Nativity, Scourging of Christ*
(c.1511-14), *Deposition*. **Rm. XXXIII:** Beccafumi's *St Catherine Receiving
the Stigmata* (c.1515) and *Birth of the Virgin* (1543). **Rm. XXXVII:**
Beccafumi's *Descent into Hell* (c.1530-35). Sodoma's *Descent into Hell* and
Gethsemene (c.1525).

Salimbeni Palace ▥

This beautiful 14thC palace is the headquarters of the Sienese-owned Monte dei Paschi bank. On the right side of Piazza Salimbeni is the Renaissance **Spanocchi Palace** (1470) by G. da Maiano, and on the left the 16thC Tantucci Palace.

Sant'Agostino †
The 13thC building, remade in the 18thC, retains important paintings, notably Perugino's *Crucifixion* (1506), A. Lorenzetti's *Madonna and Saints*, Matteo di Giovanni's *Slaughter of the Innocents* (1482) and, over the high altar, Sodoma's *Epiphany*.

Santa Caterina (Santuario Cateriniano) †
A complex of chapels created in and around the house of Catherine Benincasa, the eloquent mystic who was canonized in 1461. **The Oratory of St Catherine** (1465-74), facing Via S. Caterina, was built by the *contrada* of Fontebranda, whose symbol, the goose, adorns the facade. Inside is a wooden statue of *St Catherine* (1474) by Neroccio, and five frescoed *Angels* by Sodoma. The Oratorio della Camera is built over St Catherine's cell. The Baroque Oratorio del Crocifisso contains the 13thC *Crucifix* before which the saint received the stigmata at Pisa in 1375. The Oratorio Superiore has a ceiling by Riccio, and a 17thC tiled floor.

San Domenico †
The stark red-brick Dominican preaching church crowns the hill above **Fontebranda**. The present building, incorporating the original early 13thC church, dates from the 14th-15thC. The campanile was completed in 1340. The only authentic portrait of St Catherine, who assumed the Dominican habit in this church, is that by her friend Andrea Vanni, in a chapel at the w end. In the Chapel of St Catherine, off the right side, are Sodoma's frescoes of *Episodes from the Life of St Catherine* (1526). The *Ciborium* and two *Angels* (1475) are by B. da Maiano.

San Francesco †
As in Florence, the Franciscan preaching church stands across the city from that built by the Dominicans. An earlier church here was begun at once after the death of St Francis. The present building (1326-1475) was altered after a fire in the 17thC and again in the late 19thC. The Neo-Gothic facade was applied in 1913. In the N transept are detached frescoes (1331) by P. Lorenzetti of the *Crucifixion* and by A. Lorenzetti of *St Louis of Anjou before Pope Boniface VII* and the *Martyrdom of the Franciscans*.

On the piazza's s side is the **Oratorio di San Bernardino** (*no. 19 for custodian*). This oratory was built in the 15thC on the site where the Franciscan St Bernardino had preached. The upper chapel has elegant 15thC stuccowork, carvings and frescoes by Sodoma, G. del Pacchia and Beccafumi. The Via del Comune descends to the 14thC **Porta Ovile**.

Santa Maria dei Servi †
Piazza Alessandro Manzoni.
The building dates from the 13th-15thC; the interior naves and aisles were reworked in 1471-1528. Most important of the Sienese school pictures are: **right aisle**, Coppo di Marcovaldo's *Madonna* (1261); **right transept**, P. Lorenzetti's fresco of *The Slaughter of the Innocents*; **left transept**, Lippo Memmi's *Madonna*. Nearby is the imposing **Porta Romana** (1327), from which the Via Cassia leads to Rome.

Santo Spirito †
Via dei Pispini.
The brick Church of the Holy Spirit dates from 1498. The portal is attributed to Peruzzi and the cupola (1508) to Cozzarelli. Inside are works by Sodoma, Cozzarelli and Beccafumi. At the end of Via dei Pispini is the 14thC **Porta Pispini**, with the remains of a fresco of the *Nativity* (1531) by Sodoma.

Tolomei Palace ▥
11 Via Banchi di Sopra.
The oldest private palace in Siena, now occupied by the Florentine Savings Bank, was built in 1208 and altered in c.1267.

Other sights outside the city walls
Diavoli Palace ▥
Just beyond Porta Camollia in Via Fiorentina is a medieval building, rebuilt in 1460 by A. Federighi. This palace is one of the first and most original pieces of Sienese Renaissance architecture.

Osservanza ▥ †
2.5km (1½ miles) from Porta Ovile, beyond the railroad crossing, is the most interesting church near Siena, founded by St Bernardino in 1423 and rebuilt after damage in World War II to the original designs (1474-90) of Giacomo Cozzarelli. It contains a terra-cotta group of the *Annunciation* by A. della Robbia and, in the sacristy, a large *Pietà* by Cozzarelli.

Some of Tuscany's most beautiful old gardens are near Siena. Two that are open to the public on request are: **Vicobello** (*apply to Marchesa Chigi-Bonnelli, Via Vicobello 12*) and **Villa Palazzina** (*apply to Signor Gianneschi, Strada di Ventena 28*).

Hotels

Certosa di Maggiano 🏨
Via Certosa 82, 53100 Siena ☎ *(0577) 288180* ● *574221* ||||| *14 rms including 9 suites* 🖂 *14* ▦ ➡ 🏠 ⇥ *AE* ⊙ *VISA Closed Nov-Feb.*
Location: E of Porta Romana off the Arezzo/Rome road. An exceptionally civilized hotel around the cloister and church of a 14thC monastery. The restaurant is now open to nonresidents, but the quality of the food does not justify the prices or the formal service.
🏠 ▢ 🖉 ☙ ≈ ⅋

Park Hotel 🏨
Via Marciano 16, 53100 Siena ☎ *(0577) 44803* ● *571005* ||||| *69 rms* 🖂 *65*▦ ➡ 🏠 ⇥ *AE* *CB* ⊙ *CO* *VISA*
Location: 2km (1¼ miles) to NW. A slick, modernized 15thC suburban villa. Good restaurant.
🏠 ‡ ▢ 🖉 🐾 ☙ ≈ ⅋ ☗

Palazzo Ravizza
Pian dei Mantellini 34, 53100 Siena ☎ *(0577) 280462* ● *575304* |▢ *to* ||▢ *30 rms* 🖂 *21* ➡ 🏠 ⇥ *AE* ⊙ *CO* *VISA*
Location: 5mins' walk from the Duomo and Campo. This attractive first-class *pensione* in a 17thC villa is now part of a chain, but has kept its old-fashioned character better than most.
‡ & ▢ ☙ ≪ ♆ ⅄

Villa Scacciapensieri
Via di Scacciapensieri, 53100 Siena ☎ *(0577) 41441* ● *573390* ||▢ *to* |||||| *30 rms* 🖂 *30* ▦ ➡ 🏠 ⇥ *AE* ⊙ *CO* *VISA Closed Nov to mid-Mar.*
Location: 3km (2 miles) to N. A big, comfortable country villa set in a large garden with wonderful views of Siena. The generous breakfasts are a rare treat in Tuscany.
🏠 ‡ & ▢ 🖉 ☙ ≪ ≈ ♆ ⅄

Also: **Jolly Excelsior** (*La Lizza* ☎ *(0577) 288448* |||||); **Continentale** (*Via Banchi di Sopra* ☎ *(0577) 41451* ||▢); **Santa Caterina** (*Via Piccolomini 7* ☎ *(0577) 221105* ||▢); **Chiusarelli** (*Viale Curtatone* ☎ *(0577) 280562* |▢); **Villa Patrizia** (*Via Fiorentina 58* ☎ *(0577) 50431* |||||).
The youth hostel, **Ostello della Gioventù Guido Riccio**, is in Via Fiorentina (☎ *(0577) 52212*).

Restaurants

Siena is not one of Tuscany's gastronomic centers. But to dine in the Campo on a starlit evening is one of life's most magical experiences, though there isn't much to choose between the two restaurants, **Il Campo** (☎ *(0577) 280725, closed Tues*) and **Mangia** (☎ *(0577) 281121, closed Mon, Feb*).
Away from the Campo, try: **Le Campane** (*Via delle Campane 6* ☎ *(0577) 284035* ||▢ *closed Sun in summer, Sun and Mon in winter, Nov*); **Da Guido** (*Vicolo Pettinaio 7* ☎ *(0577) 280042* ||▢ *to* ||||| *closed Wed*); **Le Logge** (*Via del Porrione 33* ☎ *(0577) 48013* ||▢ *closed Sun, June*); **Al Marsili** *Via del Castoro 3* ☎ *(0577) 47154* ||▢ *to* ||||| *closed Mon*); **Nello La Taverna** (*Via del Porrione 28* ☎ *(0577) 289043* ||▢ *closed Mon, Feb*); **Tullio ai Tre Christi** (*Vicolo Provenzano 1* ☎ *(0577) 280608* ||▢ *to* ||||| *closed Sun dinner, Mon, 2 weeks in July*).

Restaurants outside Siena

Botteganova
Strada Chiantigiana 29 ☎ *(0577) 284230* ||▢ ⇥ *AE* ⊙ *CO* *VISA Closed Sun.*
Traditional Tuscan cooking. The vegetables, picked fresh from the proprietors' garden, are especially good.

Il Molino delle Bagnaie
Off the SS408 at Pianella ☎ *(0577) 747062. Closed Mon, Jan* ▢
Straightforward local cooking in an attractively renovated old mill.

La Taverna ✿
Via del Sergente 5, Vagliagli ☎ *(0577) 322532* ❚❚] ▭ 🚭 🛥 ⬛ 🎫
Closed Mon.
This is a warm, cheerful tavern in a small hill town N of Siena. ***Specialties:***
Homemade pastas.

Taverna do Solimano
SS 222, Querciagrossa, 2km N of Siena ☎ *(0577) 51144* ❚❚] ▭ ■■ ▬
🚗 ▬ ⒶⒺ ⬛ ⒸⒹ 🎫 *Closed Mon, Jan.*
The old inn serves its own ham and wine from the Villa Colombaio estate
of the Ugurgieri family.

Sinalunga
*Map 12G7. 103km (64 miles) SE of Florence, 45km (28
miles) SE of Siena. 53048.*
Hill town in the heart of the Valdichiana near the entrance to the
autostrada A1. Above the center, the church of **San Bernardino**,
rebuilt in the 18thC, preserves some interesting Sienese
Renaissance pictures, notably an *Annunciation* (1470) by
Benvenuto di Giovanni, and a *Madonna and Child* by Sano di
Pietro.

🍴 **Delle Grotte** ✿ (*Viale Matteotti 35* ☎ *(0577) 630269* ▢ *closed Wed*),
in the center, with tables outside in the summer.

🛏 🍴 **Locanda dell'Amorosa**
2km (1¼ miles) S ☎ *(0577) 679497* ⓖ *580047* ⓖ *(0577) 678216* ❚❚❚] ▭
■■ ▬ ⒶⒺ ⬛ ⒸⒹ *Closed Mon, late Jan-Feb.*
An unusually elegant restaurant, with comfortable rooms, in the converted
brick stables of a wine-growing estate. ***Specialties:*** *Filetto di cinghiale,
zuppa ribollita, fracosta di chianina.*

Sovana
*Map 8J6. 226km (141 miles) S of Florence, 82km (51 miles)
SE of Grosseto. 58010. Grosseto.*
A solitary, semi-abandoned village with Etruscan-Roman
foundations on a plateau 8km (5 miles) NW of *Pitigliano*. The
Rocca was built by the Aldobrandeschi lords in the 13thC. The
main street is flanked by medieval houses. At one end is the
13thC **Palazzo Pretorio**, modified in the 15thC, and the
Romanesque church of **Santa Maria**, which contains a
c.8th-9thC **ciborium**, a rare example of pre-Romanesque
sculpture. At the far end is the splendid and dramatically situated
Romanesque **Duomo**, with a beautiful, austere interior, which
gave one writer "the overall sense that one day soon this
cathedral, already looking impossibly ancient in experience and
wisdom, will shrug its stone shoulders and amble off into the
countryside, never to be seen again."
 The **Etruscan necropolis** (✿) is in cool birch woods 1.5km
(1 mile) below the town (*a guide can be found at the Taverna
Etrusca: allow a minimum of 1hr.*) The architectonic tomb fronts
are carved from the rock face of the gorge with burial grottoes
beneath. The most sophisticated is the 2ndC BC Tomba
Ildebranda in the form of a temple facade.

🛏 🍴 **Taverna Etrusca** ✿ (*Piazza Pretorio* ☎ *(0564) 616183* ▢ *closed
Mon, 2-3 weeks in June-July*).

Stia

Map 12E7. 49km (30 miles) E of Florence. 52017. Arezzo. Population: 3,023.

At the head of the Casentino just below **Monte Falterona**, where the Arno has its source. Its central Piazza Tanucci is a piece of first-class town planning, and the Romanesque church preserves a *Madonna and Child* (1437) by A. della Robbia and an *Annunciation* (1414) by Bicci di Lorenzo.

Nearby sights

In the late Middle Ages Stia was closely surrounded by the castles of the Guidi lords who ruled the upper Casentino and with whom the exiled Dante took refuge. The noblest of the ruined castles is the **Castello di Romena**, 3km (2 miles) s. Nearby, on a parallel road, is the 10th-12thC **Pieve di Romena** (*custodian in house next door*), the finest Romanesque church in the Casentino but over-restored. A magnificent 4hr walk N from Stia will take one to the summit of Monte Falterone via the source of the Arno.

Loris ✿ (☎ *(0575) 58680*▢ *closed Tues, Sept*) is 2km (1 mile) N at Papiano Alto.

Talamone

Map 8J5. 164km (102 miles) S of Florence, 24km (15 miles) S of Grosseto. 58010. Grosseto. Population: 485.

A fishing village and tourist harbor guarded by a grim medieval fortress on a headland s of *Monti dell'Uccellina* overlooking Monte Argentario.

The Sienese purchased Talamone from the Abbey of San Salvatore in 1303; their intention to make it into a port rivaling Pisa and Genoa was derided by Dante (*Purgatorio, XIII*). It became part of the Spanish Garrison States in 1556.

❧ **Corte dei Butteri** 🏨
58010 Fonte Blanda, Grosseto ☎ *(0564) 885547* ◉ *580103* ◎ *(0564) 886282* ⅡⅡⅡ *87 rms* ▭ *87* ▦ ▣ ⌂ ⥤ AE ⊙ ⅦⅥ *Closed mid-Oct to Apr.*
Location: Fonte Blanda, 4km (2½ miles) NE. A modern luxury hotel.
⌂ ✦ ♿ ▱ ☙ ⋙ ☃ ♒ ▅

❧ On the promontory is the **Capo d'Uomo** (*Via Cala di Forno 7* ☎ *(0564) 887077*ⅡⅠ▯ *closed Oct-Mar*).

═ The best in the center is **La Buca** (☎ *(0564) 887067*ⅡⅠ▯ *to* ⅡⅡⅡ *closed Mon, two weeks in Jan*). 2km (1¼ miles) NE at Fonte Blanda is **Il Bracconiere** (☎ *(0564) 885523* ⅡⅠ▯ *closed Tues, Nov*).

Torre del Lago Puccini

Map 14E3. 95km (59 miles) W of Florence, 16km (10 miles) N of Pisa. 55048. Lucca. Population: 5,450.

Just to the E of the dull little village of Torre del Lago Puccini is **Lake Massaciuccoli**, the largest of the few lakes in Tuscany. The opera composer Giacomo Puccini, who settled here in 1891, once described this place as his "supreme joy, paradise, Eden, the Empyrean, turris eburnea, vas spiritualis, kingdom." He built himself a house on the shore of the lake, where he lived until shortly before his death in 1924.

Event   A festival of Puccini operas is held in early Aug (*for information and reservations contact Segreteria del Festival Pucciniano, Piazza Puccini, 55048 Torre del Lago, Lucca* ☎ *(0584) 342006*).

Villa Puccini ☆
The villa is preserved as it was in Puccini's lifetime, and he is buried here in a mausoleum built, appropriately, between his piano and his gun-room. The house is a shrine as well as a vivid testimony to this likeable genius.

≕ Next to the villa are **Butterfly** (☎ (0584) 341024 ▯□ closed Thurs, late Oct-early Nov) with rooms; **Da Cecco** (☎ (0584) 341022 ▯▯ closed Mon, late Nov to mid-Dec).

The food is more interesting at **Il Pescatore** (Viale Europa ☎ (0584) 340610 ▥▥▥ closed Mon, Tues in winter).

Vallombrosa
Map 12E6. 33km (20 miles) SE of Florence. 50060. Firenze.
In the NE Pratomagno Hills, reached by beautiful twisting roads, is the monastery of Vallombrosa, the mother house of the order founded in the early 11thC by the Florentine religious reformer San Giovanni Gualberto.

Monastery ▥ †
The imposing monastery, like a finely designed symmetrical castle, has a facade (1635-40) by G. Silvani. The campanile is 13thC, and the tower 15thC; the church itself is mainly 17thC. A plaque records that the poet Milton stayed here in 1638. All around is the magnificent deciduous forest that inspired Milton's description of the gathering devils in *Paradise Lost*: "Thick as autumnal leaves that strow the brooks/In Vallombrosa, where th'Etrurian shades,/High-overarch'd, imbower."

Nearby sights
9km (6 miles) above, near the summit of **Monte Secchietta** at 1,449m (4,216ft), is fine walking country, also equipped for skiing. **Saltino**, a modern summer and winter sports resort, is 2km (1¼ miles) W, and **Consuma**, another vacation resort, is 10km (6 miles) NE.

❧ **Croce di Savoia**
50060 Saltino, Firenze ☎ (055) 862035-6 ▯□ to ▯▯▯ 80 rms ▭ 52 ⌂
≕ ᴁᴇ Open July and Aug only.
Location: 1km to W. A comfortable wooded summer retreat.
⌂ ≵ ⛰ ☙ ⫶

❧ ≕ **Sbaragli**, at Montemignaio (☎ (055) 8306500 ▯□ closed 15 Nov-15 Apr, restaurant closed Tues except in summer).

❧ **Villa Rigacci**
15km (9½ miles) s at Vaggia, Via Vaggio 76 ☎ (055) 8656718 ▥▯□ 17 rms ⌂ ⚊ Closed Feb.
A country house situated high on a hill and surrounded by mature trees.
⌂ ☙ ⫶ ≋ ☙ ♙ ⫶

❧ ≕ See also **Pontassieve** and **San Giovanni Valdarno**.

Vetulonia
Map 11I5. 141km (87 miles) SW of Florence, 29km (18 miles) NW of Grosseto. 58040. Grosseto. Population: 615.
Vetulonia is the most enigmatic of the great Etruscan city states. Like *Roselle*, Etruscan Vetulonia was a maritime city situated on an island rising from the navigable waters of the gulf that then filled part of the Grosseto plain. Its culture flourished from the 8th-6thC BC and then seems to have died out with mysterious suddenness. The Roman symbol of power, the fasces, was borrowed from archaic Vetulonia.

Sights and places of interest
Museo Archeologico
This small, interesting museum occupies the site of the acropolis at the

entrance to the village. Above are remains of the **walls** (6thC BC) built of huge polygonal blocks of stone and commanding a magnificent view.
Necropolis ☆
3km (1.75 miles) to NE ✗ compulsory (inquire about tours at museum)
The most important tombs are the **tumulo della Pietrera**, domed in the manner of Mycenaean tombs, and, 400m (¼ mile) below, the **tumulo del Diavolino**; both are probably late 7thC BC.

Viareggio
Map 14D3. 97km (60 miles) W of Florence, 27km (17 miles) W of Lucca. 55049. Lucca. Population: 59,460.
The capital of the Versilia Riviera is one of the oldest seaside resorts in Italy. The climate is healthy and mild in winter, but the atmosphere today is that of a tough, citified seaside strip masking a sleazy but more congenial port area. Stately Liberty buildings and palm-fringed avenues were laid out in the 19thC in strict parallel roads where the medieval King's Highway (Via Regia) once ran through the pine woods. The fine-sand beach is over 100m wide and divided into well-equipped and expensive bathing establishments. The harbor is lively with fishing and tourist boats.

To the N, Viareggio merges with the modern and less expensive Lido di Camaiore. To the S, a protected pine wood stretches as far as *Torre del Lago*, and there are free beaches.

The monument to Shelley in Piazza Shelley records that the poet's body was washed up on the beach in 1822.
Event Viareggio Carnival, the most elaborate in Tuscany, takes place throughout the month before Lent. Festivities include processions of allegorical floats, masked balls, fireworks and a soccer tournament.

⌂ Astor
Viale Carducci 54, 55049 Viareggio, Lucca ☎ (0584) 50301 ⊙ 501031
||||| *120 rms* ⬚ *120* ▦ ⬚ ⬚ ⬚ AE ⊙ ⊙ VISA
This ultramodern luxury hotel is part of the SINA chain. Service apartments available.
♨ ⅃ ⬚ ⬚ ☙ ⟪ ⇗ ⬚ ➤ ⛲

⌂ Palace
Via Flavio Gioia 2, 55049 Viareggio, Lucca ☎ (0584) 46134 ⊙ 501044
⊛ *(0584) 47351* ||||| *200 rms* ⬚ *200* ▦ ⬚ ⬚ ⬚ ⬚ ⬚ ⬚ VISA
An attractive first-class hotel decorated in red, white and gold, Second Empire style.
⬚ ⬚ ⛲

⌂ Principe di Piemonte
Piazza Puccini 1, 55049 Viareggio, Lucca ☎ (0584) 50122 ⊙ 501283
||||| *123 rms* ⬚ *103* ▦ *partial* ⬚ ⬚ ⬚ AE ⊙ *Closed Oct-Apr.*
A spacious turn-of-the-century grand hotel decorated in sugared-almond colors with polished mahogany and fresh flowers.
⬚ ☙ ⟪ ⇗ ⬚ ⛲

⊟ Buonamico
Via Sant'Andrea 27 ☎ (0584) 961038 ||||| ⬚ ⬚ ⬚ AE ⊙ ⊙ VISA *Closed Mon, Aug.*
A small, dark restaurant on a side street near the fishing port. Next door is a tiny fish store where you may choose what you want for dinner. Reserve.

⊟ Oca Bianca
N toward Lido di Camaiore, Via Aurelia Nord 312 ☎ (0584) 64191 |||||
⬚ ■ ■ ⬚ ⬚ AE *Closed Wed, Thurs lunch.*
One of the great, unforgettable Italian restaurants in three small, tastefully decorated and professionally staffed rooms. The culinary style ranges successfully from sophisticated simplicity to intriguingly fanciful.

⇌ Il Patriarca
Viale Carducci 79 ☎ (0584) 53126 ⅢⅢ ☐ ■ ♠ ☰ ⟋ ▾ ⅋ AE CB ⊙
⊙ ⅦⅢ *Closed Wed in winter, mid-Nov to early Dec.*
One of the super-smart restaurants of the Versilia. Good soups, risottos,
baccalà.

⇌ Romano
Via Mazzini 120 ☎ (0584) 31382 ⅢⅢ ☐ ➤ ♠ ☰ AE CB ⊙ ⊙ ⅦⅢ
Closed Mon, 2 weeks in Jan.
Skillfully inventive variations on the fresh fish motif. Ask advice.

⇌ Also recommended: Gusmano (*Via Regia 58 ☎ (0584) 21233* ⅢⅢ
closed Tues, Nov); **Margherita** (*Piazzale Margherita ☎ (0584) 42553* ⅢⅢ
closed Wed in winter); **Montecatini** (*Viale Manin 8 ☎ (0584)962129* ⅢⅠ☐
to ⅢⅢ *closed Mon, 2wks in Sept, 2wks in Jan)*.

Vinci

*Map **15**E5. 43km (27 miles) w of Florence. 55009. Firenze.
Population: 13,577.*
Leonardo's birthplace is on Monte Albano, N of *Empoli*.

Museo Vinciano
The town has dedicated rooms in its restored 13thC *castello* to a small
museum about its famous son, displaying models made from his designs.

Nearby sights
3km (2 miles) N at **Anchiano** is the farmhouse where Leonardo may have
spent his childhood, in a ravishing setting amid olive groves.
  The drive N over Monte Albano to *Pistoia* is spectacularly beautiful.

⇌ See *Artimino* and *Lastra a Signa*.

Volterra ★

*Map **10**F4. 81km (50 miles) sw of Florence, 57km (35 miles)
w of Siena. 56048. Pisa. Population: 14,911.*
Volterra was the northernmost and one of the most powerful of
the federated Etruscan city states. Its name was Velathri, it was
three times the size of the present town, and it controlled a
territory stretching from Pisa to Populonia and from the sea
inland as far as the Pesa valley. 522m (1,712ft) above sea-level
and protected by 7km (4½ miles) of walls which were in places
12m (39ft) high, it became a prosperous Roman municipality in
the 4thC BC, but supported Marius against Sulla in the civil war
and was conquered by the latter in 82-80BC.
  During the Middle Ages, Volterra's struggle against the
ecclesiastic lords for communal independence was bitter and
protracted but, in the 13thC, successful. Although taken under
the "protection" of Florence from the mid-14thC the Republic of
Volterra remained technically independent until 1470. This was
the year when Lorenzo de' Medici, desperate to safeguard the
crucial Florentine rights to alum mining in Volterra's territory,
hired the Duke of Urbino to invade the city. The brutality of the
siege remained one of the few blots on Lorenzo's diplomatic
career; one of his would-be assassins in the Pazzi Conspiracy
8yrs later was a Volterran.
  Lorenzo built a new fortress, known as the Fortezza Nuova or
"*Il Maschio*" (now a prison) and fortified the old 14thC tower, the
Fortezza Vecchia or "*La Femmina*." The city waited in the
shadow of these loathed symbols of foreign domination until the
final and futile rebellion of 1530, which was quickly subdued by
the Florentine general Federigo Ferrucci.

Many travelers have remarked on the uncanny atmosphere of Volterra, where a chill wind can spring up from nowhere on the balmiest summer day, and where the hill on which the town stands has sheered off, forming the cliffs, the *Balze*, to the NE, and carrying parts of the Etruscan city with them. D.H. Lawrence saw the city "that gets all the wind and sees all the world" as "a sort of inland island, still curiously isolated, and grim." It is certainly very much its own place. Unlike its neighbor and traditional enemy **San Gimignano**, Volterra does not primp for tourists. The inhabitants are courteous, but there is about them an air of brooding energy which can prompt the fancy, especially when the wind is high, that Volterra is still waiting, and for something more important than tourists. Meanwhile, the town is economically if not politically independent. The quarrying and carving of alabaster is the chief occupation.

Sights and places of interest

The medieval city is contained within 13thC walls. The views, on a clear day, extend to the mountains below *Carrara*, to Corsica and inland to *Monte Amiata* and the Casentino.

The parking lot nearest the central Piazza dei Priori, the main square, is in Piazza Martiri della Libertà, the s entrance to the town. The following itineraries assume a day's visit, half devoted to the medieval town and half to the remains of the Etruscan city and to visiting the *Balze*.

Duomo ▥ †

The simple facade is 12thC, adapted to the Pisan style in the 13thC. The interior, altered in the 16thC, has an attractive painted wooden ceiling. In the right transept is a polychrome wooden *Deposition* (1228), an unusual larger-than-life-size folk-Romanesque scene made by Pisan sculptors, more religious theater than art. Over the high altar is Mino da Fiesole's exquisite **ciborium** (1471), flanked by his two charming *Angels* resting on 12thC twisted columns. In the left aisle is the **pulpit**, remade from 12thC carvings, and an *Annunciation* (1497) by Albertinelli.

In the chapel off the entrance to the nave are two niches containing 15thC polychrome terra-cotta groups by Zacchi Zaccaria of the *Epiphany* (right) and *Nativity* (left). The background to the *Nativity*, a delightful panoramic fresco of the *Magi*, is by Gozzoli.

Inside the 13thC **Baptistry** is a **baptismal font** (1502) by A. Sansovino.

Museo di Arte Sacra

Via Roma ☎ *(0588) 86192.*

A display of architectural fragments, sculptures, reliquaries and paintings, next to the Duomo. Notice particularly Andrea della Robbia's bust of *St Linus*, the silver bust of *St Octavian* by A. Pollaiuolo, and a gilded bronze *Crucifix* by Giambologna.

Museo Etrusco Guarnacci ★

Via Don Minzoni 15.

This is one of the largest and most important Etruscan collections outside Florence and Rome. There are some 600 cinerary urns in tufa, alabaster or terra cotta, dating from the 6th-1stC BC. For D.H. Lawrence these urns were like "an open book of life"; for scholars they are like a book about Etruscan beliefs about the afterlife. They are arranged according to subject matter of the carvings. In Rm. 24 on the first floor is the tiny Giacometti-like *Ombra della Sera* and other Etruscan bronze votives.

Piazza dei Priori

The central square retains its character thanks partly to some modern imitations of the medieval architecture. The **Palazzo Pretorio**, on the NE side, is a 13thC complex but much restored; its crenelated tower, adapted in the early 16thC, is known as the "*porcellino*" (piglet).

Palazzo dei Priori

The town hall (1208-54) is the oldest civic building in Tuscany; on the lower facade are the terra-cotta emblems of the 15th-16thC Florentine commissioners. Climb the tower for stunning views.

Museo Civico

Via Sarti.

The 15thC Palazzo Minucci-Sarti houses a collection of 14th-17thC

Florentine and Sienese pictures by, among others, D. Ghirlandaio and Signorelli; but the museum is worth visiting if only for Rosso Fiorentino's vivid, whirling *Deposition* (1521) (★).

Quadrivio dei Buomparenti

The intersection of Via Roma with Via Ricciarelli and Buomparenti is the most picturesque corner of the medieval town. The 13thC tower-houses of the Buomparenti are remarkably intact.

San Francesco †

The **Cappella della Croce di Giorno** is entirely covered with frescoes of the *Legend of the True Cross* (1410) by Cenni di Francesco Cenni.

≈ **Nazionale**
Via dei Marchesi 2, 56048 Volterra, Pisa ☎ *(0588) 86284* ⌷ *34 rms*
▱ *34* ⌷ ⇌

"The hotel is simple and somewhat rough, but quite friendly, pleasant in its haphazard way." D.H. Lawrence's description of 1927 still fits.
& ‡ ⌒

≈ **Villa Nencini** (*Borgo S. Stefano 55* ☎ *(0588) 86386*⌷) is quiet and has a garden.

⇌ **Da Beppino** (*Via delle Prigioni 15/19* ☎ *(0588) 86051*⌷ *closed Wed, Nov*) is the locals' favorite, which also serves the best food. **Etruria** (*Piazza dei Priori 8* ☎ *(0588) 86064*⌷ *closed Thurs*) is on the main square.

Shopping

There are dozens of stores selling objects made of alabaster. The central outlet and information center is the **Cooperativa Artieri Alabastro** (*Piazza dei Priori 2* ☎ *(0588) 87590*).

Walks

Walk 1/Etruscan and Roman Volterra

Just to the w of Piazza Martiri della Libertà is the **Arco Etrusco**, the s entrance to the Etruscan city. The uprights and bases on the inner side are Etruscan; the archivolt was rebuilt by the Romans who reincorporated the three Etruscan heads. Via Porto dell'Arco lies on the cardinal axis of the Etruscan-Roman city which continues with Via Matteotti, lined with medieval tower-houses, and into Via Guarnacci, which was the site of part of the Roman Forum.

Turn left into Via Lungo le Mura del Mandorlo, which overlooks the **Roman Theater** (1stC BC) and **Baths** (3rdC BC). Beyond the Porta Fiorentina, the pretty Via Diana leads to the Porta Diana, the N Etruscan gate of which only fragments survive. Beyond is the site of the **Necropoli del Portone**. The empty underground tombs are mostly unmarked, but some, in the middle of a farm, are signposted "*Ipogei dei Marmini.*"

Walk 2/To the Balze

Start at the church of San Francesco; the *Balze* are 2km (1¼ miles) by foot from Porta S. Francesco. Taking Borgo S. Stefano, turn left under Vicolo della Penera, then sharp right behind the hand railings. You will find a path running along the base of the stretch of the **Etruscan walls** known as the Mura Etrusche di S. Chiara, which in summer are festooned with flowering capers, to the **Balze**, the cliffs formed by repeated landslides. The views to the w are superb, and on a peaceful summer midday when the scent of broom is sweet and strong one may wonder at Augustus Hare's description of the **Balze** as "an arid and ghastly desert." But if you go just before sunset you could share his vertiginous apprehension "that the flowery surface on which you are standing may be hurled into destruction tomorrow."

Biographies

A selection of major 13th-17thC Tuscan artists.

Alberti, Leon Battista (1404-72)
Influential Renaissance architect, theoretician and scholar.

Ammannati, Bartolomeo (1511-92)
Florentine sculptor and architect influenced by **Michelangelo**.

Andrea del Sarto (1486-1531)
"Flawless painter" of the early Florentine High Renaissance.

Angelico, Fra Giovanni (active c.1418-55)
Dominican monk and Renaissance painter.

Arnolfo di Cambio (before 1245-c.1302)
Gothic architect and sculptor, a pupil of **Nicola Pisano**.

Baccio d'Agnolo (1462-1543)
Florentine Renaissance architect and woodcarver. His son
Giuliano (1491-1555) was a fine Mannerist architect.

Baldovinetti, Alesso (c.1426-99)
Florentine Renaissance painter and mosaicist.

Bartolommeo della Porta, Fra (1472/5-1517)
A leading painter of the Florentine High Renaissance.

Beccafumi, Domenico (c.1486-1551)
The outstanding Sienese Mannerist painter and sculptor.

Botticelli, Sandro (1445-1510)
The greatest linear painter of the Florentine Renaissance.

Bronzino (Agnolo Allori) (1503-72)
Florentine Mannerist painter, a polished portraitist.

Brunelleschi, Filippo (1377-1446)
The creator of Florentine Renaissance architecture.

Buontalenti, Bernardo (1531-1608)
Florentine Mannerist architect to the Medici grand dukes.

Castagno, Andrea del (active c. 1442, died 1457)
Renaissance painter strongly influenced by **Donatello**.

Cellini, Benvenuto (1500-71)
Florentine sculptor, goldsmith and autobiographer.

Cimabue, Giovanni (c.1240-?1302)
Florentine painter and mosaicist who may have taught **Giotto**.

Civitali, Matteo (1436-1501)
The most important Renaissance sculptor of Lucca.

Cronaca (Simone del Pollaiuolo) (1457-1508)
Florentine architect and stonemason.

Daddi, Bernardo (c.1290-c.1348)
Florentine painter influenced by **Giotto** and the **Lorenzetti**.

Della Robbia, Luca (1400-82)
Sculptor who invented a method of applying vitreous glazes to terra
cotta. Nephew **Andrea** (1424-1525) and sons **Giovanni** (1464-
c.1529) and **Girolamo** (1488-1556) continued the family workshop.

Desiderio da Settignano (1428-64)
Renaissance sculptor of delicate reliefs and portrait busts.

Donatello (1386-1466)
The greatest Italian sculptor of the early Renaissance.

Duccio di Buoninsegna (active 1278, died 1318/19)
The greatest and most influential of early Sienese painters.

Ferri, Ciro (1620/34-89)
Baroque painter, **Pietro da Cortona's** most important pupil.

Francesco di Giorgio Martini (1439-1502)
Sienese architect, military engineer, sculptor and painter.

Gaddi, Agnolo (active c.1370, died 1396)
Florentine painter, son of **Taddeo**.

Gaddi, Taddeo (active c.1325, died 1366)
Giotto's most important disciple.

Biographies

Ghiberti, Lorenzo *(1378-1455)*
Florentine early Renaissance bronze sculptor.

Ghirlandaio, Domenico *(1449-94)*
Florentine Renaissance painter, a teacher of **Michelangelo**, and master of a large studio run with his brother **Davide** (1452-1525) and son **Ridolfo** (1483-1561).

Giambologna (Jean Boulogne) *(1524-1608)*
Flemish-born court sculptor to the Medici.

Giotto di Bondone *(1267/77-1337)*
The first great innovatory genius of Florentine painting.

Giovanni da San Giovanni *(1592-1636)*
Tuscan Baroque painter of frescoes in Florence and Rome.

Giovanni di Paolo *(1403-82/3)*
A leading 15thC Sienese painter working in 14thC style.

Gozzoli, Benozzo *(c.1421-97)*
Florentine narrative painter, a pupil of **Angelico**.

Guido da Siena *(active mid-13thC)*
Founder of the Sienese school of painting.

Leonardo da Vinci *(1452-1519)*
One of the greatest figures in the history of Western art, with an apparently limitless power and range of intellect. Engineer, anatomist, sculptor, architect and creator, with **Michelangelo** and **Raphael**, of the High Renaissance style of painting.

Lippi, Filippino *(1457-1504)*
Son of Filippo and distinguished quasi-Mannerist painter.

Lippi, Fra Filippo *(active c.1432, died 1469)*
Florentine Renaissance painter; disciple of **Masaccio**.

Lorenzetti, Ambrogio *(active 1319-47)* and **Pietro** *(active 1320-45)*
The Sienese Lorenzetti brothers worked in a style that synthesized the prevailing Florentine and Sienese schools.

Maiano, Benedetto da *(1442-97)*
Florentine Renaissance sculptor, especially of fine reliefs. His brother **Giuliano** (1432-90) was an architect.

Margaritone d'Arezzo *(active mid-13thC)*
One of the earliest Italian painters to sign his work.

Martini, Simone *(active c.1315, died 1344)*
The leading Sienese exponent of International Gothic painting.

Masaccio *(1401-c.1428)*
A founder of Florentine Renaissance painting.

Michelangelo Buonarroti *(1475-1564)*
Painter, architect, poet and sculptor of deeply expressive human figures.

Michelozzo di Bartolomeo *(1396-1472)*
Cosimo de' Medici's favorite architect.

Mino da Fiesole *(1429-84)*
Florentine Renaissance sculptor in marble.

Nanni di Banco *(c.1384-1421)*
Late Gothic-early Renaissance Florentine sculptor.

Orcagna, Andrea (Andrea di Cione) *(active c.1343, died 1368)*
The greatest mid-14thC Florentine painter, sculptor and architect.

Piero della Francesca *(1410/20-92)*
One of the outstanding Tuscan painters and theorists.

Piero di Cosimo *(1462-1521)*
Idiosyncratic Florentine painter of mythological subjects.

Pietro da Cortona *(1596-1669)*
Painter and architect; a founder of Roman High Baroque.

Pisano, Andrea *(c.1290-1348)*
Sculptor known for the bronze s doors of Florence Baptistry.

Pisano, Giovanni *(c.1245-c.1315) and* **Nicola** *(c.1223-c.1284)*
Nicola and his son Giovanni created modern figure sculpture.
Poccetti, Bernardino Barbatelli *(before 1548-1612)*
Florentine painter, the leading master of *sgraffiti*.
Pollaiuolo, Antonio *(c.1432-98) and* **Piero** *(.1441-96)*
Florentine painters, sculptors, engravers and goldsmiths.
Antonio, one of the great draughtsmen of the Renaissance, is
considered the more talented of the brothers.
Pontormo, Jacopo Carucci *(1494-1556)*
Deeply religious painter and one of the creators of Mannerism.
Quercia, Jacopo della *(1374-1438)*
The greatest Sienese sculptor of the early Renaissance.
Raphael *(1483-1520)*
Umbrian pioneer of High Renaissance painting.
Rossellino, Antonio *(1427-79) and* **Bernardo** *(1409-64)*
Brothers whose sculpture exemplifies the "sweet style" of the
Florentine Renaissance. **Bernardo** worked also as an architect.
Rosso Fiorentino *(1495-1540)*
A founder of Mannerism; important religious painter.
Salviati, Francesco (or Cecchino) *(1510-63)*
Florentine Mannerist painter and friend of **Vasari**.
Sangallo
Florentine family of architects. **Giuliano** (c.1443-1516), a
follower of **Brunelleschi**, was Lorenzo the Magnificent's favorite
architect. His brother **Antonio the Elder** (c.1453-1534)
introduced the Roman High Renaissance style to provincial
Tuscany. Both were military architects, as was their nephew
Antonio the Younger (1483-1546).
Sansovino, Andrea *(c.1460-1529)*
High Renaissance sculptor in terra cotta and marble.
Sansovino, Jacopo *(1486-1570)*
Andrea's pupil and namesake and city architect of Venice.
Sassetta (Stefano di Giovanni) *(c.1423-50)*
The most important early 15thC Sienese painter.
Signorelli, Luca *(c.1441/50-1523)*
Tuscan painter; an influence on **Michelangelo**.
Silvani, Gherardo *(1579-1675)*
One of the best High Baroque architects outside Rome.
Sodoma *(1477-1549)*
Interpreter to Siena of **Leonardo's** style of painting.
Spinello Aretino *(active 1373, died 1410/11)*
Narrative painter in the style of **Giotto**.
Starnina, Gherardo *(c.1354-before 1413)*
Florentine painter, a modest anticipator of **Uccello**.
Tacca, Pietro *(1577-1640)*
Sculptor to the Medici grand dukes after **Giambologna**.
Tino di Camaino *(c.1285-1337)*
Sienese sculptor who also worked in Pisa, Florence and Naples.
Tribolo *(1500-50)*
Florentine sculptor and designer of gardens.
Uccello, Paolo *(1387-1475)*
Florentine Renaissance painter famous as a perspectivist.
Vasari, Giorgio *(1511-74)*
Architect, painter and author of the first history of art.
Vecchietta *(1412-80)*
Sienese sculptor, painter and architect.
Verrocchio, Andrea del *(1435-88)*
Painter, goldsmith and the leading bronze sculptor of his day.
Volterrano *(1611-89)*
Tuscan Baroque painter influenced by **Pietro da Cortona**.

Tuscan wines

Wine has been an element of Tuscan life for ages. We know that the Etruscans made wine three millennia ago. The Romans followed suit, and though vine cultivation lapsed during the Dark Ages, wine was back in prominence through the Renaissance, flourishing as nutrient of body and soul and as a source of inspiration for who knows how many works of art or grandiose ideas.

Tuscans in their time have contributed notably to the development of wine-making as art and science, to techniques of bottling and shipping wine and establishing the rituals that have grown around its service and consumption. Over the last two decades Tuscany's vineyards and cellars have been transformed from generally rustic to prevalently high-tech, as the region has seized the lead in the styling of modern red wines. But since the hills have a broad range of microclimates and wine-makers insist on expressing individuality, wines often show variations in type from one place to another. This diversity makes Tuscan wine lists especially fascinating.

Tuscany's 22 wines of controlled name and origin or DOC (for *denominazione di origine controllata*) include three of the six with Italy's highest classification, the government-guaranteed DOCG. These are Brunello di Montalcino, Vino Nobile di Montepulciano and Chianti. The latter is Italy's most prodigious classified wine, with seven zones covering much of the region, from N of Florence to S of Chiusi and from Pisa inland to Arezzo. Chianti became famous in its rounded straw flask, but today most wine, including the *riserva*, which must be aged 3yrs before being sold, comes in straight Bordeaux-style bottles.

Montalcino and Montepulciano also lie within Chianti's territory, although Brunello stands proudly as one of the world's longest lived and most expensive reds, and Vino Nobile is gradually regaining the status it held in the 17thC when it was called "of all wines king."

All Tuscan DOC red wines are based on the versatile Sangiovese grape, sometimes used alone (as in Brunello and Morellino di Scansano), sometimes mixed with other varieties (as in Carmignano, Chianti, Elba Rosso, Montescudaio Rosso, Parrina Rosso, Rosso delle Colline Lucchesi and Vino Nobile). Not all the fine reds are DOC, however: Tignanello, Le Pergole Torte, Flaccianello, Coltassala and Rosso di Cercatoia are but a few of the prized Sangiovese-based wines sold under individual names. Other varieties have also gained status, none more than Cabernet, which is the base of such renowned table wines as Sassicaia, Sammarco, Solaia and Tavernelle.

Tuscan whites have gained stature as new wine-making methods have improved quality. Among DOC whites, Vernaccia di San Gimignano stands out, although foreign varieties have instilled class in such appellations as Pomino and Montecarlo. Other DOC whites such as Bianco di Pitigliano and Bianco Vergine della Valdichiana are gradually reaching markets beyond the region.

Among the many unclassified whites produced, the modern light Galestro is increasingly popular. But by now every Tuscan estate or winery, large or small, makes a special white, although type and quality vary markedly. Outside varieties, especially Chardonnay, but also the Pinots, Riesling and Traminer, have added fragrance and fruitiness to the rather bland native Trebbiano and Malvasia.

Among sweet dessert or aperitif wines, Vin Santo, made from semi-dried grapes and well aged in small sealed barrels, is beloved by Tuscans, but, alas, production is painstaking and there is little of this true "holy wine" to be found. Lately, though, there have been signs of a comeback, as even large producers concentrate efforts on limited stocks of prestigious Vin Santo. There are, as well, a great many curiosities, experiments, and esoteric wines to be discovered. Although most such wine is unclassified, moves are afoot to create new official categories for modern red and white wines by a consortium of producers who use the term *Predicato*.

Everywhere local wine of the latest vintage is served as the natural accompaniment to the local food. The authorities of a zone, or even an individual estate (*fattoria*), sometimes boast the added attraction of an *enoteca*, or wine store, where the wines can be bought. For those who like to combine the enjoyment of art and history with the pleasures of food and wine, few regions offer such exciting possibilities. All major zones are within easy reach of Florence.

Chianti Classico

For all the violent history that transpired in this buffer zone between Florence and Siena, Chianti Classico, the most important of the seven Chianti zones, is today one of the most peacefully handsome of all places where wine is made. Follow the Via Chiantigiana (SS222) s from Florence through Strada, Greve, Panzano and Castellina to Siena, through wooded hills where vines and olive groves, cypresses and pines surround medieval castles, villas and stone farmhouses. The complete Chiantigiana route includes a detour through the domain of the original Chianti League, founded in the 13thC by the feudal barons of Castellina, Gaiole and Radda. This can be extended to take in the Castello di Brolio near San Regolo, where modern Chianti was "invented" in the last century by Baron Bettino Ricasoli, and the villages of Castagnoli, Villa a Sesta, San Gusme, Castelnuovo Berardenga and Vagliagli.

Most Chianti Classico estates welcome visitors, though to assure a reception it would be wise to arrange appointments with the Chianti Classico *consorzio* (*Via de' Serragli 146 in Florence* ☎ *(055) 229351/2/3*). Three historically important houses, Castello di Brolio-Barone Ricasoli (☎ *(0577) 749710*), Marchesi Antinori (☎ *(055) 282202/3*) and Ruffino (☎ *(055) 8302307*) are not in the *consorzio*. Ricasoli and Antinori will accept group visits if arranged ahead of time. Ruffino conducts regular tours through its cellars at Pontassieve or, by arrangement, to its properties in Chianti Classico. Antinori's wines are served at the Cantinetta Antinori in the center of Florence (see **Florence/Restaurants**).

A complete selection of Chianti Classico is sold at the Enoteca del Gallo Nero in Greve, the hub of Chianti and the setting of an annual wine fair in early Sept. Other stores with a good selection include the Bottega del Chianti Classico at Greve, the Enoteca del Chianti Classico at Panzano and the Bottega del Chianti Classico at Castellina. Several estates have a *trattoria* or *osteria* on the premises. Noteworthy examples include the Trattoria di Montagliari near Panzano (see **Greve** in **Tuscany A to Z**); the Badia a Coltibuono near **Gaiole** (see **Tuscany A to Z**); and the Tavernetta Serristori "Albergaccio" (where Niccolò Machiavelli spent much of his exile from Florence) at S. Andrea in Percussina. Some estates have quarters for *agriturismo*, with houses or rooms to let for a few days or longer, sometimes with full board. The *consorzio* can provide information.

Siena/Montalcino/Montepulciano/San Gimignano

Siena is sometimes called the capital of Italian wine, partly because it is the center of Tuscany's most important production zones and also because the **Enoteca Italiana**, the public national wine library, is located in its Medici fortress. Though the *enoteca* is open only by appointment. (☎ *(0577) 288497*), select wines can be tasted at a bar that is open daily. The city makes a convenient headquarters for traveling enophiles — in Siena's province are the original sector of

Tuscan wines

Chianti Classico, the Chianti Colli Senesi zone, the vineyards of the exceptional Brunello di Montalcino and Vino Nobile di Montepulciano, and the white Vernaccia di San Gimignano.

Montalcino, a hill town 45km (28 miles) S of Siena, is the home of the fabled red Brunello and the even older but currently less renowned Moscadello di Montalcino. The Medici fortress in the center of town houses an enoteca and tasting bar of Brunello. Outside Montalcino, visits to one of the leading producers and what ranks as Italy's most famous wine estate, Il Greppo of Biondi-Santi, can be made by appointment (**☎** *(0577) 848087*), and the Fattoria dei Barbi has an *osteria* on the estate (see **Montalcino** in **Tuscany A to Z**). Poggio Antico (**☎** *(0577) 849200*) also has a good restaurant on the premises. Villa Banfi (**☎** *(0577) 864111*) welcomes visitors to its ultramodern cellars and vineyards. A wine museum and restaurant are being prepared in its Castello Banfi.

The lovely Renaissance town of Montepulciano, 37km (23 miles) farther E, is surrounded by the vineyards of Vino Nobile, whose *consorzio* (**☎** *(0578) 757844*) will arrange tours to the various cellars. And in San Gimignano, whose towers jut over a landscape of vines and olives, many producers of the vigorous white Vernaccia sell bottles in individual shops.

Florence/Rufina/Carmignano

Florence is itself a wine town, center of the Colli Fiorentini Chianti zone and headquarters of many important Tuscan wineries. Italy's outstanding collection of wines (including French and Californian) may be viewed by clients in the cellar of the restaurant Enoteca Nazionale of Giorgio Pinchiorri (see **Florence Restaurants**).

Rufina, a small DOC zone 20km (13 miles) E of Florence, makes some of the finest Chianti. Within its limits are some of Tuscany's best-known wine houses: Marchesi de' Frescobaldi (**☎** *(055) 218751*), with estates of Pomino and Nipozzano, and Ruffino (see under *Chianti Classico*).

Carmignano, a zone some 25km (16 miles) W of Florence, produces a scarce red wine that some consider Tuscany's most consistently impressive DOC. There are only about a dozen producers whose wine can be sold as Carmignano only if approved by experts in a rigorous annual blind tasting. The wines are displayed at a small *enoteca* in the center of town. The Fattoria di Artimino, in the Medici villa of the "Hundred Chimneys," is open to visitors.

Other itineraries

The Chianti Putto *consorzio* (*Lungarno Corsini 4, Florence* **☎** *(055) 270168*) can help arrange visits to estates in the other six Chianti zones: Colli Aretini, Colli Fiorentini, Colline Pisane, Colli Senesi, Montalbano and Rufina.

Nearly every center of interest to tourists has a wine area nearby. Pisa has Bianco di San Torpe to the SE. Lucca has two DOC zones, Rosso delle Colline Lucchesi, to the N, and Montecarlo, a white wine produced around the village of that name. From farther E, near Montecatini Terme, comes Bianco della Valdinievole. In Arezzo province, the broad Chiana valley between Cortona and Montepulciano is the home of Bianco Vergine della Valdichiana.

The Tuscan coastal strip also produces good wines. Not far from Viareggio and the Tuscan Riviera is the DOC zone of Candia dei Colli, with red, white and Vin Santo, and the island of Elba, with red and white DOC wines and a sweet red Aleatico di Portoferraio, which Napoleon supposedly liked. In the Maremma hills of Grosseto province there are three DOCs: Morellino di Scansano, Bianco di Pitigliano and, adjacent to the Argentario peninsula, Parrina.

Sports, leisure, ideas for children

There is much in Tuscany besides sightseeing, as those with small children may be relieved to learn; and you can usually buy temporary membership of private sports clubs and organizations.

Bicycling

Bicycles and tandems can easily be rented by the hour or week. **Federazione Ciclistica Italiana** (*P. Stazione 2, 50123 Firenze* ☎ *(055) 283926*) is the organization for serious cyclists.

Camping

Helpful organizations include the **Centro Nazionale Campeggiatori Stranieri** (*at exit 19 of Autostrada del Sole, Calenzano* ☎ *(055) 882391*); **Campeggio Club Firenze e Toscana** (*Viale Guidoni 143* ☎ *(055) 419940*); **Club Alpino Italiano** (*Via del Proconsolo 10* ☎ *(055) 2340580*); and **Touring Club Italiano** (*Viale Lavagnini 6* ☎ *(055) 474192*).

Fishing

Fishing is a popular sport even in Florence. The clear waters off the rocky southern coast are excellent for snorkeling, and underwater fishing is allowed anywhere except harbors. For fishing in most lakes and rivers, an inexpensive license is required, as is membership of the **Federazione Italiana della Pesca Sportiva** (*Via De' Neri 6, 50122 Firenze* ☎ *(055) 214073*).

Gardens

Tuscany is richly endowed with great historic gardens, some regularly open to the public, especially around Florence, Lucca and Siena. Others may be visited through **Agriturist** (*Piazza S. Firenze 3* ☎ *(055) 287838*). Serious enthusiasts can join the rather exclusive **Garden Club of Florence** (*Palazzo Strozzi* ☎ *(055) 282245*) for tours in summer of gardens not otherwise open to visitors. See the *Index* p218 for a list of Tuscan gardens.

Golf

18-hole greens open all year: at **Punta Ala**, and at **Ugolino** (*Strada Chiantigiana 3, 50023 Impruneta* ☎ *(055) 2051155*).

Gymnasiums

There are many gyms in Florence, though some are private clubs. Open to temporary members is the **Palestra Ricciardi** (*Borgo Pinti 75* ☎ *(055) 247844/2478462*) from 9am-8.30pm, with a full range of equipment as well as saunas.

Horse racing and trotting

There are two racecourses in the Cascine in Florence, with trotting races in summer and racing in winter. Information from **Centro Ippico Toscano Le Cascine** (*Via Vespucci 5* ☎ *(055) 372621*). There are also racecourses at San Rossore, Montecatini and Punta Ala, and trotting races near Follonica.

Horseback riding

There are many opportunities to ride in rural Tuscany. You will find horses at the **Centro Equitazione Rendula Riding** (*Montevarchi (Arezzo)* ☎ *(055) 987045*); **Azienda Agricola Montescalari** (*Figline Valdarno* ☎ *(055) 959596*); **Fattoria Le Cannelle** (*Talamone (Grosseto)* ☎ *(0564) 887020*); **Podere Casa del Monte** (*Mercatale Val d'Arno*); **Podere Romena** (*Stia Casentino (Arezzo)* ☎ *(0575) 987045*); and **Fattoria Anqua** (*Radicondoli (Siena)* ☎ *(0577) 790722*).

Hunting

A hunting reserve is open to foreigners near Capalbio.

Italian

Since the purest Italian is spoken in Tuscany, it is an ideal place to learn the language. Most of the schools will help enrolled students find accommodations. The many schools in Florence include the **British Institute** (*Palazzo Lanfredini, Lungarno Guicciardini 9, 50123 Firenze* ☎ *(055) 284031*) and the **Centro Linguistico Italiano Dante Alighieri** (*Via de' Bardi 12, 50125 Firenze* ☎ *(055) 2342984*).

Music

Florence is one of the musical capitals of Italy; the Florence Maggio Musicale, which runs throughout the summer, is a festival of international importance; and the **Accademia Musicale Chigiana** at Siena is among the most distinguished Italian music academies. Lucca and Prato are musically active too, and Barga, Batignano, Cortona, Gargonza, Montepulciano, S. Gimignano and Torre del Lago Puccini have summer festivals.

Nature parks, reserves and zoos

Some reserves can be entered only with permission, usually obtainable from the communal government offices nearest the site. The Maremma is well supplied: see *Ansedonia*, Monte Argentario and, especially, *Monti dell'Uccellina*. Other reserves are at Bolgheri, Cavriglia, Migliarino (near Pisa), Montecristo and Orechiella (Garfagnana). There are zoos at Pistoia, Poppi, at Tirrenia near Pisa, and a small one in Florence.

Rowing

Rowing on the Arno is a popular sport. Information: **Società Canottieri Firenze** (*Lungarno de' Medici 8* ☎ *(055) 282130*).

Sailing

Tourist harbors are at Cala Galera, Castiglione della Pescaia, Elba, Giannutri, Viareggio, Port'Ercole, Giglio, Talamone and Punta Ala. Report to the *Capitaneria di Porto* (Harbor Master). A useful book is *The Tyrrhenian Sea* by H.M. Denham (John Murray).

Skiing

The best skiing is in the Apennines, at Abetone, Cutigliano and S. Marcello Pistoiese. Nearer to Florence, in the Pratomagno hills, there are winter sports facilities at Consuma, Stia and Vallombrosa. Monte Amiata has some 20km (12 miles) of piste; its principle resort is Abbadia S. Salvatore.

Swimming

Beaches vary from superb to squalid. The best sandy beaches are shown in the *Orientation map* in *Planning*. Below Livorno and on Elba the coast is mostly rocky with small sandy bays. Although there are some free beaches, those that provide facilities are fairly expensive. Most inland towns have well-maintained public pools: in Florence, the **Piscine Bellariva** (*Lungarno Colombo*); **Piscine Costoli** (*Viale Paoli*); **Piscine Pavoniere** (*Viale degli Olmi*); and at the **Circolo del Tennis** (*Via Visarno 1*), a private club in the Cascine.

Tennis

Public courts and tennis clubs are widespread. The Circolo del Tennis in the Cascine is not keen to take temporary members, but there are also good courts on the Campo di Marte. Information (also about skating and track and field) from **Associazione Sportiva ASSI** (*Viale Michelangelo* ☎ *(055) 6812686*).

Walking

Near Florence there is pleasant country walking in the Fiesolan hills and around Arcetri. There are marked trails through the protected forests at Abetone, Camaldoli, La Verna and Vallombrosa. Maps showing footpaths are obtainable from **Istituto Geografico Militare** (*Viale Strozzi 14, Firenze*). Information about mountain walking from **Club Alpino Italiano** (*Via Proconsolo 10, 50123 Firenze* ☎ *(055) 2340580*).

A guide to Italian

This glossary covers the basic language needs of the traveler: for essential vocabulary and simple conversation, finding accommodations, visiting the bank, shopping and using public transportation or a car. There is also a special menu decoder, explaining all the most common descriptions of food terms.

Reference words

Monday	lunedì	Friday	venerdì
Tuesday	martedì	Saturday	sabato
Wednesday	mercoledì	Sunday	domenica
Thursday	giovedì		

January	gennaio	July	luglio
February	febbraio	August	agosto
March	marzo	September	settembre
April	aprile	October	ottobre
May	maggio	November	novembre
June	giugno	December	dicembre

1	uno	11	undici	21	ventuno
2	due	12	dodici	22	ventidue
3	tre	13	tredici	30	trenta
4	quattro	14	quattordici	40	quaranta
5	cinque	15	quindici	50	cinquanta
6	sei	16	sedici	60	sessanta
7	sette	17	diciassette	70	settanta
8	otto	18	diciotto	80	ottanta
9	nove	19	diciannove	90	novanta
10	dieci	20	venti	100	cento

First	primo, -a	Six o'clock	le sei
Second	secondo, -a	Quarter-past....	....e un quarto
Third	terzo, -a	Half-past....	....e mezzo
Fourth	quarto, -a	Quarter to....	....meno un quarto
One o'clock	l'una		

Mr	signor(e)	Ladies	signore, donne
Mrs	signora	Gents	signori, uomini
Miss	signorina		

Basic communication

Yes	sì	Today	oggi
No	no	Tomorrow	domani
Please	per favore/per piacere	Next week	la settimana prossima
Thank you	grazie	Last week	la settimana scorsa
I'm very sorry	mi dispiace molto/mi scusi	....days ago	....giorni fa
		Month	mese(m)
Excuse me	senta!(to attract attention), permesso!(on bus, train, etc.)	Year	anno
		Here	qui
	mi scusi	There	lì
Not at all/you're welcome	prego	Big	grande
Hello	ciao(familiar), pronto(on telephone)	Small	piccolo, -a
		Hot	caldo, -a
Good morning	buon giorno	Cold	freddo, -a
Good afternoon	buona sera	Good	buono, -a
Good evening	buona sera	Bad	cattivo, -a
Good night	buona notte	Beautiful	bello, -a
Goodbye	ciao(familiar), addio (final or familiar), arrivederci	Well	bene
		Badly	male
Morning	mattino	With	con
Afternoon	pomeriggio	And	e, ed
Evening	sera	But	ma
Night	notte(f)	Very	molto
Yesterday	ieri	All	tutto, -a

209

Words and phrases

Open aperto
Closed chiuso
Entrance entrata
Exit uscita
Free libero
On the left a sinistra
On the right a destra
Straight on diritto
Near vicino
Far lontano
Up su
Down giù
Early presto
Late tardi
Quickly presto
Pleased to meet you. Molto lieto/piacere.
How are you? Come sta?
Very well, thank you. Benissimo, grazie.
Do you speak English? Parla inglese?
I don't understand. Non capisco.
I don't know. Non lo so.

Please explain. Può spiegare per favore.
Please speak more slowly. Parli più lentamente per favore.
My name is.... Mi chiamo....
I am American/English. Sono americano/inglese, -a.
Where is/are....? Dov'e/dove si trova/dove sono....?
Is there a....? C'è un, una....?
What? Cosa?
When? Quando?
How much? Quanto?
That's too much. È troppo caro.
Expensive caro
Cheap a buon mercato
I would like.... Vorrei....
Do you have....? Avete....?
Just a minute. Un momento.
That's fine/OK. Va bene/benissimo/OK
What time is it? Che ore sono?
I don't feel well. Non mi sento bene/sto male.

Accommodations

Making a reservation by letter

> *Dear Sir/Madam,*
> *Egregio Signore/Signora,*
> *I would like to reserve one double room (with bathroom) —*
> *Vorrei prenotare una camera doppia (con bagno) —*
> *— a twin-bedded room, and one single room (with shower)*
> *— una camera con due letti, e una camera singola (con doccia)*
> *for 7 nights from 12 August. We would like bed and breakfast/half board/full board*
> *per 7 notti dal 12 agosto. Vorremmo una camera con colazione/mezza pensione/pensione completa*
> *and would prefer rooms with a sea view.*
> *e possibilmente camere con vista sul mare.*
> *Please send me details of your terms with the confirmation.*
> *Sarei lieto di ricevere dettagli del prezzo e la conferma.*
> *Yours sincerely,*
> *Cordi ali saluti,*

Arriving at the hotel

I have a reservation. My name is....
Ho già prenotato. Sono il signor/la signora....

A quiet room with bath/shower/WC/wash basin
Una camera tranquilla con bagno/doccia/WC/lavandino

....overlooking the sea/park/street/the back.
....con vista sul mare/sul parco/sulla strada/sul retro

Does the price include breakfast/tax/service?
E tutto compreso/colazione/tasse/servizio?

This room is too large/small/cold/hot/noisy.
Questa camera è troppo grande/piccola/fredda/calda/rumorosa.

That's too expensive. Have you anything cheaper?
Costa troppo. Avete qualcosa meno caro?

Floor/story piano
Dining room/restaurant sala da pranzo/ristorante (m)
Manager direttore, -trice
Porter portiere
Have you got a room? Avete una camera?
What time is breakfast/dinner? A che ora è la prima colazione/la cena?
Is there a laundry service? C'è il servizio lavanderia?
What time does the hotel close? A che ora chiude l'albergo?
Will I need a key? Avrò bisogno della chiave?

Is there a night porter?   C'è un portiere di notte?
I'll be leaving tomorrow morning.   Parto domani mattina.
Please give me a call at....   Mi può chiamare alle....
Come in!   Avanti!

Shopping (La Spesa)

Where is the nearest/a good....?   Dov'è il più vicino/la più vicina....?
   Dov'è un buon/una buona....?
Can you help me/show me....?   Mi può aiutare/Può mostrarmi....?
I'm just looking.   Sto soltanto guardando.
Do you accept credit cards/travelers cheques?   Accettate carte di
   credito/travelers cheques?
Can you deliver to....?   Può consegnare a....?
I'll take it.   Lo prendo.
I'll leave it.   Lo lascio.
Can I have it tax-free for export?   Posso averlo senza tasse per
   l'esportazione?
This is faulty. Can I have a replacement/refund?   C'è difetto. Me lo
   potrebbe cambiare/rimborsare?
I don't want to spend more than....   Non voglio spendere più di....
Can I have a stamp for....?   Vorrei un francobollo per....

Shops

Antique store negozio di antiquariato	Jeweler gioielleria
Art gallery galleria d'arte	Market mercato
Bakery panificio, forno	Newsstand giornalaio, edicola (kiosk)
Bank banca	Optician ottico
Beauty parlor istituto di bellezza	Perfumery profumeria
Bookstore libreria	Pharmacy/drugstore farmacia
Butcher macelleria	Photographic store negozio fotografico
Cake shop pasticceria	Post office ufficio postale
Clothes store negozio di abbigliamento, di confezioni	Shoe store negozio di calzature
Dairy latteria	Stationers cartoleria
Delicatessen salumeria, pizzicheria	Supermarket supermercato
Fish store pescheria	Tailor sarto
Florist fioraio	Tobacconist tabaccheria (also sells stamps)
Greengrocer ortolano, erbivendolo, fruttivendolo	Tourist office ente del turismo
Grocer drogheria	Toy store negozio di giocattoli
Haberdasher merciaio	Travel agent agenzia di viaggio
Hairdresser parrucchiere, -a	

At the bank

I would like to change some pounds/dollars/travelers cheques
Vorrei cambiare delle sterline/dei dollari/dei travelers cheques
What is the exchange rate?
Com'è il cambio?
Can you cash a personal check?
Può cambiare un assegno?
Can I obtain cash with this credit card?
Posso avere soldi in contanti con questa carta di credito?
Do you need to see my passport?
Ha bisogno del mio passaporto?

Some useful goods

Antiseptic cream crema antisettica	Shampoo shampoo
Aspirin aspirina	Shaving cream crema da barba
Bandages fasciature	Soap sapone(m)
Band-Aid cerotto	Sunburn cream crema antisolare
Cotton cotone idrofilo(m)	Sunglasses occhiali da sole
Diarrhea/upset stomach pills pillole anti-coliche	Suntan cream/oil crema/olio solare
Indigestion tablets pillole per l'indigestione	Tampons tamponi
Insect repellant insettifugo	Tissues fazzoletti di carta
Laxative lassativo	Toothbrush spazzolino da denti
Sanitary napkins assorbenti igienici	Toothpaste dentifricio
	Travel sickness pills pillole contro il mal di viaggio

211

Words and phrases

Bra reggiseno
Coat cappotto
Dress vestito
Jacket giacca
Pants pantaloni
Pullover maglione (m)

Shirt camicia
Shoes scarpe
Skirt gonna
Stockings/tights calze/collants
Swimsuit costume da bagno (m)
Underpants mutande

Film pellicola
Letter lettera
Money order vaglia

Postcard cartolina
Stamp francobollo
Telegram telegramma (m)

Motoring

Service station stazione di rifornimento (f), distributore (m)
Fill it up. Faccia il pieno, per favore.
Give me....lire worth. Mi dia....lire.
I would like....litres of gasoline. Vorrei....litri di benzina.
Can you check the....? Può controllare....?
There is something wrong with the.... C'e un difetto nel/nella....

Accelerator acceleratore (m)
Axle l'asse (m)
Battery batteria
Brakes freni
Exhaust lo scarico, scappamento
Fan belt la cinghia del ventilatore
Gear box la scatola del cambio

Lights fanali, fari, luci
Oil olio
Spares i pezzi di ricambio
Sparking plugs le candele
Tires gomme
Water acqua
Windshield parabrezza (m)

My car won't start. La mia macchina non s'accende.
My car has broken down/had a flat tire. La macchina è guasta/la
  gomma è forata.
The engine is overheating. Il motore si scalda.
How long will it take to repair? Quanto tempo ci vorrà per la riparazione?
I need it as soon as possible. Ne ho bisogno il più presto possibile.

Car rental

Where can I rent a car? Dove posso noleggiare una macchina?
Is full/comprehensive insurance included? E'completamente assicurata?
Is it insured for another driver? E'assicurata per un altro guidatore?
Does the price include mileage? Il kilometraggio è compreso?
Unlimited mileage kilometraggio illimitato
Deposit deposito
By what time must I return it? A che ora devo consegnarla?
Can I return it to another depot? Posso riportarla ad un altro deposito?
Is the gas tank full? E'il serbatoio pieno?

Road signs

Accendere le luci in galleria lights
  on in tunnel
Autostrada highway
Caduta di massi falling stones
Casello toll gate
Dare la precedenza give way
Divieto di accesso, senso vietato
  no entry
Divieto di parcheggio no parking
Divieto di sorpasso no overtaking

Divieto di sosta no stopping
Lavori in corso roadworks ahead
Passaggio a livello level crossing
Pedaggio toll road
Raccordo anulare beltway
Rallentare slow down
Senso unico one-way street
Tangenziale bypass
Tenersi in corsia keep in lane
Uscita (autocarri) exit (for trucks)

Other methods of transportation

Aircraft aeroplano
Airport aeroporto
Bus autobus (m)
Bus stop fermata
Coach corriera
Ferry/boat traghetto
Ferry port porto
Hovercraft aliscafo
Station stazione (f)

Train treno
ticket biglietto
Ticket office biglietteria
One-way andata
Round trip andata e ritorno
Half fare metà prezzo
First/second/economy prima
    classe/seconda classe/turistico
Sleeper/couchette cuccetta

When is the next....for....? Quando parte il prossimo....per....?
What time does it arrive? A che ora arriva?
What time does the last....for....leave? Quando parte l'ultimo....per....?

Which track/quay/gate?   Quale binario/molo/uscita?
Is this the....for....?   E'questo il....per....?
Is it direct? Where does it stop?   E'diretto? Dove si ferma?
Do I need to change anywhere?   Devo cambiare?
Please tell me where to get off.   Mi può dire dove devo scendere.
Take me to....   Mi vuol portare a....
Is there a dining car?   C'è un vagone ristorante?

Food and drink

Have you a table for....?   Avete un tavolo per....?
I want to reserve a table for....at....   Vorrei prenotare un tavolo per....alle....
A quiet table.   Un tavolo tranquillo.
A table near the window.   Un tavolo vicino alla finestra.
Could we have another table?   Potremmo spostarci?
I did not order this.   Non ho ordinato questo.
Breakfast/lunch/dinner   prima colazione/pranzo/cena
Bring me another....   Un altro....per favore.
The check please.   Il conto per favore.
Is service included?   Il servizio è incluso?

Hot	caldo	Dry	secco
Cold	freddo	Sweet	dolce, amabile
Glass	bicchiere (m)	Salt	sale (m)
Bottle	bottiglia	Pepper	pepe (m)
Half-bottle	mezza bottiglia	Oil	olio
Beer/lager (draft)	birra (alla spina)	Vinegar	aceto
		Mustard	senape (f)
Fruit juice	succo di frutta	Bread	pane (m)
Mineral water	acqua minerale	Butter	burro
Orangeade/lemonade	aranciata/limonata	Cheese	formaggio
		Milk	latte (m)
Carbonated/noncarbonated	gassata/non gassata	Coffee	caffè (m)
		Tea	tè (m)
Flask/carafe	fiasco/caraffa	Chocolate	cioccolato
Red wine	vino rosso, vino nero	Sugar	zucchero
		Steak	bistecca
White wine	vino bianco	well done	ben cotto
Rosé wine	vino rosé	medium	medio
Vintage	di annata	rare	al sangue

Menu decoder

Abbacchio	baby lamb	Bistecca alla fiorentina	grilled T-bone steak
Acciughe	anchovies		
Affettati	sliced cold meats	Bollito misto	boiled meats
Affumicato	smoked	Brace (alla)	charcoal grilled
Aglio	garlic	Braciola	chop
Agnello	lamb	Branzino	sea bass
Agnolotti	pasta envelopes	Bresaola	dried salt beef
Agro	sour	Brodetto	fish soup
Albicocche	apricots	Brodo	consommé
Amaro	bitter	Bruschetta	garlic bread
Ananas	pineapple	Burrida	fish stew
Anatra/anitra	duck	Burro (al)	(cooked in) butter
Anguilla	eel	Cacciagione	game
Animelle	sweetbreads	Cacciucco	fish stew
Antipasto	hors d'oeuvre	Calamaretti	baby squid
Aragosta	*langouste*, lobster	Calamari	squid
Arancia	orange	Calzone	half-moon-shaped pizza
Aringa	herring		
Arrosto	roast meat	Cannelloni	stuffed pasta tubes
Arselle	baby clams	Capitone	large conger eel
Asparagi	asparagus	Cappelletti	stuffed pasta hats
Baccalà	dried salt cod	Cappe sante	scallops
Basilico	basil	Capperi	capers
Bianchetti	whitebait	Carciofi alla giudia	artichokes fried in oil and lemon
Bianco	plain, boiled		
Bietola	Swiss chard	Carne	meat
Biscottini di Prato	small, hard almond biscuits	Carote	carrots
		Carpa	carp

213

Words and phrases

Carpaccio raw lean beef fillet
Carrello (al) from the trolley
Casa (della) of the restaurant
Cassalingo, -a homemade
Castagnaccio chestnut cake
Castagne chestnuts
Castrato mutton
Cavolfiore cauliflower
Cavolini di Bruxelles sprouts
Cavolo cabbage
Ceci chick peas
Cenci fried pastry twists
Cervella brains
Cervo venison
Cetriolo cucumber
Cicoria chicory
Ciliege cherries
Cima cold stuffed veal
Cinghiale wild boar
Cipolle onions
Cocomero watermelon
Coda di bue oxtail
Coniglio rabbit
Contorno vegetable side-dish
Controfiletto sirloin steak
Coppa cooked pressed neck of
  pork or an ice cream sundae
Cosciotto di agnello leg of lamb
Costata di bue entrecôte steak
Costolette cutlets
Cotto cooked
Cozze mussels
Crema custard, cream soup
Crespolini savory pancakes
Crostacei shellfish
Crostini small savory toasts
Crudo raw
Diavola (alla) in a spicy sauce
Dolci desserts, sweets
Espresso small black coffee
Fagiano pheasant
Fagioli all'uccelletto beans with
  tomatoes and garlic
Fagiolini French beans
Faraona guinea fowl
Farcito stuffed
Fatto in casa homemade
Fave broad beans
Fegatini chicken livers
Fegato liver
Ferri (ai) grilled
Fesa di vitello leg of veal
Fettina slice
Fettuccine thin flat pasta
Fettunta garlic bread
Fichi figs
Filetto fillet
Finocchio fennel
Finocchiona fennel-flavored
  salami
Focaccia dimpled savory bread
Formaggio cheese
Forno (al) cooked in the oven
Fragole strawberries
Fresco fresh
Frittata omelet
Frittelle fritters
Fritto fried

Frutta fruit
Frutti di mare shellfish
Funghi mushrooms
Gamberetti shrimps
Gamberi big prawns
Gelato ice cream
Giorno (del) of the day
Girarrosto (al) spit-roasted
Girello topside of beef
Gnocchi small pasta dumplings
Grana Parmesan cheese
Granchio crab
Granita water ice
Gran'pezzo roast sirloin of young
  beef
Graticola (alla) grilled
Griglia (alla) grilled
Indivia endive
Insalata salad
Involtini skewered veal and ham
Lamponi raspberries
Lampreda lamprey
Lasagne baked flat pasta
Lenticchie lentils
Lepre hare
Lesso boiled (meat)
Limone lemon
Lingua di bue ox tongue
Lombata, -ina loin, loin chop
Lonza cured fillet of pork
Luccio pike
Lumache snails
Macedonia di frutta fruit salad
Magro lean
Maiale pork
Mandorle almonds
Manzo beef
Marmellata jam
Medaglioni rounds of meat
Mela apple
Melagrana pomegranate
Melanzane eggplant
Melone melon
Merluzzo cod
Miele honey
Minestra soup
Minestrone vegetable soup
Misto mixed
Mostarda pickle
Muscolo alla fiorentina beef
  casserole with beans
Naturale (al) plain
Nocciole hazelnuts
Noci nuts
Nodino di vitello veal chop
Nostrale, nostrano local
Oca goose
Orata gilt-head bream
Osso buco veal knuckle
Paglia e fieno green and white
  tagliatelle
Paillard thin grilled steak
Palombo dogfish
Panforte di Siena hard cake with
  honey, fruit and almonds
Panino imbottito roll
Panna cream

Panzanella salad of soaked bread and fresh vegetables
Pappa al pomodoro thick tomato and bread soup
Pappardelle long flat pasta
Passato purée
Pasta e fagioli bean and pasta soup
Pasticcio layered pasta pie
Pasto meal
Patate potatoes
Pecorino hard ewes' milk cheese
Penne all'arrabbiata short pasta tubes with a fiery sauce
Peperoni sweet peppers
Pera pear
Pernice partridge
Pesca peach
Pesce fish
Pesce persico perch
Pesce spada swordfish
Pesciolini small fry
Pesto green basil sauce
Petto di pollo chicken breast
Pezzo piece
Piacere according to taste
Piatto del giorno today's dish
Piccante spicy, piquant
Piccata thin escalope
Piccione pigeon
Pinzimonio oily vegetable dip
Piselli peas
Polenta maize porridge
Pollame poultry
Pollo chicken
Polpette meatballs
Polpettone meatloaf
Polpo octopus
Pomodoro tomato
Pompelmo grapefruit
Porchetta roast suckling pig
Primizie spring vegetables
Prosciutto ham
Prugne plums
Quaglie quails
Radicchio red bitter lettuce
Ragù meat and tomato sauce
Rane frogs
Ravanelli radishes
Ravioli stuffed pasta squares
Razza skate
Ribollita thick vegetable soup
Ricciarelli almond biscuits
Ricotta cheese — similar to cottage cheese
Rigatoni ridged pasta tubes
Ripieno stuffed
Risi e bisi pea and rice soup
Riso rice
Risotto savory rice dish
Rognoni kidneys
Rombo maggiore turbot
Rosmarino rosemary
Rospo (coda di) tail of angler fish
Salsa (verde) (green) sauce
Salsiccia sausage
Saltimbocca alla romana veal escalopes with ham and sage
Salvia sage

Sarde sardines
Scaloppine escalopes
Scelta (a) of your choice
Schiacciata alla fiorentina vanilla sponge cake
Scottadito grilled lamb cutlets
Selvaggina game, venison
Semifreddo frozen dessert
Semplice plain
Seppie cuttlefish
Sgombro mackerel
Sogliola sole
Sottaceti pickled vegetables
Spaghetti
  all'amatriciana spaghetti with bacon, tomatoes
  alla bolognese with *ragù*
  alla carbonara with bacon, eggs
  alla napoletana with tomato
Spezzatino meat stew
Spiedini skewers, kebabs
Spiedo (allo) on the spit
Spigola sea bass
Spinaci spinach
Squadro monkfish
Stagionato hung, well-aged
Stagione (di) in season
Stoccafisso stockfish
Stracciatella clear egg soup
Stracotto beef in red wine
Stufato braised, stew(ed)
Sugo sauce
Suppli rice croquettes
Susina plum
Tacchino turkey
Tagliatelle thin flat pasta
Tartufi truffles
Tegame (al) fried or baked
Telline cockles
Timballo savory pasta pie
Tinca tench
Tonno tuna
Tordi thrushes
Torta flan, tart
Tortellini small stuffed pasta
Tost toasted sandwich
Totano squid
Tramezzino sandwich
Trancia slice
Trenette flat, thinnish pasta
Trifolato fried in garlic
Triglia red mullet
Trippa tripe
Trota trout
Uccelletti grilled beef on skewers
Umido (in) stewed
Uova eggs
Uva grapes
Verdure green vegetables
Vitello veal
Vongole clams
Zabaglione egg yolks and Marsala whip
Zucchini zucchini
Zuccotto ice cream liqueur cake
Zuppa soup
Zuppa inglese trifle

215

Index

Index

Index

Index

221

Index

222

Index of restaurants in Tuscany

Index of restaurants in Tuscany

FLORENCE AND TUSCANY

1

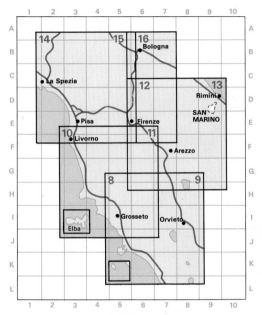

LEGEND

Area Maps

0   5   10   15   20 Km

- ⦾ Motorway (with access point)
- ═ Main Road-Dual Carriageway
- ═ Other Main Road
- ─ Secondary Road
- ─ Minor Road
- ─ Scenic Route
- SS73 Road Number
- --- Ferry
- ══ Railway
- ✈ Airport
- ✦ Airfield
- ▓ International Boundary
- ▬ Province Boundary
- ⛪ Abbey, monastery
- ∴ Ancient site, ruin
- ♛ Castle
- ⚑ Good Beach
- **12** Adjoining Page No.

City Maps

- Major Place of Interest
- Other Important Building
- Built-up Area
- Park
- † † Cemetery
- † † Named church, church
- ✡ Synagogue
- ✠ Hospital
- *i* Information Office
- ✉ Post Office
- 🖐 Police Station
- 🚗 Car Park
- → One Way Street

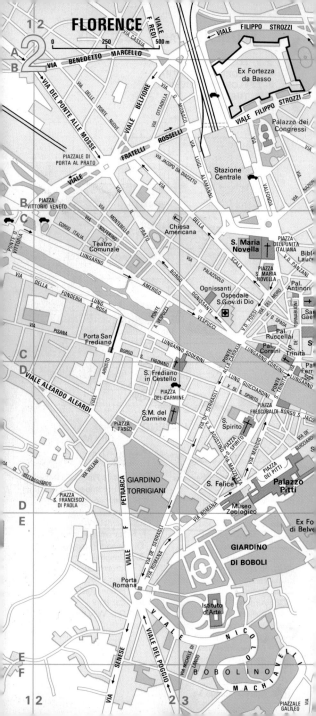

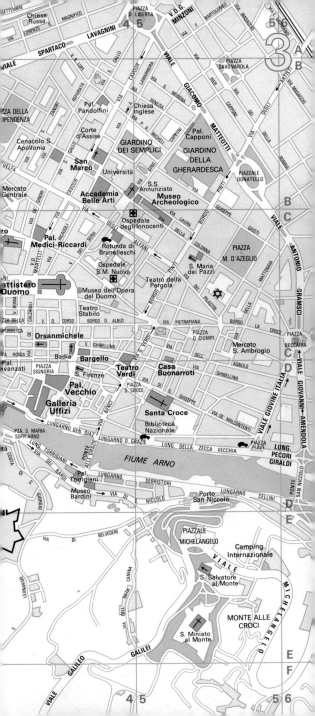

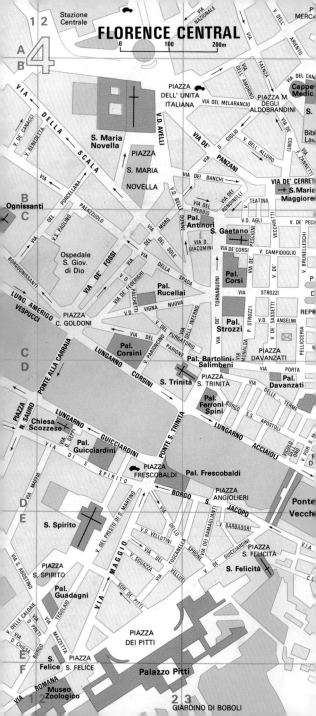

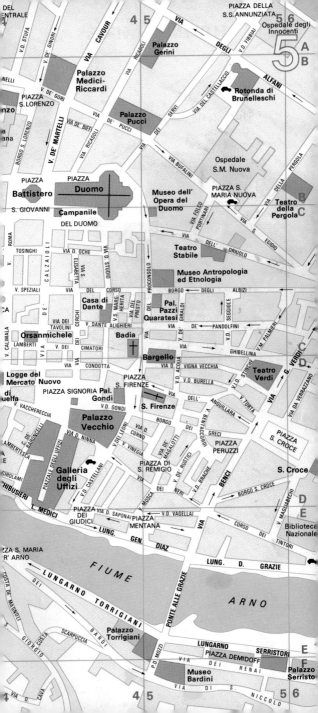

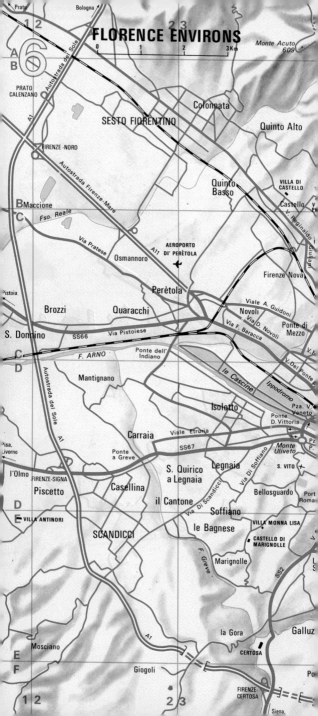

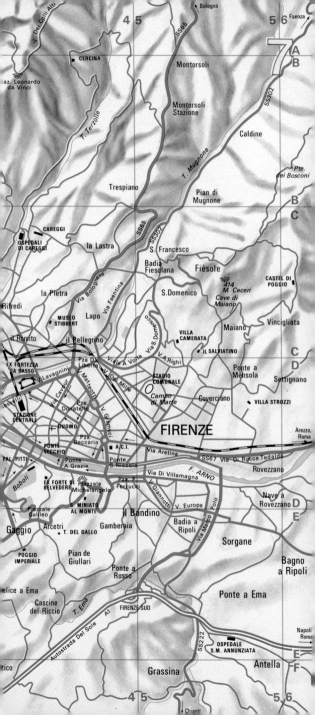

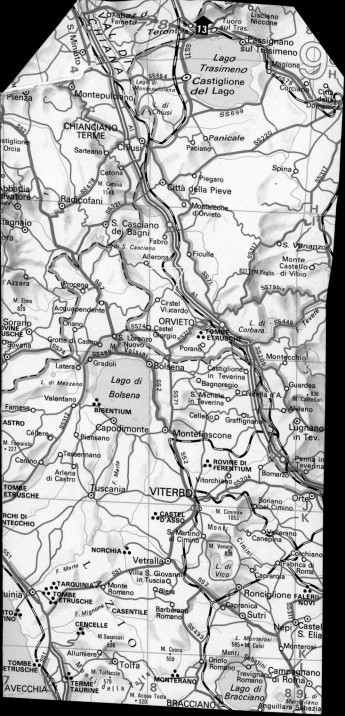